TO

HARRISON RANDOLPH

REMEMBERING GOLDEN DAYS

NELSON W. ALDRICH

A LEADER IN AMERICAN POLITICS

KENNIKAT PRESS SCHOLARLY REPRINTS

Dr. Ralph Adams Brown, Senior Editor

Series in
AMERICAN HISTORY AND CULTURE
IN THE NINETEENTH CENTURY
Under the General Editorial Supervision of
Dr. Martin L. Fausold
Professor of History, State University of New York

NELSON W. ALDRICH

NELSON W. ALDRICH

A LEADER IN AMERICAN POLITICS

BY

NATHANIEL WRIGHT STEPHENSON

KENNIKAT PRESS
Port Washington, N. Y./London

NELSON W. ALDRICH

Copyright 1930 Charles Scribner's Sons
Renewal copyright © 1958 Mary Mazyck Robertson
Reissued in 1971 by Kennikat Press by
arrangement with Charles Scribner's Sons
Library of Congress Catalog Card No: 72-137928
ISBN 0-8046-1490-3

Manufactured by Taylor Publishing Company   Dallas, Texas

KENNIKAT SERIES ON AMERICAN HISTORY AND
CULTURE IN THE NINETEENTH CENTURY

PREFACE

I wish to acknowledge the kindness of many people who have assisted me either directly or indirectly in the preparation of this biography. The whole manuscript was read and criticised most helpfully by Professor W. B. Munro, Professor F. L. Paxson, Professor C. L. Lingley, and Professor H. B. Learned. Other generous friends read considerable portions of it. Professor R. M. Story trained his keen analytic faculty on the mode of handling political forces; Professor H. P. Willis made a careful examination of the factual basis of the financial narrative; Professor G. S. Burgess and Professor Felix Frankfurter gave me the benefit of their legal attitudes toward 1906; the Honorable Carter Glass, the Honorable A. P. Andrew, Mr. P. M. Warburg, Mr. Frank Vanderlip, and Mr. A. H. Shelton reviewed the portions dealing with the Federal Reserve; Miss Ida M. Tarbell discussed with me those portions that invade the field of her particular interests; Professor Allan Nevins made interesting suggestions about the orientation of the whole matter.

Of course it does not follow that all my correspondents approve all the interpretations here expressed. For example, Mr. Robert S. Owen, commenting on the chapters dealing with the Federal Reserve, expressed views that are severely at variance with those of his own associates, and which I find myself unable to accept. He denies flatly the importance attributed to Mr. Bryan in Chapter XXVII, and thinks that I overestimate the significance of other leaders on the Democratic side. Senator Glass, though very guarded in his comments on my interpretation of Senator Aldrich, at least goes along with me in being quite unconvinced by Mr. Owen's views. Professor Willis, I am happy to say, accepts the main lines of the story of the Federal Reserve movement as here indicated.

In accordance with the provisions of our copyright law, letters found among a statesman's papers cannot be printed without permission of the person who wrote the letters or his heirs. In two instances I had to cut out of my tentative manuscript letters of this sort because permission to print was refused. Fortunately, no serious loss of fact was the result. But vivid details had to be sacrificed, and these it was a pity to lose.

There is a long list of persons who control manuscript sources, or who have contributed first-hand information, whom it is impossible to thank adequately. To no one am I more indebted than to Mrs. Roosevelt, who has permitted extensive search in the rich mine of the Roosevelt papers. Would that it were still possible to thank the late Chief Justice of the United States for opening freely his personal papers, which are of inestimable historical importance. Mr. George B. Cortelyou showed every courtesy in connection with the vast mass of the McKinley papers. The Allison papers, the most voluminous collection of all, were not only opened for research by Mr. Edgar R. Harlan, in whose custody they are, but so far as quoted were carefully checked by him. For access to other collections of manuscripts, without which the history of the time cannot be written, I am deeply indebted to Senator George H. Moses (Chandler papers); Professor Robert M. McElroy and Professor J. Franklyn Jameson (Cleveland, Morrill, and Sherman papers); Mr. Otis G. Hammond (Cummings papers); Mrs. Joseph B. Foraker (Foraker papers); Mrs. Benjamin Harrison (Harrison papers); Mr. Roger Howson (Holls papers); Mrs. L. T. Michner (Michner papers); Mr. Victor H. Paltsits (Morton papers); the late Mrs. Orville H. Platt and Mr. George S. Godard (Platt papers); Mr. Charles P. Spooner (Spooner papers); Mr. Arthur B. Shelton (Shelton papers); Mr. P. M. Warburg (Warburg papers); Mr. Frank Vanderlip (Vanderlip papers). The Honorable Elihu Root has permitted the use of a significant letter.

The list of those who have put me under obligation by incidental contribution is so long that the full recital of it

is impossible. Of first importance is the frank discussion of
the events here set forth by certain veteran newspaper men,
including Mr. Richard Hooker, Mr. G. G. Hill, and Mr.
R. V. Oulahan. Some very valuable newspaper contacts
would not have been possible except through the kindness
of Mr. Adolph S. Ochs. Among the senators, past or present,
it is due to mention particularly Senator Moses, Senator
Smoot, Senator Clapp, Senator Beveridge, Senator Over-
man, Senator Warren, Senator Burton, Senator McCumber,
and Senator Simmons. Professor Volwiler, now at work on
the definitive life of President Harrison, made it possible to
determine several perplexing points. Of great value are the
recollections of Colonel E. H. Halford, secretary to President Harrison, and Miss Kathleen Lawler, secretary to Senator Platt. At various places in the text are indicated the aid
given by Mr. W. A. Slade, Mr. G. M. Reynolds, and Mr.
Vreeland. I must also make grateful mention of the kindness of Miss Mabel Boardman, Miss Josephine Patten, Miss
Grace C. Lynch, Mrs. Edith Newlands Johnson, and Mrs.
Cornelius Vanderbilt. Mr. and Mrs. J. C. Fitzpatrick gave
freely of their time at the Library of Congress. No one could
have been more generous of time and energy than Mr. Percy
E. Budlong and Mr. Charles E. Alden. Mr. Charles Moore
contributed richly to the comprehension of the neglected
figure of Senator McMillan. Colonel David Corser made
possible the recovery of some unique facts. No one person
has given more valuable suggestions than President Nicholas
Murray Butler.

It is a pleasure to praise unreservedly the assistance I
have had from Doctor Jeannette Paddock Nichols, for whom
I want to coin the term research secretary. The art of the
professional specialist in research, who gathers material for
some one else to use, is still so new, its technic so fluctuating, that there is in many minds much doubt as to its prac-
ticability. Doctor Nichols is one of those who have learned
how to use it. She has that ardor of pure investigation which
waxes stronger and stronger as the demands upon it grow
more unmerciful. I remember a letter of hers in which she

speaks with delight of the way I was "bombarding" her with requisitions.

Doctor Nichols gave her whole time during five years to this work. With a very few exceptions she has explored and fully reported upon all the manuscript collections—excepting a few entirely inaccessible ones—of which there is any reason to suspect that they contain Aldrich material. Among the exceptions are the Hanna papers, which have mysteriously disappeared, and the Hale papers, which are not yet in a condition to be used. In some cases long and painstaking examination has ended negatively. In other cases the results are precious, and new light has been thrown on American history. Altogether, I estimate that near a half million pieces of manuscript have passed under Doctor Nichols' eye and have been reported upon. The skeleton calendar in the list of abbreviations, prepared by Doctor Nichols as introduction to the notes, shows the quantity, the location, and the main characteristics of these masses of manuscript. Doctor Nichols also conducted many interviews with survivors of the Aldrich period, thus accumulating much valuable information that is now incorporated in the Aldrich papers.

Naturally, my final thanks are due to the Aldrich family. The notes indicate the great consideration of the more distant members who, with old friends of Senator Aldrich, have made it possible to reconstruct so much of his early environment. His immediate family have rendered every possible assistance, which also is shadowed in the notes. They have opened all their manuscripts without reserve, and without placing upon the author the slightest restriction in the use of these materials.

N. W. S.

CLAREMONT, CALIFORNIA,
29 March, 1930.

CONTENTS

xi

NELSON W. ALDRICH

A LEADER IN AMERICAN POLITICS

CHAPTER I

IN THE WAKE OF THE CIVIL WAR

I

In the seventies of the last century the State of Rhode Island was ruled in the main by Henry B. Anthony. That is not the conventional way to put it, but much nearer the truth than the usual way. Mr. Anthony was a sedate and reputable person, a senator of the United States, with a fine political machine all his own. He was generally able, in the days of his eminence, to tell the Republican party of Rhode Island just "where to get off." He had rivals, of course—especially one Lippitt, of whom, hereafter—but for the most part he was too strong for them. None knew better how to manage that after-war psychology with its hysteria, its disillusion, its truculent mental aimlessness, that had followed the dreadful days of the sixties. A scrupulous trafficker in votes, he always gave good weight in political deals, and any one serving him was sure of his just dues by way of patronage. His idea of statecraft was the orthodox one expressed by a notorious countryman of his—"What are we here for if not to get the offices?" And as a rule, Mr. Anthony got them—for himself or his friends.

Mr. Anthony had a lieutenant, a General Brayton, faithful to his chief with that amazing fidelity which is sometimes the redeeming feature of professional politics. Harsh things have been said of General Brayton—whether truly or falsely has nothing to do with this story. There was an absence from the State—a two years' absence—due to furious quarrels over his mode of providing the party with funds. But all that was cleared away, largely through the influence of Anthony; there was generous forgiving and forgetting; the General returned to the fond embrace of his

3

native State and to a long career of further political skilfulness.

As acknowledged henchman of the great boss, Anthony, it was part of the General's duty to find the right recruits for the Antonian forces. He had a shrewd instinct for coming men and he kept his ear very close to the ground. The governorship of Rhode Island was not in those days considered a great plum. But it had its uses. It was chiefly valuable as purchase money, when some rising young politician might be assumed to be on the make; for such, the offer of the governorship was the same thing as a gracious assurance that he might have his place in the sun—or, in home-spun American, the bandwagon—if only he would behave himself and play the game according to rule—in this case, Anthony's rule. In 1877, with the election for governor approaching, there was no claimant for the honor about whom there could not be two opinions. Apparently, it was Brayton, peering deep into all the currents and eddies and backwashes of party sentiment, as well as watching narrowly every movement of his chieftain's enemies within the party, who determined the course of the Anthony faction. What reasons he gave to the boss, and how the boss came to a conclusion, has not been recorded—at least, so far as is known. The result, at this distance, seems curious. But perhaps those two arch students of human nature were keener men, who saw further beyond their noses, than they have had credit for being. They decided to make overtures to relative obscurity.

There was a newcomer in politics, a Mr. Aldrich, of Prov-idence. He was a quiet young business man, something of an independent, who was supposed to incline to the Lippitt faction rather than to Anthony's. Altogether he was an unknown quantity from the Brayton point of view, and perhaps he was worth purchasing. At that moment, the politicians had no inkling, or very little inkling, of what was the central fact of this unostentatious young man. Before all else he was deeply independent in spirit, determined to live his own life his own way and not to purchase success on any other man's terms. Furthermore, he had an insight into men, and in certain ways a knowledge of conditions, far more illuminating than General Brayton's or Senator Anthony's. He had his own views of the political possibilities before him. They did not include subservience either to the great boss or the lesser one. When the General, quite unsuspicious of Mr. Aldrich's foresight, proposed to him the nomination for the governorship, Mr. Aldrich calmly declined the honor.

And who, pray, might this cool Mr. Aldrich be?

The political managers had become acquainted with him eight years before when he was elected to the town council of Providence. He was then twenty-eight. His story previous to that time had little to differentiate it from the stories of ten thousand young New Englanders whose youth was cast in the middle third of the nineteenth century. New England was convulsed at that time by the final adjustments of the last of the industrial revolutions; its fine old farming or seafaring communities were fading away, or being violently disrupted, while manufacturing communities were taking their places. It was a time when the old stocks that had the flavor of the stern soil bred in their bone, often found themselves thrust rudely out of the picture, often had to struggle with want. Nelson Wilmarth Aldrich was a child of that hard transition. His early life was silent; his people were of the unvocal phase of New England; and no one to-day can tell how he felt the changes going on all about him in his boyhood. Did he sense the ruthlessness of economic transformation and did it lay deep in him a resolve to master fate under a new régime? An orthodox motive that would befit the opening of a great career! But he has not recorded it. His childhood was spent largely in the mill town of East Killingly; though his parents were in straitened circumstances, they managed to give him a common-school education; later, came a year at the East Greenwich Academy; and then at the age of seventeen he made a start in business at Providence.

Of the school days there are legends, of course. One of

these would have it that at the East Killingly school, while still a mere lad, Nelson Aldrich, on those Friday afternoons when it was the rule to declaim "pieces," invariably chose passages from political orations such as the immortal one by Webster at Bunker Hill. These stories are better based than are many of the similar ones concerning the early fancies of men of genius. The family preserves a duodecimo volume which he purchased at the age of nine. His mother had given him a circus ticket and money to buy luncheon. He went without luncheon and instead bought this little book, one of the moral tales popular in those days entitled "The Tinker's Son, or I'll Be Somebody Yet."

His first infatuation was with oratory. "I remember when a small boy," he wrote to his wife long afterward, "in the old Church at E. K., hearing some man preach who possessed to my untaught imagination a wonderful eloquence, and as he pictured in glowing terms the future world, its rewards and punishments (à la Calvin) I felt an uncontrollable yearning to become at some time a public speaker, to wield myself this wonderful power." [1] He was not destined to achieve this first ambition.

Though he has left on paper very little in the way of reminiscence, the old church of his childhood fastened itself in his memory. "How distinct to-day are my memories of that country church I attended years ago. The immense pulpit, the choir from whence the same maiden voices had discoursed sweet music for many a year, and most of all the white-haired patriarchal man that was the shepherd of the flock. No matter if he was *very* puritanical in his notions. No matter if the harsh dogmas of eternal damnation furnished a text for most of his discourses. I had not then heard of the new-fangled ideas of a liberal religion. Then, a continual awe of God's justice and fear of His dreadful judgment was the lesson taught by inspiration, and the thunderings of Sinai would not have seemed more prophetic than the voice of this 'old man eloquent' seemed to me." [2]

The scanty record of his youth reveals little in the way of character origins except as matter for speculation. Far behind him in the ghostly company of his ancestors one glimpses Peleg Williams, a member of that General Assembly which passed the act called the Rhode Island Declaration of Independence, May 3, 1776. At the head of his American pedigree stands no less a person than Roger Williams, from whom he could trace descent through three lines. Another of his forebears raised sufficiently above the general level for his name to be remembered was Gideon Burgess, a major in the militia in the good old days when militia commissions signified local influence, and who also saw long-time service in the State legislature. Of selectmen and town officers in the Aldrich pedigree there is any number.

There still stands in the town of Foster an old white farmhouse, high upon a hill—it is reputed the highest house in Rhode Island—and open to all the winds of heaven. There in 1841 lived Anan Aldrich and Abby, his wife, born Burgess, daughter of Major Gideon and great-granddaughter of Peleg Williams. Anan appears to have been easy going, not in love with the strenuous sides of life. Abby was his opposite. Remembered as a tall commanding woman, Spartan, fearless, she was willing to face any hardship, bear any burden, in the pursuit of her duty. For her, with her true New England faith, nothing was too hard, nothing was beneath her dignity, if imposed by necessity. It was she apparently, whose strong will carried both of them through the troubled forties, when they had left the farm, when a fresh start in town was hard to effect, and poverty threatened to engulf them. It is quite possible that we find in the son of these two, born in the farmhouse on the high hill November 6, 1841, traces of both his parents. His silent, slow-maturing youth will be succeeded by a gradually opening manhood which at length shows a relatively luxurious nature, one that gives itself more and more, in later years, to the delights of art. But along with this, at all stages, an iron will, a contempt for difficulty, a belief that everything adverse can be overcome, no toleration for any one who surrenders to his fate. If we trace these two sides of him re-

spectively to father and mother, is there not good color for
such a conclusion?

When Nelson Aldrich was growing up Americans loved
to speak of their conspicuous figures as "self-made men."
A misnomer, of course! It was merely their way of saying
of a popular favorite that he had risen by his own merit, his
own force. As far as any man ever deserves such a description, this quiet young man who set out on the quest of fortune
at Providence in 1858, may claim the distinction. He had no
pull of any sort. Only natural wit, good habits and unfaltering industry were behind his start in business. The
precise nature of his start fluctuates in tradition. Three
years later we find him in the employ of the important firm
of Waldron and Wightman, wholesale grocers. They had at
the time no commercial superior in the State. Young Aldrich was comfortably placed on the lower rungs of a ladder of sure promotion. If tradition is to be trusted, what
gave him his start was first of all character—his easy self-
confidence, the impression he made of inherent power, his
"poise," as people said. Furthermore, from the very beginning of his career there was always about him the flavor
of personal charm. His pleasant manner and quiet smile
were instantaneously part of his impression. Said his employer, Wightman, in the early days of their acquaintance,
"See, he'll make his mark." And again, "I'd do anything I
could to help him." [3]

II

The fated year 1861 arrived. There was nothing of poise
or serenity in the atmosphere at Providence, any more than
elsewhere. The trumps of doom had blown in South Carolina, and even as the year opened it was plain that the
Gulf States, if not all the South, were going to follow her
over the precipice of secession to what result God only
knew. Horace Greeley was shrieking hysterically, "let the
erring sisters go in peace," while far off in Illinois, a strange,
shambling man, newly elected to be President of the United
States, had issued an ultimatum which made it plain that

nothing of the sort could happen; and everywhere in men's consciousness invisible fingers were clutching nervously at the sword hilt. It was a time when many people, overcome by the tension of the hour, revealed new selves, when old friendships cracked, and sudden personal enmities flashed into bitter life.

By contrast an interesting light is thrown upon the personality of young Aldrich. He did not lose either the charm or the firmness that characterized him—that peculiar impression which he made of calm power. The occasion focussed a disagreement in his family upon politics. Both parents were Democrats. Anan Aldrich was one of the last of that type of New Englander who centred his whole literary interest upon the history of his political party, whose mind revelled in its traditions and was a treasury of local political record. In the old days when the town store in New England was the centre of a casual debating society—when its function of barter might be compared with its function as forum, in the ratio, say, of one to ten— it seems that Anan was a devotee of the store. His son in boyhood had not been excluded from the scene. In the intervals of schooling, he found lucrative employment at a store in East Killingly. The true milk of the Democratic gospel must have been fed to him from his youth up. And yet, when the crisis arrived in 1861, Nelson Aldrich though not yet of age, repudiated his father's politics and counted himself a Republican.

Had Anan been the only authoritative voice in the family politics, this might not appear significant. The dim figure of Anan Aldrich, as it floats in recollection, suggests charm but does not suggest force. Very different the figure, no matter how vaguely remembered, of that heroic woman, Nelson's mother. Though she had no part in the debating society of the town store, she was as keen and devoted a political partisan as her good-natured husband. Her brother remembered, long afterward, how excited she would get in political discussion, "shaking her head rather violently while speaking and winking her eyes at the same time." This same

good authority tells us that "she took politics seriously and
loved to argue upon the virtues of the Democratic party."
It was a source of delight to Abby Burgess Aldrich that
another son, Clarence, followed her lead and became a devout Democrat.

The spiritual relations between this positive woman and
her gifted son Nelson appear to have been close, even to
the end of her life, but she did not affect him politically.
Still more significant is the fact that for all her excitable
partisanship, his apostasy produced no breach. Much as
she deplored his fall from grace, her pride in him kept her
from becoming unhappy. In this we may find a prophecy
of the ease with which in after days, he kept the regard, the
personal friendship, of many men who as partisans were as
far from him as the poles.

Apparently there was a deep ferment of new thought,
of mental independence, among the younger members of the
Aldrich-Burgess connection in those stirring years of the
fifties, when the Republican party was born. Theoretically,
the personal record being what it is, East Greenwich Academy ought to be the mental keystone of the arch. In fact,
there is no evidence that it was. The debating society of
the town store, the tense emotion of the family politics, and
the great things that were in the air, were what counted just
then. These, and that wonderful enthusiasm of a youth
for a young man which Kipling estimated correctly when he
said that it passes the love of woman—while it lasts. Nelson Aldrich as a boy had one of these deep attachments.
His cousin, Albert Burgess, ten years older than he, felt the
touch of the mystic shadow cast by coming events, thrilled
to that singular premonition, gave himself up to a passion
for new things, joined the new political party. He con-
verted his younger cousin in whom from boyhood he had
taken the greatest interest. Youth goes to youth—or to
genius!—and thus young Nelson was initiated into the new
world of the late fifties. He and Albert Burgess were not
destined to continue in close association, but their friendship survived every separation. Long afterward, when the

one was a great power, the other, dwelling quietly and happily in rural Rhode Island, was the faithful guardian of his cousin's political influence in the neighborhood where he was born.

Eighteen sixty-one passed out. The invisible fingers on the sword hilt became grim realities; war broke in a terror of rolling drums; 1862 came in amidst the roar of cannon. In Providence as everywhere throughout the land, the one appeal was for soldiers—and more soldiers—and yet more soldiers. Nelson Aldrich had joined the First Regiment of the Rhode Island National Guards. From this and other militia organizations was formed the Tenth Rhode Island Volunteers. In the spring of 1862, when this new regiment was being trained, Nelson Aldrich—still six months short of twenty-one—was a private in Company D. Two great Confederate generals planned a psychological *coup* that was to terrify Washington, paralyze the Federal strategy, and give Lee his most promising opportunity. They were completely successful. An hysterical Secretary of War, still new to his job, telegraphed the State governors begging for troops because in his excited imagination the Confederates "in great force" were marching on Washington. The Tenth Rhode Island was one of the new regiments hastily mustered into service (May 20, 1862) and hurried to the front because Stanton expected every minute to see Stonewall Jackson come galloping along Pennsylvania Avenue.

Sentry duty amid driving rains and carelessness about drinking water terminated for young Aldrich in hospital with typhoid fever. He was mustered out of service in September and returned to Providence. In the light of his subsequent career a curious interest attaches to a passage in one of his letters from the front. Having obtained freedom to visit the Capitol he "went up a splendid white marble Staircase into the House of Representatives. Took my seat among many other soldiers in the gallery. It was hard to believe that in the humming, noisy, ever-moving crowd below us was congregated the wisdom and the talent of the country. It was very much like a country town meeting—a perfect chaos. Members talking, writing letters, franking speeches, etc., etc., seemingly perfectly indifferent as to what was being done. Important business was before the House—the new Naval Bill—but none were interested, except a very few. Sedgewick of N. Y. (Chairman of Com. on Naval aff.), Noell of Missouri and several others spoke. Many military and naval officers were on the floor. Grow, the speaker, was the only man that seemed to know what was going on. But what a contrast the Senate was. There everything was calm and dignified, no noise, no confusion. Every man of them looked as if the existence of the nation depended upon the length of his face and the whiteness of his vest. Towering above every man there, conspicuous for his noble manly bearing, was Charles Sumner. The question before the Senate was the removal of the Naval Academy from Newport. Anthony attempted to make a speech. It was sensible but poorly delivered. He was opposed by nearly all. . . . When Sumner spoke all were attentive."

Back in Providence, the steady ascent of the ladder with Waldron and Wightman was resumed as if no break had taken place. He was handsome, athletic, a lover of baseball, and more popular than ever. One may guess with safety that his return in uniform made him for the day a hero. Was it a teasing impulse that led him to wear that uniform when he went home to see his mother? In later life, humor is one of his constant characteristics. Perhaps this is its first appearance in his recorded history. If that be so, it must also be the earliest record of something else. He was always capable of displaying what Walter Pater called the prime evidence of being civilized—the power to hold one's ideas lightly. That was a by-product of his humor. His mother may have had the same quality. To suppose that he wore his uniform in this interview unless he knew she was able to see it without offense, is to contradict all the rest of the evidence upon his character through a lifetime. Ruthlessness, if necessary, he was capable of; to wound sensibilities without necessity was beyond him.

What should guide surmise further is the pregnant fact that Mrs. Aldrich was now a pronounced Copperhead. Putting all this together, one is scarcely going too far if one glimpses in imagination a bit of robust comedy, two strong natures laughing at each other's convictions and loving each other none the less. The substance of their interview was an "altercation" on the merits of the war. However, the valiant amazon of Democracy, now in passionate opposition to the government, continued to be fondly proud of her cool and handsome son. As always, his personality enfolded and colored and rendered harmless all their mental differences.

Three years passed; the dreadful war wore itself out; able and devoted attention to business at Providence had its reward; Mr. Wightman got his chance to advance young Aldrich's fortunes; in 1865 or 1866 he was made a junior partner. It may be that the last straw which turned the scale and enabled Mr. Wightman to bring his young friend into the firm was a curious incident which lingers somewhat confusedly in several memories. A Providence man had fled the city owing money to several firms including Waldron and Wightman. The renegade was traced to New Orleans. What happened next is uncertain except that Mr. Aldrich went to New Orleans and brought him home— whether through persuasion on the strength of their common membership in the Masonic order, or by force, with the police at his back, is in dispute. What seems plain is that the difficulties he had to overcome were of such a sort that his success increased decidedly his reputation at Providence, because of "the ability and energy displayed." [4]

It seems also probable that another consideration both served as an index of his growing reputation and accounts for Mr. Wightman's success in getting him into the firm. At the opening of 1865, Aldrich had contemplated removing to New Orleans for good. One of his earliest letters that have been recovered was addressed to an old friend stationed at New Orleans in April, 1865. That his mind had not been idle during the war time is evidenced in the first political comment of his known to be on paper. He writes in this letter, "The year that has past has been crowded with important events which will help to make our times the most memorable in the history of the world." He passes on to discuss Southern conditions. He is so convinced that the advantages for a young man South are more promising than in the North, that he has "nearly, if not quite, made up" his mind to go there. "It seems to me that the immense business of New Orleans before the war must return gradually with peace, and in the not distant future be immeasurably increased. If I mistake not, many who have been the leading men there are incapacitated by death, absence or opinions, from returning to their old positions." He is keenly "aware that to succeed there—as well as elsewhere—requires skill, an untiring perseverance, a determination to succeed and perhaps not least capital." [5]

But things changed rapidly the next twelve months. Before they were past, he had his junior partnership, and was so committed to Rhode Island that never after did it occur to him to shift his base. Just what lessons he had learned from the war one would like to know. Of course he had observed the rapid continuation of those industrial changes that had been going on around him ever since he could remember. He had seen—it is hardly believable that he had not pondered—the beginning of that joint destruction and reconstruction which the war set going in Northern, no less than in Southern, life; as keen a mind as his must have noted sharply the terrible thoroughness with which Northern business exploited the war conditions, noted the rise of profiteering, the rush of the new industries to control legislation, the gathering predominance of manufacture over commerce. Unless he was widely different from what he afterward became, there must have waked in him an ironic mirth as he listened to the diapason of insincerity, the grand chorus of the profiteers masquerading as patriots. Perhaps it was thus early that he formed a contempt—an amused contempt—for all those who would capitalize sentiment, especially the sentiment of public service. During the war that masquerade had been the main business of the

New England spinners—with dividends at forty per cent!

The last word of this range of his experience lies embedded between the lines in that letter to New Orleans. He assumes that what is done is done. For him, the war with its last gunshot became ancient history. Its events, its issues, its hopes, fears, animosities were as dead as Hecuba. Whether the fact was pleasing to him personally or displeasing did not concern him. What's done is done! He not only accepted this principle as his own rule but assumed it in others. Thereby he revealed what was ever to be his dominant characteristic, what was to prove many times an incomparable source of power, but also, now and then, a disastrous limitation.

III

When young Aldrich was thinking of New Orleans as a place where a fortune might be made more quickly than at Providence, he had the personal incentive to seek that result which most young men are fortunate enough to have. The lady's name was Abby Chapman, though she was commonly spoken of as Abby Greene. She had lived since infancy with a childless uncle and aunt—Mr. and Mrs. Duty Greene—wealthy people from whom eventually she inherited a comfortable little fortune.

One first catches sight of her in the later war years—a brisk gay young girl, full of spirits, generally attractive. She is much sought after. Among her suitors is a great fop, and Abby threatens to cut off his curls. One gets the impression that for a penny more, she would have done it. There are rich young fellows dangling after her, and Nelson Aldrich is still only a clerk with Waldron and Wightman, his future not yet assured; but that does not matter to Abby. They take rides together and walk and read together and at least one recollection is of a lovers' quarrel—Abby with her high spirits all aflash in her eyes; her temper soaring; vehement commands to Nelson; and he, quietly biding his time, keeping his temper with a firm rein and a smiling eye.

It is plain that both the young people took themselves
and their affair with the increasing seriousness natural to
such affairs, and at last the predestined point was reached
in the summer of 1865. Calling upon her, he was told she
was not at home when he knew she was; that same night he
wrote her a letter that was an ultimatum. It still exists in
the small package of letters addressed to "Miss Abby P.
Greene," which, with one other package containing letters
written to her seven years later, form about the whole of
his intimate revelation of himself now to be found on paper.
He was in a high mood, very youthful but very natural—
and somewhat mid-Victorian be it remembered—when he
wrote that letter which was the beginning of the end. Perhaps it has a psychological significance as well as an amatory
one. In the after days he developed—or did he merely reveal?—an uncanny power to determine the precise strategic
moment at which to demand the "dernier ressort." He used
that potent phrase in this letter but implied that it applied
to her course and her employment of "the not uncommon
subterfuge." While the letter plainly is both hurt and
angry, may it not have been also the first instance of his
faculty for divining the psychological moment?

Soon afterward they were engaged. But more than a
year elapsed before they were married. During much of
this time she was away from Providence and it is through
the letters which bridge this interval that many glimpses
into the man's real self are given. So much of his life was
encased in a serene reserve quite impervious to scrutiny,
that all these little windows inward are peculiarly valuable.
It is in one of these letters to his betrothed that he describes
incidentally the white-haired patriarch and the choir of
maidens in the old church of his childhood. His religion,
in the days of his eminence, was not paraded to the world.
He never became a professing member of any church. But
there was in him a vein of concealed mysticism that gave
him his own form of response to religious suggestion. That
reminiscence of early days in church was written on a Sunday. It came to mind following the remark "No Sabbath

ever seems as sacred to me as a New England Sabbath. At New Orleans the universal and continued bustle and confusion seemed completely to change the nature of the day. In the bright stillness of a day like this God seems nearer to us. His presence more perceptible, our adoration of Him is instinctive." That he has already drifted far from the mood in which he had once listened to the white-haired patriarch is made plain in this same letter.

I suppose it is for some good purpose that we are cut loose from the trusting faith of youth and set adrift upon the sea of doubts and fears which overspreads our maturer years. I wonder if these doubts and fears are conquerable. I fear not by mortals. Perhaps without them any great disappointment would be fatal, and we should curse the Power that gave us such delusive and groundless hopes. We are receiving continual installments which lessen the effect of the final catastrophe and we suffer in imagination for all conceivable evils which *may* befall us. I wish it was not so. We are trees gnarled and dwarfed by fear of a tempest which may never come. Better be a prostrate and scarred trunk awakening conceptions, at least, of past greatness than be an insignificant shrub afraid of its own growth.

What I want most is faith. If that Superior Creator *would* only give to my ideal creations the vital essence of realities, would make me always hopeful never despondent, *would* continue and multiply these occasional hours of an unalloyed happiness! I will make an effort which with His help must succeed. I will ask, expect happiness—more—I will *be* happy.

It will not do to generalize upon a subject which thereafter he shrouded in a deep reserve. But surely in reading letters like this which was written in 1866 one should remember what the world was speculating upon, that while, when the tide of agnosticism was in full flood contending in every mind with every inherited belief. It should be remembered, seven years later, when, in a peculiarly susceptible mood, shaken by ill health, he found in the architecture of the Pantheon with the magic circle of its open dome, a glorious symbol of the eye of God. Intense religious sensibility, joined with uncertainty upon religious dogma, was characteristic of the most typical Americans of that day. It is a pity he could not have read the intimate papers of Lincoln and comprehended the mood in him that was so similar to his own.

Already, fanaticism in religion had become an offense which he would not tolerate. On another Sunday he was sharply annoyed. He had driven to East Killingly to attend a memorial service for a cousin who had died in Libby Prison.

It was in the old church all unchanged since the days when my youthful self sat bolt upright upon its hard board seats, and heard with fearful wonder—without understanding—the unsparing denunciation of sin and emphatic warnings of the eternal punishment that threatened all sinners. . . . All except the church had changed. I knew hardly any one. Those which I had known as boys and girls were fathers and mothers; many prematurely old, most unmistakeably entering into that dreary monotony of drudgery and toil from which they never could emerge.

The minister was a southern refugee who had evidently misunderstood his calling, and with whom I could associate no ideas of reverence or religion.

He might be adrift in his formal belief at this time but he had no impulse toward any of the "new-fangled" religions which were flourishing all about him at the very moment when agnosticism and the heady new wine of the doctrine of evolution were cracking so many old bottles. With a quiet humor he describes a convention of Spiritualists at Providence which

comprises men who have believed everything and nothing at times, from fanatical superstitions, through nominal Christianity to atheism. If we can believe the statement of their speakers all the good spirits of the world are gathered in our favored city.

I must confess that I have never felt their presence, not the first inspiration, not the first friendly rap upon my head board.

What a contrast with the mystic excitement of which we shall hear later in the Pantheon. Allowing for all the differences in health on the two occasions, the contrast is of the heart of the matter.

These letters are plentifully enriched by tender passages and yet, withal, there runs through them the true New England fear of emotional display. "Do not fear I am going to write a sentimental love letter, not that I would detract from the importance of love which I believe to be the noblest, divinest part of our nature. But you know I *might* commit some extravagance which might not look well in this ink." Just the same he has learned the great lesson "how little there is in life away from those we love." His ideal man had once been a cold creature "above the reach of circumstance, above the whirlwind of common passion," but now he can say "love transformed me."

In one who has been conceived by the world almost as sheer adamant it is rather startling to find that in these early days he counted himself "unfortunately constituted, alternating between faith and despondency." Just the same even now, the unfaltering self-confidence of the great men of action is beginning to appear. His doubts arise only when he is in a mood of dreams, pondering the unseen things. The moment he turns to the practical world he is himself again. "Five years of this imprisoning alliance to traffic and then I *will* be free. My commencement in business life has been, beyond my most sanguine expectations, successful, and if some dreams of my boyhood may never be realized, more *power* for good than I ever hoped for seems within my reach."

In 1866 they were married. By this time he had attained financial independence. On his wedding day he had every reason to feel that Fortune was not his foe. Whether it is true that Mayor Doyle, the Antonian lieutenant for Providence, had already taken favorable note of him and said that day, as report has it, "Nelson Aldrich is the smartest man in Providence and some day is going to be heard from"—whether that is true or not, Nelson Aldrich knew his own mind in many ways and had no fear of the future. He had the old-fashioned American belief that the man

should support the family. He was ready to help his wife
invest her fortune—some of it was later put into the business of which he was part—but he steadily refused to live
on her income. That purpose was immediately made plain.
As the young couple were about to take the train for their
wedding journey, the bride's brother, who was seeing them
off, presented the groom with an envelope. "Your wife
asked me to hand you this," said he, "she would like you
to use it if you find it convenient." Mr. Aldrich tore the
envelope open and found a thousand-dollar bill. He handed
it back to his brother-in-law saying, "You may return this
to my wife and tell her that when I feel the need of using
her money, I shall ask for it."

A perfect simplicity and straightforwardness about his
resources always characterized him. He never made any
bones about just what he could or could not afford. His
wife's sister—who like so many others including Mrs. Duty
Greene, his wife's foster mother, had implicit faith in him—
preserved with admiration this incident of his complete
freedom from pretense. He had asked her to go with him
to pick out Abby's wedding present. After examining many
jewels he selected a set of pearls. "These are the ones I can
afford," said he, "do you think she would like them?" "Indeed she would," was the reply. All the years of their life
together he held to his belief that his income should be the
one they lived upon. Mrs. Aldrich fell into his humor. At
first, while his income was less than hers she cheerfully contracted her scale of living. It expanded rapidly with his
widening prosperity until, presently the distinction between
his and hers ceased to have significance. A few years later
she was living as luxuriously as ever she had, perhaps more
luxuriously, in a fine house in a fashionable part of the
town.

These were pleasant years while he mounted slowly but
steadily the golden ladder. His wife was a true fortune
irrespective of her money. Her dauntless spirit, her quick
wit, her good looks, her taste—all of which she had in full
measure—benefited him at every turn. Until now he had

cared little about dress, was inclined to be careless. She put an end to that. As fast as money and children came to them—the gods being generous at the same time in both respects—she wove about them all a charmed circle of home delights. He had none of the responsibilities of the household and all its pleasures. His children were a joy and he loved to play with them.

IV

Presently, in a small way, he got into politics. And here, as in business, his start did not come from pull. It may be traced to an institution that has vanished from American life. A few elderly people still remember that in their youth every thriving American town had a "lyceum." Webster preserves the fact by recognizing the word as an Americanism with the definition "An association for popular instruction by lectures, a library, debates, etc.; also its building or hall." It is rather the thing to be mentally snobbish to-day about all these American beginnings of culture, but just the same the lyceums of the middle third of the century formed a vast popular university as significant as anything in our history. The one at Providence was founded as far back as 1829 by a few students of Mr. De Witt's school who met in one another's houses. In 1832 it adopted the name Franklyn Lyceum. Its first course of public lectures was given in 1840 "through the kindness of Emerson." For more than thirty years it maintained its lecture courses and also sponsored public concerts. There is a long list of celebrities, speakers and musicians, who were brought to Providence by the Franklyn Lyceum. But it had another function even more significant in the lives of any number of young men. Every Monday night from October to June the members took part in a debate. It was in the debates of this and other lyceums from 1840 to about 1870 that the thinking of America was in no small part determined. When one reflects what subjects convulsed the world, those momentous years, when one remembers that Emerson and the Concord radicals were the zealous sponsors of the popular university and that Darwin rose before it passed, one ceases to be condescending with regard to it.

Young Aldrich joined the Lyceum soon after his arrival in Providence. In 1864 he was elected secretary; in 1866 vice-president. The contemporary account of the meeting at which he became vice-president is too characteristic of the journalism of that day to be overlooked.

The annual election of officers of the Franklyn Lyceum took place last evening. Nearly three hundred votes were cast and the canvass was one of much interest and considerable excitement . . . vice-president, Nelson W. Aldrich. . . . At the close of the meeting at the rooms (of the Lyceum), and after the installation of the newly elected officers, the members of the Lyceum, under the leadership of Colonel S. H. Wales as marshall, proceeded to the saloon of Mr. S. Goff on Westminster Street to partake of the annual supper. The tables were laid in the finest style, and the quality, variety and abundance of the fare will give this well-known caterer a still higher place in popular favor.

The city and state authorities, the present, past and would-be officers of the Lyceum were then successively called upon for a representation. Many humorous and some serious speeches were made, and the best of feeling prevailed on the part both of those whom fortune had placed at the head of the poll and those who were characterized as the "unburied dead" of the conflict. The excitement of the contest has awakened, as it nearly always does, a new interest in the affairs of the Lyceum, and may well be expected to exert a favorable influence upon the future prosperity of this ancient and useful institution.[6]

Such reports of Lyceum meetings—their semi-social character, their boisterous *camaraderie,* their good humor, their intense delight in club politics, coupled with the fact that they were debating societies—make plain the other significance they had, which was quite as important as their intellectual significance. They were seminaries of parliamentary law. They educated a whole generation of Americans—perhaps two generations—in the procedure through which representative government has expressed itself. Through a dozen years and more young Aldrich was a devoted member of the Lyceum. In it he became, at an astonishingly early age, a master in the tactics of the manipulation of assemblies. The youths who found their delight in the weekly tournament of the Lyceum included many of the brightest and most ambitious of the rising generation. Trust them to learn all the tricks of the leaders of assemblies and to practise them with the ruthlessness of their years. To test a presiding officer by unmerciful heckling was part of the game. But when it happened that Nelson Aldrich was called to the chair and the usual game began he was so entirely master of the situation that "they missed their usual fun in confusing the new presiding officer."

The debates of the Lyceum were the special training of this resolute mind. From the first days in Providence his nights were often crowded with laborious reading. Many a night he would go to bed with a lamp beside him and read until he could keep awake no longer. His memory was sure and capacious. He had a passion for books and bought as rapidly and as freely as he could afford. Almost as soon as he began to take part in the debates, he established a reputation for accuracy and thoroughness in the presentation of whatever he discussed. This continued to be his reputation in many intricate debates of his later career. But it is to be noted that he was a debater at the Lyceum, not an orator. A perfectly friendly critic, in his early days in politics, said that he did not know how to make a good popular speech. If this means that he was wholly devoid of the sympathetic illusions of the orator, wholly incapable of histrionic reactions, it is borne out by all his subsequent career. Gladstone says that an orator gives back to his audience in a stream what he gets from them in a vapor. In this sense, young Aldrich—and still more truly, old Aldrich, long afterward—was not an orator. At the beginning of a speech he knew exactly what he meant to say and very seldom, at the end of a speech, had the "vapor" of his audience clouded his purpose. He would have made a consummate legal advocate. Naturally, therefore, he became— rather, by instinct he always was—a debater of the first rank.

When, and in what way, he admitted to himself that his oratorical ambition was futile is not known. Perhaps it was the Lyceum that forced home upon him the bitter truth. That it was bitter is shown by a passage in the same letter which preserves the incident of his childish admiration for the terrible preaching Calvinist. Immediately after telling the anecdote he adds, "Alas! disappointments come to us all. Our lives are continually twisted from the current in which we would like to have them run, and perhaps we can only ask God that we may not in the end find ourselves on some unknown sea." It is possible that oratory was not the only art which he attempted in vain. A few surviving fragments among his papers seem to indicate that he tried his hand, unsuccessfully, at imaginative writing. These were the days of his omnivorous reading, and there are passages in some early letters which show how much books meant to him. "Is not Irving splendid!" he exclaims. "He is so talented, so grand yet so simple, so eloquent without affectation and withal so original that he universally wins the affection of his readers." He thinks that "all the heroes in 'Pendennis' are too much of that type which Thackeray is always berating—snobs." He thinks the "second volume of 'Pendennis' much the best. The XIVth chapter is particularly good—I think it is the fourteenth." He uses phrases like "Vanity Fair" in the discriminating way of a reading man. He writes his sweetheart of an evening at the Lyceum reading the *North American Review,* and gives her in another letter an outline of a lecture by Holmes. A hard-worked old woman with whom he falls into conversation and who talks philosophically of her troubles, has a face that "resembles Emerson." Books and writers in imagination are all about him. His early letters reflect the writing impulse; he slips easily into meditations or homilies. There is a touch in them here and there which both intimates scientific reading, and shows some real ingenuity in expression, though of a grandiloquent, Emersonian sort no longer in fashion, as when hunting for an image he exlaims somewhat rashly,

"The brightness of solar light becomes darkness when dif-
fused through all space."

If his first ambition to be an orator, melted into a second
ambition to be a writer, both were renounced so completely
that except for the early letters to his wife one could hardly
believe that they had existed. He gave himself up to the
enjoyment of success as a debater. This was paralleled by
another gift that completes the roster of his political equipment. He had the trick of holding in hand the results of his
hard work without parading how he got them. For all his
accuracy, his thoroughness, he never smelled of the lamp.
A genial casualness—or what seemed to be that—hovered
in his atmosphere. Early in life, people began mentioning
his urbanity. Again, Pater's test of the civilized man—the
power to hold one's ideas lightly.

Active politics were first suggested to him by his friends
in the Lyceum. Among minor historical ironies is the quaint
fact that the political party which Mr. Aldrich had repudiated, which was to become his object of inveterate attack,
gave him his political start. He resided in a Democratic
ward, the Fifth. He had a brother-in-law who was a Democrat, also a close friend, a Democrat. These with his Lyceum friends persuaded him in 1869 to stand for the Common Council. He consented and was elected by a handsome
majority without, it would seem, any definite party commitment.[7]

The city government was in a bad way. Mayor Doyle,
who according to tradition had already detected in young
Aldrich a coming man, was having his troubles. In the de-
pressing after-war conditions the purchasable voters had
been mobilized and boldly used. The devices whereby a
local machine may secure its ascendancy through skilful
use of those departments which employ much labor—such
as a highway department—were being ably developed. At
the same time, the local politicians were studying the influence of corporations as a factor in politics and were doing
juggler's feats with taxation. Property values were falling

and tax rates were rising. The Fifth Ward put a sound
young business man into the Council because people of substance were getting out of patience with the government
of the day. Republicans as well as Democrats contributed
to a temporary defeat of the Doyle organization. In the
Fifth Ward Mr. Aldrich had been indorsed by the Republican primary without opposition.[8]

As a Common Councilman, he had a further training in
parliamentary strategy. He found himself as a rule in the
minority—as when he strove in vain to induce economy in
the purchase of a new site for the City Hall. Though not
inflexibly either of the minority or the majority—voting
now with one, now with the other—his general attitude was
in opposition to the machine because wholly inspired by the
desire for economy and good business in municipal finance.

He continued to represent the Fifth Ward until 1871,
when he removed to the Sixth Ward which promptly chose
him as a councilman and chose him again the next year,
and the year following. He was president of the Council,
1871 to 1873.

For all his independent temper, he was unmistakably a
Republican. There is a curious illustration of the political
good humor which always enveloped him. In the days of
torchlight parades, it was the rule to illuminate one's home
on the night when one's own party paraded, but to make it
sternly dark when the opposite party was marching past.
The Aldrich house would be illuminated on both occasions.
This gracious course is attributed to Mrs. Aldrich and at a
little later time, it used to anger her small children who
were true blue Republicans, as Papa was. But the double
illumination may as justly be attributed to both the Aldriches. While most Americans in their party affiliations
remained at the age of the Aldrich children, the father in
this case as well as the mother had progressed to the age
where fury is not an essential of conviction. Once more,
we hold our ideas lightly—if we are civilized.

This pleasant-mannered young man could be positive
enough when the need arose. In the Republican State Con-

vention of 1872 he was present and a candidate for selection as delegate to the national convention. "During the progress of the ballot, Mr. Aldrich stated that it was circulated on this floor that he was not friendly to General Grant. He wished to state unqualifiedly that he was for General Grant first, last and all the time and for nobody else." He was chosen a delegate. At this same State Convention he compassed the nomination for secretary of state of an old friend of his, Joshua Addeman. The election soon afterward put Mr. Addeman into office. He was to figure again, more significantly, in his friend's story.[9]

The Philadelphia Convention which has the doubtful distinction of renominating General Grant for the presidency, witnessed the first definite association of two men who did not at the moment suspect how close their subsequent relations were to be. These were Mr. Aldrich and General Brayton, both delegates from Rhode Island. Neither has recorded their relations at Philadelphia. What impression the convention made on Mr. Aldrich we do not know. It occurred near a turning point in his development. Later in this same year he set out upon a lonely journey in which he made discoveries of first importance to his development —the old world and art, and in himself, the wanderlust; and all this so soon after attending for the first time a national convention, the most prodigious symbol of organized popular power that modern democracy has invented. One may risk a good deal that in the next year and the year after, many things, actual and imaginary, practical and visionary, of the present and of the future, were "changing pickets" —as Kipling impudently expresses it—in his head.

V

Mr. Aldrich was suffering from a deep grief. His eldest child, a bright boy, had been the idol of both father and mother. At the age of four, suddenly, he died. That was in 1871. The father was not quite thirty. He had worked hard; apparently he had not entirely recovered from the

typhoid fever of the war time; and now profound grief
wore into his spirit. His quiet buoyancy deserted him. At
length he was persuaded to try Europe as a tonic. Whether
that first wandering, on which Mrs. Aldrich was unable to
accompany him, really healed the wound we do not know.
But it certainly fixed upon him a new habit—or else, it gave
an outlet to something within him of which hitherto he was
not aware. Was there, after all, deep beneath his apparent
serenity a submerged restlessness, an imaginative vagrancy?
Was it that which drew him so often in afterdays to the
open road, and the windy sea, and the far side of the horizon? At least we know that thereafter, whenever occasion
permitted, he was an inveterate traveller.

From this journey dates his active interest in art. There
had been little if any of it in his life hitherto. Native
American art in Rhode Island has not much to show except
for the beautiful doorways of old Newport and a few old
houses at Providence. Such things were not pointed out
and set in the world's eye in 1872. It is not fanciful to
guess that the rituals of the Masonic order were the only
artistic influences with which, as yet, he had been at home.
And now, of a sudden—the Louvre and the National Gallery, and the Capitol, the pomp of Whitehall, the clink and
glitter of Paris afternoons, the Carnival at Rome. He fell
in with some delightful and cultivated people, to whom the
vocabulary of art was a natural language. When he came
home he brought back a number of admirable things, a few
of real distinction. He had discovered the noble art of en-
graving, the magnificent art of painting.

This journey is recorded in a package of letters to his
wife. In their changing moods they sum up and dismiss
the story of his formative time. Personally, they reveal a
tender man, homesick for wife and fireside, the sort that
was plainly foreshadowed in the letters of seven years before. Intellectually, here is evidence that the Lyceum, and
nights of reading, could produce as much and no more, in
the way of appreciation of art, as could Beacon Hill and
Harvard College, and Fifth Avenue, in those "green" days

when Americans still regarded the European tour as evidence of a superior social position. Though these letters abound in shrewd comments, though he is honest enough to confess that he likes Turner and Constable better than the old masters of the National Gallery, he is also capable of gazing thrilled at Roubillac's sensational memorial to Mrs. Nightingale in Westminster. But so were all his countrymen then—so are many of them still. It is in yet another vein that the letters speak out strong and bold, promising unintentionally far more than the writer suspected they did. Here and there, they ring deep with the inner resonance of a mind that is predestined to great things.

He seems to have gone abroad reluctantly. Homesickness was often his companion. If only his wife were with him! Would the time come when he, she, the children, could enjoy all this together! But home and the far countries were not the only things that touched his imagination. What was he really thinking of, we wonder—this young politician with the vision of political greatness so fresh in his eyes!—when, just after his arrival in Ireland he fell into meditation over the news of the death of Horace Greeley. One glimpses between the lines, the charm there is for him in the political career. Also, here is deep sympathy for the leader that has failed. What moves him most is the spectacle of Greeley—whom he had helped to defeat—repudiated by the party he had himself been mainly instrumental in creating.

Though the noble sights of Europe roused his reverent admiration, there were other sights that also struck deep which aroused observation that was keen, and reflection that was acute. In a desolate hour, when he was peculiarly lonely in his mind, he writes:

The mysteries of life and the greater and deeper mystery of death stand out in stronger relief to me every day. Why is all this?—and where will it end?—are questions which I am continually asking, but the answer never comes. Here in this great Maelstrom of passion and excitement, where the life of a man or of a thousand are valued as a rush light, the relationship of hu-

manity with Divinity has a new and a terrible interest. This
morning at breakfast at a regular French cafe, the table next to
me was occupied by two Frenchmen of the middle or lower class
drinking absinthe. As I looked upon their dull wild stupor I
wondered what dreams were evolved from the depths of the bitter
glass. Multiply this scene and you have the possibility of the
wildest revolution or the most terrible outrages.

He was destined, in after days, to think much upon the
place, and the power, of the excitable multitude in modern
civilization. There is no evidence that he had done so hitherto. It may well be that the impressions made upon him
in days of physical pain and spiritual depression, while he
looked into the maelstrom of European decadence, were the
beginning of a disdain of weakness which he never outgrew.
He was taking himself back to health partly through sheer
force of will, writing in his gloomiest moments that he had
no fear for his own recovery. Men who abandoned themselves to their fates must have filled him then as they continued ever after to fill him, with disgust.

A few fervent passages in these European letters are so
different from all the utterances that come after, as to compel one to close the door upon speculation. So much of his
later life was sealed in a smiling taciturnity that these
revealing passages are like windows inward where curtains
were very soon to be drawn down forever. It is always food
for thought when one finds in the early life of a statesman
hidden springs of feeling, too real to be considered accidental, but which do not reveal themselves subsequently except
by indirection. Furthermore, the men who begin, as this
man did, with an ambition that was never gratified, are
always to the analytical mind delicate challenges. In this
case, how did the deeper emotions and the frustrated ambition transmute their power into something rich and strange.
Who shall say? There is a letter written at Rome in 1873
that is the most surprising, also the last, of his self-revela-
tions. Rome had taken possession of him. "If I have felt
at other places impressed by the many objects of interest
around me, *here* I am completely overwhelmed." The

Capitol with its memories of "the men who for centuries ruled the world" stirred in this American the enthusiasms of the essential ruler. But something else was stirred still more deeply. The scenes around him called back his earlier, now suppressed, desire to excel in an art. They brought out of distant shadow and touched again with the light that never was, the vivid reality of that day when the thundering Calvinist waked in his heart the desire to be an orator. And he had come to believe that it was all a mere dream, a hopeless phantasy. "But now, to-day, in Rome the same feeling renewed and intensified takes hold of me. Oh, if I could *only* paint in words the visions that have passed before me during this one day. If I could *only* catch and retain in a tangible form the inspired life that has filled and surrounded me. Never before have I—as during these few days in Rome—lived so little in the present, the real. I have not, I trust, forgotten my duties and relations to the few loved ones, to whom alone my thoughts or doings are of consequence. I know at best the dream is a short one. At home, governed by the exacting, unfeeling, I almost said unscrupulous, laws of business, I would have no right, could not afford to have such dreams. But here, in the balmy, intoxicating air of Italy, to dream is the normal condition and whether you will it or no, you find yourself borne away from the present into some new state of existence, peopled with strange yet familiar forms, find yourself grappling the great mysteries of our nature with new emotions. It is these strange weird combinations and impressions that I would like to weave into an ineffaceable picture before they elude my grasp. But this is beyond my power."

His thoughts pass to the Pantheon. It is a curious, perhaps a significant, fact that the only piece of architecture which affected him strongly was this singular building. Westminster had carried him away because it was the shrine of the world's "greatest civilization," but it did not lay hold of him as architecture. In Paris, the boulevards, the Place de la Concord, high mass, all had their effect; but Notre

Dame was not mentioned. Did this strong, typically American mind find its footing in the Renaissance more easily than in the Middle Age? Was symmetry more akin to it than variety? Or was there something in the vast open dome of the Pantheon, defiant of all tradition—the one contribution of the real Rome to religious art—that seized upon the countryman of Emerson as if a piece of nature transcending nature. "Then the Pantheon, to me the most sublime of all temples or churches in its simple grandeur conveying an impression of the Presence and Power of Divinity which I have never felt elsewhere. Your view *upward* is unobstructed by any device of man's. Surrounded by perfect symmetry and beauty, you can look trustingly into the clear bright all-seeing Eye so beautifully symbolized here. I feel a strong impulse, each visit, to throw myself prostrate on the marble pavement under the dome, to acknowledge His supremacy, and to hold for a moment near communion with the Father."

At bottom, still unconquerable, the mysticism that is the basis of the American character, its bequest from the seventeenth century. It is not for nothing that this man is the direct descendant of Roger Williams. And yet, along with these deeply suppressed feelings, which so seldom were allowed to escape, is the invincible modernism which was his obvious characteristic. In him, as in some few others, practicality and mysticism had no antagonism. This letter broke off short in order to catch the mail.

VI

Things now moved swiftly toward that time when Brayton, in his own estimation, offered him all the kingdoms of the Earth, locally speaking, and got an answer that surprised him. Five years of rapid advancement both in business and politics bridge the interval. By the time Brayton's offer is made his business standing has increased so much that he has become president of the First National Bank and also president of the Providence Board of Trade.

His political advance these years between 1872 and 1877 is not so easy to make out. One surmises that it was rather overshadowed by the business advance. His service as councilman closed in rather sharp antagonism to Mayor Doyle. The next year he went to the State legislature where he manifested a tendency to exalt sheer efficiency by advocating a general State system of liquor licenses instead of local option. The year after, as chairman of the Republican State Convention, he addressed it "in a very earnest manner upon national topics, taking the most decided views of the necessity for purity and ability in the standard bearers of the party, and insisting on honesty in the individuals and honor in the government and a speedy return to a sound currency." [10] Shortly afterward, he took part in an obscure political affair, the explanation of which is still to seek. The Anthony machine was in opposition to the weaker but considerable faction headed by Henry W. Lippitt, who had been elected governor the year before. A month after his earnest speech to the Republican Convention, Mr. Aldrich was chosen speaker of the State House of Representatives. The election for governor had been held, no one had received a majority, and the choice of governor had devolved on the legislature, which was also to elect a senator. Mr. Aldrich retained the speakership only fourteen days, being excused from further service to attend the National Republican Convention of 1876. In those fourteen days, Lippitt was re-elected governor and Anthony was re-elected senator. What is the meaning of the incident—or whether it has any meaning—no one can now say. It is asserted—but on very slight authority—that until this time Mr. Aldrich was a "Lippitt man" rather than an "Anthony man."

Whether this bore upon the great event of the next year is a matter of speculation. Though the Republicans in the State made a pretense of harmony, though the Anthony men had voted for Lippitt for governor and the Lippitt men had voted for Anthony for senator, their good relations were of the surface only. Anthony had every reason

to want to undermine Lippitt. Brayton had every reason
to want to recruit good men, to draw them away from the
Lippitt organization. But none of these schemers ever put
their motives on record. As to what actually happened,
let Brayton tell the story.

I met Senator Aldrich on the street one day and said: "Do
you want to be governor? Because if you do you can get it."
He said he didn't know, he'd think it over. "Well, there's no
time to lose," I said. "If you want to be governor, say so." But
he never said it. He never really wanted to be governor.[11]

Mr. Aldrich consulted his friend Addeman—the same to
whom he wrote about New Orleans in 1865, for whom he
had secured the nomination as secretary of state, and Mr.
Addeman urged him not to accept the offer. The governorship might prove his political eclipse. The venturesome
mind of Mr. Aldrich inclined him to the same conclusion.
Mahomet had beckoned to the mountain but the mountain
was too securely based.

CHAPTER II

SHADOWS BEFORE

As the mountain would not come to Mahomet, Mahomet did the sensible thing. The next year General Brayton proposed to back Mr. Aldrich as a candidate for the National House of Representatives.

He was thirty-six and locally somewhat of a personage—president of the First National Bank, president of the Board of Trade, partner in a vigorous commercial concern, generally liked and admired. In direct contacts with men, in a relatively small community, he was a conspicuous success. His rise in fortune had been happy, without so far a slip. In the little world of Providence he had arrived.

Now, at last, the chance to try his luck in the greater world outside. What did it portend? Would he be equal to more relentless tests? Though quite without egoism he had faith in himself. He decided to take the new chance.

Oddly—considering what a name he has for boldness—the first step was taken fearfully. As the time for the nominating convention drew near he became desperately nervous. He left the stage, went down to New York, and there waited for Brayton's telegram that was to be the voice of fate.[1]

Brayton had assured him that the prospect was certain. The arch manipulator had canvassed all the local bosses. Mr. Aldrich had done his share, driving from place to place, talking with the men of importance, the men whom Brayton alone could not account for.

The career of Aldrich bridges the central span between an old America and a new, and there were scenes in this first campaign for the congressional nomination that were typical of the old America which was passing, of which he was destined to see the end. A fine specimen of the old-fashioned Rhode Island Quaker was Nathaniel Peckham.

35

He lived at Middleton. Both Brayton and Aldrich felt that his support was much to be desired. Brayton found him one day—the day of the celebration of the battle of Rhode Island—at a wayside blacksmith shop. When Brayton had explained his purposes, and had told him that Aldrich might be found at the scene of the festival, Peckham at once rode off to find him. He greeted the candidate with the words, "It's time you went to Congress." Whereupon Mr. Aldrich "held a reception there and left every one his friend." When Brayton's telegram finally came to him at New York it contained the delightful news that his nomination was unanimous. When the election came he polled a handsome majority.[2]

And all this was in spite of the fact that he had not done well as a public speaker. That was not, never became, his forte. The very poor showing which he made at a flag-raising had inspired pity in political veterans to whom glib talk was as the air they breathed.[3] Now, as always, it was the individual not the mass to whom Aldrich instinctively addressed himself, with whom he was irresistibly at home. The clew to his success was put into homespun by his friend Addeman who explained his early elections by saying he was a "great mixer."

From the Providence of 1878, Washington was a far cry. The man who, for all his boldness could become so nervous over his first nomination, had no intention to play the rash provincial. Intuitively, he was never a provincial. The cosmopolitan instinct was part of his make-up. It led him, now, to go slow, to measure his new environment, to become for a season the careful, assiduous apprentice learning a job. The day he arrived in Washington with his family, and took rooms at the Arlington Hotel, he was in a mood to be as cautious as he was brave.

The Forty-sixth Congress gave him a place on the relatively inconspicuous District of Columbia Committee[4] made up otherwise of routine politicians, men vastly less original than this newcomer whom they regarded as an amateur. Nevertheless they showed quick recognition of something in him that impressed them, for it was upon this newest member that the committee allowed the defense of the tax bill of the District to devolve. He acquitted himself well, stating the matter simply, clearly, with apt brevity.[5]

He was cool and shrewd while he took the measure of Congress. Was this national arena any different except in size from the local one he knew so well? Was the parliamentary character of the House of Representatives any more impressive in the eyes of a serene and objective mind, than the town council of Providence or the Franklyn Lyceum? One may risk it that Aldrich did not take long to weigh the House in a balance and conclude it was poor stuff. Who can doubt that this miscellaneous assemblage, in which the majority were the creatures of political gambling, was less distinguished than was that company of keen young fellows, self-selected, who had taught him what was what in parliamentary procedure.

The Fates had conspired—and continued to conspire—to give him a low estimate of the mentality revealed in practical politics, to reaffirm his instinctive impulse to think in terms of the individual, not in terms of the mass. The characteristic thinking of his time was drifting that way. Charles Darwin was in full career, both his masterpieces bywords in the Lyceums. The doctrine of the survival of the fit was in the air. An unvoiced but none the less real demand, communicating itself somehow throughout the land, was for some new mode of determining *vox deii* other than the traditional one of counting the noses of the crowd. Some day some courageous historian may link all this back to the lyceums, self-perpetuating as they were, with their unconscious propaganda for a selective process that should draw intelligence together and make it co-operative, that should weed out unintelligence in the seats of the mighty. Or, he may discover some other less obvious base for the political mood of which Mr. Aldrich in course of time is to become a conspicuous exponent.

In his first term in Congress, his business besides learn-

ing the new job was also to make doubly sure of his hold
on his constituents, to clear the way for another election,
to have time in a second term to finish his apprenticeship.
He watched carefully the interests of his district. His
qualities of affable friendship were exhibited whenever any
of his acquaintances visited Washington. Many a time he
delighted them by coming up into the visitor's gallery of
the House, sitting with them, and pointing out the celebrities.[6]

He captured a second election with relative ease. That
was in 1880—the year the Republicans got a President without a popular majority and with a plurality of only
9,000; when the congressional elections gave them a majority of one in the next House while it became plain
that the Senate, except for the casting vote of the Vice-
President would be tied. It was a memorable year because
for the first time since Andrew Jackson there was a national
ticket in the field that made no bones about its proletarian
appeal. And both the "Greenback" nominees, Mr. Weaver
of Iowa and Mr. Chambers of Texas, were so far removed
from all the social and economic ideas that were orthodox
in Rhode Island. The country at large had no appreciation how significant this was, could not read the handwriting on the wall, did not make out the dim forms upon a far
horizon of those appalling coming events that were casting
their shadows before.

Mr. Aldrich, the hard-working political apprentice,
studying his job as a congressman, had no more second
sight this year than had the rest of his countrymen. The
business of being a congressman, and the business of making a fortune—the constant delightful occupation of sin-
gling out the men who were really the strong ones at Providence, of drawing them to himself as his real constituency
—these were the tasks that possessed his mind. He did not
allow himself much time for diversion—that would come
when the apprenticeship was over. He had hesitated, the
year before, about joining the Hope Club of Providence but
had finally accepted an invitation.

His family was his chief diversion. His children in after time remembered how when they were little their father would often play cards with them, and how he guarded against their sensibilities by never appearing to condescend, by seeming to be just as eager to win as they were. A delicate consideration of other people's feelings lives in a number of anecdotes. Once when a friend was desperately overwrought with grief and could not be talked out of visiting the cemetery, Mr. Aldrich followed at a distance without it being known, merely to be within call should a need arise.

His absorption in his family was the basis in part of a purpose that even now was pointing straight toward a far but sure objective. He wanted to found an estate. His family feeling, his love of beautiful things, and an innate class sense which was always strong in him, combined to give him a fondness for the figure of the country gentleman. As far back as 1869 he had fixed upon the location of his dream. Some day he would own an estate on Warwick Neck overlooking Narragansett Bay. Years were yet to pass before that lovely site was to be occupied by the house, the gardens, the spacious living of his country-seat, Indian Oaks. But all that, though an unfulfilled desire was a clearly perceived desire while this natural aristocrat was hard at work learning the ways of Congress in his political apprenticeship.

The year 1881 was one of his fateful years. Being only an M. C., he took no part in the duel between President Garfield and that brilliant apparent master of the Senate, Conkling, over appointments during the first month of the new administration. Instead, he and Mrs. Aldrich made a trip to the Pacific Coast. With his keen eye for the practical he observed the soil of what was still called the Great American Desert, and concluded it was not worth fifty cents an acre.[7] With a keen eye for the beautiful, he gazed upon the wonders of the Yosemite.

Two deaths this year profoundly affected his career. With the passing of President Garfield and the elevation of the Vice-President, Mr. Arthur, to the presidency the

Republicans lost his casting vote in the Senate and therefore it happened that when Mr. Aldrich entered the Senate, a little later, there was utmost need for his party to walk warily, to tread on eggs without breaking them.

In September of this year died General Burnside, who had been Anthony's colleague in the Senate. As was quite natural both Mr. Anthony and Mr. Aldrich attended his funeral. It is tradition that they drove away together. What they talked about tradition does not record.

The following Sunday, in the office of the Providence *Journal*, Mr. Anthony held a council of his allies and henchmen to discuss the senatorial succession. Apparently they were all at outs upon the subject, quite unable to pool their interests, to agree who should have the plum. Mr. Aldrich had not been invited. Suddenly he walked in upon them. He had come to announce that he was a candidate—this quiet young man, not forty, with only one term in Congress for his national record. They were surprised. They declined to give him encouragement. He told them he thought he could get the vote, that he intended to try, and then he politely withdrew.

The machine was in a quandary. It seems plain enough that they could not come to an understanding among themselves, that they let the matter go by default. They did not offer him visible opposition, but neither do they appear to have given him much assistance. They let him try out his strength. It was proven that he knew his constituency, and his hold upon it. When Congress at the call of President Arthur met in special session, Mr. Anthony presented to it a new colleague, the successor of General Burnside, Senator Aldrich of Rhode Island.[8]

II

The man who now steps forward as a person in the drama of American politics has the ironic distinction of having lived and died in a spiritual remoteness from the crowd, and in a degree of indifference to its praise or blame, scarcely paralleled in the life of any other American statesman who ever attained great power. The failures and the successes of the thirty-five years before he entered the large arena are the clew to all that follows. He had been formed in direct contact with individuals, and nature had denied him the two gifts, oratory and literature, that enable the politician when in search of a clientele, to strike beyond the individual and affect the crowd. The qualities that made him so easily a leader in the Lyceum—coolness, keenness, aloofness, mental combativeness, the instinct for debate— made it impossible for him to lose himself in the collective passion of his audience, to become its inspired voice, to find a great delight formulating not his own thoughts but theirs. In some of his famous achievements long afterward, he worked side by side with men who could do this—moulding and being moulded in the same breath—and his contrast with such men, with McKinley for example, while at the same time he was extremely close to them, draws the main lines of his perspective.

Intellectually, the guiding clew is plain enough. His early passion for books and his deeply imaginative sense of life are the two strands of it. Literature, reinforced by logic, books and debating, organized his mind. He had mental courage to see things as they are. To have no misunderstanding of one's own motives, to dare to act, first, last, always, out of confidence in one's own inward vision, these for him, were the cardinal virtues. When he met these virtues he gave admiration, no matter what views, what purposes, what animosities, went along with them. He could be your close friend, while, in a political way, your enemy to the death. But when he did not meet these qualities, even in the most valuable ally, he felt contempt. It was because he found—or thought he found—but few men in his day possessing these virtues, that he turned a deaf ear when the multitude of the negative ones—so he conceived them—cried out that they were The People, commissioned of God to rule the world.

"Most people don't know what they want" was one of

his maxims. There is a passage in Cromwell which if he ever noticed it must have deeply pleased him: " 'Tis the general good of the kingdom we ought to consult. That's the question, what's for their good, not what pleases them." Had he lived in the seventeenth century he would have stood by the Lord General through thick and thin, believed with him that toleration and a firm hand balancing interests made a closer approach to the kingdom of heaven than did the reign of the saints.

Humor was of the fibre of his nature. But it obeyed the general law that had predestined him to a place in that smaller, more reserved congregation commonly labelled the aristocrats. He was not a joker; he despised guffaws. Jesting, with him, took the form of irony. The quiet amusement of his youthful account of the convention of spiritualists was ever his note. His irony seldom, if ever, became sarcasm. Even anger could not, except rarely, and then for a moment only, unseat his humor. It is dangerous, always to try to pack any man's significance into a single case. Those writers who are fond of the simile of the little vase in the Arabian tale which imprisoned magically the whole of a supernatural being, those writers are too easily satisfied. But if there is one incident that might serve to give the very central hint in the comprehension of Aldrich it is the following:

Late in his career when Senator Smoot had become his lieutenant, Mr. Smoot and some others behind his back got up courage to amend a bill in a way which they knew he would oppose. At the last moment of the eleventh hour they showed their hands. Aldrich, for once, was taken by surprise. In a swift attempt to head them off he got the Senate to adjourn half an hour. But it was too late. They had formed a secret majority. When the Senate reassembled for voting, Aldrich walked in and stood beside his desk looking at Smoot. Plainly he was in a rage—it was one of the few times when anger was seen on his face in the Senate.

Mr. Smoot was terribly excited. He was trying to rearrange the text of a bill, clipping and pasting into it the

notes of the new amendments now to be voted upon. As
Mr. Aldrich looked at his unhappy revolted lieutenant, the
comedy of the situation suddenly broke upon him. He
laughed. Every trace of anger vanished from his face.
Walking across to Mr. Smoot whose fingers were all thumbs,
he said: "Here, let me fix it for you." Quickly, deftly, he
pieced together the monument of his own defeat, tossed it
upon Smoot's desk and walked back to his own. The incident was ancient history. His interest in it was gone forever.[9]

His reticence and his scorn of the multitude had its reward. No one was ever more consistently translated in the
public mind from a man into a monster. During most of his
public life he was truly "the bogey man," the wicked being
who was always in reserve as the possible scape-goat when
anything went wrong. Curiously, this began in his own
party. We shall see a famous Republican very early in the
story extricate himself from responsibility for unpopular
legislation by blaming it all upon Aldrich. But we shall not
hear a word of explanation from him. As time passes and
he commits himself to various unpopular measures, while
furious enemies depict him in the popular prints the very
reverse of what he actually was—successful when he was
not successful, defeated when he was completely the victor
—there will be smiling silence as to all these matters on the
part of the bogey man.

Reticence, as far as the world is concerned, will grow
upon him with the years. The mystical basis of his character, his instinctive dreaming upon the strangeness and the
beauty of human life, will be covered over by his reticence
as by a coat of mail. It will express itself only indirectly—
through his delight in art, through his enjoyment of religious ritual, through his horror of ugliness. Few of his utterances came more directly from his heart than those sad
remarks upon the changed congregation in the church of
his childhood where so many of his old friends were entering upon hardship and desolation in a cheerless middle age.

Statesmanship, to his mind, was largely the prevention

of all that. Was he right or was he wrong? The answer is a matter of partisanship, not of history. His lot was cast in an age when, though many people did not perceive it, the basic question was, which is more of the essence of happiness, political freedom or richness of personal experience? It was an age of transition when all the formulations of the age before were breaking up, when not a few of the strongest minds were falling back on still older ideas, on the formulations of the age before the age that was passing. The creed of Andrew Jackson and democracy, in conflict with problems it had not learned how to solve, was confronted by the resurrection of Hamilton and aristocracy.

The age was hysterical. It witnessed the collapse of an economic order not really ancient but which it had been taught to think was ancient; it sensed unsteadily the rising of new powers and principalities, "phantoms of other forms of rule"; it was not sure of its own mind and spent much of its energy—some of its best energy—trying to discover its mind, trying to determine whether to go with the old or with the new or to reject them both and plunge desperate into some third course where the landscape of the mind was still uncharted. It was one of those bewildering, changeful, multiform and contradictory periods so well intimated by John Morley when he wrote: "In such a crises as England was now entering it is not the sounder reasoning that decides; it is passions, interests, outside events, and that something vague and undefined, curious almost to mystery, that in bodies of men is called political instinct."

III

We have a picture of the new senator in the report of an interviewer from the New York *Tribune*. He wore a heavy black mustache and side whiskers close cut. "He had brilliant dark eyes which he fastens closely upon the person with whom he is conversing. His manners are genial and attractive." But he would not talk for publication. "No, don't ask me any questions," said he, "let's talk about something else." He adroitly put aside questions that he did not want to answer, was clear enough in several answers that did not tell more than was known already, and when the interviewer asked leave to print these answers he laughed and said he might.[10]

Among his earliest duties as senator was the obligation to add his tribute to that of Anthony at a memorial service in honor of Burnside. It was a notable occasion. From the point of view of senatorial tradition he was very young —only forty—and so far as experience went a mere tyro. It was the sort of occasion that has occurred only now and then in the history of the Senate—when a young man of talent who has made his way in through exceptional and quite unorthodox methods focusses the curious scrutiny of a body not inclined to be tolerant of what it regards as youth. But there was nothing youthful, neither was there anything of conventional eulogy in the strong, discriminating, well-poised utterances that drew something of his own portrait in his choice of things to say about his predecessor.

He had been the trusted and familiar friend of all classes, and all felt that they had suffered in his death an irreparable loss. There was something phenomenal in the attachment of our entire community to General Burnside. It was the affection of a people proud of their history and traditions, clinging with peculiar tenacity to their conservative institutions, slow to change or to give their confidence, for a man who came to them in mature years, a stranger from a distant State. . . .

The brightness of his military record was never tarnished by exhibitions **of** petty jealousy, or by unseemly strife for personal preferment. He had courage, a resolute steadfast determination which was superior to all obstacles, and an unwavering faith in the justice of his cause. . . . He never sought to evade the full measure of accountability for his acts and opinions, and his exceptional magnanimity often led him to assume the responsibility for failures and faults properly chargeable to others. . . .

His conclusions as to the line of public duty to be followed were reached not as the result of profound study, but by accepting the promptings of his own generous and manly nature, and these seemed to lead him instinctively to correct decisions.

We may not claim for him great genius or brilliant achieve-

ments as a soldier or statesman. He had neither the arrogant
pretensions, the impracticable theories, nor the infirmities of
temper which are sometimes accepted as evidence of genius, but
he had an intelligent comprehension of the important duties of
American citizenship and a sincere desire and honest intention to
advance the interests and improve the condition of his fellow
countrymen. . . .[11]

CHAPTER III

A STRUGGLE FOR A CONSTITUENCY

I

To get into the Senate was one thing; to get a chance, after he was in, was another. Could he—this irregular politician, not quite of the orthodox sort—so impress the powerful old senators who controlled legislation that they would let him show what was in him? Fortunately, this was a special case among Senates. The peculiarities of the moment were such that the party leaders did not dare to be arrogant. The withdrawal of the Vice-President, the vacancies that had occurred owing to death and resignation during the summer, the political vagaries of Senator David Davis, conspired to create a condition of unstable equilibrium. So nearly were the parties balanced that Mr. Davis who proclaimed himself to be superior to party could make the Senate Republican by voting that way, or he could tie the parties by voting with the Democrats. In such a situation the Senate of the United States will dicker like a pack of fishwives. As the upshot of shrewd bargaining, the Republicans got the chairmanships of committees, the Democrats got the administrative offices, and Mr. Davis got the seat vacated by the Vice-President. The Republicans at last established a majority of one. Some important measures were carried by that single vote. Government by one vote is among the beauties of majority rule.

Such a precarious dominance prevented the party leaders from practising condescension. The inexperienced senator from Rhode Island was watched as closely as any newcomer ever was, but far more sympathetically than is usually the case. When every recruit counted, it was to be hoped that the fates had sent them a fighting man.

By the same token, these were just the conditions in which to develop Mr. Aldrich in the very way most suited

to his natural bent. When a single vote might determine the
fate of the nation, the debater in the Senate had no incentive to go in argument beyond the men before him, to talk
over their shoulders to the country. The immediate audience was too deadly real! And that was just what Mr.
Aldrich liked. To talk over the shoulders of the man before him, to harangue an unseen "Public" beyond, he always resolutely refused to do.

His personal success in the Senate was instantaneous.
Two friendships that were to last many years began at
once. He had been appointed to a place on the Finance
Committee—doubtless through the influence of Anthony
—and there he met William B. Allison, a masterly politician
in the narrower sense, a man considerably older than he,
who was destined to owe much to him and to serve him
well. Almost immediately, he discovered an affinity in Orville H. Platt, still older than Allison and more entirely of
Mr. Aldrich's own sort. One of his earliest displays of policy
was in standing with Platt against the majority and the
Chinese Exclusion Bill of 1882. California was clamoring
for the bill. The East opposed it. Mr. Platt held that it
went far beyond its professed object, the protection of
American labor, and would inflict hardship beyond all justification. The Senate passed the bill, Aldrich and Platt reg-
istering against it. Though this was a minor measure, it is
notable inasmuch as the clash of interest between East and
West is to be the most significant undertow working through
all the political tides of Mr. Aldrich's career.[1]

He continued to be closely watchful of the interests of
Rhode Island. Newport was almost the rival of Annapolis
and Mr. Aldrich saw to it that Newport suffered no neglect.
At the same time he kept a sharp eye on efficiency. He
wrote the secretary of the navy intimating that certain
naval officers consulted their pleasure rather than the welfare of the service by "summer cruising in our waters" instead of long voyages.[2] Any constituent who wanted to
reach the secretary could do so through the Senator, as
when Mr. Aldrich wrote him on behalf of a rash youth "of

good family who had enlisted in a branch of the service and who has become thoroughly tired of it. I think there is much force in his appeal (to be released) and if the interests of the service will allow I should be glad to have you give him favorable consideration." [3]

But things of this sort were incidental. The true concern of the moment, politically, was—where did the parties really stand? The long backwash following the Civil War was beginning to be astir with innumerable eddies, social, economic, emotional. The great parties were drifting still in the channels of their traditional achievement, but new parties were threatening to arise, and even within the old ones there was doubt, hesitation, and pain. Shrewd politicians felt, all round them, the shadows of cats unseen—cats that were getting ready to jump—but these same politicians, for the life of them, could not guess the natures of those cats, nor in which direction they would jump. Naturally, their hearts were troubled.

Meanwhile, a newly created Tariff Commission was at work considering a problem forced upon it by a clamor over the surplus revenue of the government. The federal taxes were $100,000,000 in excess of federal expenditure. Why should this be? The Tariff Commission, dominated by Republicans was thinking hard upon the surplus. It made a report that was a surprise. It recommended "a substantial reduction of tariff duties." This Tariff Commission had something like prophetic vision. To head off a controversy which it saw dimly on the economic horizon, it pointed the way for the Republicans to withdraw from their war-time commitment to high tariff. The Senate accepted its advice. In the spring of 1883 by a vote far from merely partisan, the Senate devised a new tariff with noteworthy reductions of duties.[4]

But the House had other views. The bill was taken in hand by a conference committee of the two Houses and reworked until it ended practically in leaving the tariff where it was. The action of this Conference Committee is one of the obscurities of tariff history. Mr. Aldrich, though

still an apprentice statesman, was a member of it. Long
afterward, he defended its action on the ground that the
resulting bill at least did not make any real increase in the
tariff and that such changes as were accepted were due to
convincing representations made to the conference by interested industries.[5] Thus began for Aldrich an activity
which with the increase of experience he was to develop
into a fine art. Few men have been as successful in the
moulding of legislation through "hearings" in which the
parties on whom the legislation was to bear argued their
cause before committees.

In helping frame the tariff of 1883, this interesting be-
ginner established at once a committee reputation. And
this remained to the end his forte. In committee, in caucus,
in conference—as well as in the masterly handling of debate before an assembly—he was wonderfully skilful. Before 1883 had passed, his reputation among senators both
as a committeeman and as a debater on the floor was solidly
based, never to be shaken. The accuracy of his mind and
his immense knowledge of industrial conditions gave the
new member a position that was almost central in the deliberations of the Finance Committee. On the floor of the
Senate, it was soon evident that Mr. Aldrich was the man
who could speak of the bill with authority. Though Mr.
Morrill, chairman of the Finance Committee, was the bill's
ostensible architect, he frequently gave way to Mr. Aldrich
when some bewildering industrial tangle had to be made
plain.[6]

An American tariff bill is the special product of the Evil
One for evading lucidity. Chief among its abominations
are difficult questions of the classification of goods, and
these in the tariff of 1883 were sometimes too abstruse for
the chairman. Senator Ingalls snapped him up with testy
words, "If the chairman . . . does not know what it is intended to include . . . I think before we are called upon to
vote we ought to have some information."

"Without undertaking to say anything about the propriety of it," Mr. Aldrich volunteered, "I can explain what

it is for. It is"—and the rest was sharply technical, but so
lucid that Senator Ingalls understood.[7]

His quick reputation for clear thinking became also a
reputation for fair dealing. His most distinguished opponent in debate was Mr. Beck of Kentucky, especially upon
the intricate cotton schedule of which Mr. Bayard, in a moment of petulance, exclaimed, "I doubt very much whether
any one but a very close and practical student of cotton
manufacturing can make head or tail of it." Other opponents made the point that Aldrich had permitted Rhode
Island cotton manufacturers to argue their cause before a
sub-committee that was charged with the cotton schedule.
Thereupon Beck, the generous Kentuckian, rose to his defense.

So far as the senator is concerned, I not only have deferred
to him, but I have referred everybody to him, and have regarded
him as not only a true representative of his people, but I have
publicly and privately said that he knew more about the subject
than anybody else, and I admire the earnest activity with which
he stands up for his people; but that does not make me agree
with him.[8]

Incidentally in the course of debate he revealed a tolerably definite theory of the tariff—its justification, what
ought to be its scope, and the touchstones for trying proposed legislation. In a debate upon the duty on steel files
he repeated the general idea that it should be high enough
to enable American manufacturers to compete with English and Swiss. He went on to calculate for the benefit of
the Senate what labor signified in the manufacture of files.
His conclusion was that it was ninety per cent of the cost.
These figures were brought out in reply to Mr. Vance who
was holding a brief for the importers of files. The argument of the ninety per cent labor cost defeated a proposed
Vance Amendment.[9]

In a very sharp tilt with Senator Gorman—an amusing
detail in the light of coming events that are still far into
the future!—he opposed raising the duty on bichromate of
potash.

I say there is nothing in this article, in its character, in its surroundings, in its past history, in its present condition, that should lead the Senate of the United States to select it out for their special care and preservation. . . . It is not a national industry; it is not a State industry; it is hardly a neighborhood industry. . . .[10]

Clear, consistent, playing fair, he was nevertheless capable at times of sharp words and now and then of quiet ridicule. A bill that the Finance Committee had passed upon was so simple that "it might even be understood by the Senate." [11] When Mr. Vance quoted poetry he declined to follow him "into the realms of fancy and imagination." [12] With regard to the duty on gunpowder even Beck received a sly dig.

I hope my friend from Kentucky will not allow this to pass without criticising it. . . . I do not object to it at all, but it is the sort of increase which has been objected to constantly by senators on the other side of the chamber.[13]

On a rare occasion he showed vengefulness. While defending a provision designed to prevent evasions of the law, he was interrupted by Mr. Vance who tried to brush his point aside. "It is my desire and that of the committee," retorted Mr. Aldrich, "that they should not be allowed to evade the law. If the Senator from North Carolina has any contrary wish or opinion, I suppose he will vote in that direction." [14]

Altogether, within two years, he was a man of mark in the Senate.

II

The delicate balance of parties at Washington gave warning to a few quick-witted politicians that the clock was running down. The impetus given by the dreadful issues of 1860 was wearing out. Party allegiance was growing slack. Among the Republicans especially a long tenure of power was making them indifferent to fate. The danger was seen by a brilliant politician—one of America's most crafty manipulators of mass feeling. Mr. Blaine determined to gal-

vanize the Republican party. He set out to revive the passions of a day that was dead. He would wave "the bloody
shirt" until it fanned into a new diabolic brightness the
embers of sectional hate, the things that had made the
Civil War. In 1884 it was plain that he had built up on
this evil basis a power that was dangerous.

Mr. Aldrich—now within two years of his next election
—was squarely against Blaine. He could not be himself and
be otherwise. The man to whom the war was ended at its
last gunshot—who if anything erred on the side of regarding animosity as irrational—had no place in his thoughts
for the Bloody Shirt. He went to the Republican convention at Chicago, hoping to prevent the nomination of
Blaine.

As all the world knows he accomplished nothing. Nevertheless the summer of 1884 has a curious significance in his
biography. Other good Republicans had hoped to save
their party from the hero of the Bloody Shirt. One, Theodore Roosevelt, of New York, who was just arriving in
politics, was at Chicago working against Blaine. Mr. Foraker was busily and almost successfully trying to unite all
the anti-Blaine men behind John Sherman. There were
many conferences. One of these included both Mr. Aldrich and Mr. Roosevelt and both men joined the Sherman
forces in their futile last stand against the idol of the crowd,
the rhetorician that the crowd called lovingly "the Plumed
Knight." [15]

Their destinies—or chance—had in store for these two
great men one of the most interesting rivalries of our political drama. We shall see them, many years later, cordially co-operating in great tasks; then as cordially in deadly
opposition; again in co-operation; and at last each indirectly will have been the main instrument frustrating the
dearest hope of the other.

And this is but one of the fateful coincidences of the
year 1884. In the course of the political campaign, a young
man in Iowa did some speech-making that arrested the attention of the Plumed Knight. Thus Jonathan Dolliver

steps into history. To him eventually will come a seat in the Senate, and the rôle of henchman to an inner circle dominated by Mr. Aldrich. But he will never stand high in the Aldrich scheme of things. The younger Senator will be too florid intellectually, too tense, too susceptible to illusion, for the cool New Englander. Mr. Aldrich, at a crucial moment will treat him disdainfully, a bit cruelly, and thereafter—just twenty-five years from this portentous summer—Mr. Dolliver will get his revenge. The Aldrich-Dolliver drama will be strangely interwoven with the Aldrich-Roosevelt drama—Mr. Dolliver will have his turn as Mr. Roosevelt's lieutenant—and, as a whole these complicated political adventures will read like a tragedy upon predestination.

III

It is hard to-day to appreciate the feelings of innumerable Northern Americans in November, 1884, when it was known that the Republicans, for the first time in twenty-four years, had lost the presidency. Despite a deal of talk about signs of the times and handwriting on the wall, the complacent mass had laughed it away as the mere grumbling of extremists, or as the fanciful chatter of "highbrows." And now the bottom was out of the universe! But the sun still shone and the seasons apparently would keep their wonted course. Obviously, the kingdom of God and His saints was not of this world.

Fate was conspiring with accident to keep Mr. Aldrich in the relation to political action that was begun by the peculiar conditions of his first session in the Senate. A party balanced on the knife-edge of a single vote had been tumbled clean over into a party of opposition. The Democrats had the presidency and the House. The only consolation of the fallen Republicans was their more secure hold on the Senate. Their majority rose to six votes; but only to fall again two years later by the loss of four seats. Here was a situation in which inevitably such a man as Aldrich would concentrate his thought upon two things, logic and the natures of individual senators. To hamper the victors, to force them to play their cards badly, to drive their apologists in the Senate into false positions, man for man to be cleverer than they were—this was the rôle of political common sense for the leaders of the Republican chamber. What school of politics would have served better to develop to the last degree all the subtleties of parliamentary strategy? No wonder that the rising Senator before the end of his term became a past master of that difficult art. What began in the Franklyn Lyceum was perfected, as a leader of opposition, in the United States Senate.

The long vacation of 1885 was a soul-racking time for the depressed Republicans, a time in which to take stock anew, to cast with care the political horoscope. It was a critical moment for Mr. Aldrich. Mr. Anthony had died the previous year and General Brayton had succeeded to a large part, if not to the whole, of his power as Boss of Rhode Island.

The career of General Brayton is the reverse of explicit, his purposes are obscure. His relations with Mr. Aldrich, especially in the years before 1885, are particularly obscure, There is a letter among the Aldrich manuscripts dating back to the time when Mr. Aldrich was still an inconspicuous representative which indicates that at one of Brayton's several moments of crisis the young representative rendered some sort of aid for which, at the moment, Brayton was very grateful. It is a pathetic and discouraged letter. In 1880, when this letter was written he had fallen momentarily from power. "I, of course know not what is before me but feel well, have a good constitution yet, and a stout tho heavy heart." [16] But even in his valley of humiliation, he cannot refrain from giving shrewd political advice with the accent of authority.

The next four years there were parallel ascents by these two men so utterly unlike. While Aldrich was establishing himself as a man of mark in the Senate, Brayton was recovering confidence in himself and regaining his hold on the machine. When Anthony died in 1884, Brayton was a man to be reckoned with. To assume that a politician of the boss type was permanently inspired by sentimental gratitude may be rash. But many men of this sort contradict the conventional impression of them. It is plain that General Brayton appeared to be friendly to Mr. Aldrich. His first act of consequence was picking a successor to Anthony in the Senate. He went through the form, at least, of consulting the junior Senator. His decision to support the worthy Mr. Chase, who was regarded by all Rhode Island as incorruptible, was evidence that he was not in a cynical or defiant mood. The choice was an appeal for support to the best classes of the State.

The local political situation was immeasurably complex due to a variety of causes—rival factions among the Republicans, the appearance of the prohibition issue, a popular demand for reform of the State constitution, growing discontent among the laboring classes. Mr. Aldrich had been very skilful in not creating opposition for himself in any of the factions; but at the same time he had not allowed any of them to put him where it could control him. The question of the hour in Providence was whether his influence, at a crucial moment, might prove to be the makeweight in the trembling political scales, with so many factions pulling in so many directions.

As to his dangerous friend, a highly picturesque character is this General Brayton. He deserves a permanent place among those interesting Americans who will some day be taken seriously by historians precisely as we now take the "despots" of the Italian cities of the Renaissance. The methods that at last gave him great power were much the same as theirs, both among good people and bad. One day, at the height of his success he chanced to meet a professor of Brown University with whom he was slightly acquainted. They had a pleasant talk; the charm of the personality of that delightful scholar warmed the heart of the Despot. Presently he remarked, "By the way, professor, what do you think the university needs of the legislature?" The scholar made the most of his opportunity. Brayton jotted the points down. "You shall have them all," said he. And the legislature obeyed. Telling the story long afterward the professor admitted ruefully that a Despot was easier to deal with than the mass of the electorate as represented in the legislature.[17] Like most of the practical politicians in democratic countries, he had no respect for the masses. Unlike the "highbrows" of the universities he could not see what harm there was in buying votes that were openly offered for sale, that would go to some one else, and be used against you, if you did not purchase them.

There is a delicious story of an election in an English rotten borough, which had but six electors, one of whom was the local barber. Lord Somebody and Sir William Somebody Else were the candidates. My Lord stepped into the barber's shop and had himself shaved. Later Sir William followed suit. He paid fifty guineas. The barber mentioned that this was just what His Lordship had paid. Sir William stroked his chin thoughtfully and came to the conclusion that he needed a second shave. A second time he paid fifty guineas. He was elected to Parliament. It is to be hoped that Mr. Brayton's scant historical reading included that classic tale. It would have greatly pleased him, and yet, the price of a vote, in the story, would have seemed to him shockingly high.

Like every true boss he had a great virtue and a great talent. He was perfectly faithful to his confederates. He had a genius for knowing what the people below the average would do—how they could be bought, what they would stand for, when they would rebel. Also, he was fairly shrewd in sensing the states of mind of the people above the average, the people of numerous interests, who are willing up to a certain point, to pay blackmail to a machine in order to escape the less intelligent despotism of direct action by the crowd. He understood the basic principle of all the bosses, the need to combine the interests of these two groups.

Brayton's power, in the days of his eminence, rested on three things. He gave good government, so far as it touched the man of business and all those good people who avoid politics. They would reason time and again, that he was the least evil of bosses. The age accepted the boss as a fixed term in politics. The rebellion against him as an institution had scarcely begun. A few hotheads ran amuck with him; the rest came to terms—as was the wise course with a despot. And Brayton was a generous Despot who made lavish contributions to all sorts of good causes. Thus he got a certain indirect support from the best people; but he was too shrewd not to see that this was largely negative.

His second reliance was the State Senate. The constitution of Rhode Island made the upper house of the Legislature very like the National Senate, its membership distributed equally among the towns. The shifting of population had all but emptied certain towns of their electors. They had become pocket boroughs as truly as were the historic pocket boroughs of the eighteenth century. A few salable votes might name the town's senator.

The electorate generally gave Brayton a more indiscriminate opportunity. It was drearily corrupt—that is to say, its members, very largely, either had lost, or had not yet found, the political conscience. The immense outflow from New England in the middle third of the century had drained away a great proportion of the independence of the lower class, especially in Rhode Island. What was left behind was in no small degree, a class of broken people, dispirited, who had lost their traditions, who had been herded by poverty and lack of enterprise off the farms into new, coarse, industrial communities. What did politics mean to them? The Rhode Island of Aldrich's eulogy upon Burnside was the Rhode Island of the upper classes and of none other. Furthermore these crowds of broken people, overstocking the labor market had been reinforced by crowds of foreigners, who were in even worse plight, who had not lost their political tradition because they never had had any, to whom the right of suffrage was a meaningless group of words.

Brayton, in time, became the head of an elaborate business that dealt in votes. He had his middlemen in the shape of the local bosses, and through them he herded voters wholesale.

In last analysis this was Brayton's power. The purchasable voters were the foundation on which the whole fabric of his despotism was based. With this power in his hand, with the good-will if not the active support of the people above the average, he was in a position to plunge heavily, any way he pleased, in the desperate game of State politics.

IV

In 1885, Brayton was not as powerful as subsequently he became. Whether he and Aldrich may be termed political equals, that year; whether Brayton was still patiently working up hill, not yet in possession of the Antonian inheritance; whether he was skilfully trying to manipulate Aldrich without any open rivalry; whether he was really his friend—is a shadowy tale that concerns the despot rather more than the Senator. Whatever, beneath the surface, were the true relations of these men, it behooved Mr. Aldrich to hold a strong hand of trumps. And in politics, no cards reveal their true value until after they have been played. It was plain that Mr. Aldrich's strength was his appeal to the business classes. Was this enough to make him master of the moment?

The really significant part of his first term in the Senate lay in his own thoughts upon the relation of business to government. The tariff of 1883 marked the point at which a few men in America began to think hard, in a new set of terms, about some fundamental problems of government. The Tariff Commission could probably plead not guilty. Doubtless the secretary of the treasury, Mr. Folger, was equally good-humored and unconcerned. If the spirit of prophecy had been in him he might have pondered long, perhaps turned to the Scriptures and reread the account of Belshazzar's feast—in those days statesmen read such things—before he pigeon-holed a letter signed by congressmen from Louisiana. It scrutinized the members of the

Tariff Commission in terms not of States, nor of sections, nor of parties, but in terms of the industries to which, it might be assumed, their main allegiance should be given. Then, not in the name of the South, nor of Louisiana, but in the name of "Sugar which represents Three Hundred Millions of invested capital" the signers earnestly requested "that this important industry have representation on this committee." [18]

There was a debate on sugar in 1883 that signifies little in tariff history but has sidelights that signify much. In the course of it Mr. Aldrich read to the Senate a letter signed H. A. Havemeyer. The language with which he introduced this letter showed that he was among those who were beginning to think in the new terms, were beginning to look on economic interests as the statesmen of the elder day looked upon geographical interests. He spoke of "the largest sugar refiner in this country, one whose influence upon legislation has often been properly felt in this Chamber and at the other end of the Capitol." [19] The fact that he and Mr. Havemeyer disagreed, that Aldrich was for a low tariff on raw sugar, that he wanted to reduce "the cost of manufactured articles to consumers throughout the land" by reducing Labor's cost of living, is interesting but in Aldrich's development relatively unimportant.[20] Many men thought that way. What really matters is his power to think of sugar imaginatively as a social and political entity, as a vast assemblage of interests, an economic commonwealth with its rulers, the investors, and its population, the workers, a commonwealth which he was willing to treat with.

What Mr. Aldrich was capable of thinking about one industry he was capable of thinking about all. He saw that the time was coming when America would have to redefine the word "constituency." Brayton might think of a constituency in the old way, as a piece of the map with all its people, houses, appurtenances, interests, magically combined into one thing. Undoubtedly there had been a time when it was proper to think of Rhode Island in that way.

Aldrich had not ceased to think of it in that way. But for him, for many men, the geographical constituency was less real than it once had been. The idea of an economic constituency was becoming very real indeed. Did this idea point the way toward building a clientele of business interests that should be the firm foundation on which he might stand as a statesman, a true "constituency" which all such men as Brayton would not dare ignore?

The idea of surrendering to Brayton, of accepting the Purchasables as his masters never entered his head. Contempt for that sort of humanity was instinctive in him. It was not only the people below the average, it was the whole vast congregation of the easily led, the easily deceived, the easily betrayed people, that roused his scorn. But it was not his way ever to have direct dealings with them. He would not even disabuse them when they misunderstood him.

At this very moment, while he was pondering his home problems, he had an opportunity to reveal this frame of mind. The woolgrowers of Ohio had resented the tariff of 1883. Mr. Sherman was standing for re-election to the Senate. He cleared his skirts by loading upon Aldrich the whole responsibility for the wool tariff.[21] It was the beginning of Aldrich the bogey man. But not a word of defense, or explanation, came from Aldrich. To the huge audience of the general nation he was stubbornly silent. He would talk to his constituency—whatever that might be—and he would talk to the Senators, but as to the world at large, he snapped his fingers. A temperamental attitude that was part of his destiny.

He looked about for opportunities to make Rhode Island business regard him as its own, to see that he was, first of all, the business man in politics. His aim was to bring business and politics together. Especially, he stood for manufacturing, for a cautious union between manufacturers and workmen. He was frankly not an agrarian. In a speech at Providence, late that year, he expressed this position advocating low duties on raw sugar.[22]

Still more clearly he made himself the champion of Rhode Island manufacturers—of all eastern manufacturers—in opposing the Interstate Commerce Bill early in 1886. This famous statute was one more indication that the country was in transformation. How and why it had been proposed to extend the power of the national government over all the procedure of the interstate railways did not concern either Aldrich or his friends in Rhode Island. It was from the West that the cry for this drastic statute had gone up. In the West the railroads formed a government under the government—truly an *imperium in imperio*—cruelly powerful. They had made and unmade towns, they had given wealth to this man and denied it to that through favoritism in the making of rates. They had established pools and combinations which the Westerners believed were pernicious.

None of these things touched Rhode Island. But there was one provision of the bill that gave Mr. Aldrich an opportunity. The Eastern manufacturers were beginning to fear that they might be crowded out of the Western markets by younger competitors situated beyond the mountains. Obviously, freight costs might be the determining factor. They wanted to be free to make any agreements with railroads that they desired and that the railroads were willing to accept. The bill proposed to compel all the roads to charge uniformly for carrying freight in proportion to the distance. With such a system in force New England would have no way to offset its great disadvantage, competing with Chicago or Detroit in shipments to Arizona or Colorado or Oregon.

Mr. Aldrich ranged himself with his true constituency, the New England manufacturers, irrespective of party, by his vigorous opposition to this bill. He protested against depriving the railroads of all freedom in adjusting rates to the demands of different localities. Unable to defeat it altogether, he aimed to narrow the scope of the bill by introducing an amendment limiting the sort of freight to which its severe provision was to apply.[23]

It was while the Interstate Commerce Bill was pending in Congress after Aldrich's attack upon it that the time arrived for choosing a senator in Rhode Island. Mr. Aldrich, with his championship of the manufacturing interest so clearly in evidence, had placed himself in a good strategic position. There was every reason why he and Brayton should each be a little—perhaps a good deal—afraid of getting at cross purposes. Each had everything that the other lacked; each found his pleasure in things to which the other was indifferent. Aldrich had social position, the confidence of business, the high regard of his brethren in the Senate. Brayton was a man of irregular life, who had no connections with the recognized occupations of men; he was looked upon as a political adventurer. Aldrich had no talent for direct popular appeal, no faculty for manipulating the crowd; Brayton was a past master in manipulation. Aldrich, the exponent of the manufacturing interests, could command the solid support of the classes that signed checks and contributed to the exchequers of political parties; Brayton knew how to obtain the solid support of a great host of Purchasables whose votes created legislatures.

For these two merely to agree not to fight each other would have been a happy solution on either side. But there was another consideration. No local boss could be sure of his machine unless he had a voice at least in the disposition of federal patronage. Brayton dearly longed to control the patronage. Aldrich was peculiar in having an intense dislike for that sordid subject. It was part of his general contempt of the Purchasables, of the crowd.[24] And thus he had in his hand a trump card that he was quite willing if need be to toss over to Brayton.

There was some sort of a concordat. But it would have been utterly unlike Brayton if the terms were anywhere preserved on paper. Nevertheless the subsequent relations of the two men give a broad hint. If they did not agree to divide the field of politics between them, Brayton always to see that his legislatures gave Aldrich the senatorship, Aldrich to keep his hands off local politics; furthermore, if Aldrich did not tell Brayton that he and the Representatives might do what they pleased about patronage provided they never got in his way upon the real business of government, then circumstantial evidence has again proved a delusion and a snare.

Whatever happened, the understanding which they reached brought about Brayton's support of Mr. Aldrich for the senatorship. In June, 1886, the Rhode Island legislature re-elected him.[25] Immediately he received this telegram: "I don't usually believe in men who have no enemies but am glad to see you re-elected just the same."[26]

CHAPTER IV

ON THE VERGE OF GREATNESS

WE are traversing the age of the barren congresses when almost always, in one way or another, legislation is at stalemate. This Forty-ninth Congress, Republican in the Senate, Democratic in the House, could accomplish nothing except on some peculiar issue, like that behind the Interstate Commerce Bill, which broke through the deceitful semblances of politics and grounded itself on a clash between economic constituencies.

But nothing further was done about Interstate Commerce the remainder of the session though Congress dragged on, talking interminably until August. In one connection Mr. Aldrich came out with his natural frankness, in a blunt insistence on recognizing the economic constituencies. A bill was up that favored granulated tobacco at the cost of "fine cut." He killed the bill by getting it referred to the Finance Committee whence it never returned. He told the Senate "that a very large portion of the trade, in all parts of the country, I think with a single exception of one or two small manufacturers in the city of New Orleans, was strongly opposed to the bill on the ground that it opened the door to the gravest and grossest frauds. The committee have not determined whether that state of affairs is true or not, but considering . . . the fact that almost without exception the manufacturers of the country believe that the bill ought not to pass, . . . the committee by a unanimous vote instructed me" to get the bill before it for deliberate consideration.[1] He had previously made the same point upon the Interstate Commerce Bill. When Senator Cullom tried to rush that bill through, Aldrich had picked him up sharply. ". . . there are a great many important interests to be considered; the representatives of those interests should have a

65

right to see this bill in print more than twenty-four hours, as well as the members of Congress, before we are called upon to vote on it." [2]

But if Congress was barren the country was not. New ideas upon government were astir at both ends of the social scale. Even while Aldrich was arguing for the recognition of a group of manufacturers, employers of labor, as an informal legislative assembly, that should have contact with a formal legislative assembly through one of its committees, a group of furious agitators, in the midst of a strike of 40,-000 employees had made a wild appeal for a different method of influencing government. "Revenge! Workmen to arms" was the watchword of confessed anarchists at Chicago. There had followed the famous Haymarket riots, bomb throwing, dead policemen, the arrest of men charged with being anarchist leaders. A stormy summer, a country shocked out of its complacent belief that such things were impossible in America, and in the autumn, the execution of the anarchists while an encompassing mob sang the "Marseillaise."

Here were interesting matters to be thought upon by every senator. Probably there was not one of them that did not owe his seat to some sort of roundabout compromise with the Purchasables. In a State like Rhode Island the Purchasables were well under control, and it was the obvious interest of their masters to play in with the manufacturing interest. But it was not so everywhere. The incidental cause of the Haymarket riot was an uprising of the employees of the McCormick reaper. What next? Might the Purchasables everywhere pass from the control of men like Brayton to the control of the sort of men who were executed that autumn? Was the crowd around the Chicago scaffold and the haunting strains of the "Marseillaise" an ominous prophecy—or was it all froth and moonshine?

Few Americans were thinking clearly and firmly on these disturbing subjects when Congress reassembled in December. But every one was aware that he had seen ghosts on the horizon.

The ensuing session kept up the record for barrenness. A foregone conclusion was the passage of the Interstate Commerce Act. Aldrich was still in opposition to what is known as "the long and short haul clause." He thought that the way he had changed its phraseology made the bill a little better than it had been but that it still was "revolutionary in its character and in violation of the sound principles which should govern transportation charges, and that the rigid enforcement of its provisions would demoralize business, change the channels of trade, destroy values through vast areas, and cripple both internal and external commerce." He denounced the commission created by this act because through its power to suspend the act at its discretion, these "five men, a majority of whom shall belong to one political party and selected partly on that account," were to have "the power, to be exercised without appeal, to make or unmake States, to build up or destroy communities, and to increase or extinguish the earnings of railroad companies." Other functions of the commission, such as enforcing the publicity of rates, prohibiting the exaction of unreasonable charges, and shielding the public "from undue and unjust discriminations" had his "hearty approval." [3]

The wave of feeling against the railroads which was sweeping the country had a good deal of justification and Mr. Aldrich was scarcely fair to it. There is an interval in his life when he is not quite the same man that he was before and after. A mood of impatience, a sort of mounting recklessness, comes and goes among his actions during the years 1887 and 1888. Possibly his personal victory in the senatorial election, uniting with the exasperating condition of the country, created in him a reaction of momentary intolerance, of over-confidence in the power of strong men like himself to straighten everything out if only they could get the chance. There is also a shadow of ill health over these years, a shadow that lifted before long but that may have had more significance for a time than has ever been attributed to it. He came as near as ever he came to voicing sheer irritation when he exclaimed that "those gentlemen who believe that a long and short haul provision furnishes a panacea for all railroad troubles will sooner or later find out that this bill is a delusion and a sham, and the country may as well understand that it is an empty menace to great interests, made to answer the clamor of the ignorant and the unreasoning." [4] It was in this same mood that he confronted another manifestation of the furies of the hour. A bill was passed prohibiting members of either House from acting as railroad attorneys—so prevalent was the belief that the railroads were indirectly traducing the government. Twice Aldrich attempted unsuccessfully to amend the bill by restricting its prohibition to "suits in opposition to the interests of the United States." [5]

This session had a gloomy significance for him. Its close marked the breaking of a comradeship. He now had some fast friends in the Senate—Mr. Allison, already his firm ally in the Finance Committee; Mr. Platt with whom it was becoming habitual for Mr. Aldrich to find himself in cheerful accord; Mr. Spooner, whose clear strong mind and idealistic temper were a solace to the Rhode Islander; Mr. Harrison, who probably was the senator with whom he was in closest terms of intimacy. Aldrich and Harrison had much in common. Both were natural aristocrats, both were instinctively in opposition to the crowd, both were firm, quiet, unexcitable, without the qualities that captivate men in the mass. Both lacked and both despised all the arts of the rhetorician, the mere orator, and the demagogue. Each was predestined to unpopularity and each was indifferent to the fact. Through the caprice of the electorate in Indiana it was plain that Mr. Harrison would not return to the Senate in December. But it did not follow that this was the end of Mr. Harrison's career. [6]

When they parted in the spring of 1887, and Aldrich set his face toward Europe, did he look into the future and speculate on what might happen in a Republican National Convention but little more than a year distant? He never for a moment thought of himself as a presidential possibility. He sensed politics too well not to be aware that tiny

Rhode Island would never by any turn of chance be of sufficient importance in a convention to impose a candidate. He had no illusions about the lack in himself of the qualities that might create a personal following outside his State and the Senate. Mr. Harrison had no better chance as a personal "spell binder." But he was the "favorite son" of one of those powerful and "doubtful" States whose propitiation will sometimes determine an election. There was more than one man in America who thought that the Republicans might be induced to choose this friend of Aldrich's as their next candidate.

Perhaps this train of thought was passing through his head in June when, from a resort in the Vosges he wrote to another senatorial friend, Eugene Hale, telling him his summer plans—"We shall leave to-morrow for Geneva and after a stay of a few days in that neighborhood shall go to Thun and Interlaken and on to Lucerne." He hopes that Hale will join him.

He hasn't yet discovered the unbeaten paths of travel, but what of that? The traditional ones, while still the new ones, are as thrilling as any. As he wandered leisurely that glorious route across the Oberland, his forecastings of his friend's future—if, as yet, he permitted himself to have any —are lost in his habitual reticence.

II

A curious succession of ironies filled the next twelve months. American politics were so nearly stagnant in 1887 that one strong man may be credited with a great change. Cleveland opened a new chapter not because he stood for this or that but because his powerful nature was sick of political frivolity. His party was not with him and he knew that it was not. It wanted to go on playing the old cheap game, to the classic tune of "what are we here for if it's not to get the offices?" The Republicans had coquetted with an economic issue in 1883, had gone with the tide on

Interstate Commerce in 1886, and now like their enemies were not clear in their own minds what they wanted to do.

There are fairy tales of magic trumpets that shatter castle walls, and loose vast powers, and draw sudden lines of battle. Such was Cleveland's message, of December, 1887, making tariff reduction the issue of the hour.

Unaware, Cleveland had given Aldrich his opportunity. The President's views were approximated by the Mills Bill that was promptly introduced in the House. The Republican Senators at once began holding confidential meetings considering what to do by way of counter-blast. They met in the room of the Finance Committee. Morrill nominally was chairman of the committee. He was in poor health. His place, and more than his influence, devolved upon Aldrich. In time, Morrill named the measure which was the Republican answer to the Mills Bill "the Aldrich substitute."

Cleveland and Aldrich were pitted squarely against each other, not through direct controversy, but indirectly through their works. Poles asunder in so many ways, they were alike in their courage and their realism. Neither ever winced; neither ever—or scarcely ever—saw his field of battle other than as it actually was, and both—whether wise or foolish, good or bad—were sportsmen of the first water. How hard to resist quoting that fine passage in Kipling which closes: "When two strong men stand face to face though they come from the ends of the earth . . ."

Aldrich was not the only man to whom unaware Cleveland gave the chance of his life. Now that there was to be a fight between parties on a real issue, doubtful States were of first importance. None was more doubtful than Indiana —and yet, the Republicans had a chance there. Blaine, arch-wizard at forecasting popular caprice, wrote from Paris, picking the logical candidate. He was the man who might carry Indiana—Mr. Harrison.

A troubled spring, that of 1888, in which the Republican senators were laying their heads together over Blaine's advice! Mr. Aldrich was hard at work devising a tariff for use in the coming election. Whether he agreed with Blaine at the start is uncertain. He may have been tempted, as some men were, to put forward that other friend of his, Mr. Allison. But it was Harrison, before long, to whom he pinned his faith. When the convention met, Mr. Aldrich was there quietly working for his friend from Indiana.

No nomination and election were ever compassed by more surprising means than were the nomination and election of Harrison. Things were done of which that proud aristocrat and his friend from Rhode Island were probably not informed. If there was ever any intimation to them of what went on among the negro delegates from the South, they must have fallen back, the one upon gloomy disgust, the other upon satiric amusement. Aldrich had no illusions about the purchasable elements in politics. He was content not to be personally responsible for their use.

Certain politicians, who had nothing to learn about the game, bid against each other in the South buying negro delegates. That huge pocket borough, the fictitious Republican party of the South, was a standing political scandal those days. It was controlled, when the Republicans were in power by the administration. The Southern office holders picked out manageable negroes and sent them to the party conventions as administration delegates. But with a Democrat in the White House, delegates were for sale. The managers for John Sherman tried to corner the market. An astute friend of Harrison's was too quick for them. A hundred negro delegates were secured, bought at fifty dollars the head.[7]

But all this is of the unofficial part of the political story that usually goes untold. The other side contains a conference—an anxious conference—of utmost propriety. It met at the Grand Pacific Hotel, Chicago, on a Saturday night. Aldrich was there, along with President Butler of Columbia. The shrewd bargainers who had corralled the precious negro votes were not included. They had laid a firm foundation—or helped lay such a foundation—that might now be taken for granted. What would settle the matter was a variable group of respected white delegates who must be got in line before the convention reassembled the following Monday. And not all these men were satisfied with Mr. Harrison's views on this, that, or the other. The anxious conference at the Grand Pacific rushed off an envoy to Indianapolis.[8]

A momentous day in the lives of many men was Sunday, June 24, 1888. One would like to know—if, that is, one enjoys the comedy of politics!—what the invaluable but ignored dusky cohort did that day. There were restaurants of all sorts in Chicago—and other places—and prohibition had not been heard of. If some one whispers something about shooting craps, it is not incredible.

What a chasm separates that scene from the one at Indianapolis. There was no conference until after church. The organ tones, the classic evangelical hymns, a congregation that stood for fashionable righteousness, a sermon that was edifying. After church, eager but sedate talk between the envoy of the conference and the calm, reserved, precise man who might be the next President. He rang true upon every question propounded to him.

Back in high spirits went the envoy. Swiftly the report of the day's proceedings spread among the delegates. Before nightfall on Monday, Mr. Aldrich was again a happy man, and Mr. Harrison was the Republican nominee.

III

Irony continues to be the note of this episode. Harrison's election, as all the world knows to-day, was compassed by methods still more disconcerting than those which had nominated him. That brilliant, unappreciated genius, Matthew Quay, manipulated deals that were the last word for political Machiavellianism. But he was shrewd enough to keep the knowledge of all this from Mr. Harrison. The aristocratic temper is a real thing not to be trifled with, and when it is joined with evangelical piety—one needs beware. Mr. Quay did not question Mr. Harrison's sin-

cerity when he said after the election that Providence must
have been on their side; but Quay remarked to a third
person that "Providence hadn't a damn thing to do with
it," adding, with the delightful simplicity which is ever the
mark of genius, "that he supposed Harrison would never
learn how close a number of men were compelled to approach the gates of the penitentiary to make him President." [9]

Quay and his amazing strategy were not the only bril-
liancies of the campaign for Harrison. His friend in the
Finance Committee was also a power. Never had that
friend thrown himself into any task with such ardor, such
confidence, such masterful ability as he now displayed.

The Mills Bill was passed by the House, July 21. The
Republicans of the Finance Committee drove ahead un-
tiringly with their counter-blast, the Aldrich substitute.
Presently Morrill was writing Aldrich: "I have received the
Tariff Report of the majority of the Finance Committee,
and it is in all respects a most creditable performance, re-
flecting special honor upon yourself and great credit upon
the other members of the Committee for the wise conclusions reached. I fully comprehend the Herculean task of
preparing this substitute as well as the merciless logic with
which the Mills Bill has been torn into pitiable fragments
by your report." [10]

The Republican counter-blast was at once published as
a campaign document: "Protection against Free Trade:
Report of Nelson W. Aldrich from the Committee on Finance
to the Senate of the United States, October 4, 1888." [11]

This bill is of no consequence in the scientific history of
the tariff. It was absorbed into the Act of 1890 of which
contemporaries said that it might just as well have been
called the Aldrich Tariff as the McKinley Tariff. [17] The
"Aldrich Substitute"—to use Morrill's term—is a stepping
stone in political, not financial, history. It was the real
platform on which the Republicans stood when they drove
their enemies from power in November, 1888, electing
House, Senate and the President.

The joy Mr. Aldrich took in creating it is apparent between the lines, and often on the line. Congress remained in session until October 20 and there were passages at arms in the Senate all that while. Mr. Aldrich's tongue was never sharper nor did he ever show quicker wit catching enemies at a disadvantage.

As Congress reassembled December 3, the year 1888 has the strange honor of having had a Congress in session almost the whole time—quite sufficient cause for remembering it as an awful year. The seven weeks without a Congress were a riot of joyful expectation on the part of the Republicans. Mr. Aldrich's part in the general campaign these weeks was confined mainly to his own State. Like many other Republicans he was doubtless over-confident expecting a more complete victory than was finally obtained.

Whether he was made acquainted with those singular performances attributed to Mr. Quay—assuming that they took place—we do not know. If it is really true that Mr. Quay and Mr. Hill made their reputed deal—the Republicans to help elect Mr. Hill governor of New York, the Democrats to help elect Harrison President—that joyful news must surely have been communicated to the leading members of the Republican Congressional Campaign Committee. Mr. Aldrich was a member of the executive committee of the committee.[18] It was during these seven weeks that he heard—with what glee may be imagined!—the roar of indignation which greeted the indiscreet letter of the British minister telling a pretended Briton who was aiming to trap him that the election of Cleveland would probably be beneficial to England.

Harrison's victory of course delighted his stanch friend but even his confident mood should have perceived the hint of danger which the vote contained. Though so distributed that it gave the Republicans a majority of sixty-five in the electoral college the combined popular vote for six other tickets—Democratic, Prohibition, Union Labor, United Labor, American and Socialist—exceeded their own by half a million. Harrison's popular vote was less than Cleveland's. The majority of the Republicans in the House was perilously small. They were still a minority party for which any mistake in strategy might spell destruction.

CHAPTER V

MIRAGE

THE note that is never quite silent in politics, that often peals up to the top of the register, is irony. Politics are so terribly human! And men are so often doing just what they think they are not doing. That "dramatic irony" which the playwright delights in, is so much of life, so much of politics. The Republicans in 1890 were a case in point. They were in high feather. They walked straight into a trap without, until it was too late, any true comprehension of what they were doing.

For our two friends, Aldrich and Harrison, the moment was peculiarly ironical. The man of all men whom they least wanted to trust was the one man they would have to trust. When Aldrich came home after his futile attempt to defeat Blaine in the convention of 1884 a jesting letter from one who was "always a Republican but badly disgruntled" wondered whether he had "recovered from the hard struggle you must have undergone—swallowing the nomination, plume and all." [1] And now, after four years on the off horse he would have to swallow—plume and all. Blaine had made Harrison's nomination possible. Blaine had swung the mass of the intemperate people whom Aldrich despised into the Harrison column. American politics being what they are, it was not safe for Harrison to make any one but Blaine secretary of state. Nevertheless, his private secretary urged him not to do so—temperamentally it would be so hard for the two men to get on together. But Harrison had his own shrewd sense of things. "Brother Halford," said he, "you and I will not have so good a time in Washington with Mr. Blaine out of the cabinet as with him in it." [2]

The appointment was made. Two men as dissimilar as any that ever held these great offices at the same time became President and secretary of state. Harrison, an aristocrat, intensely reserved, cordial to his friends but frozen to the world, a legal intelligence, a man of piety, severely upright, was almost naïve as a politician. Blaine, demagogue on a grand scale, brilliantly forthcoming, magnetic with his barber, his bootblack, his coachman, looking on all life as an amusing game of wits, was the last word for astuteness. The one should have been a Cromwellian general with a peculiarly severe taste in hymns; the other should have been a Renaissance cardinal greatly amused at the simplicities, which passed for subtleties, of that bishop who ordered his tomb in St. Praxed's Church. Harrison faced the most frivolous matters in a gravely high mood; Blaine, until he lost his temper—which he was capable of doing—confronted the most serious problems with that "naughty little twinkle in his eye" of the rollicking modern song. Can there be any doubt of the truth of the adage about politics and bedfellows!

Harrison's shrewdness, such as it was, was personal not political. He opened his administration by making the mistake of his life, the mistake that temporarily ruined his party. Before he was inaugurated Blaine had urged him to call an extra session.

I venture to state my impression that the general feeling among the wisest men in Congress is that the subject of the tariff cannot safely be postponed until the regular session unwelcome as the prospect of an extra session is. The best judgment is that to throw the tariff over to December next will surely continue it until the summer of 1890 and make it again the bone of contention when the congressional elections come.[3]

To Harrison this advice seemed rash. He did not want an extra session because it would "bring a strain upon us before we get our cables out. I fear too that with our narrow margin we may be successfully obstructed or may even divide over a tariff bill."[4] This was the wisdom of timidity. Blaine's was the wisdom of boldness. Twice in this era the Republicans undid themselves by listening to the voice of the timid, conventional politician instead of to the boldly original politician. In this first instance, Blaine's prophecy was fulfilled to the letter—and worse. By putting off an evil day instead of rushing to meet it, there happened— what we shall see.

During ten months—precious months that might have saved them!—the Republicans twirled their thumbs. When they met in December they took up at once—too late—the thorny subject of the tariff. The Congressional elections were less than a year distant. On that fact history depended.

II

The House formulated a tariff bill—the famous Mc-Kinley Bill. As contemporary observers said, it might as well have been called the Aldrich Bill. It was the Aldrich "substitute" of 1888 expanded, tampered with, made into a comprehensive attempt at a working tariff.

Mr. Aldrich defended the provisions of this bill—so nearly his own child—with a gaiety and a confidence that glimmers like bright sunlight across the dingy pages of the *Congressional Record*.[5]

There is another note that hovered in his mood during the debates—sometimes savage, sometimes amusing—upon the McKinley tariff. A change, a very subtle change, had come over this confident young senator. He has become audacious. Perhaps his quick and brilliant ascent to power has just a little dazzled him. Perhaps he over-values the skill, the strength, the good fortune that have been his portion the past three years. It is more than likely that he, and most if not all his party, thought their victory more complete than it proved to be. But all this is wholly atmospheric, wholly an impression of the observer's sensibilities. In debate Aldrich was as cool as ever. He knew when and how to be entertaining.

The Democrats tried to make out that the rates proposed in the new tariff could be translated into "equivalent" values that were indefensible. They assumed that a given

article cost abroad a very small sum; they calculated the
proportion between this cost and a specific duty—ten,
twenty, thirty cents—and called the result the "equivalent"
rate of duty.

Aldrich made merry at their expense.

For example, a species of cloth known as "cotton velvets"
came in two grades and the cheaper which was assumed to
cost 12 cents a yard in England, was made dutiable at 14.1
cents a yard. A more expensive grade, costing 40 cents a
yard carried a duty of 17.6 cents the yard. Working out the
ratios that may be found among these prices and these
duties the consciences of the opposition were outraged. The
figure 17.6 is forty-four hundredths of 40; the figure 14.1
is one-hundred-eighteen hundredths of 12.

You see! The wicked Republicans were levying a duty
of 118 per cent on the cheap cotton velvet which would be
bought by the poor but honest son of toil—in this instance
generally a colored man—while on the more expensive cloth
bought by the wealthier person there would be a duty of
but 44 per cent. But advocates who reasoned thus not un-
naturally forgot to make sure that their feet were on solid
earth. That was the mistake Aldrich never made.

For the purpose of ascertaining the magnitude of the benefit
which the poor colored people who are said to be the principal
purchasers of these goods derive from the present low rate of
duty upon cotton velvets, I had a very careful inquiry made
a few days ago as to prices at the various dry goods stores in
the city of Washington and the lowest price at which a yard
. . . could be bought was 70 cents. I was desirous of finding out
just how careful these importers were of the welfare of their
wards. . . .[9]

He found that these cheap "velvets" netted the Washington retailer, on the average, 53 cents a yard profit. "Who
is to-day engaged in robbing these poor colored people in
Washington and throughout the South through the sale of
this article?" The existing duty was 4.8 cents the yard.
Could not that profit of 53 cents be reduced by 10 cents,

in the way of increased duty, with no purpose to grind the face of the poor?

He tested his case by visiting himself a number of retail shops. He challenged the good sense of the assumptions on which the "equivalent" rates were calculated by his enemies. Spectacles gave him a good target. "In this case the rate is placed at 300 per cent. They say that if spectacles were worth 1.4 cents per pair, the duty on them would be equivalent to 300 per cent. (Laughter.) The lowest-priced spectacles I could find anywhere in Washington were 25 cents per pair, and the man who offered them for sale was candid enough to say of them, 'The glass is window glass and the bows are worthless.' "

He struck with a sharper edge commenting on a delegation of importers to whom he attributed the method of calculating duties which the Democrats had taken up. Importers as a group had detached themselves from the general business community and had drawn together in a fraternity of their own. A flock of them came to Washington to argue against the proposed tariff. Aldrich, in one of his most skilful speeches, packed with calm disdain, gave an account of this hearing. It

was a notable one. It was the first time in the history of this country that importers as a class had undertaken to dictate what its tariff laws should be. The spectacle was one which will long retain a place in my memory. A large number of men, filling the reception room and the corridors of the Senate to overflowing. . . .

One could not help admiring the aggressiveness of this unique delegation. Intelligent—knowing precisely the limitations of their own wants; skilful—the promptings of selfish interests having trained them to master the intricacies . . . of our tariff laws; astute—with all the inherited shrewdness which belongs to generations of merchants; famous—bearing names familiar upon every exchange in Europe; no such collection of men ever before appeared at the doors of the American Senate to influence its legislation.[7]

Aldrich was quite frank admitting that the proposed tariff was more in favor of the manufacturers than the farmers.

His defense was that even the agricultural interest would be better served by an abundance of American labor and by busy factories and teeming markets than by legislation supposed to be more directly for its own good.

The Democrats raised a storm of rhetorical protest: he was practically admitting that the tariff was in the interests of the wealthy classes; money controlled manufacture; to favor manufacture was to confess yourself the agent of the rich.

Aldrich scoffed at such reasoning. But other Republicans did not. With his luxurious, artistic tastes, he must have been deeply amused—it is a wonder he was not irritated!—when his party, as a reply to the charge that they were catering to the rich, decided that works of art must not be allowed to come in free.

Being articles of luxury we do not deem it wise nor in the interests of the Republican party to place these articles on the free list. . . . If this is done several congressional districts may be lost in the West . . . it being too obviously in the interests of the rich, and indefensible before the people.[8]

It was characteristic of the man that he did not resist this move, merely let it pass—something incomprehensively silly that he could not prevent.

What lay back of such fatuousness? Chiefly, the slow realization by the Republicans that they had been overconfident, that with each day's delay the eventual problem of defending their tariff before the country took on a more formidable aspect.

The precious days raced past and the elections drew nearer, while the Democrats strained every nerve to fulfil Blaine's prophecy, now more than a year old, and keep the hubbub going until close to election time. Meanwhile, in their fear of seeming to be the aristocratic party, the Republicans had recourse to other measures besides the tariff on works of art. The Sherman Anti-Trust Act was rushed through. As it aimed to have some sort of magical effect—

no one knew quite what—curbing the power of the rich, perhaps it would silence their detractors. This new willingness to denounce aristocrats was spreading wildly, dangerously, through the country. A talisman was needed to offset it.

From the Republican point of view this summer might be called the time of the great mistake. But Mr. Aldrich, in his high mood, would not admit that things were going wrong. To the end of his days he was always most serene when the tide was against him. While other senators grew tense and haggard, he shrugged his shoulders. Sleepless nights were many a senator's portion, the summer of the great mistake. For Mr. Aldrich, a vigorous lonely walk late at night gave him sound sleep, and the next morning he was blithely his strongest self.

It did not trouble him because the tariff was not going to be "entirely satisfactory . . . to every senator, or to any individual senator." All he demanded was to have it "fairly represent the average judgment of the majority of Congress upon the interests of the whole people as well as upon the claims of sections and industries."

He held that tariff was a difficult science that must be viewed as a whole; its aim was to create a balanced system of duties in which all activities would be guarded by the central purpose; he "sought to equalize, so far as legislation can do this, the conditions under which the various industries of the United States are carried on, in competition with similar industries in competing countries."

III

Mr. Blaine, ordinarily so bland, was badly upset this summer. There was a provision in the tariff bill that incensed him. It dealt with sugar. Mr. Aldrich was faithful to his traditional views favoring sugar refiners more than sugar growers. With that understanding he was willing to advocate a general reduction below the rates established in 1883. The House bill—whether on his advice or not, is uncertain—adopted his policy. It made a sweeping reduction while retaining the traditional advantage to the refiner. Raw sugar was made free; refined sugars were made dutiable at four-tenths of a cent a pound. The average duty on such sugars hitherto had been two cents.[6]

For the moment the Republicans fell into two factions barking at each other over this question of sugar. Each side insisted that it was being guided by tenderness for the West—as were those brave advocates of duties on art. The McKinley faction defended free sugar on the ground that it would placate the West, offset the high duties on manufactures, and help meet the charge that they were framing a rich man's tariff. Blaine violently opposed free raw sugar. His argument also had the West in mind.

This peculiar and brilliant man was one of those who never permit us to gauge them upon surface evidence. He must not be dismissed as insincere. His reasons convinced himself. But did they always arise in his mind in the way he believed they did? In this case, was his tenderness for the West the mainspring or the dial face of the clock of his policy?

He was naturally grandiloquent. He thought to the tune of rolling drums. He saw policies as if they were magnificent cycloramas. Also he wanted to be the next President of the United States. A policy that should inspire himself, and that should captivate the imagination of the country— and Blaine's views were always in terms of the imagination—was his condition of success.

He believed that he had devised such a policy. Even before Congress met he had assembled at Washington the first Pan-American Congress. He had brought all his faculties into action. Never did the delegates of foreign countries meet a more fascinating secretary of state. Under his deft touch some abstruse matters, such as standards of weights and measures, became almost human. He intrigued his visitors with other matters not abstruse. Why not draw the Western nations together in, say, a great Customs Union, or what would amount to that? Why not play into each other's hands, trading chiefly among ourselves? Of course, the foundation of this glittering dream would be a system of economic reciprocity—opening each other's markets to the members of the fraternity without tariff bars.

Was it all to benefit America, or to make Blaine President? Who knows! Probably, he could not have told just how the two motives intertwined. And thus arises the question, when did he discover that in this scheme lay the salvation of the Western farmer, whose wheat might find a new market in South America? When did he discover that in the Western farmer lay the salvation of the Republican party?

The stages of his thought are not on view. But this we know, when McKinley and his fellows accepted free raw sugar, Blaine scented danger. Sugar was one of the few Latin-American products that were not already free. Blaine wanted it as a trump card with which to play the game with his new friends. Quickly he persuaded himself that the party would be ruined if it did not arm him with the sugar tariff as an item to be traded off in return for the abolition of Latin-American duties.

This was what Blaine told a House committee, told it passionately with all the energy of his powerful nature. For once, the twinkle was out of his eye. This was life or death for the present administration—remembering the shortness of the interval that would elapse between the bill and the election, remembering how much easier it is with the crowd to dissect than to construct, to pull down an argument than to build up a defense—and hardly any one but himself appreciated it. The House committee that had the bill in charge would not listen to him.

He took refuge in the Senate Finance Committee. A picturesque tradition has it that he let himself go in a way which brightens the cold page of history with a burst of temper like a lightning flash, "smashed his silk hat in baffled rage and flung its crushed remains across the chamber as he denounced McKinley and his colleagues." [7]

IV

For the moment it seemed as if Mr. Aldrich's high mood was justifiable. His party, in the main, seemed to be with him. And then out of what he had thought was a clear sky, came the unexpected thunderbolt. Sugar was relatively a trifle. But the West was not. Mr. Aldrich had not learned the lesson he ought to have learned in 1886, when the Interstate Commerce Bill was the handwriting on the wall.

On the one point where Western interests clashed with his own he had seen things clearly. But he had failed to generalize what he saw. He had failed to make real to himself the fact that a great new constituency was forming in the West and that it had a predominant interest for which as yet no protection was afforded in his scheme for the equalization of industrial interests.

The silver industry was peculiar. Seen from one side it might have been regarded as coal and wheat were regarded —as the production of a raw material that did not have a manufacturing despot aiming to keep down the price. But the analogy would not quite apply because silver had been in the past, and might be again in the future, used as money. The one great market that might be opened to it as a manufactured article was the mint of the United States. This fact hitherto had found no recognition in the Aldrich scheme of things.

What was ardently believed by the silver-bearing portion of the country was bluntly stated by Senator Wolcott of Colorado in a tilt with Aldrich on the day that was perhaps the most crucial moment in the parliamentary history of the year 1890.

I wonder how long the Republican majority in Rhode Island, for instance, would last, if the interests upon which the people depend for their livelihood were no longer fostered and protected by the party in power. The worm of Democracy seems already to have made some headway in that commonwealth, possibly because duties are not yet high enough, and how long does the

senator from Rhode Island (Mr. Aldrich) expect the miners and
farmers of the West will continue to help protect the industries
he represents, while he and other senators who agree with him
can find for us only words of criticism and denunciation? [12]

When these strong words were used the most determined
of the silver advocates were trying to force upon Congress
a bill that would open the mint-market to silver without
restriction. In other words they wanted free coinage of silver. Obviously Wolcott was not quite fair in his comparison of the silver interest and the Rhode Island manufactures. A silver dollar may be a manufactured article—not
only physically but economically—but its function as money puts it in a different class from a silver teaspoon. This
the Easterners saw with quick alarm. The Westerners also
saw it, but from a different point of view and without
alarm. To their minds it was but another mode of convert-
ing their energies and their natural resources into purchasing power. As to economic and financial theories—they
were not in order. The only practical question was, who
had the votes in Congress?

> . . . The good old plan
> That they shall take who have the power
> And they shall keep who can.

Again the story swings back to Mr. Blaine. In this silver
complication he had a second reason for being terribly
afraid of what might happen after Congress adjourned,
when the members would scatter to their homes and the
real work of the year politically would begin, the work of
defending the new tariff before the electorate. The silver
Republicans were grimly in earnest. They were ready to
make a deal with the Democrats. They would throw all the
fat in the fire, drive the tariff men into ignominious defeat,
send the party before the electorate with a record of absolute futility, if their demands were not met.

Meanwhile the alarmed Republicans of the House had
sent up a bill designed to head off free silver. Early in June
the Republican senators held a caucus on the subject, dis-

cussing the possibility of compromise. Then, ten days later, in broiling hot weather, when everybody—Aldrich excepted —was more or less hysterical, the Senate revealed the startling fact that a majority was in favor of voting for free silver.[13]

All this while Blaine had been working against free sugar.

It was a moment of crises. Here was the Western power bluntly displayed. If it did not exactly prove Blaine's point, at least it was a grim warning that the other wing of the party did not understand the West as well as they had thought they did. So complicated was the Republican confusion that President Harrison decided to accept Blaine's dictation. He consented to present to Congress a Blaine ultimatum. His message of June 19, advised the virtual Customs Union that Blaine desired; he also accepted Blaine's views upon sugar. The duty should be restored but provision should be made for removing it through reciprocal commercial treaties giving this country equivalent commercial advantages.[14] Senator Hale introduced in the Senate an amendment to the tariff bill restoring the sugar duty.[15]

The President was not alone in his conclusion that the anti-Blaine faction had lost the day. Mr. Aldrich had reached the same admission. So had the Plumed Knight. He left Washington and sought a lovely retreat at Bar Harbor confident that he had won the game. He was destined to a curious surprise.

In this discouraging turn of affairs, Mr. Aldrich had encountered a type of situation that was to tax his powers time and again in after years—the unexpected break in an advance that can be retrieved only through a desperate flank movement or by a strategic retreat. He pulled himself together realizing that his plans must be swiftly reorganized. It was his first test as a strategist. He rose to the occasion. He would execute a strategic retreat.

Mr. Aldrich had a confidential talk with his friend the President. In view of the menacing vote in the Senate on silver, he felt that the tide had turned and was racing the

wrong way. There seemed to be nothing for it but to surrender raw sugar as the first step in a general compromise.
And then the President surprised him. Much as he admired Harrison, Aldrich does not appear to have thought
him a constructive politician. Harrison suggested what Professor Taussig calls the new type of reciprocity. He proposed to leave sugar free but to arm the President with
power to levy duties upon it if the countries exporting to
the United States would not give us advantages equivalent
to the remission of the sugar duty. Aldrich seized upon the
idea. The tide began to flow back.[16]

V

Had Mr. Aldrich been a conceited man—in addition, had
he been a superstitious man—he might have thought that
a special Providence was trying him out, testing him severely, by way of introduction to the task of legislation.
How different it was from the clever opposition, the glori-
fied nagging—just what the Democrats were now doing—
in which hitherto he had been engaged.

The next stage in this introductory ordeal was a startling
lesson in the incalculable caprice of circumstance.

Washington was possessed by a blazing summer—the
summer of destiny that Blaine had foretold. The Democrats were delaying the game by all those skilful devices
that hardened parliamentarians know so well how to use.
It was their cue not to appear to be holding up legislation,
but to do so none the less with apparent innocence, until
the very eve of the elections. The silver men were bolder.
They did not disguise their purposes. And now appeared a
third factor in this amazing instance of political fatuousness.

The Greek certainly knew what was what in his epigram
upon whom the gods would destroy. The final aftermath
of the sectional furies of Reconstruction chose this strange
time at which to reappear. Mr. Henry Cabot Lodge in the
House of Representatives was responsible for what has

come to be known as the Force Bill, more accurately known
as the Elections Bill, a punitive measure designed to give
the federal government complete control over national
elections in the South. Consequently there were pending
in the fierce heat of Washington in July the three antagonistic measures—the Tariff Bill, the Silver Bill, the Force
Bill. And every minute, for the Republicans, was precious.

The whole story of what happened the next two months
still eludes the historian. A furious parliamentary battle
was fought, to a large extent, under cover. It was carried
on through a succession of truces arranged we know not
quite how. Aldrich having got the new reciprocity policy
from the President, engineered an amendment expressing
it; he led a victorious compromise vote putting through the
Silver Purchase Bill, which provided for huge purchases of
silver bullion by the government but not for free coinage.[17]

But this was but one of the truces. The solution seemed
still so far away, the time before the elections was vanishing so rapidly, that the administration senators made a
move which is final evidence that they were desperate. To
shut off debate is the last offense against the most treasured
of Senate traditions. A few days before the passage of the
Silver Purchase Bill a caucus of Republican senators appointed a committee that was to consider the reorganization of the Senate rules so as to permit shutting off debate.
Mr. Aldrich was made chairman. With his characteristic
thoroughness he at once asked the Library of Congress for
everything to be had on legislative procedure in England
and France.[18] But there were no results. There could not
be any, for it was soon evident that the silver men and the
Southerners were in alliance and that they could block legislation indefinitely.

Again a truce was effected. Senator Quay is credited
with having brought it about. The Southerners received a
promise that the Force Bill should lie over until the next
session[19]—until after the dreaded elections—and they released the silver men from whatever agreement they had
made: the silver men thus came under the full effect of what-

ever agreement lay back of the Silver Purchase Act; and at last in the fatal month of September, 1890, even later than Blaine had prophesied, the McKinley Bill was passed. One of its sections provided for the new type of reciprocity. Another offset free sugar by promising a bounty to the growers equivalent to the duty that was taken off.

VI

When Mr. Aldrich was baiting the Democrats over their feeble dialectic upon "equivalent" rates he forecast their attempts "to prejudice the farmers of the West against the measure by the pretense that the articles in every-day use by them will be greatly increased in price by its provisions." He had divined correctly just what their course would be. But he had not allowed for two things: the shortness of the time remaining for the popular discussion—less than six weeks—and for the different values of certain modes of argument in the Senate and in a village. His prophecy that the farmers would quickly "learn to value correctly the gloomy forebodings and croaking of the whole brood of tariff reformers" proved to be a delusion.

In a brief, furious campaign the assailants of the McKinley Bill rang the changes on three related points—there is more protection for manufacturers than for farmers, rates are lower proportionately on articles consumed by the rich than on articles consumed by the poor, the whole thing is an expression of the power of money. Simple-minded country folk were visited by hired peddlers hawking pots and pans at exorbitant new prices "due to the McKinley Bill." Surely no one in America can be ignorant of what followed. Blaine's prophecy of eighteen months before was ruthlessly fulfilled. The "landslide" as the elections were called, changed a Republican House with a majority of 20 into a Democratic House with a majority of 138.

Legislatively, Harrison's administration was at an end. His one initial mistake had destroyed him. His friend Aldrich was also, for the rest of this administration, a ruler with nothing to rule.[20] The Republicans were again the futile party. The next two years was their *descensus avernus* until in 1892 they lost both the presidency and the Senate and were once more sunken deep in the lethal waters of mere opposition.

A sterile time it was for the two friends who had been so unwise as to undervalue Blaine's intuition of the crowd and its ways. A few pleasant performances they could still conduct together. Reciprocity treaties were negotiated under that provision in the McKinley Act from which at one time they had hoped so much, but which in the long run served them not at all.

There was a controversy with England over Behring Sea and a treaty for the Senate to ratify. There was considerable talk about closer relations with Hawaii—even whispers of annexation and rumors that the Sugar Trust wanted to bring it about—but not until the last moment anything tangible. The first of our strained relations with Germany was a quarrel over Samoa and some astonishing opera bouffe played out by her agents there.

A recognition that the silver question had come to stay —at least for a good while—was Harrison's appointment in 1892 of delegates to an International Monetary Conference that was held at Brussels, and accomplished nothing. A clamor for more direct popular control of the government took the form of propaganda for the election of senators by the people.

Some consolation for all their woes was found by the orthodox Republican leaders in a select little card club which they playfully named "The School of Philosophy." Senator McMillan was the most frequent host. This delightful man, neglected by historians, made of the School of Philosophy an informal political salon. It was an unique salon, being wholly male. For ten or a dozen years it continued. Several cabinet ministers were added to its membership. A powerful force behind the scenes was this coterie of the elder statesmen in which policies were outlined and the senators and the cabinet—when the cabinet was Republican—kept in touch.

The last word upon the Harrison debacle, like the first, should be Blaine. For a while, in a futile effort to rebuild the administration fortunes, he poured his energies into foreign affairs. But it was all in vain, and he knew it was in vain. The Republicans, as a party, had lost the game; he, as a leader, had lost the game. His health broke—the outward sign of a broken spirit—and he parted with Harrison almost an open enemy. As the curtain fell upon this brilliant and picturesque character, there were stormy rumblings all over the country of the new class animosities, the new sectional animosities which had been invoked and fostered with such little scruple in the bitterness of the debates of 1890.

CHAPTER VI

THE RESURRECTION OF ALEXANDER HAMILTON

I

A SADDER and generally a wiser man was every Republican leader as Harrison's administration approached its inglorious end. Mr. Aldrich was no exception. He had learned that politics was not all beer and skittles—to repeat the famous old saying!—and he was not quite sure that he wanted to stay in the game. With his party dished so completely, the fickleness of the crowd so brutally in evidence, was the game worth the candle?

He was now pretty well off. He had moved recently into a pleasant house on Benevolent Street in the most desirable part of Providence. It was, and is, one of those charming architectural fragments that gives distinction to the old New England town. You may call it late Georgian or Early Republican, just as you please. Airy, cheerful rooms, high ceilings, good woodwork, black marble mantels. There was an old-fashioned garden full of sunshine and roses. It is the home to-day of one of the Senator's daughters and contains many beautiful objects which he selected.

His fortune was growing steadily. But he had expensive tastes—he discovered the beauty of Persian rugs and began buying them long before it was fashionable in America to do so—his family was numerous, he was ambitious for them no less than for himself, and always there was that dream of a landed estate on Warwick Neck. Why not give up politics and go back to mere money making?

It was the spring of 1892. A great newspaper was also thinking hard about Aldrich's fortunes. The New York *World* had recently discovered that the temper of the Americans of the later nineteenth century had certain resemblances to the temper of the English of the seventeenth century. It did not express its conclusions historically but that does not matter. What it had discovered was that the rôle of professional informer could be revived.

The World was a Democratic newspaper. Years after, Mr. Pulitzer was asked why *The World* became the persistent enemy of Mr. Aldrich. He replied that he was against the Republican policies and he never wasted time attacking the small fry among his enemies; he struck only at the real leaders.

But this was only part of the explanation. The history of the nineties, in American politics, has some astonishing similarities with the political story of exactly one hundred years earlier. In each case a Revolution had been succeeded by a reconstruction of society. The two reconstructions were much alike. They were promptly denounced in much the same ways. In the nineties of the eighteenth century, Hamilton organized property and used it as the cement to hold together a stately social edifice based on the economic pre-eminence of the intelligent few. He was accused of class despotism.

In the nineties of the nineteenth century a new order had issued out of the economic chaos which followed the Civil War. It was using Hamilton's methods to recover and re-establish the type of community he had founded. It provoked the same furious assault that Hamilton had provoked.

The outcry against the tariff makers of 1890 was the straw in the wind. A social battle was on in America. Before long no one would have any peace with regard to it.

Mr. Aldrich was the sphinx at the back of the Republican policies. He had nothing to say to the propagandists who cried out that the Republicans were the party of the rich. Perhaps he realized that his instinct of silence was a handicap in the political game. Perhaps his momentary disgust with politics was part of such a perception. But if he felt that way, he had no intention to alter his methods. He might leave politics. He might not. But whatever he did he would continue to be himself, the man who refused to play to the crowd, the firm Hamiltonian, the rebuilder of the old social régime. That régime had been overwhelmed in the middle of the century by apparent democracy. Why should it not revive? Its recovery was a natural faith in any man who like Aldrich instinctively appealed to the few, to the ones whom evolution and heredity had selected to be leaders. Such men have no fear of the rôle of the political sphinx.

Mr. Pulitzer had another reason for herding his professional informers into Rhode Island this year. Mr. Aldrich would come up for re-election just about the time when the Republicans would be nominating a candidate for the presidency. If the Democrats should be so fortunate as to defeat him, what a spectacular event it would be! What an omen of Democratic success.

Furiously, *The World* blew its clarions and rushed into battle.[1] Its cue was Aldrich, the bogey man! He was the voice of corrupt wealth. He had made a fortune through nefarious relations with the Sugar Trust. He must be defeated. "An editor and staff of reporters specially detailed for the work will make the fight on the spot and remain until the battle is won. . . . Come on, Democrats! We must carry Rhode Island."[2]

With this challenge flung in his face, Aldrich for the moment forgot every thought except to win. He marshalled all the allies he could find. Knowing that he had no faculty for public speaking, Aldrich did not attempt to play spellbinder. But for once he admitted the necessity to put up a popular fight. Late in March he was at Providence. He wrote Harrison that Secretary Tracy who had promised to go to Rhode Island and make a speech must not be allowed to change his mind.

You can *have no idea* how much harm it would do us if the Secretary should fail to come now. We have a very serious and uncertain contest on our hands . . . the chances of success are no more than even.[3]

His telegrams to party leaders asking for speech-making visits drew forth answers such as McKinley's promising to come and deploring his possible defeat as a calamity to the party.[4] One of those who had come to his aid before the episode closed was that Jonathan Dolliver of Iowa who appeared in 1884, who was now a Representative in Congress, a brilliant magnetic man, of whom much hereafter.

Meanwhile *The World* continued to the tune of "Money against men. Boodle the sole dependence of the Rhode Island Republicans."[5] It published a cartoon of Aldrich as an auctioneer selling the Rhode Island governorship to the highest bidder.[6] The fact that Brayton was working hard for Aldrich was used in the most sinister way.

Against this background of calculated hysteria rises the calm and dignified figure of the great Cleveland. He paid Mr. Aldrich the high compliment of coming to Providence and speaking against him.[7] On the same day Cleveland, Thomas B. Reed and William McKinley all spoke in Providence. As *The World* pointed out there was "a remarkable mixture of party leaders" at the Narragansett Hotel. We glimpse Cleveland, Aldrich and several others leaving the dining room "all in a bunch."[8]

A striking group, in the mind's eye, against the background of that hotel which still stands, typically gorgeous, typically pretentious, the very expression of its time. It was a day when fashionable American hotels had "rotundas" and vast marble staircases, and enormous French paintings—either battle pieces or scantily attired ladies—with golden frames a foot thick. Imagine those great realists, the dour Cleveland, the quietly massive Aldrich, both of them powerful in physique as in mind, descending together the frivolous grandeur of that meaningless marble stair. Did either comment on the way their lives had interlaced, how they had begun their political duel in the fight over the Mills Bill? Probably not. It would scarcely have been in key for either.

The election was obscure in its ultimate causes as were most elections in the nineties, in States ruled by Despots. The honors were divided. The Democrats got the two seats in the National House. This was due apparently to having captured the working classes of the larger cities. Through what influences Brayton had been deprived of his hold on these industrial communities is not clear. Posters advertising Aldrich as "The People's Candidate and Workingman's Friend" did not check the rush of Labor into the Democratic camp.[9] But the country districts were another story. There Brayton was as powerful as ever. He captured the legislature. The legislature returned Mr. Aldrich a third time to the Senate.[10]

II

A few days earlier his old friend Harrison had been nominated for President the second time. In response to Aldrich's "friendly words of approval," the President wrote him a note that for him was almost affectionate, reminding Aldrich that he knew "in an especial way what my work here has been and what my positions have been upon all public questions." He was much gratified over Aldrich's re-election.[11]

The two friends were parting company. The President made a feeble attempt to keep up the delusion that he had a chance of re-election. Mr. Aldrich did his duty in the way of party gestures, speaking boldly upon Republican principles in the Senate and at campaign meetings. November came and Cleveland swept the country a second time. A dreary moment it was for all Republicans.

There was still in the mind of Mr. Aldrich the doubt whether it was sensible for him to stay in politics. Though prosperous he was far from rich. The connections he had made at Washington had not brought him money. Bogey man though he was, and always would be, the Sugar Trust had not lined his pockets. He was fifty-one years old.

It now became apparent that he had captured his true constituency, the Rhode Island business men, in a double way. He had more than their political confidence. He had also won their confidence as an executive. A proposal was made to him that was the true turning point of his career. Some friends of his who were believers in Aldrich the statesman, were bent on keeping him in politics. They were shrewd capitalists and saw that there was a great opportunity in giving Rhode Island a modernized equipment of street railways. They needed an administrative genius, skilled in all the devices both of business and politics, who could use their money and realize their dreams. They invited Aldrich to join them, combining his abilities and his influence with their wealth. It is not clear whether this was done just before or soon after his re-election. But some time, in the course of 1892, the bargain was struck. Mr. Aldrich went in for a great speculation in what used to be known as "traction"—that is, transportation in other ways than by railroads. He was immensely successful. Presently, he had interests in traction not only throughout Rhode Island but far afield. From the moment of his entrance into this field of investment, he climbed rapidly into the ranks of the millionaires.[12]

The incident was the first clear instance of his power to use imagination in business no less than in politics. Also, it showed that he knew how to play the sphinx as subtly in one rôle as in the other. He blew no trumpets of advertising, made no announcement of what were his ultimate purposes. He and his friends wanted to buy street-railway stock: who would sell? They persuaded a large holder to sell at $250 the share. That seemed to most people a large price. It was a large price assuming things were to go on as they were. Other shareholders fell over their feet selling out at the same rate.

As soon as Aldrich was in control, he altered his tactics. But it was not the public to whom he spoke out. To the banks he explained his purpose. His powers of vision and of convincing argument were irresistible. He easily obtained all the money he needed for financing his purchases, and for transforming the horse railways into electric railways.

When his plan became public property, the people who had sold out set up a wail. He was accused of over-reaching them. Their former opinion of the price paid was forgotten. Another touch was added to the popular picture of

Aldrich, the Bogey Man. He made no reply and again turned his eyes toward Washington.

Was he ever really in earnest about quitting politics? Or was the idea one of those surface impulses, which mere Prudence is forever attempting to foist upon natural bents? There is a good deal to say for the latter interpretation.

If Mr. Aldrich could have been forced into business exclusively he would doubtless have made a conspicuous success. Such success as he had, giving it only a fraction of his time and very little of his thought, warrants that conclusion. He had the business imagination, the power to foresee possible economic conditions, and to create them. Sometimes the boldness of his ventures was taken up by his enemies and made the bases of accusations—as when his insatiable enemy, *The World,* eighteen years later made its final attack upon him because of his investments in rubber.

Nevertheless, the evidence that business was anywhere near as great a delight to him as politics, does not exist. Like all the great men of action he was fundamentally an artist. And the artist is animated first of all in every line by the joy of the working. During the days of hesitation in 1892, the real, fundamental Aldrich, the artist Aldrich, in his stronger moments when the temptress Prudence seemed an unreality, must have anticipated one of the most famous meditations of Mr. Thomas Atkins, that one in which he concludes—

> For to admire and for to see
>   Whatever makes this world so wide,
> It never done no good to me,
>   But I can't drop it if I tried.

III

The year 1893 came in. The unhappy Republicans set their faces toward another season of eclipse. Mr. Aldrich and the President took their last step in common, acquiescing in the revolution in Hawaii, and preparing a treaty of annexation to the United States—the treaty which was pending when Cleveland was inaugurated, which he promptly quashed.

The long vacation of 1893 may be regarded as the time when Mr. Aldrich closed his apprenticeship as a statesman. He had committed himself. He was in politics now, as his major interest, for good and all. It behooved him to formulate his views in his own mind with finality. How he would have done so, even had the events of 1893 been other than they were, can hardly be doubted. The train of thought, at the back of his actions that can be traced through the ten years since he entered the Senate is plain enough—the perception of the inconsistencies in the popular definition of "constituency," the belief that industries and "interests" as such have a right to representation in government, the willingness to mould, even create, economic conditions through legislation; a contempt for the delusions of the crowd; a great respect for the exceptional man.

The elections of 1884, of 1890, of 1892, had all shown him the volatility of the electorate. For Blaine to have got the power he did get even though he missed election, was a grim warning to men of the Aldrich temperament. The "landslide" of 1890 had given him a shock which we may assume he never forgot. And to cap the climax, by what wretched methods had not the electorate been swayed in Rhode Island in the last election! Even under the cynical hand of the Despot, the purchasable men were a poor basis of power. How easily a considerable part of them—or some other group not yet clearly perceived—had responded to the sensational appeals of the professional informers. How it had happened, whether through gold or emotion, does not matter. Assuming that the virtuous Democrats had not spent a dollar in the buying of votes, there was a dark menace in the ease with which they had invoked a class issue, had captivated the tired imagination of the city workmen. Merely to depict their enemies as the tools of wealth was sufficient to raise up a power out of the dust.

Mr. Gresham who abandoned the Republicans, this year,

had written two years before, when he still counted himself a Republican, that the laboring men at least in the West were looking upon the Republicans as the aristocratic party; he felt that the outlook was not encouraging. "Our boat will have to be rowed against the stream while the Democratic boat will run with it." [13] Very completely recent events had verified Mr. Gresham who since his doleful prophecy had broken with the Republicans and was now secretary of state in the Cleveland cabinet. This year 1893 marks the general recognition that American society had been stratified anew, that out of the economic reconstruction, fruit of the Civil War, a new social system had emerged. A long series of sporadic symptoms of discontent, mainly in the West, too frequently ignored by the East, had failed to impress the nation, failed to link themselves, in the general imagination, with those haunting strains of the "Marseillaise" that now and then blew along the air from some tempestuous labor meeting, and reminded one, though faintly, of the scaffold at Chicago in 1886.

All along, the question, hardly phrased, just audible at the back of men's heads—what if the hosts of the Purchasables break out from under the hands of their Despots? And now the genius of *The World,* and of others in the new-fangled "yellow press," was aiming at a party of the proletariat. It was on that basis that the campaign had been fought in Rhode Island. Though the antiproletarians had won, how narrow was their margin, how treacherous the instrumentality they had had to rely upon! In last analysis the final battle was between *The World* with its army of professional informers, and Brayton with his Purchasables. Were these the alternates to be expected of American democracy, of government by the counting of noses?

While Mr. Aldrich was ranging himself, in his own mind, on all these great questions—the questions that were to be the basic, though sometimes the invisible political tides all the rest of his life—the panic of 1893 fell upon the land. Amidst the breaking of banks and the crash of great fortunes, the bottom fell out of the world of labor. In most parts of the country unemployment became the order of the day. The clamor of idle workmen crying for food—their wives and children crying—formed another reminder of the "Marseillaise."

It was in the stress of this tragic year that Mr. Aldrich found a sudden unexpected opportunity; out of it, he issued a statesman with a definite creed. The opportunity was in using his traction speculation as a means of tiding Rhode Island over the panic. Swiftly, with sure judgment, the work of transforming the street railways of Providence into electric roads was pushed forward. An emergency market for labor was created.[14] The distress of the panic year was reduced to a minimum in Rhode Island.

Everywhere else, or almost everywhere else, the distress was a godsend to the proletarians. *The World* and all it symbolized, won hosts of converts for the creed of—Down with the Rich!

By these events the thinking of Mr. Aldrich was finally cast in its enduring form. His success in meeting the panic was all that was needed to complete a fusion of two ideas characteristic of the man, the place, the time. In many a mind besides his the break-down of the popular conception of democracy had coincided with the spread of the doctrine of evolution. For better or worse, rightly or wrongly, here was the genesis of a new type of American statecraft—new, that is for the period since the war. In reality it was not new. At bottom it was Hamilton's gospel of a hundred years before. Though Hamilton had not heard of evolution, did not talk about the survival of the fit, he had similar ideas, by instinct, so far as society was concerned—as all the great aristocrats have had—and no man ever was more splendidly the despiser of the rule of the crowd. It was the spirit of Hamilton returned to earth that animated Mr. Aldrich's thinking from this year to the end.

There is a passage in a momentous historical document which Mr. Aldrich did not write but which it is fair to as-

sume he inspired. It expressed not only his general attitude toward the relations of business and government, but
the ineradicable impression made upon him this year.

Successful enterprise, of the type which benefits all mankind,
can only exist if the conditions are such as to offer great prizes
as the rewards of success . . . the business ability of the man
at the head of any business concern, big or little, is usually the
factor which fixes the gulf between striking success and hopeless
failure. . . . Moreover, it cannot too often be pointed out that to
strike with ignorant violence at the interests of one set of men
almost inevitably endangers the interests of all. The fundamental
rule in our national life—the rule which underlies all others—
is that, on the whole, and in the long run, we shall go up or down
together. . . . It surely ought not to be necessary to enter into
any proof of this statement; the memory of the lean years which
began in 1893 is still vivid. . . . The mechanism of modern business is so delicate that extreme care must be taken not to interfere with it in a spirit of rashness or ignorance. Many of those
who have made it their vocation to denounce the great industrial combinations which are popularly, although with technical
inaccuracy, known as "trusts," appeal especially to hatred and
fear. These are precisely the two emotions, particularly when
combined with ignorance, which unfit men for the exercise of
cool and steady judgment. In facing new industrial conditions,
the whole history of the world shows that legislation will generally be both unwise and ineffective unless undertaken after calm
inquiry and with sober self-restraint.[15]

The conception of society as an economic hierarchy,
which is the heart of Hamilton's vision, Mr. Aldrich had
rephrased for himself out of his own experience; henceforth he was always to hold the belief that prosperity per-
colates downward from the actions of the directing few in
the upper stratum of the social pyramid, through all its
stages from top to bottom.

CHAPTER VII

THREE FRIENDS AND A DIFFICULT SITUATION

I

MR. MCMILLAN, the delightful host of the School of Philosophy, reminds one in many ways of an older and riper social order than that which underlay the crackling politics of 1893. Had he lived a hundred years earlier, in those brilliant days when Philadelphia was the capital, he would have been a solace to General Washington and a conspicuous figure in Mrs. Bingham's drawing room. Mr. Hamilton would have loved him.

Conventional critics have disdained to speculate upon what his deft touch counted for, harmonizing the party chieftains around his card table. But this was not his only service. There was another little group that has eluded history. It was smaller than the School of Philosophy and it was not altogether Republican. The Triad, it might have been called—or even by a playful satirist the three graces of politics. The three were Mr. McMillan, Mr. Aldrich, and Mr. Gorman.

There were two or three reasons why this little group should be particularly close in the years 1893 and 1894. As the Republicans were on the shelf, the political activities of their leaders were reduced to the minimum. The School of Philosophy, temporarily, ceased to be an unofficial legislative chamber. Cards are all very well, and all its members were devoted players, but cards without politics—in the older day we should have said they were like Mrs. Bingham's drawing room without Mrs. Bingham. This while, with their party in opposition, Mr. McMillan and Mr. Aldrich were giving most of their energies to business. Each had staked a great deal upon traction. Mr. Aldrich had found a wise counsellor in his friend McMillan whose

104

traction interests were wide-spread. Mr. Gorman had similar interests. These men who so often antagonized each other in public were good cronies in private, even business associates. Mr. Gorman was virtually the partner of Mr. Allison in a mining venture.[1]

The friendliness and the common business interests of the three were curiously cemented when the new Congress assembled. The chairmanships of the major committees passed of course from the Republicans to the Democrats. But senatorial tradition is rigid that all the leaders must have chairmanships—for a chairman is entitled to a special room of his own. On few subjects are the grave rulers of the Republic more touchy than on this matter of the allotment of rooms to chairmen. At times, the fate of legislation has been materially affected by promising Smith or Brown the room he wanted. Mr. Aldrich in 1893 was assigned a minority chairmanship.

The second and third members of his committee were Mr. McMillan and Mr. Gorman.[2] The significance of their coming together is revealed by the title of the committee, "On Corporations organized in the District of Columbia." Politically it counted for nothing. But it afforded a pleasant opportunity for these good comrades, all of whom were interested in the public utilities of cities—traction, and others—to talk together time and again testing their views by the municipal development of the Capital. In a way, it was their commercial club the next two years.

There was still a deeper significance in the membership of the Committee on Corporations. Again, the underlying fact of the whole period, the difference between the obvious territorial or theoretical constituencies and the unacknowledged but far more real economic and social constituencies. These three were divided in theory by political labels but at heart they were a unit in their social and economic affiliations. As individuals they could act together in complete accord. The problem of their lives just now was how far they could bring their political action into tune with that accord.

Surely, even in short-memoried America, it is not yet forgotten that Congress met that year in August. Mr. Cleveland had called it in extra session. The panic was the cause. Those same staggering events which had brought about in Rhode Island the final definition of Mr. Aldrich as a statesman, had challenged the entire country. While, in Rhode Island the crisis which they had created could be thought about mainly in terms of employment, the country over it was thought about mainly in terms of money. It was to deal with the financial quandary of the nation that Cleveland called his extra session.

Strange things had happened since the passage of the Sherman Silver Act three years before. America was not alone in its preoccupation with silver. The European capitalists who had many millions invested in this country had taken alarm. They had begun to be afraid that America might pay them in metal the value of which was steadily falling as compared with gold, and which was not accepted as equivalent for gold in other countries. The failure of the bimetallic conference of 1892 to place silver internationally on an equality with gold was followed by an increased anxiety of the foreigners to get their investments out of America. Foreign creditors who had hitherto accepted American securities in settlement of trade balances ceased to do so and demanded gold, only gold.

A stream of gold was flowing out of America toward Europe. The government was borrowing desperately to keep redeeming in gold the paper money presented to the treasury. American banks, especially the great Eastern banks that did international business, found themselves in danger. Loans were called in. Applications for new loans were refused. As a consequence business failures became the order of the day. Railroads went into the hands of receivers. Six hundred banks broke in the year 1893. Even before that, it had become the custom of the American money lenders to stipulate in business contracts that indebtedness should be paid in gold.

It was against this tense background that appalling news

came to America from India. The great Indian Empire had
closed its mints to silver. Shortly before the closing of the
Indian mints, Cleveland had had confidential warning of
what was coming. August Belmont had the news from
England. He told the President "the race between India
and the United States to get upon dry ground first is all in
favor of India, unless we act with the greatest prompti-
tude." [3] Four days after the closing of the Indian mints the
extra session was called to meet August 7. The purpose was
the repeal of the purchasing clause in the Sherman Silver
Act.

And now once more a real issue broke through the spider
web of the party labels and revealed briefly real constituencies behind the veil of the labels. The three friends in the
Committee on Corporations had this while no trouble in
pooling their interests. Though few men were keener judges
of the value of these labels they were clear enough as to what
it was that controlled their deepest allegiance.

There must have been a deal of good-humored banter in
Mr. Aldrich's committee room while the three watched the
progress through the House of Representatives of a bill to
put an end to the government's purchase of silver. Mr. Aldrich and Mr. McMillan had good ground for twitting their
friend Gorman about what was happening to his party. As
his interests would give him no choice but to vote with
them when the time came, why not drop the Democratic
party altogether and come over to a party that knew its
mind?

What may have served as the text for such irony was a
rival bill introduced by Mr. Bland ordering instantaneous
free coinage of silver. Two bills both sponsored by leading
Democrats aiming at directly opposite results! What was
now the true constituency of that storied party? But Mr.
Gorman was not quite helpless under the teasing that we
may assume his friends indulged in. He could point out
that the issue had been defined by a Democratic President,
that Republicans of the stamp of his two comrades were
meekly following the leader of the opposite party. And Mr.

Aldrich with his valiant sense of humor must have gaily
admitted that the laugh had been turned upon him.

At the time he had no suspicion that August 16, 1893,
was one of the crucial dates of his career. Exactly twenty
years later the dearest hope of his life would be brought to
naught, because of a man who this day stepped suddenly
into a great place before the world's eye. Mr. Bryan made
a speech three hours long. In the gracious words of Cleveland's authorized biographer, "the magic of his personality,
the unrivalled beauty of his voice, and the compelling eloquence, which were later to charm millions, were fully in
evidence." [4] Silver had found its leader.

A great parliamentary battle ensued. By the end of the
month, repeal had been driven through the House, almost
the whole Republican membership siding with the President, while a goodly number of Democrats and a handful of
Republicans sustained Mr. Bryan. It took two months
more to get repeal through the Senate. There was much
stormy talk, much defiance of the wealthy East by the poor
West and South, before the three friends got their chance
to vote for the repeal of this short-lived Sherman Silver Act.

A threatening lesson was this episode for all our three
friends in the Committee on Corporations. Cool experienced politicians that they were, it gave them a new sum
to calculate. Of those men who had broken ranks for the
moment how many could be relied on to continue breaking
ranks? And will any of the three themselves abandon their
party labels? You, Gorman, for example, would anything
ever induce you to quit calling yourself a Democrat? And
yet how can Cleveland and Bryan both lead your party?

And this reintroduces the deepest question of the hour—
who is tired of the make-belief of the old apparent constituencies, and who is not? These fellows who play politics as
a game have a double affiliation, one-half their minds gives
allegiance to a label, a tradition, a constituency that has
lost its reality; the other gives allegiance to a reality; and
often the two are irreconcilable. Our deepest issue is this
matter of double affiliation in politics. Who is honest about

it, and wants to sweep it away? Who is deceiving himself in the belief that it does not exist, that the present deceitful political order is not an illusion? Who—to repeat! Cleveland is honest, he has had enough of double affiliation. So is Bryan. What of us—of these three fast friends—are we in earnest or are we not?

II

They had good reason to face the music. Cleveland had been elected on a platform that denounced "the Republican protection as a fraud, a robbery of the great majority of the American people for the benefit of the few," and asserted without conditions that "the federal government has no constitutional power to impose and collect tariff duties, except for the purposes of revenue only." [5]

To what extent these words, in the minds of the men who subscribed to them, had been mere verbiage, accepted without thought, it is impossible to say. The year 1893 had put many things in new lights. All sorts of talk that had been indulged rashly before then, were far more significant thereafter. Ideas and grievances that had been brewing in all sorts of vague ways, took on reality. And all these, in a sort of witches' dance began revolving around one central idea.

It was an idea that the three saw plainly enough, a terrible idea, but one from which they did not shrink. The country was dividing itself—had already divided itself—into two vast constituencies, debtors and creditors. How often or how steadily either group could act together, impose its will upon the machinery of the ostensible government, no man as yet could say. But for once, under sudden pressure that result had been accomplished. Mr. Aldrich, Mr. McMillan, Mr. Gorman, when the time came to quit joking about silver had stood shoulder to shoulder not as party men in the ordinary sense but as representatives of the creditor classes, of the part of the country where the creditor classes were in the saddle, as Easterners. [6]

This was an application on a great scale of the thinking Mr. Aldrich had completed the year before dealing with his

local conditions in Rhode Island. In contrast Mr. Bryan
and certain revolted Republicans took their stand as the
symbols of classes or regions where the debtors predominated. Westerners and Southerners, Silver Republicans,
Populists, and a new type of Radical Democrat, made up
the opposition to repealing the Silver Act.

The truly significant words in the Democratic platform
were "a robbery of the great majority of the American people for the benefit of the few." Right or wrong, wise or foolish, those words were a blazing truth to Mr. Bryan and all
his followers. Silver had no very clear meaning to its partisans outside the silver-mining States. But as a symbol, as
the sign of the debtor against the creditor, it suddenly became sacred.

Now that silver had been given a class significance, what
of the tariff? In Cleveland's mind it was essentially a class
issue. Ever since the message of 1887, he had preached
that gospel. Wealth was reaping the harvest of tariff profits.
Cleveland's programme was free raw materials which should
reduce the cost of living for the mass of the nation.[7] This
idea was embodied in the Wilson Tariff Bill framed in the
House as an expression of the President's views.

As our three friends turned from their achievement holding together on the Silver question, they realized that in the
tariff question lay a far more difficult test. Broadly speaking they were as well convinced of the community of their
interests on almost all phases of the tariff as on finance.
But there was a long-standing interweaving of traditional
with actual interests in the case of the tariff that produced
a situation which if they had been less clear headed than
they were might have been called bewildering.

The Senate was so delicately balanced that two or three
votes might determine everything. It was quite plain that
a complicated criss-cross of motives would underlie every
ballot. There would be infinite opportunity to bargain
among factions whose existence was not always acknowledged. Everything was on the knees of the gods. The most
serious and problematical feature of it all was due to a pro-

vision in the Wilson Bill that had only a slight connection
with tariff. It is an old and, to the clear minds, an irritating fiction that tariff bills are devices for raising revenue—
when all the world knows that they are primarily devices
for advancing economic interests. But because of this fiction extraneous matters are easily pushed into them for reasons purely strategic. On the tariff stem of Mr. Wilson's
bill had been grafted an income tax. Its advocates in the
House were frank. They wanted to put the burden of government on the rich. Thus temporarily the two ideas were
linked together—taxation of the rich through an income
tax, and abolition of high duties supposed to be the bulwark
of the rich.

The two Republicans and the one Democrat in the fraternity of the three were assailed by very different but
equally serious temptations. Mr. Gorman, traditional
Democrat—and still, as events were to prove unable to escape double affiliation except now and then—was tempted
to break away from his genuine economic interests and let
his party label be his halter—as thousands of other men
did. But, for this moment, Mr. Gorman was possessed by a
reckless devil of consistency—the politician's most dangerous friend unless honestly married to him, indissolubly and
of free choice. Mr. Gorman momentarily set his party traditions at defiance and did what he wanted to do. He committed himself to assist his two friends in making over the
low tariff of the Wilson Bill into an approximately high tariff—the "unconstitutional" thing of the Democratic platform. And yet he had not the least intention to give up his
Democratic label. Unlucky Mr. Gorman!

Mr. Aldrich's temptation was voiced by many tongues
clamoring all to the same effect: the Democrats are making a huge mistake in strategy; don't oppose their bill; give
them plenty of rope and let them hang themselves.[8] This
was the cry of the Eastern politician of the creditor class
who was as blind in his way as Mr. Bryan was in his.

Mr. Aldrich did not play politics in the ordinary fashion.
The artist in him pervaded the politician. The end of poli-

tics was to create conditions—the conditions he foresaw in imagination as the desirable ones. He was secure against the personal appeal of politics as a game to attain power. Rhode Island was practically a known quantity. The greatest power he could attain was as a manager—perhaps, the chief manager—of the Senate, and that he was sure of for many a year to come. No small part of the clew to him is the double fact: perfect confidence in the possession of a certain measure of power and a calm acceptance of its limitation. This is partly the explanation why his policy is so consistent, so unwavering, so steadily the expression of his mind.

While the House was wrangling over the Wilson Bill and the three friends were laying their heads together ominous things were happening. The woollen mills of New England had shut down waiting grimly to see what would happen in the shape of a Democratic tariff bill.[9] In many parts of the country unemployment stalked like a spectre. It was in the winter of 1893–1894 that groups of desperate men, without work and without food, formed themselves into "armies" to tramp to Washington and demand relief. The most famous, "Coxey's army," reached the Capitol grounds, only to be scattered by the police in an ignominious anticlimax that struck thoughtless people as comic.

III

Mr. Aldrich had decided what he would do about the Wilson Bill. He preferred no tariff bill at all—leaving the McKinley tariff still in force—but if that was impossible he would do all he could to get what he regarded as a good bill. He was not so narrow a politician as to want his enemies to frustrate his own desires merely to put themselves in a bad position at the next election. He might help Gorman out and not commit himself at the end to accept responsibility for his bill. The amiable traditions of the Senate do not bind a senator to support in the final voting a bill he has contributed to form.

It is unbelievable that the three friends did not talk over

the ultimate possibilities of their relation to each other and to the bill. The whole of what they agreed upon no one knows, but as will presently appear, they could not agree to abandon their party labels. And on that, a word is to be said in their defense. While it was the indirect economic system in the background that guarded their interests, it was the obvious political system of the foreground that endowed them with power. To form a working balance between the two was the task that every politician of that day was endeavoring, more or less successfully, to accomplish. They could not agree to stick together to the end of the chapter. They could agree that whatever bill was adopted by the Senate should be in the majority of its provisions approximately satisfactory to them all.

On this understanding they set to work. A great deal of futile anger has been poured out upon all of them because they did exactly what it was natural for them to do. The Wilson Bill was made over in committee, savagely debated in the Senate, altered in hundreds of particulars, rejected in a conference of the two chambers, but finally accepted by the House in the form the Senate had given it. The House committee protested bitterly but had not courage to do more. The bill had been so craftily recast that braver men would have hesitated to reject it.

First of all the income tax had been retained. That in itself was enough to float the bill through the House. The issue which it involved—which we shall meet next year as the central fact of the time—was already a ruling purpose in the new coalition forming around Mr. Bryan. It was on this point that Mr. Gorman and his two friends had their first disagreement. He sacrificed his economic convictions and his class prejudices to the need to placate other Democrats, while Mr. Aldrich and Mr. McMillan expressed the point of view of the creditor class of that day, severely disapproving an income tax.[10]

The Cleveland theory of free raw materials received scant courtesy. The one conspicuous exception was wool. What appears to have been a compromise among the three was in

taking the tariff off raw wool while keeping it upon manufactured wool. Here Mr. Aldrich and Mr. McMillan stuck
to their labels while Mr. Gorman stuck to his. In all the
votes upon the subject Aldrich and McMillan were consistently for a tariff on wool.[11] And in so doing, as party men,
they were far-sighted. Their record in the votes on wool
will prove a useful counter in the political game a year from
now.[12]

The most immediate furore created by this tariff concerned sugar. It began before the bill was reported by the
Finance Committee. Everybody knew that the Sugar Trust
was lobbying at Washington as never before. They had a
special opportunity because the Louisiana Senators had for
this moment, frankly repudiated double affiliation, were
acting as sugar men pure and simple, treating their Democracy as a fiction. They were confessing the hope of the time
that the subterranean constituencies might yet become the
basis of real politics as distinguished from the mere game of
politics. And this while, they were after the reality not the
game. And they had their State behind them. "Have our
friends make Caffery and Blanchard understand," said a
Louisiana telegram, "that they need have no fear of retalia-
tory legislation if they vote against [Wilson] tariff bill.
Everybody here working hard to get them to do it." [13]

It was Mr. Allison to whom the Louisianians chiefly appealed. He played their hand so skilfully that Mr. Clarkson
two years later charged them with ingratitude because Mr.
Allison in 1894 saved them from bankruptcy.[14] At the time
Mr. Manderson gave a delicious account of the way things
were going.

Brother William B. Allison with the feet of his debate clad in
list slippers, is talking on the Wilson Tariff Bill, and with soft
gloves on the hands of his arguments is pounding the face off the
speech made by Brother Dan Voorhees a day or two since. The
great debate has opened and if you should drop in upon us two,
even three months hence, I think you would find it still going
on.[15]

There were hearings galore while the bill was with the

committee. The great Mr. Havemeyer himself made a futile attempt to appeal to Cæsar. "Sugar is fighting for life, here, now, not for big boodle," wrote his secretary begging for an interview with the President. "It can't get on with less than it has agreed to accept. I don't want to join with the opponents of the tariff bill. Mr. Havemeyer can show the President in half an hour's interview the exact situation." [16]

This appeal was made through the secretary of war on March 6. Ten days earlier the Democratic senators had held a caucus. It had refused to instruct the Democratic members of the Finance Committee what to do about the tariff bill. Thereupon Senator Gorman showed his hand. He rejoiced openly that the protection Democrats "were within three votes of getting higher tariff instructions from the caucus." [17] Aldrichism was in the air.

At this time *The World* was watching with fierce eyes the progress of the Aldrich influence in the Senate. It was ready for another bout with its enemy from Rhode Island. It saw plainly enough the reality of the unacknowledged combination that was defying party labels and was typified by the three political Graces. *The World* was thriving upon the rôle of professional informer. It boasted of the growth of its subscription list since it had dedicated itself to exposure.

The 6th of March, the day Havemeyer's secretary wrote his distressed letter to the secretary of war, was a day of surprises. There were sharp unexplained flurries in sugar stock—up 12 points, and down 9. How to put two and two together explaining this, no one knows to this day. But the next morning *The World* made the most of it. With an air of charming innocence, it printed a lot of rumors— carefully assuring its readers that doubtless they meant nothing at all. And yet—if you must know!—it was said yesterday on the stock exchange that Senator Brice came often to Wall Street (and Senator Brice, Democrat though he was, was for high duties, especially protection of sugar!); and Senator McPherson "is credited" with having recently bought 10,000 shares of sugar stock; and "rumor says" that Senator Vest is buying sugar stock; and of course everybody knows that the wicked Havemeyer is in Washington hard at work corrupting the government.

There was a sudden epidemic of newspaper cynicism. The grave *Tribune* permitted itself very serious insinuations. The jumping of stock quotations was attributed to "secret conferences" with members of the Finance Committee. This ordinarily conservative paper went so far as to say that "the feature which made the speculative episode one to cause regret was the common opinion in Wall Street that the big rise and the big break had lined the pockets of some shrewd national legislators." [18] Two days passed and then Senator Peffer, the new member whom the Kansas Populists had sent to Washington, brought *The Tribune's* insinuations into Congress. He moved for an investigation. Senator Morrill objected that the Senator had no moral right to make such a motion unless he was convinced of the truth of the charges. Senator Quay wished to lay the motion on the table. Nothing came of this first attempt at an investigation.[19]

Before Senator Peffer had brought in his resolution, Senator McPherson, wounded and indignant, had made a statement to the Senate denying the insinuations of *The World*. And then Aldrich did a singular thing. He was oddly irregular in his reading of newspapers. He liked journalists better than journalism. He asked McPherson what paper had made the charges. He was enlightened. When the time came, he gave his contemptuous vote against the tabling of the Peffer resolution.[20]

He was already using all his art of parliamentary warfare to put into the bill as much protection as he could get. His tactics were largely delay—thrusting other business to the front—letting every one understand that the protectionists would hold the bill back until it took a form which, at least, would not be an offense to them.[21] Scornfully retaliating upon the yellow press, he made the sugar schedule the crux of the debate.

A group of senators—not all of them Republicans but all for the moment hand in glove—held frequent conferences at the house of Mr. Chandler, one of the senators from New Hampshire. The central figures were Mr. Aldrich and a famous Democrat, an eager aspirant for the presidency, Senator Hill of New York.[22] Really, it seemed—to the uninitiated!—as if double affiliation might be passing away.

Of course, there were endless negotiations behind the scenes of which to-day very little is known. In the middle of May the Republicans held a caucus followed by confidential conferences among senators. Here, probably, is the end of a chapter. Aldrich was so well satisfied with the prospect that presently a change appeared in his tactics. He slackened his pressure upon the Democrats. He began to allow things to take their course. The situation was summed up by Senator Dubois who said that "as the principle of protection had been recognized by the dominant party, there was nothing now left but a quarrel over schedules." [23]

And then, suddenly arose another instance of the difficulty of putting two and two together. The sugar scandal flared out again. The Philadelphia *Press* drew a lurid picture of the octopus of the sugar lobby, of Mr. Havemeyer, in rooms at the Arlington Hotel "convenient" to the Finance Committee, and implied that the President was in the conspiracy, and would let the trust and the Louisianians write the sugar schedule.[23] The New York *Sun* which was then a Democratic paper, was still more courageous. It charged senators with having accepted bribes.[24] So furious was the temper of the hour that *The Tribune* thought "the public generally is inclined to believe the charges." [25]

The Senate was thrown into a fury—or something near that. Senator Lodge proposed a resolution to investigate the charges, both of bribery and of speculation. It passed without a division.[26]

Throughout the sugar scandal Mr. Aldrich pursued his natural bent, treating the matter either with indifference or with scornful irony. His Puritan ancestors, whom he had

almost forgotten, survived in his willingness to believe that
the heathen rage and the people imagine a vain thing. In
the midst of this legislative hurricane, on the day the Lodge
resolution was passed, a newspaper correspondent recorded
one of the best pen pictures of him.

The Commander-in-chief of the forces of protection is Mr.
Aldrich. . . . But technical knowledge . . . exhaustive and unusual as it may be, does not alone fit any man for leadership in
the United States Senate. To this essential foundation Mr. Aldrich adds the gifts of a ready command of the English language,
of a clear and well modulated voice, and of a facility in speaking which while not exactly deserving the name of eloquence is
logical, incisive, and always perfectly lucid. Add to these qualities a wonderful capacity for patience, a marvelous self control
under provoking aspersions, and an ideal perfection of manner,
and you have the best equipped man in an all around sense for
the leader of a minority struggling for the salvation of American
labor and American homes.[27]

The bribery investigation soon ran upon a snag. The investigating committee had summoned two newspaper men
and demanded their sources of information upon senatorial
affairs. They refused to testify. The committee submitted
a report which was an appeal to the Senate to consider
these men in contempt. The Senate was inclined to acquiesce. Aldrich set the sensationalists at defiance. If *The
World* and its similars thought they could affect legislation
through lurid journalism, they might know that he, for one,
was totally indifferent to such performances. He calmly
but firmly opposed the reading of the report.

He had a further reason. It was very characteristic. Several veteran journalists have testified to his faculty for
trusting men. He would talk to correspondents with a candor that lesser men dared not risk. There are no traditions
of his confidence having been abused. He had the subtle
quality that prevents such abuse. The press gallery, when
Aldrich was opposing the report, knew that there was no
pretense in his words:

The value and character of the information which is sent out
from this Capitol, and the information which is collected all over

the United States, in which the public is so deeply interested, depends very largely upon a certain relation of confidence between the party who gets the information and the party who imparts it; . . . it is as important to the public interests that that confidence should be at least in some degree respected as it is that the confidence between a lawyer and his client, or a physician and his patient, should be maintained.[28]

But he could not prevent the reading of the report. He revenged himself by speaking of the sugar schedule as "this contemptible juggle." [29] Shortly afterward in his more usual temper he ignored an article in *The Tribune* which intimated that he had put through the sugar schedule of 1890, in return for a subscription of $100,000 to be used in Harrison's campaign.[30]

We have now come to the most curious phase of this extremely curious episode. One of the clews to Aldrich was his moderation. Granted his assumptions he was always for the middle way. He was too astute a statesman not to understand the danger of overleaping his intent. His friend Gorman was a simpler soul. Having allied himself with the Louisianians, whose votes he dared not estrange, he let them take the reins in their hands. They drove hard. They demanded a general duty on all sugar of forty per cent; also a special additional duty of one-eighth of one cent per pound on refined sugar and a further additional duty, one-tenth of one cent per pound on refined sugar from countries that gave export bounties.[31] Aldrich thought that the two additional duties were unnecessary.

"I desire that the American refiners should have the American market," said he, "but I do not want to give them any more than an adequate protective duty upon their product." [32]

The group of senators meeting at Mr. Chandler's house stood with Aldrich in the attempt to shut off the imposition of the additional duties. There followed a series of votes that are amusing. Aldrich, with Chandler and McMillan were joined by the great Democrat, Hill, in vote after vote against the additional sugar duties. Gorman that arch

Democrat, of the party of free trade, together with those other true blue Democrats from Louisiana, voted time after time to impose the additional duties. A hot fight, and at last Chandler recorded in his diary, "We are beaten." [33] In spite of Aldrich the three sugar duties were all at last incorporated in the law.

Meanwhile, the committee on investigation summoned many men before it. Mr. Havemeyer made his famous contribution to the history of American political method revealing with delightful frankness that the Sugar Trust contributed to the campaign funds of both parties regulating its contributions by the size of the party votes. As to the talk about bribery of senators, this of course came to nothing. On the subject of speculation, Mr. Aldrich was among those who testified. He stated on oath that he had not speculated in sugar. More than one senator frankly admitted that he had done so.

In this connection the most dramatic event of the session occurred. It is probable that each speculating senator gave his testimony with regret except one. There was one man of whom we may risk it that he was delighted to be able to "call" the newspapers—as card players might say—in the astonishing way circumstance had offered him. A faculty for estimating delusion, for detecting its insubstantiality, an ease in forgetting himself in his problem, a brilliant fluidity of determination—if that means anything!—characterized Matthew Quay. There is scarcely a more striking moment in the history of congressional investigation than that one in which Quay told the committee that he had been speculating in sugar, that he intended to go on speculating in sugar—or in anything else he pleased. What would the Senate do about it? The Senate could not do anything. For the moment, at least, the newspapers were answered. They had intended to scare some timid old sheep: they had encountered an amused lion. The balloon of their propaganda broke loose and went sailing down the wind.[34]

Was ever a parliamentary battle more confused apparently than was this! Of course, if we knew it all, knew what sharp trading went on behind the scenes, what cool understandings were established among various interests—the wheels within the wheels—all sense of confusion would disappear. Because Aldrich did not have his way with the sugar schedule it does not follow that he was not relatively successful. On the day when Quay made that confession which was such a poser for the committee on investigation, Aldrich made a statement that fits the classic phrase—"half reveals, half conceals."

The cotton schedule was under consideration. Senator Dolph turned upon Senator Aldrich "who sat smiling in his seat and had not uttered a word," and asked him why this schedule that occupied ten pages of the proposed law, was passed in thirty minutes.

Mr. Aldrich said that the average rate on cotton goods in the McKinley Bill was fifty-five per cent and the rates just adopted averaged about forty per cent. He had no hesitation in saying that the schedule just adopted was the most scientific ever prepared. While the rates were lower than he should like, the methods of levying the duties were most satisfactory, and therefore he and other senators who knew the rates would not be fixed in accordance with their ideas were glad to accept the schedule on account of the methods of levying them. He declared in conclusion that the cotton manufacturers owed the committee a debt of gratitude for the schedule.[35]

Our three friends had travelled together as far as they could go. The bill had been recast. It was now to be voted upon as a whole. Here they shook hands and parted. After all, party labels were party labels. The day had not come when double affiliation could be quite dispensed with. While Mr. Gorman voted for the bill Mr. Aldrich and Mr. McMillan voted against.[36]

Just the same a great step had been taken toward the day when the ostensible constituencies and the subterranean constituencies should be less absurdly at variance.

CHAPTER VIII

REALIGNMENT

I

ALDRICH the business man always gave way to Aldrich
the statesman. It was in those periods when his public
activities were reduced to a minimum, that he consoled
himself with active attention to business. In this period
following 1893, when the Democrats were in power, the
wide-spread traction ventures that were such keen interests to all the Graces were for the time Aldrich's chief concern. During the winter he frequently raced back from
Washington to Providence to attend board meetings. In
summer, when he was not in Europe, he kept his eye on all
the details of his ventures.

By all accounts he was a very pleasant man of business.
The charm that was so generally recognized was not kept
in reserve for his family and his political associates. It was
felt by every clerk in his offices. When he reappeared after
an absence of any length he would shake hands all round.
"He would come breezing in with quick step and air of
much to do but without an appearance of hurry." He called
all the clerks "Mister," even the youngest. At times, when
there was much to do, he would seem absent-minded. He
had been known to start out to seek his barber, forget his
errand, and return to his desk and its preoccupations. When
addressing some one or when presiding at a board meeting,
he would look at the person speaking keenly, penetratingly,
then look away and bring his eyes back again, many times.

He impressed those with whom he came in contact as
being alert but not aggressive. He did not exude authority
as some lesser men did. "He never swore, but used 'my
goodness gracious' in place of an oath."

At board meetings he would often handle objects on the
table, in a sort of busy way while the conference went on,
giving less the impression of nervousness than of a man with

122

much to do who was impatient to get on with it. His dress is described as "simple, an open collar being used in the old days, and he gave no evidence of thinking particularly about his appearance, although always neat."

He had a few particularities as to dress. His colored butler, George Wallace—one of the last of the old-time colored servants to whom "the family" is an article of religion—remembers the care he took in shining the Senator's shoes and how well it was appreciated.

Throughout his life all his observers noted his eyes. The secretary of Senator Warren remembers them as "dark brown and beaming. They expressed his personality." Years afterward Anders Zorn said that they were extremely difficult to paint, so individual were they, so changeable.

This period of business success marks the turning point in his private fortunes. Almost the first definite evidence that he felt himself a made man financially came three years later in his first purchase of land on Warwick Neck. What was known as "the Hoppin place" had been rented by the Aldriches during several summers. The pleasant old farmhouse marked the exact spot on which Mr. Aldrich hoped some day to build his great mansion. A lovelier piece of land it would be hard to find, rolling downward as it does from the crest of a ridge to the margin of Narragansett Bay.

Mr. Aldrich was now well established both in politics and in finance. But he was not yet in the first rank in either field. Financially, he never made any very startling further advance. The increasing range of his political activities kept his business activities incidental. As a statesman, he was now to make his turning point, to establish himself in the front rank.

II

For all his boldness, Mr. Aldrich was always instinctively tentative in the opening move of an advance toward new ground. He was one of those highly consistent people who are the same in all walks of life, in his family, in his office, in the Senate. The most characteristic thing about his con-

versation was not so much what he said himself as what he
made others say. People who talked with him remembered,
so often, that they had done most of the talking but that
they had not picked the subjects of talk. Subtly, delicately,
he had determined these. And yet they never felt that they
had been manipulated. Instead they had a delightful sense
of having fallen in with the mood of a charming man. His
effect on them was atmospheric. His family say the same.
His influence pervaded and persuaded but was not expressed in words; "Papa never preached to us," says one of
his daughters, "and yet, somehow, we were all so eager to
do just what he wanted us to do."

It was a very subtle master of the innerness of strategy—
if one may put it that way—who now addressed himself to
the task of putting his party in a strong position on the
money problem.

The one absorbing question was now whether silver—
or more truly what silver symbolized, the debtor classes, the
regions where borrowers predominated—would serve to rearrange the American political system in genuine constituencies. In a way Mr. Aldrich and Mr. Bryan were for the
same result from opposite points of view. Both were wholly
out of patience with make-believe politics. And each was
too astute not to see the main lines of safety so far as they
involved the class and the section to whose interests each
stood committed.

Mr. Aldrich opened the game with his natural delibera-
tion. Though he was firmly wedded to the East, and to
Hamiltonism, though if necessary he would take gold mono-
metallism rather than free silver, he was not going to throw
the West over unless he had to do so. He gave full credit
to the shrewd remark of the president of the C. B. & Q.
Railroad:

I think the East is a little inclined to forget that our silver
policy has been to the silver region what the protective tariff
has been to Pennsylvania and New England, and that a sudden
stoppage in the one case must have somewhat the same local
effect as a sudden stoppage in the other.[1]

The advent of Mr. Bryan, the formulation of silverism in surpassing eloquence, had not driven Mr. Aldrich as it had driven Mr. Cleveland to the opposite extreme. He took up Mr. Bryan's challenge but in an adroit way. In the midst of the sugar scandal he signed a cablegram to the Lord Mayor of London:

We desire to express our cordial sympathy with the movement to promote the restoration of silver by International agreement in aid of which we understand a meeting is being held today under your Lordship's presidency.

We believe that the free coinage of both gold and silver by international agreement at a fixed rate would secure to mankind the blessing of sufficient volume of metallic money and what is hardly less important secure to the world of Trade immunity from violent exchange fluctuations.[2]

This was a skilful adaptation of the Republican platform of 1892, which had clung to "the parity of values of the two metals" assuming that it could be effected through the action of the United States alone. But that was before India closed her mints. Now after repealing the purchase clause of the Sherman Act the Republican leaders were prepared to offer the West, and incidentally the South—all the borrowing part of the country—an astute compromise. The lines of the controversy were redrawn. "International bimetallism" became the shibboleth in opposition to "free silver."

A year passed while the two cries went on exchanging echoes. It was a lurid year, from the summer of 1894 to the summer of 1895. Watching coolly the progress of events— at first from the Senate; then in the midst of petty political quarrels in Rhode Island; through a pleasant brief ramble in Europe; from Washington again—Mr. Aldrich marked the Civil War at Chicago when Cleveland showed the iron that was in him suppressing the famed Pullman strike. Do we remember those haunting strains of the "Marseillaise" in that same Chicago seven years before? Already, from a far Western State an excitable governor had earned the nickname "Bloody Bridles Waite" because, denouncing the

suppression of another strike, he had said that he was willing in the People's cause to see their horses ride bridle deep
in blood.

Wild echoes all this sort of thing had, and the world
listened aghast. The government ran short of money. Its
bonds went begging. At last—in February, 1895—Cleveland called in Mr. Morgan and through him borrowed gold
to save the nation's credit. Mr. Morgan offered to take three
per cent interest instead of four if Congress could be induced
to guarantee payment in gold. But Cleveland knew it was
useless. After this, a fury of talk denouncing the President
as having sold out the nation to "money lenders," Mr.
Bryan leading the bacchic chant. And then, the great event
of the hour——

The income tax was declared unconstitutional. The chief
counsel against it was Mr. Choate. And this brings up
again—as so often in the history of politics—the lamentable
fact that many of the most interesting moments in the
story are forever lost. Not long before the final argument
in the case Mr. Aldrich and Mr. Choate spent several hours
together on a railway-train. What did they talk about?
Two of the most delightful men of their day, both Easterners to the core, both aristocrats, both disbelievers in the
income tax, and one of them about to plead against it before the Supreme Court! What keen talk, that day, on a
fleeting Pullman car, through a dissolving landscape of
which we may be sure neither was aware. No rhetoric in
that talk, no platform flourishes, no useless bewailing of
conditions, just the close and careful comparison of two
points of view—the statesman's and the lawyer's.

The argument developed by Mr. Choate before the court
was full of the most skilful legal subtleties. It has been
praised by lawyers as a masterpiece. From the legal point
of view, that may be, but it was far more than that. It was
a bold appeal to class feeling and to sectional feeling. Mr.
Choate accepted the idea that the income tax was aimed at
property, and he played upon the idea with all the skill of a
consummate master of suggestion. A still more daring move

was his argument that because a great proportion of the tax would be drawn from the four States of Massachusetts, New York, New Jersey, and Pennsylvania, the tax was in effect a despotism of the poor parts of the country over the wealthy parts.[3]

The subtlety of his arguments persuaded eventually five out of nine justices. Said Mr. Justice Field, "the present assault upon capital is but the beginning. It will be but the stepping-stone to others larger and more sweeping till our political conditions will become a war of the poor against the rich; a war growing in intensity and bitterness."

This hysteric idealization of the rights of capital is startlingly similar to the argument in another Supreme Court decision made thirty-eight years before, that Dred Scott decision still familiar even to those who pay little attention to history.

What Mr. Aldrich thought of the constitutionality of the decision we do not know. All his thinking at the moment justifies the conclusion that he was glad the income tax was upset. It did not fit into the Hamiltonian conception of economic society. But he could not have shared the hysteria which the subject aroused. Hereafter, we shall see him, while still disapproving of an income tax, make use of it in his most brilliant *coup* bringing about the constitutional amendment under which the present income tax is laid.

Mr. Choate had served Mr. Bryan well. What better argument to justify his policy! The golden East, the four great money-lending States and their dependencies, to be set apart, their interests sacrosanct beyond the reach of any legislation that the vast congregation of the poor of the nation could effect. To arms, ye poor men—Western silverites, Southern debtors, Populists, Socialists, all who are unhappy and seek redress! They were not familiar with the "Marseillaise," or its strange fanatic loveliness, discordant at heart, would have rung through the land the summer and autumn of 1895.

III

With swiftly growing confidence the silvermen were drawing together all these elements of discontent. Mr. Aldrich watched them waiting for an opportunity to force their hand. Then quietly, unexpectedly—in the lingo of that card game whose terms have already served to clarify a situation—he "called" them. It was done so effectively that the gasping New York *Sun* had this to say: "Senator Aldrich of Rhode Island is the political manager of the Republican party in the Senate, and is regarded as the most influential man, all things considered on the Republican side of the Chamber. He is the virtual Chairman of the Finance Committee and was the organizer of the flank movement that in effect read" the silvermen out of the Republican party.[4]

It was a very pretty little piece of strategy to which *The Sun* alluded. The Republicans of the House had sent up a bill providing for special funds to redeem legal tender notes through sale of bonds.[5] The Finance Committee contained a silver majority. They amended the bill so as to provide for free coinage of silver.

Mr. Aldrich voted against the amendment but it was carried by a coalition vote of Democrats, Populists and silver Republicans. The bill was passed over Aldrich's head by practically the same vote.[6]

Another House bill providing for exceptional revenue through an increase of tariff was altered by the Committee on Finance in precisely the same way. If there had been the slightest chance that either bill would have been signed by the President, this double performance of the silvermen would have been singularly absurd—proposing to pass two bills identical in language, both providing that "the mints of the United States shall be open to the coinage of silver and there shall be coined dollars of the weight of 412½ grains troy, of standard silver." [7]

Strategically, both these bills were challenges to the silvermen to dare to impede legislation desired by the East, by business generally. In each case the silvermen had shown the courage of their convictions. During debate upon the revenue bill, Mr. Teller, leader of the silver Republicans, lost his temper. "We (silvermen) can get along without the party as well as the party can get along without us." [8] He protested that he would not be read out of the party until he got ready to go. He had been irritated by the quiet irony of some remarks by the aged chairman of the Finance Committee.

Mr. Allen cut into the "colloquy," remarking, "I see present my amiable and distinguished friend, the Senator from Rhode Island, who always coaches the Senator from Vermont, the chairman of the Committee on Finance, and I wish to ask the Senator from Rhode Island, who has said he is a bimetallist and that his party is a bimetallic party, whether he is willing to take the tariff bill just exactly as it comes from the House of Representatives with a free silver coinage amendment attached to it?"

Mr. Aldrich blandly replied, "Does the Senator from Nebraska wish an answer from me?"

"I desire," said Mr. Allen, "to have an answer from some responsible head of the Republican party, if it has one."

Mr. Aldrich's answer rang sharp. "I answer, then, frankly, no, with as much emphasis as it is possible for me to use."

Mr. Allen retorted, "I am glad to hear it, because it stamps the Republican party as the enemy of bimetallism. Your party has been masquerading for three years under false pretenses in this chamber." He pressed Aldrich with the further question, "Are there any circumstances under which you will take free coinage?"

Again the unconditional retort. "No, sir . . . unless an international agreement on the subject shall be first secured."

Mr. Allen interjected the Republican platform of 1892, and there was lively debate as to what it meant, especially its indorsement of "the use of both gold and silver as standard money with such restrictions . . . as will secure the

maintenance of the parity of the two metals." The introduction of the platform was the stroke of fate.

Mr. Aldrich cut in with "We stand on that now."

Throughout this altercation, Aldrich and his friends had
kept their tempers. With uncompromising serenity they
had piled up their insistence that the Republicans stood
for bimetallism, but only by international agreement. Aldrich nailed his colors in his sharp replies to Allen. And all
this had further irritated the already irritated Mr. Teller.
When Aldrich said "We stand on that now," Mr. Teller
could not restrain himself. Rashly, he struck back, "No,
we do not."

This was just what Aldrich wanted him to say. He did
not answer him, not even when Mr. Allen stormily promised that if Aldrich wanted to pass the emergency revenue
bill "with a free coinage amendment attached to it, the
Populist party stand here pledged to give you six votes to
carry that joint measure." Again, Mr. Aldrich did not answer. There was more outpouring of spirit, some of it
heated. Aldrich blandly spoke the last word, but it was
merely to point out that the Committee on Finance intended to let the bill drop and that all this talk was not
to the point, and then the debate was closed.[9]

The rest of the story of 1896 is a familiar tale to this
day. Mr. Aldrich went to St. Louis to attend the convention that nominated McKinley.[10] What was far more important in his eyes, he took part in framing the celebrated
provision in the platform miscalled the "gold plank"—the
adoption of which led to the dramatic withdrawal of Senator Teller and the Silver Republicans from the convention.
What was actually done in the famous plank was not to
declare for the gold standard—that was Cleveland's position, and among the great leaders, his alone—but to effect
a compromise restating what Mr. Aldrich and his friends
had been insisting upon ever since they signed the telegram to the Lord Mayor: "we are . . . opposed to the free
coinage of silver, except by international agreement with
the leading commercial nations of the world, which we

pledge ourselves to promote, and until such agreement can be obtained the existing gold standard must be preserved." [11]

On this understanding the Republican party at last found unity with itself, and proved that it had a mighty following. The presidency, the Senate, the House all became theirs. But the way their power was based showed that a great shifting of political centres of gravity had begun. Nearly a third of the McKinley's popular vote was in the four States fixed upon by Mr. Choate as being par excellence the creditor States. These four with the rest of New England and the States which might be called the suburbs of the East—Ohio, Indiana, Illinois, Michigan, and Wisconsin—gave him altogether four and a half of his 7,000,000 votes. Even thus he led Mr. Bryan, the nominee of the poor men in league with silver, by little more than half a million. The East had beaten the West. The spirit of Hamilton repossessed America. But there was a great multitude that did not believe in him. What was to be the future of the statesman who, more than any other, reincarnated Hamilton?

CHAPTER IX

THE DAY OF THE ELDER STATESMEN

At last the Republican ship had reached a port. Sixteen years had passed since the young Senator from Rhode Island came aboard. The stormiest sort of sailing had filled those years. The young Senator was beginning to think of himself as an old senator—old, at least, in experience. Had he been classically inclined he might have compared himself to the much wandered Ulysses; he might even have pushed the parallel so far as to find a simile for the brief gleam of insubstantial glory that had seduced his party in 1890. He would have been within the bounds of truth—rhetorical truth—had he called it the Circe's isle of his long and perilous voyage as a minority statesman.

He was so inured to disaster in politics that doubtless he had no suspicion he was entering upon a halcyon time, that the Republican ship had dropped anchor off the Islands of the Blest, that he had before him twelve years of the full delight of power. The situation in the Senate was unique. Those political storms that had raged so furiously since 1881 had not been so universal as, to the casual eye, they may have appeared to be. Rather, they had been epidemics of storm that attacked some regions and avoided others. Or, to change the image, they were inundations that swept over plains and valleys, but left certain strong islands untouched. The country had divided itself senatorially into stable and unstable States. Consequently there were now two classes of senators—experienced, elderly men who with stable States at their back had survived the storms, the inundations; younger, inexperienced men who had come or gone as the caprice of their electorates blew this way, blew that. Consequently in 1897 the Senate was composed of a core of elder statesmen and a fringe of novices.

No great assembly has ever been more sensitive to its

prerogatives, has ever had a more intricate body of unwritten custom, has ever been more difficult for a novice
to influence, than the Senate of the United States. A brilliant satirist, once the joy of all America through his im-
personation, Mr. Dooley, sensed the power of the Elder
Statesmen in an essay of inimitable impudence forecasting
the future of a talented young man who came into the
Senate from Indiana this same year, 1897. His prophecy
was not fulfilled; but none the less Mr. Dooley had an accurate impression of the gentle, irresistible way in which
the Elder Statesman would take a novice in hand, either to
teach him the game, or to make it impossible for him to
learn the game.

Among the Republicans, the School of Philosophy was
pretty much the heart of the matter. Among the lost trea-
sures of history are the memories of what things were discussed in that unique male salon and how they were decided. We may risk it, that any novice of the day would
have parted with one of his eyes to become a member of
the School of Philosophy.

The power of the Elder Statesman was not circumscribed by the Senate. From that rock of Republican prestige, influence had ramified into many local machines. The
Representatives, with their short terms, their difficulty in
forming contacts with the President, depended so largely in
their political fortunes upon their senators. It should never
be forgotten that the Senate is not merely a legislative body.
Through its participation with the President in the power
of appointment, it comes near to being an administrative
body. The experienced old men of the Golden Age—for such
in Senate history this period may be called—had taught
the Senate as a whole how to lay its strong hand indirectly
but authoritatively on the House.

The very peak of senatorial happiness was a period of a
few years when there were in the House enough Representatives under the shadow of their senators to enable the
Senate leaders on most occasions to direct the balance of
power in the House this way or that. There is a sort of

analogy to the relation of the two Houses of Parliament, once upon a time, in the history of England. In those far off days when the great landholders of the House of Lords could determine the majority in the House of Commons, the aristocracy of England had a power in legislation not wholly dissimilar to the power of our Senate about the close of the last century and at the opening of this.

Nevertheless it was a time of uncertainty in the organization of the Upper House. The Republican majority had only to close its breaches to be irresistible—except for one thing. It is an old and in the main a fiercely guarded tradition that the freedom of debate in the Senate is inviolable. Consequently, no assembly is more tolerant of the obstructionist, the "filibuster," who prevents voting by talk. One of the few attempts to break this tradition will form a striking detail in the career of Mr. Aldrich. Still more significant will be his vain attempts to close the party breaches. Within the dominant majority, the School of Philosophy formed the next circle, the aristocracy of the majority. But there was still an inner circle. The most interesting and unusual body in the Senate's history is an alliance of very dissimilar men who are to be known hereafter as the Four.[1]

The Four were Aldrich, Allison, O. H. Platt, and Spooner. Their fraternity had been full sixteen years in the making. Mr. Allison and Mr. Platt were in the Senate when Mr. Aldrich arrived. Mr. Spooner, who had come in four years after Mr. Aldrich, was forced out by local quarrels in Wisconsin, but had since recovered his hold upon his State, and was now returned again. All the Four were over fifty-five. Mr. Allison was sixty-eight this year; Mr. Platt, the eldest, celebrated his seventieth birthday.

The day of the Elder Statesmen was literally a day of old men. The ones who were in power in 1897 remained in power for ten years thereafter. The ones whom they adopted, like Mr. Hanna, were of their own age. The younger men were treated altogether as lieutenants. A good deal is to be said for the idea that one cause for their eventual fall was the breach that they allowed to open between themselves and their recruits. When at last the party broke in the Senate, their quarrel in a way was a fight between old men and young men—counting seventy as old and fifty as young.

What was true of the Elder Statesmen as a group—and of the School of Philosophy—was also true of the Four. Though Mr. Aldrich and Mr. Spooner in 1897 gave no suggestion of age both were of that remarkable sort who, while they never grow old, have by intuition the point of view of the final experiences. Of Mr. Aldrich particularly this was true. Furthermore, he had the greatest affection for Mr. Platt; and for many years he had the most confident reliance upon the restraining influence of Mr. Allison.

It were a difficult—perhaps an impossible—task, to trace out all the ramifications of the interplay of these four men, one upon another. That there was something common to them all, that it was distinctive, powerful and constant, goes without saying. They could not else have formed the close fraternity they did. But like all such delicate forces it eludes the scientist. The mere historian bows and withdraws. If only he were an artist—an analytic maker of human portraits—who might do justice to things so deeply laid, so far the reverse of the obvious!

We shall see these men acting together, forming policies of their own, skilfully imposing their leadership upon the Senate. They compose a genuine cabal, perhaps the only one in the history of the Senate. While they hold together —just nine years—they are at the very heart of Republican policy. This is because collectively they come very near to being a composite of the best intentions of the dominant elements of their party.

Each contributed an essential to the composite. Mr. Spooner's contribution is the easiest to define. He was essentially the legalist. In an age when old standards were being challenged from every side, the legalist was an essential in every situation. All these men were instinctive conservatives—at least, all but Mr. Allison and he was a conservative almost to the end. None but Mr. Spooner was a genuine legalist. A sound intuition led them to value him as a constitutional want.

Mr. Allison was the one who sensed the average practical man. Until his judgment began to break toward the end, few men ever did it better. He was an opportunist, if you will—bitter Mr. Ingalls said that he was so pussy-footed he could walk from New York to San Francisco on the keys of a piano and never strike a note[2]—but there was always a limit to his opportunism. Though walking over piano keys, and sitting on fences were the true diversions of his soul, he had the faculty, which the mere opportunist does not have, of knowing when to get off the fence.

But the average practical man is no less important in the calculation of events than another type not so generally recognized, the average spiritual man. It was this potent if often unacknowledged factor in human affairs that found a remarkable expression in Mr. Platt. In him was focussed a singular and wonderful phase of humanity that New England has been peculiarly able to produce. It is made up of shrewdness, of scrupulous honesty, of rigid adherence to the principles he accepted, but with little imagination, and with an intuition of what might be called the spirit-with-its-eyes-upon-the-earth. It was Platt apparently who time and again interjected into their councils the one touch of something else that kept legalism from becoming despotic and opportunism from sinking into time-serving.

And Mr. Aldrich—his deepest instinct was undoubtedly for administration. It was he who knew how to combine the others, to make them effective jointly, to produce a resultant. His mind was as keen as Spooner's but almost humorously non-legalistic. He was large enough to trust Spooner to be his corrective, to save him from making efficiency his sole test. Lacking altogether Allison's deference to circumstance, as bold by nature as Allison was timid, he deliberately many times let Allison hold him back, apply the check rein. But it was Platt apparently that he trusted farthest. It is not at all certain that he could have told why. Here the relation was more intimate, the values subtler, than in the other cases. But there is every reason to take literally as an expression of himself the remark he made after Platt's death. "He was the best man I ever knew." In the midst of his tremendous battle in 1909, when he was wearily driving the field before him, but with his heart upon widely different matters, he regretfully exclaimed, "If Platt had been here this wouldn't have happened." [3]

CHAPTER X

CONCILIATION

I

THE key to the moment in the minds of the Four was that clause of the Republican platform pledging the party to work for international bimetallism. Apparently this was the only way to escape a tragic break between East and West. In the effort to prevent it they found an able ally. Senator Wolcott—the same Wolcott who had threatened Aldrich in 1890—had been in the silver movement and yet was not quite of it. He had begun to be fearful of whither it might lead. He was very earnest to reunite the nation through a new monetary policy.

Mr. McKinley shared the conciliatory temper of Mr. Wolcott and the Four. His inaugural address promised "constant endeavor" to secure international bimetallism "by co-operation with the other great commercial powers of the world." One of the first things he did as President was to appoint a commission of special envoys to reason with the European governments. Mr. Wolcott was the head of this commission. It was created under an Act of Congress passed very late in the previous session and approved by Mr. Cleveland the last day of his term.[1]

The journey of the commissioners was postponed until an extra session, promptly called by McKinley, had shown its hand in the matter of the tariff. Senator Wolcott had made an informal journey with a view to sounding the European bimetallists previous to the inauguration.[2] He had returned in a mood both hopeful and alarming. On the one hand his unofficial conferences with French bimetallists had led him to write home: "If we have only patience and tact, the whole question can be solved in the next few months in a way that will take the whole subject from

138

American politics and will further civilization and progress
the world over."[3] This letter was addressed to Senator
Chandler, who was working heart and soul to reunite the
Republicans on a bimetallic basis.

The ominous part of Mr. Wolcott's first journey was the
discovery that France would come into an international
agreement only if America reduced her tariff walls. In the
words of another correspondent of Mr. Chandler's, praising
a speech he had made against monometallism, "all depends
on Mr. McKinley's action in support of the plan elaborated
in Paris by Mr. Wolcott and the French bimetallists," who
felt sure that England was suffering from the closing of the
Indian mints because of her capital invested abroad and
was ready to join the movement.[4]

Mr. Aldrich and Mr. Wolcott were in close co-operation
while the tariff programme of the Senate was being put into
outline.[5] They had become personal friends and it is fair to
assume that Mr. Aldrich sympathized with the anxiety
which was felt by the senator from Colorado. The latter believed that he was cutting his own throat in opposing free
silver. He was sacrificing his future in the hope of reunit-
ing the party and preventing a break between East and
West.

I do not refer to my political future. I have ceased concerning myself as to that and fully recognize that if I had ambitions
the door is closed upon them finally. I am, however, consumed
with the desire that it shall be demonstrated to the people of my
State, nearly all of whom hate and distrust me, that the course I
have taken is right, forever right; and that the way to our prosperity and happiness lies along the path to which I have ad-
hered. . . .

The newspapers and people most influential with Mr. Teller
are extremely sectional in their utterances since election; declare
there can be no prosperity without free coinage; that this talk
of returning prosperity is a fraud and that we must continue to
suffer for four years, when Bryan will surely be elected.[6]

At the same time there was well-founded alarm over the
tendency of the Eastern press to demand the single gold

standard and relentlessly to disregard the West. It is impossible to say which was the more firmly sectional, those rabid silverites in Colorado who were after Mr. Wolcott's political head—who eventually drove him into retirement— or the uncompromising monometallists of the great creditor States.

To steer between these furious antagonists and to find a policy that would commend itself to the majority of the nation, was the difficult task of senators like Chandler and Wolcott and Aldrich and the others of the Four. The silver Republicans were in command of the situation. They did not want to quit the Republican party. They wanted to terrorize it into giving them control. Though their support of the Party of the Poor Men had been of greatest importance to Mr. Bryan, they were ready at any moment when it should serve their turn to stab their new allies in the back, and desert home again. They were protectionists. It was all very well to unite with Mr. Bryan denouncing the tariff when both were in opposition, when both aimed to break down the organization that was in power. But now, when a revision of the tariff of 1894 was certain to take place, when these silver Republicans could throw the vote in the Senate either way they pleased, they meant to use their power. They were steadily in favor of protection of four articles, silver, wool, lead and hides—silver by free coinage; the other three by the tariff.

The desire of the Senate conciliators to harmonize the two groups of protectionists—Eastern and Western—and at the same time to get a tariff that would not offend the French bimetallists, determined the amended form imposed by the Finance Committee on a bill sent up by the House and known in history as the Dingley Bill.

This bill had aroused instant alarm in France. So outspoken was the French resentment that the Associated Press, at Paris, put a number of questions to M. Hanoteaux, the minister of foreign affairs. He answered rashly, "The co-operation which France could give the United States in the assembling of a monetary conference would naturally depend upon the state of the relations between the two countries." Furthermore, "the federal government at Washington will succeed without any doubt in drawing closer the bonds which unite France and the United States by abstaining from overtaxing imported French goods, such as sparkling and still wines, brandies, silks, woollens, gloves, works of art, etc. To shut out from the United States by quasi prohibitive tariffs the product of French industry and art will have a contrary effect." [7]

The American friends of a French agreement did not lose their tempers because of this blunt threat. They laid their heads together to see what could be done about it. Aldrich took the Dingley Bill in hand. He and his fellows in the Finance Committee made it over. Though they had many ends in view the most far reaching was this one of satisfying the French. In this they succeeded—temporarily. The recasting of the bill was well under way when Mr. Wolcott sailed, a second time, on his mission of international conciliation. His sailing was preceded by a conference with the Republican members of the Finance Committee who made an agreement with him which "involved the adherence to certain reasonable and moderate duties upon the products of France and the retention upon the free list of certain French products in accordance with the general principles upon which the tariff bill is being framed, and with the further idea of preventing adverse feeling or delay in the preliminary work of our Bimetallist Envoys in their conferences with the French ministry." [8]

As Mr. Aldrich was the most conspicuous member of the Finance Committee he must have taken part in this conference. As the tariff debate progressed he grew impatient of the uncompromising sectionalism of all factions, of the narrow interests of most economic groups. Perhaps the deepest significance to him of the years between 1896 and 1900 was the widening of his horizon. He entered the period without any vivid concern with American interests abroad. He issued from it with an international horizon. It was the maddening criss-cross of purely domestic interests in connection with the Dingley Bill and their conflict with international interest that began his transformation.

This whole episode is permeated with illusion and disappointment. At first Mr. Wolcott met with great success abroad. It was paralleled by relative failure in the experience of Mr. Aldrich. "I believe that it is extremely important to the country," he had written to Mr. Frick, "and to the iron and steel industry that there should be no excessive rates levied in any portion of the new tariff bill, and I cannot help thinking that some of those suggested by the Ways and Means Committee in the metal schedule are unnecessarily high." [9]

In his speech opening the discussion of the bill, in the Senate, Aldrich took the same tone. "It was, I believe, thoroughly understood throughout the country in the last political campaign that if the Republican party should again be entrusted with power no extreme tariff legislation would follow. . . . The rates suggested by the committee's amendments are considerably below those imposed by the House bill. . . . Industrial conditions in this country with a very few exceptions do not demand a return to the rates imposed by the Act of 1890. . . . Without relinquishing a particle of our devotion to the cause of protection, we feel that we have a right to ask that the cause shall not be burdened by the imposition of duties which are unreasonable and excessive." [10]

He was unable to carry out this programme. The silvermen held the whip handle. Ruthlessly, they carried through a second remaking of the bill, transforming it back again in the direction of the wishes of the House. Aldrich spoke scornfully of the trooping of the beggars of high protection through his committee room. It is possible that his surrender to an attack of illness may have been induced in part by his disgust at the way things were going. For a while, in June and July, he withdrew from the contest and the management of the tariff bill devolved upon his less strenuous colleague, Mr. Allison. "Senator Aldrich has been seriously sick (June 10) and does not appear to be getting any better. I am doubtful if he will appear again in tariff matters for some time, not merely because of his health, but because, I suspect, he feels keenly the manner in which the Republican Senators are treating the tariff bill— so largely the work of himself. The general character of the bill is being changed at committee meetings which are more like town meetings than like meetings of the Finance Committee, and it must be humiliating and galling to him in the extreme. I have not heard him say a word, and I may be wrong in my surmise. He has not read his mail for ten days and that is one reason for my thinking as I do, although his sickness is doubtless sufficient to account for that." [11]

II

A peculiarity of Aldrich was his power to step back and forth from public to private life without letting either affect the other. His power to accept the fiat of circumstance was even more extraordinary. Of this trait, as of so many others, his taciturnity makes it hard to generalize. His friends fall into argument trying to determine whether to call him a fatalist or not. But all are definite upon his ability to feel as well as to say, "What's done is done." His serenity in the face of adverse fortune which in other men would be put down to strength of will may in him be attributed to a quality much deeper, much more subtle, more unusual.

And there is another quality that is germane to the explanation of the summer of 1897. He did not need the faith in victory in order to fight well. He was an artist in all his activities. He fought well because poor fighting would have made him unhappy—as the poor painting of an off day plagues the painter and compels him the next day to scrape it out.

Who can say whether Aldrich in his efforts to get a Francophile tariff was hopeful of success, or merely doing his best, and leaving the result to take care of itself? If ever a man, in all respects, great and small, lived in the temper of Milton's most famous lines, it was he. Granted his own standards—

> "Nor love thy life nor hate, but what thou live
> Live well. How long or short permit to heaven."

When he left the field in the middle of June, and while he absented himself from the battle, there is no evidence of gloom or unhappiness in his mood. During the first fortnight in June he was mainly in seclusion at the Arlington. He managed to get out and attend a caucus on June 8, at which it must have been quite plain to him that the rebels in the party led by the silvermen had got control. He does not appear to have attended another caucus, four days later, when the rebels took the bill out of the hands of the Finance Committee and started that series of fierce discussions which have been described as "more like town meetings than meetings of the Finance Committee."

Aldrich was not critically ill. His health, throughout his career, is a contradictory matter not fully explained. Nearly six feet in height, weighing over two hundred pounds, extremely active, fond of sports, he appeared at most times finely robust. But there were other times when suddenly he dropped below par. He was subject now and then to very severe attacks of indigestion. This is all the more curious because he was abstemious in his food. He never used wine or liquors—though providing both abundantly for his guests —he hated tobacco (one of his few real aversions) and his family remembers with amusement that he never ceased to insist, once a week, on having for himself only an old-fashioned New England boiled dinner.

This fortnight of inaction at the Arlington was taken up chiefly in playing solitaire. Turning his back on the confusions in Congress he invoked the strong power he had to accept the inevitable and forget it. Only one exception is reported. An appeal was made to him to check a Democratic attack on a schedule of the tariff bill. Mr. Aldrich called up Mr. Gorman by telephone. If memory does not err, what he said was—"Gorman that schedule is all fixed. You keep your hands off it."

The middle of June he left Washington. Fortunately for him there were other matters this summer in which he could take delight. The property which he had purchased the year before—the Hoppin place—included fourteen acres of land and a comfortable old house. This was the start of his country seat of Indian Oaks. He was fifty-six, and though the great house he had in mind did not arise until he was past seventy, it continued to be a solace, on the other side of the horizon, all that time. Meanwhile the estate grew in size and in beauty, year by year.

The first farm he bought contained the central portion of the estate. He was not yet rich enough to build the sort of residence he wanted—no where near rich enough—and therefore he had laid out a plan of gradual approach to his desire. By degrees he would acquire more land until all the slope of the beautiful ridge east of the Bay should be his. Instead of building a mansion at once he would begin with its outbuildings. The first of these was a boat house. This year it was the absorbing interest of Aldrich the private man. A large enjoyable building, containing several rooms, a sort of private club, it rose in the course of 1897. Speedily, the boat house was filled with beautiful things, and became his especial care. "He loved it," say his family, speaking of its destruction by fire a few years later.

Mr. Aldrich did not reappear in the Senate until shortly before the final vote on the tariff bill. But he was back in Washington at the opening of July. He was consulted by Mr. Chandler who read him some discouraged and unhappy letters from Mr. Wolcott.

This charming though somewhat temperamental person now, for a while, becomes the doleful centre of the episode.

III

"Of exceptional analytical capacity," said Mr. Aldrich of Mr. Wolcott, "he was quick in the perception of the points involved in any issue, and when once he arrived at a conclusion he permitted no consideration of expediency or self interest to change him. . . . Mr. Wolcott was a man of charming personality, vivacious, well-read, quick-witted, and broadly sympathetic, association with him was always delightful." [12] This charming person had gone back in high confidence to resume those conferences with the French ministers which had begun before McKinley became President. Capable of enthusiasm and susceptible to dismay, his mood was destined to dramatic reverses the next four months. He watched eagerly the progress of the tariff battle.

"We are moving along," he wrote to Mr. Allison, "not rapidly but we are moving."

The bill as it passed the House had roused "a good deal of feeling" in France. He was delighted with the changes proposed by "our committee" which had made "the reaction all the greater. . . . I am assuring friends here that there will be no change, and I am relying on you and Aldrich to make my assurance good. . . . I am without any information about what you are doing in the Senate, except that I read in the New York *Tribune* Aldrich's opening statement which was admirable." [13] Before leaving America he had introduced the French consul-general at New York, M. Bruwaert to Chandler for the purpose of establishing a reliable connecting link with the French authorities.[14]

On the 20th of June, the tariff had taken its unfavorable turn; Aldrich was disgusted and ill; Allison was holding the reins somewhat feebly; and Chandler wrote to M. Bruwaert: "We have mutual sympathy on account of your disappointments in connection with the new tariff bill. You properly sought to secure low duties in order to benefit your country. Mr. Wolcott and I endeavored to ameliorate the duties on such products in order to smooth the pathway to bimetallism and because, moreover, to impose only moderate duties which would produce revenue and not prohibit importation is in accordance with the present policy of our party." He went on to show how difficult it was "to stem a very strong current in favor of high protection." [15]

July came in. There was a long conference with M. Bruwaert at Chandler's house followed by the reading of Wolcott's letters to Mr. Aldrich.[16] A few days later the American ambassador at Paris reported that "the ministers of the Government manifest a deep interest in the tariff bill and ask me many questions about its prospects. . . . Senator Wolcott presented the matter with signal ability to the officers of the Government . . . here as with us there are too many who believe that the short cut to bimetallism is free coinage of silver." [17]

Rumors of the opposition in the Senate, though they did not as yet discourage Mr. Wolcott, led him to report such a change in attitude at Paris that there was danger the "present friendly feeling toward our efforts may be checked." [18] He had sent over an anxious letter begging his allies to keep things in hand, and Chandler warned him that Aldrich and Allison had found it impossible "to make use of an agreement between you and the French consul-general" which could not be stated "openly to any one." [19]

Mr. Wolcott shifted his headquarters from Paris to London. There were long interviews with the British ministers; an audience with the Queen at Windsor; conferences with the French ambassador to Great Britain; and out of all this two plain facts: that France was essential to success, and that the course of England would depend upon whether India would reopen her mints to silver.[20] Chandler wrote Wolcott that in the absence of Aldrich the Senate had been at sixes and sevens.[21]

At a critical moment word reached Europe that the work of "our committee" had been undone. The Senate had recast the recasting of the bill. The features agreeable to the French had mainly disappeared. The understandings between Wolcott and Aldrich, on the one hand, and Wolcott and Bruwaert, on the other, were lost illusions. The French flew into a rage. A letter from Wolcott to Chandler indicated a stormy scene in London. "Thiebault came over (from Paris) yesterday in hot haste, sent by Maline who is our friend. He showed me eighty changes, twenty of them

most important to France, where the Senate had raised the
duties reported by the Finance Committee. He implied bad
faith, and it is true that I had been constantly assuring the
French ministry that the committee report would stand in
the Senate. It seems that silks even had been raised. I
didn't know what to say to him. I stand in a very bad light.
. . . Thiebault was somewhat offensive." [22]

Meanwhile, at Washington, the bimetallists had made a
last desperate attempt to keep their hold upon France.
They shifted their ground from low duties to reciprocity.
They got reciprocity—but the duties were irrevocably lost.
As Chandler cabled, "Reciprocity clauses are broad and
especially calculated for arrangements with France and
valuable to that country. Tell them to reserve their judgment." [23] He was whistling to keep up his courage. Three
days later he sent over the final doleful news expressed in
such comical fashion. "Dingley insisted paintings to be
dutiable at 20 per cent. Allison being coerced consented on
condition placing them specially in reciprocity clause for reduction to 15 per cent. All our losses were inevitable. A
seven hundred word letter from me to Bruwaert explains
reasons. Copy mailed you yesterday. Expect adoption of
conference report to-day; no way to change it." [24] M. Bruwaert wrote at once to Mr. Allison a veiled threat of retalia-
tion. The tariff was not at all satisfactory to France.[25]

The favorable position with regard to the French authorities was never recovered. France edged away from the
monetary negotiation: England also drew out. In the autumn John Hay at London wrote McKinley, "I lose no time
in telling you the bad news, so that you need not be surprised when it comes officially. I have had a long talk with
the Chancellor of the Exchequer, Saturday and to-day. He
tells me the action of the Indian government is dead against
the proposition to reopen the Indian mints, and that it will
therefore be impossible for the British government to give
us anything but a negative." [26]

IV

Mr. Aldrich had labored hard upon the Dingley Bill not only as politics but as industrialism. The wool schedule had been his particular care. The Westerners were determined upon generous treatment for wool. Aldrich himself had the Rhode Island mills in mind. The secretary of the National Wool Manufacturers' Association, S. N. D. North, was one of his expert advisers. But he did not rest his conclusions on mere advice. He visited factories and several times spent the better part of the night studying woollen fabrics under the microscope in the company of trusted workmen.[27] The result was a schedule highly satisfactory to the Woollen interests, especially in New England.

A very tired man escaped from the turmoil of Washington, and from the relative failure of his policy, to a delightful retreat on Narragansett Bay. He was there in September with Mr. Allison as his guest, when Mr. Chandler came hurrying to Providence where the two met him for fruitless conference on the French situation. The same day Chandler "went with Allison and Aldrich to Warwick, R. I., Aldrich's new home on the bay. Sailed on the bay with them. Heat very oppressive, pleasant family party." [28]

Mr. Aldrich was devoted to the water both as a sailor and fisherman and now that affluence had come to him, his yacht was one of his constant pleasures. But nothing this autumn could quite clear the sky of the great clouds hanging over. In October came the news that the Indian mints were irrevocably closed. There followed a wail from Wolcott, "I am most despondent and disheartened about France. The bitterness toward the United States is universal and any sort of agreement between France and the United States would be hotly contested in the French chamber, and to-day probably successfully." [29]

But Mr. Wolcott had a happy disposition. When he returned in November, he had rebounded against his sorrows and again he was hopeful. Even the President in his message in December professed to believe that the cause of in-

ternational bimetallism was not lost. Mr. Aldrich did not
deceive himself. With France angered over the tariff, with
England unwilling to coerce the Indian government, the jig
was up. The next move, he clearly foresaw, would be an
attempt of the out-and-out silvermen to follow up their
good fortune. In some fashion they would give the Republican party its last chance. They would serve notice that it
must now accept free silver or lose them forever. Aldrich
braced himself for the shock. He had no doubt what he
was going to do.

The New Year came. The country was talking wildly
about many things—almost as wildly as three years before
when the bloody bridles jangled and there was rifle smoke
in the streets of Chicago. But much of the talk was about
widely different subjects. The miseries of the island of
Cuba were the topic as often as any other. It had caused
stormy discussions in Congress. But Aldrich gave no heed
to it. His eyes were fixed on the silver Senators. His
thoughts were on the one question, when, how, would they
deliver their great stroke. It was but common sense for
them speedily to dress their lines and blow their summons
preparatory to the Congressional campaign of this year.

He had not long to wait. Mr. Teller introduced a resolution empowering the secretary of the treasury to pay bonds
in silver. In the resulting debate Aldrich was in his element. His aim was to make the issue unmistakable. He
was now ready to close the door, to turn the silver Republicans out of the party, to go to a gold basis, and take the
consequences. He pointed out that the resolution granted
no new power, that its only purpose was to make silver the
issue of the coming elections. He accepted the issue. So
did the rest of the Four. The result was a further demonstration that, for the moment, a silver coalition was in control of Congress. The silvermen who had voted with the
orthodox Republicans to get their views into the Dingley
Bill now switched over and voted with the Democrats to
carry Mr. Teller's resolution. It received forty-seven votes.
Aldrich led the minority of 32 which resolutely voted No.[30]

The day of conciliation was at an end.

CHAPTER XI

ENTER IMPERIALISM

I

A BOLT fell out of the blue!

Or, it might be truer to say that all of a sudden the earth trembled, and vapors arose before the sun, and the face of the world was changed. The political forces, the powers and principalities that had seemed of late years to possess America, that had been threatening it with revolution, were covered over as in the twinkle of an eye by thick darkness. Other things took their places. A whole nation became dizzy. Three years passed before again the lineaments of the political scene were even in part what they had been before.

This astonishing transfiguration is one of those unheralded eruptions that confound the superficial historian whose fatuous delusion is that politics are a simple matter. What had become over night of the forces of revolution, whence had arisen the unsteady idealism that broke loose in America in 1898, is one of those first class historical problems which only the dull comprehend. The more one knows of human life the more subtle, the more obscure, the more bewildering is popular emotion. No glib generalities about mob psychology get us far. The fact is America went wild over Cuba in the spring of this fateful year. There had been a deal of clamor on the subject, weaving in and out amidst all the other wild talk—bloody bridles, and Chicago riots, and echoes of the Marseillaise, and the eloquence of Mr. Bryan,—but few people had taken it seriously. To be sure there was a war of independence going on in Cuba—but there was a war of independence in Cuba almost always, if one believed the newspapers. That there was much suffering in the island everybody knew. But there was a general suspicion that it was being exploited for interested motives. It was whispered that American money invested in Cuba wanted to get rid of the rule of Spain.

A Cuban revolutionary junto established at New York while it chanted hysterically the woes of the distracted isle had not captured universal confidence. The most passionate propagandists for Cuba were the two American newspapers, *The World* and *The Journal,* that were contemptuous of all the fine old traditions of journalism, that were creating "the yellow press." It was in a tired disgust of the mood of the moment that Cleveland told McKinley he was bequeathing him a war with Spain.

But all this does not explain what happened. There was a powder magazine of raw emotion in America to which the blowing up of the *Maine* in the harbor of Havana was only the lighted match. And this raw powder was not the same that had threatened to explode at the kindling touch of Mr. Bryan. A different gamut of passions became audible, the old gamut fell silent. In this double fact was a tormenting challenge both to Mr. Aldrich and Mr. Bryan. Both were taken so sharply by surprise that they were at a loss what to do.

Mr. Aldrich acted doubtless on instinct. When the Cuban fury, after repeated failures to infect Congress,[1] suddenly turned a corner and captivated the imagination of Congress, his opposition was instantaneous.

His comrades of the Four took similar views. The composite of their minds was at one with itself—Mr. Spooner, with his ardent legalism was not to be duped by the furious special pleading of the yellow press; Mr. Allison, so deeply cautious, would never be the first into a breach; Mr. Platt, the traditional New Englander was for the last word of slowness in meddling with the affairs of another nation; Mr. Aldrich, just on the edge of his interest in world politics, took up this external problem in the tentative way natural to him, and with his own profound contempt for hysteria. All were fresh from the failure of their first adventure in the commingling of foreign and domestic policies, were still keenly aware of their failure to make the two accord. Wolcott's wail over the French anger still rang on their ears.

Why recapitulate the familiar tale of the winter and spring of 1897–1898!—McKinley's protest to the Spanish government against the harsh measures of General Weyler; the insolence of Spain justifying Weyler by the citation of the reputed actions of an American general thirty-three years before; the fall of the Spanish Conservatives and the establishment of a liberal ministry; the recall of Weyler and the grant of autonomy to Cuba; the 'desperate attempts of the Cuban junto, the Cuban extremists, and the American yellow press to bring on what that press gaily called the "Yanko-Spanko" war; the rash comments on President McKinley by the Spanish ambassador; the blowing up of the *Maine* in Havana Harbor; the quiet gathering of the American navy in preparation for eventualities.

Party ranks in the Senate were broken. Mr. Chandler and a few others, who had stood with Aldrich for bimetallism against the silverites, deserted to the opposite camp. A rather engaging though somewhat incalculable person is Mr. Chandler. He may be taken as the very symbol of this new political force—the sentimental radicals who are not the same as the Bryan radicals—that is henceforth to play a great part in American affairs, that is "discovered," in the old sense of the Elizabethan drama, as the curtain rises on the Spanish War. His relations with Aldrich will be interesting. In time he will write to him, "Notwithstanding our difficulties on some large matters we never had any unpleasant words and did some things together." [2] Again, "I have had some friction with men in my day, very little of which has left any present hard feelings. One must grow old gracefully." [3]

Gradually there came about another case of strange bedfellows. Mr. Chandler and the sentimental radicals, Mr. Teller and the silvermen, the rank and file of the Democrats eager to force the President into a quandary, all fell in line for extreme measures. Against this violent coalition

the Four stood firm. Around them gathered a resolute minority convinced as were many of their most intelligent
countrymen that the war fury was a manufactured fury.[4]
In this undoubtedly they were wrong. They had not taken
the measure of the emotional forces behind Mr. Chandler.
Neither did they appreciate how easy it was to play upon
those forces.[5] They were disillusioned late in March.

The yellow press had failed in an attempt to investigate
conditions in Cuba. Several Senators were induced by the
New York *Journal* to do so. The Spanish government could
not well refuse them access to the regions where war was in
progress. Speeches by Senator Proctor, Senator Gallinger
and Senator Thurston, rang all the changes up and down in
the gamut of—pity the unfortunate!

There is no denying that what they had seen in Cuba was
enough to shock the hardest heart. Both adversaries there
waged war with a sickening ruthlessness. Senator Thurston
especially had a tale to tell that lacerated the nerves of the
Senators. He was himself in a paroxysm of grief. Mrs.
Thurston had accompanied him to Cuba. There she had
sickened and died. His intense and excitable nature was
not under control when he bitterly told the Senate that he
brought it a message from "silent lips."

His harrowing picture of what he and she had seen in
Cuba was the climax of this mounting wave of emotional
suggestion. He cried out that the only people in America
who did not want war were the heartless speculators of the
stock market.

"As Mr. Thurston neared the end of his speech he became
noticeably excited and his utterance became more impas-
sioned. The peroration was brilliantly delivered. Almost at
the instant of the conclusion of the speech his voice broke
with emotion and he finished with difficulty. As Mr. Thurston sank into his seat he buried his face in his hands, while
a tremendous and overwhelming wave of applause swept
through the galleries. The Vice-President made an effort
to restrain the demonstration but it was not possible to
control the people. Tears welled to many eyes, not only in

the galleries but those of staid and dignified senators on the floor." [6]

Despite all this extraordinary rhetoric the Four were still hopeful that they could hold the Senate steady. "The situation here may be described as serious and critical," wrote Mr. Platt, March 25. "There is a fear that the radicals in Congress might be able to override the President and pass resolutions which would lead to immediate hostilities, but I think the danger is now past." [7] He was a false prophet. A naval board of inquiry had been investigating the wreck of the *Maine*. Hitherto many people had contended that the *Maine* was blown up by an accidental explosion of her own magazine. The board reported that it had been blown up from without—in other words that it had been torpedoed.

A hurricane of emotion swept the country.

A friend of Senator Hanna's had a talk with him on the subject and found that the "burden of his talk was the danger of war and he was extremely outspoken. He said that he and Senator O. H. Platt of Connecticut were the only two senators who were absolutely and unqualifiedly opposed to war under all circumstances and that Senator Spooner and Aldrich came near to that point but did not quite reach it. He spoke bitterly of the scoundrels of the Cuban junto who were simply trying to sell Cuban bonds upon the strength of this country's power and admitted that if we intervened at all annexation was the only proper thing. While we were speaking Senator Platt of Connecticut came in and he confirmed everything which Mr. Hanna had told me.

"Going back to the Cosmos Club I then found Rear Admiral Walker, Thomas Nelson Page, Lieutenant A. W. Greely, and numerous other navy and army officers engaged in animated discussions of the crisis. The talk was extremely able and brilliant and all showed the folly of recognizing the so-called Republic of Cuba. All seemed agreed however that there was no other way out of the crisis except war." [8]

On the other hand, "The President and those who sustain him (including the Four) do not want a recognition of independence, do not want any haste, but a simple resolution directing the President to take at once such steps as may be necessary to terminate hostilities in Cuba, to form a stable government there and to this end to employ the land and naval forces of the United States. Jingoes want independence and intervention. The contest between the President and his opposers will go along this line." [9]

It was now early April. Even Mr. Platt had given up the hope of preventing war; the Four were of one mind. The real issue before Congress, and before the country was not war or no war, but whether the revolutionary organization represented in America by the junto at New York should be recognized as the "Republic" of Cuba. The episode is one of the least explicit in our politics. A most curious combination was the pro-Cuban party. This was demonstrated when the House, following the President's advice, sent up a resolution empowering him to intervene and compel the pacification of the island but making no reference to what claimed to be the Cuban government. Mr. Chandler and some other Republicans promptly deserted the President and the Four.[10] They had divined the inner motive of Mr. Aldrich and his comrades, who felt that—

"A good many of us believe the recognition of independence is entirely unnecessary and would like something in the way of a resolution which will give Spain an opportunity to back down before actual hostilities are begun on our part." [11] Mr. Chandler was against that.

As to the strange bedbellows—the Democrats had seen a chance to play politics. Mr. Bryan at a great public dinner had replied to the President's message by declaring that the Cubans had earned the right to be free and that we ought to recognize "the Cuban government." His attitude was approved unanimously amidst a storm of applause. When the issue came up in the Senate it seemed, for the moment, that the Democrats had scored a hit. The secession of Mr. Chandler's group made them momentarily irresistible. They ignored the passionate warning of Senator Hale that they would live to regret their course, that the war they were forcing upon the country would give them in the long run no political advantage.

Amendments changing the tenor of the war resolution formed the final battle ground. Eventually the resolution recognized "that the people of the island of Cuba are and of right ought to be free and independent." Previously there was a hot fight over what was called "the Turpee amendment" which sought to express Mr. Bryan's views by adding the words, "and that the Government of the United States hereby recognizes the Republic of Cuba as the true and lawful government of that island." In its final form the amended resolution also demanded the relinquishment by Spain of all authority in the island. It also disclaimed any intention on the part of the United States to "exercise sovereignty, jurisdiction or control over said island." [12]

All the changes in the resolution were opposed by the Four—except the last which was so far from anybody's attention that it was agreed to without formal vote. Every member of the group spoke upon the resolution. Mr. Spooner echoed the lesson they had learned in their bimetallic defeat, and pleaded to preserve the good opinion that had been won abroad by the President's moderation.

"I have, as an American senator, taken pride in the fact that those showering praise upon the President were but a little time ago bitterly prejudiced against him because of his economic theories, which they antagonize." [13] The bulk of his speech was an argument in international law. Mr. Allison held that there was only the skeleton of a government in Cuba and that recognition would make us catspaws of a mere faction, and that the Democratic purposes had been exposed by Mr. Hale.[14] Mr. Platt denounced the "intemperate inflammatory statements and misstatements of those who from the first have planned and desired to plunge this country into war"; he denounced the Committee on Foreign Relations because in submitting the amendment it was acting "in the name of Maxime Gomez, in the name of the Cuban Junta in New York"; he reported the charge that we were merely underwriting the schemes of a group of political plungers who would use our power in exploiting Cuba.[15]

Aldrich spoke with great restraint. "I regret extremely, and I am sure the regret is shared by a vast majority of the Senate, that we approach the final vote upon this question with divided councils. With war inevitable, with our ships on the sea and our forces on the land simply waiting for the final word of command, it is more important that the American Senate and the American Congress should be unanimous in their action than that any particular form of resolution should be adopted." He was glad that the vote on the amendments would not be the last word. "I cannot vote for a resolution at this stage which contains a recognition of the Cuban Republic."

In bland contrast with the emotional attitude of most of those who had talked about Cuba, "When I say this I do not mean to suggest that Senators who have arrived at a different conclusion are not controlled by patriotic motives." [16]

The amended resolutions were adopted by a vote of 67 to 21—all the Four voting against.[17] They had some consolation when their friends in the House struck out the Turpee amendment—which, after all, was the main thing.

Spain promptly declared war. On April 25 the Four joined the majority. An act declaring that a state of war existed passed the Senate without a division.[18]

II

Thus war came and for six months thereafter it appeared to be the one concern of the American people. In reality the leaders were taking it as a matter of course—as the day's work, and as little more—and all were trimming their sails to meet the gales that would arise when the tempest of excitement turned inward again and the war-fury once more

became party-fury. The one thing that all could be sure of
was the difficulty of understanding the moment. They perceived the truth afterward put into words by a foreign
diplomat, that he had seen two Americas, one before and
one after the Spanish war.

The most interesting and the least explicit person in
this episode is Mr. Bryan. What did that astute observer
make of the new tangle of emotional and economic interest?
Not being a literary person he probably did not quote
"where are the snows of yesteryear," but he might well
have done so considering how suddenly his former issues
had passed into eclipse. A great personal following was securely his, and yet he had no secure issue to stand upon.
Could it be that the party of the poor men was an illusion
after all? Was it necessary in order to capitalize anew his
personal following to find some new programme, some creed
of reform that did not derive from the arguments of the
Income Tax Case?

The elections of 1898 were puzzling. The most astute
politician might be forgiven if he felt he could not read
them with confidence. If ever a Belshazzar had need of
a Daniel it was now. About all he could be sure of was that
all the forecasts of the previous January might as well be
forgotten. Whatever the elections meant, it was plain that
the voting had been done on different lines from those anticipated when Teller's 47 voted Yea to free silver and
Aldrich's 32 voted Nay.

In one respect the result was a consolation to Mr. Aldrich. The Republicans had made gains in the Senate. The
silvermen had lost the balance of power. A Gold Standard Act was now possible.

But in the popular chamber, though the Republicans
still had a majority it was a very narrow one. What might
be the meaning of this realignment of the House?

Mr. Bryan was troubled by this question no less than
Mr. Aldrich. His course of reasoning as he pondered the
cryptic fact can only be guessed at. What ensued was—
as so often in sound political strategy—just what the closet

philosopher would have pronounced in advance unthinkable. When, at last, there emerged through the dissipating
war clouds a treaty with Spain, Mr. Bryan and Mr. Aldrich for the one time in their lives found themselves side
by side. Of course, no one can doubt that they reached this
position by different courses of reasoning and that they had
in view widely different objectives. It was a case of that
old situation, dear to the heart of the playwright, when two
enemies, having ultimate purposes wholly at variance find
it good policy for one moment to join forces in order to take
a single step together.

The real clew to the new situation is in a letter of Mr.
Hanna's. He felt that the situation had been saved for the
Republicans West of the Missouri river.[19] That is to say
there was a new ferment brewing in the West—as the mod-
erns would have it, a new *complex*—and this was the thing
to keep one's eye upon. Undoubtedly Mr. Bryan was
equally acute as a political observer. The war had cracked
the seals upon some sort of new unmeasured force and it
was somehow involved in an enthusiasm for Cuba and for
McKinley. How it was going to entangle itself with those
other Western forces—the enthusiasm for the poor men and
the zeal for silver and the demand for high tariff on Western products—no one as yet could say. The one certainty
in this connection was the need to avoid a clash with the
West. Mr. Bryan as a party leader was prepared to go
any length to avoid such a clash.

It is strangely ironical that the one moment in which Mr.
Bryan and Mr. Aldrich appeared to unite was really the
moment of their irreconcilable divergence. Mr. Bryan
sensed the true course of the future, Mr. Aldrich did not.
Mr. Bryan hereafter will be aiming at each new crisis
to capture the force that was stirring in the West, that in
the East was absorbing the sentimental radicals and Mr.
Chandler. Mr. Aldrich will become steadily less tolerant of
it. The deepest clew to the confusions of the next ten years
will be the growing inability of East and West, of Conservatives and Radicals, to understand each other. Mr. Bryan

will seem to lose the game entirely; he will come back in a startlingly unexpected way; at last it will be Mr. Bryan who will frustrate the dearest hope of Mr. Aldrich's life.

But neither of them in the winter that followed the Spanish war had any pre-view of what was going to happen to them. The treaty which McKinley had negotiated hung on one point. It turned the war of liberation into a war of acquisition. The question of the hour was, should the Senate ratify a treaty that gave us a colonial empire—Porto Rico and the Philippines?

In a way the issue had been anticipated. The previous summer the Four had debated among themselves the wisdom of annexing Hawaii. They could not agree. Mr. Spooner was strongly opposed. But so close and intimate was their fraternity that they were able to form an accord. Mr. Spooner would go on record as opposing the annexation but he would not vote against it. That was what happened. Hawaii was taken over as a territory of the United States, the Four leading the Senate into this result.[20]

By the time the Spanish treaty reached the Senate Mr. Spooner had advanced to new ground. All of the Four were now thinking in international terms. Mr. Spooner himself phrased their position. They must accept the bitter fruits of war. They decided to do so. Again the Four became the heart of the administration party in the Senate.

But it was long doubtful whether the necessary two-thirds vote could be secured in order to ratify the treaty. It was then that Mr. Bryan revealed his astuteness. Though the old line Democrats were for playing the same game which he had inaugurated the previous April, his political sense was far more subtle than theirs. His influence changed several votes. His motives have been debated to this day. But the treaty was ratified.

A new chapter in American history, both without and within, a new chapter in the life of Mr. Aldrich, had begun.

CHAPTER XII

THE FERMENT OF 1901

In the midst of the turmoil of 1898, Mr. Aldrich was elected senator the fourth time. On the assembling of the next Congress he became at last Chairman of the Finance Committee. He held that great office throughout the twelve years of his remaining service in the Senate.

The monument of his first session as chairman is the Gold Standard Act which closed the monetary struggle with the complete defeat of silver. It was passed in March, 1900. What a great event it would have been had it been passed four years before, following the clash in the Senate when Aldrich read the silvermen out of the party, or two years before when he accepted the failure of bimetallism! But now—what a different world! Theoretically the Act should have been one of the most dramatic events of his life and yet, in this changed mental atmosphere, it was taken almost as a matter of course.[1]

Already people were thinking of other things that had grown out of the war. How were the dependencies to be governed? What was their relation to the laws of the United States? Were they within or without the scope of the tariff? Looming big in the thoughts of the whole nation was the need for an Isthmian canal. The war had brought home the difficult naval problem inherent in our possession of two coasts separated by such vast distance. To reduce that distance by a ship canal between the Caribbean and the Pacific—what could be more sensible!

Most of the legislation, this session of 1899–1900, was close to the line of least resistance. Senator Foraker's Porto Rican Act postponed rather than solved the problem of the dependencies. The canal project inspired a tentative act looking toward a canal through Nicaragua. The President opened negotiations with England for the purpose of abro-

gating the Clayton-Bulwer treaty of 1850—the treaty that
bound each nation not to construct as Isthmian canal except in co-operation with the other.

Cautious as the session was, it marked the opening of the
moment when senatorial power was at its peak. This was
the time when the influences of the Elder Statesmen upon
their State organizations was in many cases so powerful that
their hands were felt not only in the Senate but indirectly
through the composition of the majority of the House. The
period was not of long duration. The two terms of Mr.
Henderson as speaker about cover it.

A pleasant capable man without genius Mr. Henderson
was a pale contrast to his predecessor, that "Czar" of the
House, Thomas B. Reed, than whom the time produced no
more engaging character. Mr. Reed was a close friend of
Mr. Aldrich, but he refused to accompany him into im-
perialism, and after opposing vainly the Spanish treaty
withdrew in disgust into private life. The Four had a
great deal to do with naming his successor—just how much
is surmise.[2] While Mr. Henderson continued to be speaker
their intentions were almost as authoritative in the House
as in the Senate. The fact may be due in part to that after-
war psychology of which in later days so much has been
made. A political apathy—or something approaching that
—produced a momentary lull and in that interval the
political managers appear to have had a peculiarly easy
time of it. The Senators dominated the local machines, and
the local machines picked the House. Mr. Henderson was
not a cause but a symbol. His four years marked approximately one of the periods in which Jove nods—that is,
when the mysterious something that Morley describes as
political instinct is less active than usual. Such periods
come and go. Their times of passing are the times when
storms arise.

Mr. Aldrich opened the culminating stage of his career
by contributing to the fourth annual meeting of the Academy of Political and Social Science. His paper was entitled "The Industrial Ascendency of the United States."[3]

His argument summed up the tendencies of his thought since 1893. "The great importance of an investigation of this nature must be apparent when we consider that our continued industrial supremacy depends upon the assured progress and prosperity of our manufactures." The paper revealed a very close study of American statistics. Though he did not put into words the Hamiltonian theory of the economic hierarchy, it may be found between the lines. "We can assume that the number of persons employed in our manufacturing establishments increased proportionately with the increase of production . . ." He defined protection as "not a policy of exclusion, but of discrimination. It does not seek to arrest foreign commerce but to direct its flow into profitable channels." The results of his recent adventures in foreign relations appeared in two ways. The building up of adequate foreign markets for American manufacturers now appeared to him to be of chief importance. But even more significant was his enumeration of the countries to which we should direct our attention. There was no reminiscence of the French endeavors of 1897. Instead there was a broad hint that European trade was not particularly in our line. The solution of our international problem lay in "the adoption of commercial treaties or reciprocity arrangements looking to the extension of our trade with our South and Central American neighbors and the countries of the Orient." He had perceived that the future of the United States was on the Pacific.

The year 1900 came and went with little commotion at home. Again the presidential nominees were McKinley and Bryan. The Republicans got the electoral college by a large majority and both House and Senate became safely theirs. But still the menacing fact, that these majorities and the popular vote did not tally. McKinley had little over a hundred thousand in excess of his vote the previous election. With seven other tickets on the field, Bryan lost but a hundred and fifty thousand.

The nation was drifting—apparently it was drifting quietly—into a new age. What is ordinarily called pros-

perity was running riot. A new supply of gold was discovered in Alaska. Prices rose. The South African gold
mines suddenly became more prolific. The silvermen who
had deserted the Republicans loudly asserted that rising
prices were really all they wanted. They began to return.
They had gone out like lions. Their return had a suggestion of other animals, in a famous rhyme, that came home
wagging their tails behind them. Though a few like Teller
never came back, they were exceptions. When Senator
Jones of Nevada announced that he was once more a Republican the press hailed the event as giving a date to the
reunion of the party.

Far off thunder peals on the Asiatic horizon where the
Boxer Rebellion convulsed China were but a day's excitement in America. More serious attention was given to a
pathetic little war that had broken out in the Philippines.
Native leaders aiming at independence resisted the occupation of the islands by the Americans. A small though
distinguished portion of the nation wished to give them
their way. There were harsh denunciations of the government—assertions that we had been "conquered by the ideas
of Spain"—but few people really thought so.

The world had changed. It was hard to say how, and
practically impossible to say why.

In the winter following the election public affairs became
less perfunctory. But there was so much folly mixed into
them that after time may be justified in remembering the
absurd scene presented by the Senate on its opening day.
"Friends sent flowers to both Jones and Hanna, as indeed,
friends sent flowers to almost everybody else. Hanna had a
big rose tree, five feet high, and every branch loaded with
blossoms. It was tied with a gorgeous bow of crimson rib-
bon. It was by far the most ostentatious floral offering in
the room. Jones got bunches and baskets of chrysanthe-
mums, mostly silver-colored, although one bunch was as
yellow as the gold in a double eagle. Hanna's tree sat in
triumph during the session, but a few minutes after the
Senate convened, Jones had a page take his flowers away.

At twelve o'clock when President Frye called the Senate to order, the chamber looked like a flower show with groups of well-dressed men sauntering about examining the exhibits. The chaplain prayed two or three minutes longer than usual, and a good many of the Senators shifted uneasily from one foot to the other. . . ." Camera men lay in wait at the portals of the Capitol. The same paper records that "Senators Aldrich of Rhode Island; Teller of Colorado; and Foster of Washington, came up the Northern entrance to the Senate arm in arm. The trio turned pale as they faced the charging camera experts. 'What's this for?' inquired Senator Aldrich good-naturedly. 'I haven't done a thing to warrant this.' " [4]

What a tone of opera bouffe for the opening of an assembly that had great things to decide!

It was imperative to form a stable government in Cuba where the American army was still in possession. The men who had prevented the recognition of the insurrectionary government at the outbreak of the war were responsible for the pacification of the island and for the creation of a stable government. Mr. Platt who had so resolutely opposed the war and the junto felt his responsibility very keenly. He was chairman of a new committee on Cuban relations which included two other members of the Four, Aldrich and Spooner. With Mr. Platt and Mr. Teller, Mr. Aldrich went to Cuba, made a study of conditions, and the result was that piece of legislation known as the "Platt Amendment"—a provisional scheme tacked on to the Army Appropriation Bill of 1901, clearing the way for a genuine republic of Cuba under American protection.[5]

In another way the Four showed their hand in relation to this same Army Appropriation Bill. Mr. Spooner—the member of the Four who was their proper voice on constitutional questions—submitted the "Spooner Amendment." It authorized the creation of a temporary government in the Philippines. Under this act the President shortly afterward appointed William H. Taft the first American Governor of that colonial empire.

Meanwhile the canal question had come in for a great deal of heated debate. As usual there was reckless challenging of everybody's motives. The railroads were accused of lobbying to prevent a canal. Sectional interest was attributed to those who favored it. A proposed treaty with England brought the matter to a head. The first Hay-Pauncefote treaty, though it would have got the old treaty of 1850 out of the way, did not give the United States any right to fortify the canal or to close it against an enemy in time of war.

This flaw in the treaty was instantly perceived. Mr. Roosevelt, then Governor of New York, made at once a vigorous protest.[6] When the treaty came before the Senate, Mr. Aldrich led the administration forces in a vain attempt to secure its ratification without change. But he had attempted the impossible. He was compelled to accept amendments which gave the United States complete control of the canal in time of war, and temporarily checked the negotiations with the British Ministry.[7]

There was another international complication upon which the President and Mr. Aldrich could not agree. It turned upon France. That Mr. Aldrich bore in mind the anti-American feeling in France which so disheartened Senator Wolcott is not at all likely. It was not his way to act in such fashion. He never treasured an affront. "Revenge is a boomerang that always comes back on oneself" he once told his children. The quarrels of 1897 were ancient history. Nevertheless, there was little love for France, in America, at the close of 1900. France had played her cards badly in connection with the Spanish war. Americans got the impression that she was hostile. So strong was this impression that for a moment, the country had rung with the demand for a universal boycott of French goods. The fury passed, of course. But no one could be sure how much hostility was left over on both sides—in France, because of the Dingley tariff; in America because of the failure of bimetallism and the French attitude toward the war.

The President was very eager to recover universal good

feeling. He had utilized for that purpose the clause in the
Dingley Act which empowered him to negotiate reciprocity
treaties, lowering duties with nations that would reply in
kind. This was the clause which had led Mr. Chandler to
tell Mr. Wolcott that it was designed especially to propitiate
the French. Mr. Kasson, of the State Department, had
negotiated a group of agreements with foreign powers that
are labelled "the Kasson treaties." The President sent them
to the Senate this session.

Again Mr. Aldrich stood in his way. The French treaty
was the crux. Mr. Aldrich led the Four, and the Four led
the Senate, in refusal to ratify the Kasson treaties.[8]

The year 1901 came in—not proclaiming that it was to
be a fateful year in the lives of all these men. Mr. Aldrich
had bought more land at Warwick. He had a model farm.
Most of the ridge was now his property. Another pleasant
old house had been acquired and was used as a guest house.
Though the boat house had been burned he was planning
another on a more individual design. He contemplated another building that was also to be accessory to the great
house, which he was not yet ready to attempt. The tea
house, as it was called, beautifully located beside the Bay,
was completed this year. It was the club house of the
rest of the family. At the water's edge, not far from where
the boat house was to reappear, it was designed to be
equally attractive. A spacious ballroom with a noble renaissance fireplace occupied its second story with tall windows
looking out on Narragansett Bay. His family was numerous and it was his delight to gather them about him on his
beautiful acres beside the shining sea.

The delightful life at Indian Oaks in these apparently
serene days of 1900 and 1901 was no true reflection of the
life of the nation. Neither was the apparent tranquillity
of the obvious history of the time. There is a quality of
mirage, a deceitful calm, in these years, that imposed upon
many people. They did not give due regard to two things.

One of them lay at first outside the horizon of routine
politics—as so many of the potent political forces do. It

concerned a type of person once described scornfully by an
American politician as "them literary fellers." The remote
origins of what has come to be called "the literature of protest" is in the shadowy region behind obvious history
whence issued the new American mood of 1898. A simple
but not quite correct pedigree would derive it from the sen-
sationalism of the yellow press. It is truer to say that the
two were kindred but that both derived from sources not
yet charted; also, that they commingled more or less but
that the literature of protest gradually escaped from this
méssalliance, gradually became the voice of a highly respectable portion of society.

There was another consideration explaining in part its
appearance. The yellow press was an immense success
financially. Enterprising speculators perceived another possibility, distinct but not wholly unlike. They saw that the
constituency of Mr. Chandler had no publications which
directly appealed to it. Intellectual, educated, but not
wealthy, and with a great deal of restless curiosity, this constituency was too respectable to approve the yellow press,
too volatile to be content with the staid, old-fashioned
monthly magazines. It is no accident that the writers of
the new sort who were all reformers of Mr. Chandler's
variety, and a new type of magazine, like *McClure's*, the
American, the *Cosmopolitan*, that purveyed directly at a
small cost to the same people who had applauded Senator
Thurston in Cuba, appeared together, rose and throve together.

It is also significant that they picked up and developed
the same themes that Mr. Chandler and Mr. Thurston had
introduced. Their note was idealism; their refrain, the
heartlessness of wealth in the face of popular emotion; their
cry, the undue influence of money in democracies; their
programme, the translation of the methods of yellow journalism into the terms of the polite society.

But they were not followers of Mr. Bryan. They were
looking for some other sort of leader. If Mr. Bryan was
the prophet of the poor men, of the wage earners, the au-

thors of the literature of protest were the prophets of a
social stratum one stage higher up. They remind one of
that exquisite Little Billee, in a once famous novel, who
despised every one born an inch higher or an inch lower
in the social scale than himself. So, these fastidious reformers had no tolerance for any one who paid a cent more
or a cent less for a magazine than was charged for those
which they wrote. Their ambition was to be the voice of
the middle class, that class which had not been vocal in
America for many years, but which lately had waked out
of a dream and had discovered that other classes above and
below were threatening it with destruction.

Behind the apparent calm of the moment was gathering
a deep alarm. The distrust of wealth by the literature of
protest gave the clew. Hitherto there had been plenty of
talk about the power of money, the tyranny of the trusts.
Now this mode of thinking began to influence the nation's
life. As long ago as 1890, said the protestors, we saw that
trusts were dangerous and the Anti-trust Act was passed,
but what has come of it? We have great magnates of money but the salaried men, the small merchants, those who
are neither rich nor poor, are not as well off as they used to
be; we need more money than we used to need to meet a
rising standard of living; prices are going up, but salaries
and the returns of small business are not keeping pace.
They indicted "prosperity" as a thing of class interests.
They charged the vast industrial system of America with
being a monopoly of the rich.

So much for this budding literary force that was to play
ducks and drakes with forces apparently much more powerful than itself, that was to find the Moses for which it
longed, three years later, in the election of 1904.

The other new power was a stirring of discontent in those
regions which had saved the Republicans in the elections of
1898, where as Bryan foresaw the next political storm would
be generated. What was labelled "the Iowa idea" made its
appearance in 1901. Like all the other tendencies of this
deceptive moment, it resists formal statement. It was sen-

timental and imaginary and idealistic and economic all in
one, with no clear sense of what it was driving at.

Iowa was stumbling into much the same attitude toward
"the money power" that was held by the literature of protest. The first steps had been taken so quietly, so unexpectedly, that Mr. Allison who had supposed that he kept
Iowa in his vest pocket, could not acount for them. It was
a strange surprise when one wing of the Republican party
in Iowa took up the cry that the tariff bred the trusts and
that the party must speedily mend its ways.[9]

The new note in Iowa was but the faint advance warning that a pot was beginning to boil in that upper middle
West between the Mississippi and the mountains. Only a
bubbling and a few jets of steam as yet; later, to become a
cauldron with huge spectres arising out of its whirlpools of
emotion.

Serious menaces to the power of the Four were both these
new forces. But their advent was so tentative, the bulk of
them at first so slight, they were so thin, indefinite against
the solid facts of the general prosperity, they were so thick-
ly enveloped by the glare of the sunshine of the new day
—why give much thought to such unrealities!

What seemed to be the significant cloud on the horizon
was a difference of opinion between the Four and the President. Was it possible that he and they would part company in the next Congress? The Kasson treaties still hung
in the wind. McKinley intended to press them; Aldrich
intended to oppose them.

McKinley still awaits his biographer. What purposes he
formed in the summer of 1901, just what he had in view at
the end of that summer, is all to seek. The one definite fact
was the position he took in his speech at Buffalo in September.[10] He gave notice to the country that he was firmly committed to reciprocity. Could this mean anything but that
he intended to push through the Kasson treaties?

CHAPTER XIII

THE GENTLEMEN'S AGREEMENT WITH
MR. ROOSEVELT

I

THE autumn of 1901 came in. With characteristic nonchalance Mr. Aldrich threw politics off his shoulders and turned to delightful personal affairs. He told his secretary he could take a long holiday. The secretary, Arthur B. Shelton, prepared to make the most of it by setting out with his wife on a trip to the Pacific Coast. It was quite like his chief—so consummately casual in all his doings!— that even when he bade Mr. Shelton good-by he had not mentioned the secret that was possessing his thoughts: his daughter was to be married—the first marriage in the family.

It is more than likely that all the rest of the Four were taking life seriously that autumn. Was not a new policy to be built up? Nevertheless there are other things in life besides policies.

The month was September, loveliest of the New England months, unless it be October. And all the family thrilling with the beautiful event so near at hand. An intruding nuisance politics can be—at times!

Suddenly, a thunder clap! It was not the speech at Buffalo. There was no surprise in that, nor in the attitude of the newspaper that may now be regarded as the Aldrich organ. *The Sun* was silent except for a quotation from the London *Chronicle* to the effect that McKinley was "letting his audience down gently by giving what is virtually free trade the conciliatory title of reciprocity." [2] It was what happened the next day that gave a new cast to the whole political situation and compelled Mr. Aldrich to abate a little his jaunty nonchalance. The assassination of McKin-

ley occurred September 6. On September 14, Theodore
Roosevelt reigned in his stead.

Even for one who was as bravely casual as Mr. Aldrich,
here was something that could not be ignored. But he
would not allow it to change for him the tenor of events.
While other people rushed forward to catch the eye of the
new potentate—the king is dead, long live the king!—he
went on making preparations for the wedding. There should
be no change in the family programme. Just the same, politics insisted on a place among the wedding guests. The
Elder Statesmen in and out of office knew that it was a time
for quick thinking. Notes passed back and forth between
Mr. Aldrich and a great friend of his, and presently T. B.
Reed was saying that he wanted "a bit of a talk" because
"we want to do something if we can at least find out the lay
of the land." [3] A few days later Mr. Aldrich was writing
Mr. Allison, urging him in the name of the entire family to
attend the wedding and adding "Come right to Warwick
and stay; we will have a committee (meeting) right away
after. There are a number of things I want to talk to you
about." [4] But Mr. Allison was too busy observing Iowa.
He was absent when the wedding occurred—Miss Abby Al-
rich and Mr. John D. Rockefeller, Jr.—and Indian Oaks
was all agog with joyousness. The ceremony occurred in the
great room of the tea house. The whole building was a
bower of flowers. Mr. Aldrich had taken the keenest interest in every detail, planning and arranging the artistic effect.

There was no obvious gathering of political leaders.
Nevertheless, there may have been talk on politics at Indian
Oaks, in October, 1901, which history would like to recover.
Mr. Reed was there. He brought as his gift to the bride a
beautiful copy of the "Vita Nuova." [5] And he had once been
speaker of the House of Representatives! One may risk it
that talk ranged widely and richly between those ripe disillusioned men who knew the world they lived in and were
not to be disconcerted by any turn of Fortune's wheel. As
things fell out there was an unconscious prophecy in the
choice of that copy of the New Life. How applicable not

only to the maiden but to her father—as we are destined to see—and not only to the man but to the statesman.

It was like him not to make haste to salute the new man of the hour. Mr. Allison appears to have been more prompt. Before Mr. Roosevelt was well settled in the seat of the mighty the wise old man from Iowa was writing to him, and he was replying, "Your letter of the 24th instant peculiarly pleased me. When do you come to Washington? I shall want to see you before I write my message, because there are two or three points upon which I do not desire to touch until after consultation with you." [6]

There was no corresponding overture from Indian Oaks. That should wait upon circumstances. Meanwhile there was the development of the estate, and family affairs, and if need be, Tom Reed and the "Vita Nuova."

II

Whatever one may think of Mr. Roosevelt—and it is pretty certain that he will always inspire contradictory opinions, so multiform, so versatile was he—there can be little question that no American President since the first held on his accession to power so rich a hand of personal trumps as Roosevelt held in the autumn of 1901. He had sown his political wild oats and while the energy of youth, its flair for great things, was not as yet abated, there had been added to it the more splendid energy of the man who has just arrived. The Spanish War and San Juan Hill were still real in everybody's imagination. The nation believed there was a touch of Quixote in him and loved him for it. Then, too, his literary tastes counted for something, and his aristocratic origin. Hercules and Sir Philip Sidney and Cowboy Ted—were they not all combined in the President of the United States? So buoyant, so exuberant, so much the daredevil! But this was not all. He had a streak of shrewd worldliness, he could tell a hawk from a hand saw, and he was not a fool when it came to the main chance. Perhaps his most resolute determination that moment was

never to flat the note. It is a byword that he began with
a resolve not to let his own impulses run away with him;
never, whatever his personal views, to let himself go the
way Cleveland had gone, never to split his party the way
Cleveland had split his. In the Roosevelt of 1901 there was
scarcely anything to forecast the Roosevelt of 1912.

He retained McKinley's cabinet. Secretary Wilson wrote
to Allison giving him an amusing picture of the first cabinet
meeting. The President had "taken hold of public duties
with his natural vigor"; it had been expected that the first
cabinet meeting "would be for only a few moments, but he
discovered that every secretary had matter that was entirely new to him and he found it necessary to ask extensive
explanations all along the line and he has really only begun." [7] Before the end of the month he was busy assuring
all the Republican leaders that he was a good party man,
that he did not mean to rule without their aid. His immediate concern was what to say in his first annual message. To that result he sent the most gracious notes to Aldrich, Platt, and Spooner as well as to Allison.[8] The tone
of the letter to Spooner was the tone of them all. ". . . before writing my message I want much to consult with you
on certain points. In the course of the next two or three
weeks could you make it convenient to come to Washington." This letter contained also the note of personal friendship—something to be remembered in the history of the
Four. "I hope to keep in closest touch with you and to
profit by your advice in the future as I have profited by it
in the past. You helped me a year ago in the campaign and
at our lunch at the Century Club last spring you outlined
a course which I substantially followed in my addresses this
summer."

Thus,—Mr. Allison having started the ball rolling—the
Four had all been notified of the new President's good intentions toward themselves and so far as the message was
concerned, of his willingness to let them have a finger in the
pie. Obviously it had three main ingredients—the Hay-
Pauncefote treaty, the reciprocity policy, and the problem

of a general attitude toward the great industrial questions
of the hour.

The Hay-Pauncefote treaty was not worrying him. Since
the Senate threw it back upon the President, a year ago,
Mr. Hay had been very busy. He knew just what the Senate wanted and he had got it from the British government.
So confident was he, that he assured the President "Our
canal treaty is past the breakers." [9]   He proved to be right.

Reciprocity was a horse of another color. Hitherto Mr.
Roosevelt had gone along with the later inspiration of Mc-
Kinley, gaily, in none too analytical a mood. A speech
which he had made at Minneapolis a few days previous to
McKinley's speech at Buffalo was in much the same vein.
During his first month in office he appears to have assumed
that the Kasson treaties would have to be acted upon by
the Senate and that they would not be materially altered.
He had heard a good deal that tended to confirm this impression.[10] But he had also made a discovery that was disquieting. During the latter half of September, senators and
representatives in Washington had . . . "gone over the old
ground, that they favor reciprocity but are against its application in their own State whether it be to beet sugar,
hides or fruit." [11]

In other words reciprocity as a gesture was one thing;
reciprocity as practical politics quite another. And yet there
were some astute politicians who were afraid to deny their
faith in it—at least afraid to have the Senate ignore the
reciprocity treaties. Mr. Allison was one of them. His ear
was very close to the ground. He was trying to make out
what the ground in Iowa was saying to itself. Apparently,
he was not sure. Apparently, his one clear conviction was
that the Senate must not appear to flout the issue. That
meant that it should take up the treaties, discuss them, and
keep on discussing them, until it became plain what the
country wanted done. His views were interpreted by the
President who was prone to be downright, a bit more posi-
tively, a bit more confidently, than in all probability he intended.

The President decided to take a position in his message that was about what might be expected of him as a disciple of McKinley in his final stage.

On October 16, he had Mr. Wharton lunch with him to talk over reciprocity. That luncheon was an unpleasant surprise to Mr. Roosevelt. Mr. Wharton did not approve the draft of the part of the message that dealt with reciprocity.[12]

Hitherto Mr. Aldrich had not expressed his opinion. The pleasant note from the President inviting him to take a hand in the message had not evoked advice. On the surface he was not taking the situation seriously. His ability to take this attitude was one of his deep contrasts with the rest of the Four. They were true descendants spiritually of those stern men of the seventeenth century who preparatory to a charge reined in their horses and gave out a hymn. He was more like the smiling modern who, on the firing line, ostentatiously stands up and rolls a cigarette.

President and policies are all very well, but—there are more things in heaven and earth, et cetera. And now, with apparent suddenness, Mr. Roosevelt felt that he must have the advice of this cool man who was so far the reverse of voluble. On the day when he lunched with Mr. Wharton, his secretary wrote to Aldrich: "The President is very desirous of seeing you about some matters of interest and before he completes his message would like to have an opportunity to talk with you. Will you kindly say when you expect to be in Washington." [13]

An interview was arranged for October 28. The fact became known. Newspapers speculated as to what would come of it. Platt, who had talked briefly with the President while he was on a flying trip to Connecticut, wrote to Aldrich in a tone slightly peevish, regretting that they could not meet in advance of the conference and "talk up the situation a little," because "there are a good many matters ahead that are likely to be embarrassing I think, and I have not had a soul to talk to about them all summer." There was a touch of sadness in his admission that the possibility

of such conference was all over now.[14] These two were devoted friends and always continued to be, but nevertheless
Aldrich had a way with him that troubled Platt. Now, as
at other times in their lives, Aldrich was taking things more
light-heartedly than was quite satisfactory to his dear old
friend whose sense of humor was so much less flexible than
his.

The conference of Aldrich and Roosevelt embraced luncheon and two hours of talk thereafter.[15] On the morning of
the conference *The Sun* had announced that "Senator Aldrich is one of the many men in Congress who have been
persistently opposed to the ratification of nearly all the
treaties that have been so long pending in the Senate, but
he has never said that he opposes the policy of reciprocity."
It quoted his view that the Kasson treaties were "jug-
handled affairs in which very little was obtained by the
United States for what was given away," and added that he
had never talked with President Roosevelt on the subject.

The Sun had changed its party in 1896. It was now
the especial exponent of the Aldrich point of view. Therefore, one puts two and two together. Aldrich is not the sort
of statesman who would urge reciprocity as a theory and
not as a practice. Now that he is ready to talk, his views
will be blunt enough to suit any one—too blunt for most.
Some good friends of his are going to be troubled before
long by the way he will ignore what the ground will be saying, especially the western ground. Whatever fears they
may have he will go on,—whether wisely or not is another
question—knowing his own mind and acting upon it.

Neither Aldrich nor Roosevelt has described their historic
luncheon. But it is fair to assume that both were aware of
its significance. Seventeen years had passed since their careers first crossed at Chicago in their joint unsuccessful effort to prevent the nomination of Blaine. Vastly different
their lives had been since then. Until yesterday, or the day
before, how little likelihood that they would ever meet on
the terms on which they were meeting now. But here they
were, one the leader of the Senate, the other the Chief Ex-

ecutive. How certain that Mr. Aldrich must have thought of the event as slightly amusing and that Mr. Roosevelt in whom the literary gift was not the least developed must have thought of its dramatic quality. Aldrich was indifferent to drama.

There can be no doubt that Aldrich advised Roosevelt to throw the treaties into the waste basket and that the President accepted his advice.

Herein lay the heart of a disagreement among the Four. The rumbling Western cauldron with the dim ghosts forming in its vapor were real things to Mr. Allison. He made a speech at Tama which was an elaborate argument for caution on the part of the Senate, for regarding *vox populi* as *vox Dei*, while at the same time begging the populace to believe that the Senate was a fountain of wisdom and that if the Senate did not produce satisfactory reciprocity treaties then it would be obvious that satisfactory reciprocity treaties could not be produced by human ingenuity.

The author now posted the speech to Roosevelt with a long letter describing it as "a mild reflection of the Iowa view." [17] His purpose, he told the President, was "first to relieve the Senate from the imputation of having purposely refrained from considering the treaties"—exactly what Aldrich had forced it to do—" and secondly to show that it would not do to expect too much of these treaties because of the difficulties in arranging them." How very different from Aldrich's blunt determination—eventually carried out—to cast the treaties aside and let the populace and the cauldron like it or not as they pleased.

The President sent the speech to Mr. Aldrich and wrote Mr. Allison, "I thank you heartily for your letter." [18]

Fond as Aldrich was of Mr. Allison, and highly as he valued his discretion, he was not at this time in a mood for walking over eggs. He meant to tread firmly and if the eggs were broken—that is to say, if the West got angry,—that couldn't be helped. He wrote the President that, as he knew, there was a disagreement on this subject between Senator Allison and himself, but that he would not give way. By implication he reiterated what appears to have been his advice to the President on October 28—that the treaties be allowed to lapse without further action by the Senate.[19]

In the exuberant good humor so natural to Mr. Roosevelt in his early days he wrote Mr. Aldrich:

Hearty thanks for your letter. I will follow exactly the course outlined therein and in my conversation with you. I have kept what I said about reciprocity entirely unchanged since I saw you . . . that is, after putting in the amendments you suggested. All I shall do about the treaties will be to say I call the attention of the Senate to them. I think that, if I did not make any allusion to them, some unfavorable comment would be excited.

I hate to be a nuisance but if on Monday of next week you are able to be here, I should much like to submit my whole message to you for a last looking over of certain parts." [20]

Thus reciprocity—the left-over reciprocity of McKinley's policy—went by the board.

Still to be accounted for is the very clear formulation in the message of a general attitude toward the industrial constitution of the new day. In this connection there is a detail of the moment that has generally been forgotten. Among the numerous significant bills that have never come to a vote in Congress, that have died quietly in committee, was one which was known for a time as "the Babcock Bill" and had a fluctuating notoriety in the newspapers. It was glimmering in the general mind in the autumn of 1901. Its author was a representative from Wisconsin and his bill was inspired by the same thinking that had begun to gather in the West behind the idea of reciprocity. Mr. Babcock proposed to put on the free list "all manufactures of iron and steel, imported from abroad, the like of which are made in the United States by a 'trust.' " [21]

Here was the real heart of the whole matter. Because of the vast scale of American manufacture, there was being produced more product than could be consumed at home. What may be called the surplus output was being sent abroad and sold there at lower prices than were charged in

America. The fact that this could be done, that the manufacturers found it profitable to do so was a rankling provocation that had stirred the deeps of anger. To the defender of the new industrial régime the surplus output was a logical by-product of the system, its assailants were emotional provincials with no true comprehension of industrial processes. This Babcock Bill was derided along with reciprocity itself as one of the twin temptations which the enemies of reciprocity warned the President to avoid. Nevertheless, it was such proposals as Babcock's that afforded the clew why the western cauldron was beginning to rumble, why Iowa, for example, was searching desperately its own conviction that tariff, trusts, surplus output and western hardship all went together.

The West was devouring many statistics showing that the trusts were making vast profit selling their surplus output in foreign countries. The intricate arguments in defense of these conditions—the idea of diminishing cost of production made possible only by quantity of production; of a distinction between capital charges and incidental charges all the variations, literal and figurative, of the idea of the by-product—were making no impression, or very little impression, on the general mind. The same restless eagerness to be up and doing that had scanned Cuba so passionately in 1897 was now turned upon the right of the protected manufacturers to have a surplus output.

This excitement was a fallow field to be cultivated easily by the professional informers through their medium, the Yellow Press. It also infected the talented writers of the literature of protest—who were all passionate defenders of the old, passionate enemies of the new economic system. Not yet were they regimented in a marching army though they were soon to be, and even now their influence is a factor in the situation. On all hands, the specific issues of economic politics are merging in a general denunciation of the new economies as a whole.

To men who regarded all this wave of excitement as essentially hysterical, as mere unreasoning insistence on what never could be again, it seemed of first importance to commit the administration to what they regarded as the orthodoxy—the new orthodoxy, to be sure—of industrial society. The attitude of the President on reciprocity was but a detail—relatively a minor detail—of his attitude on the general subject. In this respect they knew that they were but continuing the historical tendencies of their party. The Republicans had not always, apart from expediency, been high protectionists. They had always stood for that form of economic freedom which protected capital from exploitation at the hands of the State.

Upon this point the Four were still—if they did not always continue to be—safely of one mind. The many interviews which they had, first and last, with the President on the subject of the message could not have contained a syllable of dissent with regard to certain parts of it—those paragraphs upon capitalism which must have passed under Mr. Aldrich's eye in that last conference with the President on the message as a whole. In 1901 Theodore Roosevelt, on this crucial theme, saw eye to eye with the leader of the Senate. If Mr. Aldrich did not suggest any portion of the passage upon capitalism it was only because Mr. Roosevelt, with his notable literary faculty, had of his own motion put the senator's views into words.

"The creation of these great corporate fortunes has not been due to the tariff nor to any other governmental action, but to natural causes in the business world, operating in other countries as they operate in our own. . . . It is not true that as the rich have grown richer, the poor have grown poorer. On the contrary, never before has the average man, the wage worker, the farmer, the small trader, been so well off as in this country and at the present time. . . . The mechanism of modern business is so delicate that extreme care must be taken not to interfere with it in a spirit of rashness or ignorance. . . . There is a wide-spread conviction . . . that the great corporations known as trusts are in certain of their features and tendencies hurtful to the general welfare . . . combination and concentration should be, not prohibited but supervised and within reasonable limits controlled. . . ." [22] There cannot be the slightest doubt that these sentences, which so exactly expressed his own creed were warmly approved by Mr. Aldrich, along with all the rest of the passage, including a reference which it is hard to think he did not suggest, a reference to that year 1893 which had bulked so large in his own experience, both intellectual and financial.

The instantaneous effect of the message was an outbreak of activity in the stock market.[23]

III

Had the Four been superstitious they might well have sacrificed to Fortune for their unforeseen deliverance from an awkward, not to say menacing, situation. Instead of being at loggerheads with the President, as they had had some reason to expect to be, they were once more the front line of the Administration forces. Nothing could be more cordial, more appreciative than the President's attitude toward them all. How slight in comparison seemed the little differences that had developed among themselves over listening to, or not listening to, the ground-song of the West. To be sure, a merely literary person might have whispered to them something about:

> The little rift within the lute
> That by and by will make the music mute——

but then, literary persons are so prone to bring in apt quotations for their own sake and to be a trifle careless about their practical application. Lutes and rifts and muted music did not seem in order in the joyful atmosphere of Republican harmony in December 1901.

The session of 1901–1902 does not on the surface of its record appear remarkable. The line of least resistance is so steadily in evidence. And yet the session has an importance quite out of proportion to its visible achievements. Besides winding up the left-over projects of the previous administration, it co-operated with certain grim events to bring about a working agreement which served as the rock on which Mr. Roosevelt's first administration was founded.

Several measures of this session drew out Mr. Aldrich's personal views. He voted in condemnation of the direct election of senators. A bill to repeal war taxes received his support. He stood by his friend Platt who amended a bill extending the privileges of immigration among the Chinese. He was in favor of creating the Appalachian National Park. He advised the President to appoint Governor Crane of Massachusetts, secretary of the treasury.[24] A bill of his extending national bank charters was passed in the Senate perfunctorily and in the House without commotion.[25]

But all this was incidental. The important matter of the session was in making sure of an administration bloc that would stand by the new President as firmly as the Four intended to do—if he stood where they thought he stood. The consolidation of such a bloc involved unity among the Four. A measure that they were compelled to vote upon revealed a threat to their unity. The little rift within the lute was not a mere flourish of rhetoric after all. Though East and West, in America, had not acknowledged that they had differences which might justify the historian in recalling the differences of the North and South a hundred years before, the differences were there. That faint cloud-shadow so to speak, which had fallen upon the Four in relation to reciprocity, seemed again to drift across their mental landscape.

A bill for subsidizing steamship lines which was supported with great earnestness by Senator Hanna, which the Senate passed, split the Four on the line of East and West. Mr. Aldrich and Mr. Platt supported it. Mr. Allison and Mr. Spooner opposed.[26] Late in the session they split again, in the same way over a minor bill involving freight rates, a measure which New England and the West conceived in different ways.[27]

These faint differences among themselves did not trouble the Four. There were long thoughts and far visions at the

back of all their minds. For the moment everything turned
on making themselves indispensable to the President. They
put through the new treaty with England which Mr. Hay
had pulled into a form entirely satisfactory.[28]

When the House proposed to apply the Dingley tariff
against the Philippines but with a reduction of twenty-
five per cent—a proposition that came near splitting the
Republicans in two—the Four stood together in passing the
bill.[29]

They stood like a rock against an attempt to write the
old anti-imperialistic beliefs into the Government of the
Philippines. Senator Teller led the attack upon their position, and Aldrich by point blank questioning forced him to
reveal that his attitude was negative; that he had no plan
of his own for the government of dependencies. The Four
were a unit against declarations relinquishing sovereignty
over the islands, disclaiming permanent annexation, or extension over them of the protection of the Constitution.[30]

The Four took up a much more difficult problem when
they turned to Cuba. After-war conditions in the island
were deplorable. The sugar crop was vital to Cuba's re-
cuperation. But the crop was not selling. Its only hope
was the American market and the American market was all
but closed to it by the tariff. By way of giving to Cuba the
aid it needed, generous people in the United States were in
favor of opening the American market through a reduction
of the duty on sugar. The President was strong for this
act of generosity. So was Mr. Platt who felt that he had a
solemn obligation inherited from the dead President to look
after Cuba.[31] With most men such an idea might seem to
be a pose, but not with Mr. Platt. His friends of the Four
stood with him. Mr. Allison, doubtless, thought of the discontent in the West and thought that here was something
that might allay it. Perhaps he hoped that tenderness toward Cuba would offset the rejection of the Kasson reciprocity treaties. Certainly there were two views in the
country: there were people who shrieked at the proposal
as mere sentimentality, or as a squint toward reciprocity,

or even free trade, as well as those who applauded it
not only as pure sentiment but as reciprocity's entering
wedge. Back of all lay a business question—the question
of who if anybody in America might profit by the Cuban
reduction—which presently became the heart of the matter. And all these were entangled with the immediate party
question, how to form and consolidate a new administration
bloc.

The subject inspired an intermittent avalanche of talk
in the intervals of the consideration of other measures
throughout the winter. At the end of the spring a Cuban
bill was in the hands of Mr. Platt's committee: lobbies for
and against it were hard at work; and the Four had made
up their minds what they wanted done.

As an immediate problem of legislation it was a fight between two powerful commercial interests both of which
were well represented in the Senate. One of these was the
great American industry of sugar refining, commonly known
as the Sugar Trust. The other, not quite so well organized but equally definite, was the scattered community of
the sugar growers. In the old days all these latter would
have been Democrats and their opposition could have been
treated as party politics pure and simple. But of late years
a new phase of the sugar industry had created a Republican complication. In half a dozen Western States the
production of beet sugar demanded attention from the party
managers.

Here was another typical instance of the problem of the
economic constituencies and of double affiliation in politics.
The Republican sugar growers of the Northwest were on a
small scale as dangerous a problem for the party managers
as once on a great scale the silver Republicans had been.
Now, as then, the sense of economic community threatened
to swallow up the sense of all other sorts of community.

Again the endless criss-cross of economic and geographic
constituencies that renders so desperate the governmental
problem of this distracted country! Obviously the sugar
refiners had good reason to approve the reduction of the

cost of raw sugar; the sugar growers equally good reasons
to oppose competition by foreign sugar no matter what the
excuse. Again the strange bed fellows of politics. On
what was generally conceived to be the humanitarian side:
the Sugar Trust; the passionate popular befriending of
Cuba: the impulsive humanism of the President; the quix-
otic feeling of Senator Platt; the desire in certain quarters
to do anything whatever for reciprocity; and, uniting all
this in a common purpose, the cool strategy of the Four.[32]

There followed one of those unworthy congressional battles which are so common in our political history—motives
juggled in air like pairs of balls. The beet sugar men made
"a fight on the President" as much as on "the Cuban relief
plan" and it was conducted by men who professed to be for
the Administration policy." [33] The President on the advice
of the Four attempted to force the issue by sending in a
message urging reduction of the sugar duty twenty-five
per cent.[34] Two days previous to its arrival, Senator Teller
had produced evidence that General Wood, the Governor
of Cuba, had used government funds in a Cuban relief
propaganda aimed at tariff reduction.[35]

The revelation caused an uproar. The Democrats were in
high glee. When the message was received Senator Bailey
for the delighted Democrats slyly remarked to the Senate:
"I believe I will not do it, but I feel inclined to move to
refer the message to the Republican caucus." The presiding
officer, Senator Kean, revealed a sense of humor when he
replied: "The Chair is not aware that there is any Senate
Committee of that name." [36]

There were hasty conferences between the President and
the Four, but the game was lost. A Republican caucus resolved to drop the subject.[37]

The Administration bloc appeared to have been driven
into a corner. They were extricated partly by good fortune,
partly by their own cool determination. It was imperative
to close the session with the passage of far reaching measures that should appeal to the country and create a belief
in the largeness of the President's purposes. A pending

measure gave the Four their chance to turn the flank of his
enemies. This was the bill for the construction of an In-
ter-oceanic Canal.

In the previous January when the Canal Bill came up
from the House the country had been ringing with the controversy over the relative merits of Panama and Nicaragua
as canal routes. It was complicated by the French Canal
Company that controlled the Panama route and wanted
to make the most out of the sale of its rights. The price
asked was exorbitant. The original bill favored Nicaragua
and was backed by Senator Morgan and most of those
Democrats who had not had the heart to play politics over
the Hay treaty. Fearful that it would go through, the
French Company suddenly cut their price almost in three.
Since then, the drift of public sentiment had been in favor
of Panama.

A substitute bill which had been prepared by Mr.
Spooner was now brought to a vote. It authorized the
President to buy out the French Company for $40,000,000,
and to adopt the Panama route provided working concessions could be had from the United States of Colombia at
a reasonable price within a reasonable time.

The anti-Administration Republicans, having won their
point on the sugar question, had not the courage to go
farther in opposing the President. They meekly contributed
their votes to the passage of the Canal Bill.[38]

There was another bolt in the administration quiver. The
Philippine Civil Government Bill, which had been prepared for in the discussion of constitutional principle the
previous winter, still hung fire. This also was pushed to a
conclusion.[39] The passage of the Canal Act and the Civil
Government Act, just at the close of the session amidst a
fury of talk about Cuba, formed the solid achievement on
which the Four, for the administration, rested from their
labors. Despite the barren victory of the Beet Sugar men,
the administration stood before the country in a fairly
advantageous light. And yet, there were grave dangers both
for the President and the Four.

IV

The American people had come to a parting of the ways. Sixteen years had passed since the Interstate Commerce Act went through Congress with almost no one appreciating its true significance. Mr. Aldrich, on this count had to plead guilty with the rest. He had seen in it little more than a device that might injure the shippers of his section. He had not seen in it the beginning of the struggle between East and West; nor the still more alarming struggle between classes. It had not occurred to him at the time that out of the dreams of the West might come a new emphasis upon popular democracy, a furious challenge to the Hamiltonian conception of society. Nevertheless, in the bitterness of the West against the railways, far back in 1886, all these potentialities had lain pregnant.

Since then, one after another, they had revealed themselves. And all along the growing tendency to look upon the Republican party as just what Aldrich wished to make it, the party of Hamilton come to life again. And at the same time a movement within the party to repudiate everything Hamiltonian, to make the party the bulwark of the middle classes.

In Iowa, Mr. Allison's State, this menace to the principles of the Four was beginning to take definite form. There was a new man in Iowa, a Radical named Cummins, and it was whispered that he was after Mr. Allison's place.

With each day it became more evident that a new form of double affiliation had appeared, a far more dangerous and confusing form than any the Four had yet encountered. Before long, it would be necessary to define the term "Republican" relentlessly, without recourse. Was East or West, aristocracy or democracy, Allison or Cummins, to draw up that definition?

The position of the party in the country at large was also alarming. Great things had happened in the six months of the late session. The huge merger of the Steel Trust had been made public just when labor was fiercely excited over the imminence of an anthracite coal strike. A restless nation, staring appalled at both these towering manifestations, had heard with amazement of the suit brought suddenly by the government to dissolve the Northern Securities Company—that huge railway combine that had seemed, the day before, the last word of big business in the field of transportation. Pierpont Morgan, protesting against this suit, had had his famous interview with the President—no longer the affable amateur of the year before!—whose language came near being a command to the great banker to mind his own affairs.

The country was tingling with suppressed alarm. What had seemed, in 1901, to be a mere ferment that might perhaps evaporate into nothing, was growing upon the mental horizon with the semblance of a rising cloud. *McClure's Magazine,* soon to become the very organ of the literature of protest, had gathered into a discontented coterie a particularly talented group of adventurous writers who were preparing to attack all the basic assumptions of the new day. It was this year that Miss Ida Tarbell, in *McClure's* began issuing her manifesto of discontent, the *History of the Standard Oil Company.* The swift increase in the circulation of *McClure's* was a symptom of first importance. There had arrived one of those periodic congestions of feeling when the great American electorate, distracted by hasty thinking, is like a cat about to jump, and no human being can be sure what direction the jump will take.

How natural for the Four to be troubled. Iowa alone might have been forgotten. The Northern Securities case, much as some people raved about it, did not frighten them. They appear to have regarded it as safe enough under the circumstances and pretty sure to do no harm to the party.[40] The industrial unrest was more significant; still more, the outcry of the classes that were reading *McClure's* and everything else in the same vein; while the approach of winter threatened them with a coal famine. To any good politician it was obvious that the first need of the hour was a definite economic programme offsetting the effects of strikes, alarm, feverish literature, and the rising of the steel colossus. The Four must work out a policy that would make the party the sure refuge of a frightened nation. But where did the President stand? Already the Radicals were calling to him to forget his political traditions and become their leader. For the Four, it was life or death to come to a clear understanding with the President upon fundamental policy.

Just how and when the matter was opened with him is one of the secrets of the time—a time of so many secrets. During the month of July he was in brisk correspondence with Platt, consulting him in such terms as "Is my going to Hartford and Willimantic satisfactory to you" [41] and again, "Unless you object I want to go at some length (in a speech at Hartford) into the reasons why we should have close economic relations with Cuba in the shape of a reciprocity bill." [42] Meanwhile Hay had been hard at work "trying to get the Colombian treaty into the shape desired by our friends in the Senate particularly Spooner and Lodge." [43]

Still the blithe confidential atmosphere that had enveloped all his relations with the Four since his election to the Siege Perilous of the presidency. Just the same, it was a time when he needed friends. Senator Hanna was writing from Cleveland begging him to keep his hands off the tariff, defending the Steel Trust, and growling that he had "no sympathy with the complaints of the parties who are threatening the Republican party for what seems to be unbounded prosperity." [44]

And yet at this very moment, the anthracite strike, soon to fill Mr. Hanna and almost every one else with dark foreboding, was in full swing. In Iowa, the Republican split had gone so far that Mr. Henderson was about to withdraw from politics giving as his justification that he was "not in harmony with many of our party who believe that free trade in whole or in part will remedy the trust evil." [45] The middle classes were not convinced of the reality of Mr. Hanna's prosperity. The coal strike was a source of constant alarm to Platt.[46]

Against this background the President planned a speech-

making trip in New England which was utilized by Mr.
Aldrich to effect a quiet conference between Mr. Roosevelt
and a few men of consequence. It was arranged that he was
to be received on Mr. Aldrich's yacht, taken to Indian Oaks
for luncheon and thence that same day to Newport.

The preliminaries of the visit included an amusing disagreement. Already Mr. Roosevelt had begun his practice
of close association with the representatives of the press.
He took with him a host of them wherever he went—like
the bells on her fingers and rings on her toes of the good
old lady in the nursery rhyme. He had his secretary write
to Senator Wetmore, who was master of ceremonies for the
occasion, that he wished to bring his "entire official family"
if Indian Oaks could afford them entertainment. Mr. Wetmore who shared Mr. Aldrich's dislike of the crowd, blandly
pleaded that the Aldrich yacht could accommodate comfortably only half a dozen guests, and thus precluded an
influx of what he termed scornfully "a horde of newspaper men." [47]

V

Mr. and Mrs. Aldrich were recently home from Paris.
They had made a flying visit to purchase furnishings for
the new boat house. It was a singular and altogether delightful building. Mr. Aldrich had a passion for ships and
for the sea. This structure was a ship translated into a
building. Projected out from shore, it had water on three
sides. All its details had marine suggestions. A rotunda
with a circular well rose from the second story through the
third, the very semblance of the central rotunda which
was characteristic of so many ocean liners of that day. All
the furnishings were in the same key. Each story varied
its levels with ingenious caprice. The second floor contained
a huge common room that was also a dining-room on the
side toward the sea; a library occupied the opposite portion of this floor; the top floor besides guest rooms duplicated the great common room below; this was Mr. Aldrich's bedroom used also as an office—it was fifty feet

long—with the sea shining beyond every window, and windows on three sides.

For the next ten years this room was the senator's own. The boat house was the scene of many political conferences; it was, for him what the tea house was for the rest of the family. The old Hoppin house on the hill continued to be the general residence.

The President was received at the boat house. He made a quick tour of the estate. The different farms composing it had now been merged, their boundaries obliterated, and the whole was beginning to have a unity through its planting. Mr. Aldrich was devoted to trees. He used to say, "We can't reproduce a tree the way we can other things." His planting was one of his joys. Mr. Roosevelt was invited to plant a tree. It was conspicuously placed on the entrance side of the spot where the final mansion was to stand. Luncheon at the boat house was followed by the run across the bay to Newport.

It was a merry day and in the main a man's party. Though the President paid his respects to the ladies in the house on the hill, he was not for social loitering. He came and went in that swift gust of spirits, as of something always on the wing, which was to figure in the American scene, like a driving wind, the next seven years. No one meeting him on the hilltop, or at the old house, or while he vigorously cast his spaded earth around the roots of his tree, would have thought of politics. But at the boat house, and on the yacht—a different matter! There, none but politicians present, the talk doubtless was of the sort that makes history.[48]

The nature of it may be guessed from a letter written two days later, when the President had reached Nahant. Mr. Cortelyou, then his secretary, wrote to Mr. Hanna:

The President, after consultation with Senator Aldrich feels it vitally important to see you before he starts on his western trip. He wishes me to ask you if you can spend a night with him at Oyster Bay the 4th of September or the 15, 16, or 17, which ever date is most convenient to you. He will also ask Senators

Aldrich and Allison to come. There are matters of party policy about which he wishes to consult you.[49]

What they had in mind was a secret conference at Oyster Bay. The secret was well kept by all concerned. There is no mention of it in Mr. Croly's life of Hanna, nor in the Lodge-Roosevelt correspondence—though Mr. Lodge was there—nor in Mr. Bishop's official life of Roosevelt, nor in the Roosevelt autobiography. To be sure, Mr. Bishop came near, inadvertently, giving the secret away, but fortunately—from the point of view of an official concealer of fact—the slip was not observed until the incident had become ancient history. Mr. Bishop printed part of a letter from Mr. Hanna to the President in which he remarked "after leaving Oyster Bay I spent the balance of the week in New York" and took up the matter of the coal strike. When did he go to Oyster Bay, and with what result? At last, the manuscripts have told the story.

Mr. Hanna had sat in conference at Oyster Bay with the President, Aldrich, Allison, Spooner, and Lodge. A good deal of correspondence had been necessary in order to bring the conference about. Mr. Allison, less active than he used to be, did not want to come. Curiously enough Mr. Hanna was not eager, and wanted to be quite sure the conference would be significant, that the others would attend. However, he agreed to come while Allison was still hesitating. The date was fixed at September 16. Roosevelt wrote Aldrich asking,

In view of Senator Allison's plea shall I let him off till I get him in Chicago or somewhere further West, or do you think it best that you and I should jointly get him on for the date mentioned.[50]

Evidently Aldrich felt it was imperative for Allison to be present. The crisis was sufficiently acute not to leave out of the consultation the interpreter to the Four of the ground-song of the West.[51]

On September 16, 1902, this memorable conference took

place. That they talked of many things who can doubt? Considering the hysterical condition of the country a flippant reader may be forgiven if he remembers the author of "Alice in Wonderland" and murmurs something about a talk, now classic, "of ships and shoes and sealing wax, Of cabbages and kings, And why the sea is boiling hot, And whether pigs have wings."

Here were cool, strong men trying to make head or tail out of a world that was about as far removed from reason as was the world in which the Walrus and the Carpenter wandered hand in hand. This coal strike, and the mad attitude of the coal owners, were in everybody's mind. Hanna, as now we know, was engrossed with it. The threat of a possible coal famine and its certain, though illogical effect on votes, terrified Mr. Lodge. Only a few days after the Warwick visit, the President had written Mr. Aldrich "the labor situation caused by the anthracite coal business is bad politically as well as otherwise." [52] Then too, the factional quarrels in Iowa perplexed them all. Mr. Allison received a telegram from Mr. Henderson, while the conference was in progress, which led both Aldrich and the President to wire him futile protests against his decision to quit public life.[53] His reply was that the squabbling over "trusts and tariffs" had gone so far that he had "neither the time nor the strength for such work."

With all these inescapable problems of that difficult summer bright in the mind's eye, the six men at Oyster Bay undertook a great task. It was no less than determining the basis of the policy of Mr. Roosevelt's first administration, the policy that was to soothe the excited nation, deliver it from hysteria, win the coming election, and call to Washington a House of Representatives that would fall into line behind the administration bloc in the Senate, the leaders of which sat that day as the President's inner council. The event proved that they read the signs of the times correctly; the Republicans carried the autumn elections of 1902 in a majority of the congressional districts.

The conclusion which they reached was scarcely what

might have been expected from so bold and ardent a nature
as the President's. It sets one speculating upon the contrast in the two groups at that council table; the President and his bosom friend, Mr. Lodge, relatively "young"
men as politicians counted age in those days; the Four
elderly men—three among them much older even than their
years—the veterans of so many conflicts political and economic whose years ranged from sixty-one to seventy-two.
In a country that seemed to be threatened with chaos one
would not have been surprised had the President—the very
embodiment of the passion of constructive action!—insisted
on an obviously positive programme. Perhaps in a way
he did. A tradition that has been freely denied but that has
as many lives as a cat insists that at some time early in his
administration he and the Four agreed that he should have
his head in all things outside economics and finance, and
that they should govern his policy in the reserved subjects.
If such a bargain ever was made it may well have been
made this day. But at the present moment it is all a guess.
The President turned from this conference to the daring
stroke that established his fame—the enforced settlement
of the anthracite strike. He also went out into the open
and on his Western tour of the autumn of 1902 gave to
the country the general policy decided upon at the Oyster
Bay conference.

The heart of this pronouncement is an idea that is not
likely to have issued from the creative rashness of the
nature that is active first of all. It is the idea of continuity
in Statecraft. No matter how they had argued it among
themselves, the six had set their seals, so to speak, to an
agreement to assure the country that continuity of legislative policy was the aim of the Republican party. They
would offset the excitability and the dread of change that
was in the air by this promise of a stable attitude. They
recognized political temper as a main element in political
policy.

At the same time they pledged themselves not to be
merely stationary. It was in this connection that the

ground-song of the West—or, if you will, the bubbling of the cauldron—was recognized. They offered to the Westerners the vision of a gradually changing tariff but one that should not be subject to violent gusts of party passion. Such was the deep and subtle antidote to the panic of the moment which the six devised. The President officially summed up their conclusions!

A financial system of assured honesty is the first essential (of prosperity). Another essential for any community is perseverance in the economic policy which for a course of years has proven best fitted for its particular needs. The question of combining such fixedness of economic policy as regards the tariff while at the same time allowing a necessary and proper adjustment of duties in particular schedules as such readjustment becomes a matter of pressing importance is not an easy one. . . . What we really need in this country is to treat the tariff as a business proposition and not from the standpoint of any political party. . . . A nation like ours can adjust its business after a fashion to any kind of a tariff. But neither our nation nor any other can stand the ruinous policy of readjusting its business to radical changes of the tariff at short intervals. We need to devise some machinery by which while persevering in the policy of a protective tariff in which I think the nation as a whole has now generally acquiesced we would be able to correct the irregularities produced by the changing conditions without destroying the whole structure.

The tone, the temper, of these skilful generalities—apart from their brave insistence upon the need for continuity in Statecraft—suggest faintly the mode of answering the Western discontent intimated a year before in Mr. Allison's speech at Tama. In fact, throughout the agreement of September 16, there is the murmur of Mr. Allison's soul like the traditional far off sound of the sea in the shell. Of course, that strong central idea of political continuity was not his. Whose was it? No one has ever told, but——

We turn to another passage in Mr. Roosevelt's summary of the agreement. Continuing on the difficulties of blending continuity with progress, the conservative idea of government, he said: "My personal preference would be for action which should be taken only after preliminary inquiry by and upon the findings of a body of experts of such high character and ability that they could be trusted to deal with the subject purely from the standpoint of our business and industrial needs . . . treating the whole question primarily from the standpoint of the business interests of the entire country, rather than from the standpoint of the fancied interest of any group of politicians." [54]

Again one speculates as to which of the Four was the chief advocate of this clear-eyed application of the principle of continuity in legislation. Again, there is no recorded answer. However, thinking of the Tama speech and its echoes here, one looks about for other origins, and doing so, one is reminded of that article in *The Sun,* the Aldrich organ, which appeared as a prelude to the conference between Aldrich and the President, October 28, 1901. In that article, which formed an outline of the general perspective of an Aldrich policy, there was the following sentence: "The Chairman of the Finance Committee is one of that influential class of congressmen who believe in letting the tariff alone so far as may be, and he believes that a permanent non-partisan tariff commission, if it could be composed of the right kind of men, could rearrange the tariff schedules when necessary with less disturbance to the commercial interests than is caused by the periodic enactment of tariff laws by Congress." [55]

The agreement of September 16 was, of course, tentative and transitional, as all informal political agreements always are. But it served its immediate purpose. Upon it— and perhaps on the other more singular agreement that lives only in tradition—the first administration of the brilliant President was securely based. In the life of Mr. Aldrich this agreement was at least equally significant. It summed up the political convictions that had been growing during a number of years and it formed the starting point of a sharp new emphasis upon the idea that was sure to be most unpopular of them all, the idea that the less we leave to Congress and the more we take away from Congress the better.

Needless to say, the full implications of the agreement were never realized. It came too late to accomplish its own end, except temporarily. The country was sick of a mental fever that could not be cured except by time. In very truth the little rift in the lute had opened, and despite all the magic of Mr. Allison it grew more fateful as the years went by. Nevertheless there is a lasting historic significance in this Oyster Bay conference, so long and so carefully hidden from the world's eye. In the temper and in the main idea accepted that day by Mr. Aldrich, on the one hand, and by Mr. Roosevelt on the other, a party within the Republican party was born—the Conservative party.

CHAPTER XIV

INDIAN SUMMER

I

To the casual eye all was well with the Four again. But was their eminence as securely based as in the old days before the Spanish War? A great deal of water had run under the mill in the four years since 1898. How far the Four were aware of it is not altogether clear. Looking back from the vantage of what came after, the facts are plain enough. In 1902, 1903, and 1904, we are watching a period of illusion when there is in the political climate that deceptive appearance of a season that has actually passed, which New Englanders know as Indian Summer. Those brilliant New England days that succeed—or are supposed to succeed—the first shock of the coming winter, have a beauty and the semblance of a peace that is all their own. And yet, behind the dreamy glamour, and floating mysteriously through the sunshine, is that atmosphere of a gathering ruin whose existence the sensibilities refuse to accept even while the imagination cannot escape from it. The triumph of an unreality is Indian Summer.

We may assume that none of the Four had any such doleful thoughts in the bright happy years between 1901 and 1905—or, at least not until just as the curtain fell and the act closed. With the exception of Mr. Allison they were all inclined to live within their own temperaments, to be impatient with or indifferent to the world outside their own horizons.

Nevertheless, in the country at large, there was the undertone which they ignored, the invisible presence that was to accomplish their overthrow, the infection of discontent working everywhere like a fierce and potent ferment charging the nation with anger. The young men and women of talent who were finding careers through the literature of protest, the hopeful investors who were building fortunes out of the magazines and newspapers whose line was denunciation, the honest Democrats who believed that the economic reconstruction spelled aristocracy, the eager questioning by the people of middle rank who feared vaguely that some sort of White Terror was just across the horizon —all this fanned by a mighty wind of rhetoric was doing subtle work pervading the outer air beyond the charmed circle of Washington life.

The Four did not blind themselves to its existence. But Mr. Allison was the only one who was really anxious. Always with an ear open toward Iowa, he heard unmistakable murmus out of the Western cauldron and even the firm temper of his beloved comrades could not quite do away with his undercurrent of alarm. Mr. Platt admitted even more frankly the fact of the gathering animosity toward Conservative leadership. But he was aging—though probably none of the Four as yet perceived the fact—and his temper was becoming a little acid. By the same token he was less inclined than ever to compromise with his convictions, more than ever inclined to bid his enemies do their worst and be damned for it. Mr. Spooner, faithful, brave, impulsive, legally minded, a lover of tradition, was as always busy with his thoughts. He lived in that delightful world a little different from the real world, a little more abstract than life can ever be, which is the fairy palace of the deductive genius of the law. And Mr. Aldrich—was Mr. Aldrich.

There was pleasant life in Washington those cheerful years of the Indian Summer. The Arlington Hotel was almost a continuous senatorial house party. Mr. Hanna had a suite there; so had Mr. Platt. The Aldriches lived in what was known as the Sumner House, an adjunct of the Arlington. The Hanna suite, which occupied the entire second floor of the Arlington, was the centre, this while, of the senatorial coterie.

Everybody liked the Hannas. They kept open house to all the group of the Elder Statesmen and to many others.

Their Sunday breakfasts were gleefully labelled "Hanna Heavenly Hash." The Spooners and the Platts often breakfasted with the Hannas. The Aldriches less frequently—probably because of Aldrich's delight in his own family circle.[1] Otherwise the relation between him and Mr. Hanna was very close. He said of Hanna, shortly after his death:

> With his strong common sense, his unfailing kindness of heart, his charm of manner and unaffected simplicity, with his wide knowledge of men and affairs, and his direct and resolute purpose, Senator Hanna was the most important figure in American political life. His intimate friends are completely overwhelmed with a crushing sense of personal loss.[2]

But it was not in the spacious Hanna apartment that many of the most important conferences of the Indian Summer occurred. On the floor above, a modest little suite of only two rooms and a bath was occupied by the Platts. Though it was the proper thing, at that time, to paint every senator as a monster of ruthless wealth, one at least who was at the very centre of senatorial power was a poor man. "I would be glad to lend you if I could possibly do so," wrote Mr. Platt, in reply to an appeal for money, "but I have not had in all my life one hundred dollars ahead." [3]

In the "sitting room" of the Platts the fate of the nation has been determined. "It was not an unusual thing for the President to run away from his secret service men after dinner," writes Miss Kathleen Lawler, Platt's able secretary, "and not waiting for the elevator, climb up two flights of stairs at the Arlington Hotel, and pound upon Platt's door on the third floor. Down he would sit and spend an emphatic half hour or so. 'Now, what are we going to do?' fist pounding the chair arm, showing of teeth, seizing of Platt by the arm, etc., etc. A very interesting but turgid conference would follow. Hanna might come in from the floor below or perhaps Aldrich from the Sumner House. Probably, by the time the President left Platt's apartment, his secret service men had caught up with him, but that was no indication that he would not run away from them again, another evening, if some problematical situation arose for the handling of which he felt the need of Platt's conference powers." [4]

Very intimate were Roosevelt's official relations with all the Four, but there was a difference in temperament that prevented him and Aldrich from having quite the free informal cameraderie that existed not only between Roosevelt and Platt but also between Roosevelt and Spooner. The feeling of the latter for the President amounted almost to hero worship. It took all Mr. Spooner's resolution to hold out when he and the President disagreed. Mr. G. G. Hill, who knew as much about Washington as any man of his time, records a typical instance.

One morning the senator rode down to the White House in a towering state of anger toward the President. This was about 1906, and Spooner felt that the proposals of Roosevelt were verging toward the precipice of anarchy. A close intimate of Mr. Spooner, who also knew Roosevelt well, accompanied Spooner in his carriage, listened to his denunciations, and waited. After an hour or so in the White House, Spooner emerged and silently took his seat in the carriage. Nothing was said for some time, then Spooner demanded of the one beside him, "Why don't you say something?" The other replied, "I am listening." Spooner broke forth explosively, "Hill, that man in the White House is stupendous. I went in as angry as a hornet, and before I was through in there I was liking him again in spite of myself." That typified just what Roosevelt knew how to do—make men intensely angry with him and yet get and keep their liking in spite of themselves. [5]

Mr. Spooner had his troubles with Aldrich also. They were fast friends and Spooner might be described as Aldrich's legal conscience. But Aldrich's mind was too searching, his knowledge of life too varied, for him to accept a legal idea without severe testing of it in all its bearings. Again, Mr. Hill is an admirable authority.

After quite an argumentative tussle in a room by themselves, Spooner was likely to get through rather weary but rewarded by having persuaded Aldrich of the correctness of Spooner's interpretation. Sometimes one might enter Spooner's committee room to find the place looking as if a cyclone had struck it, books on the floor in every direction where Spooner had thrown them after use. If then asked what had happened, Spooner would be likely to reply, "Oh, I have been trying to get some law into Aldrich." [6]

The Four in those days worked together with systematic regularity. Their meeting place "for thrashing over the next step in some legislative programme" was likely to be the little apartment of the Platts at the Arlington. Miss Lawler attended these sessions and took stenographic notes.

This because as likely as not they would strike a snag and be uncertain as to the exact phrasing of some point agreed upon earlier in the discussion. At such a juncture Miss Lawler would push over under Platt's fingers a transcription of what had been said and there they would have it. [7]

The Four kept very sharp ears wide open for rumors. What the world outside thought or did not think seldom troubled any of them but Mr. Allison. What Washington thought was another story. The rumors that deserved most attention concerned the President and it was frequently Platt who was the one to warn him. "When other men had informed him of their fears he would seek out Miss Lawler's room for the confidential dictation, thus wise: 'Dear Mr. President (or perhaps sometimes, To the President): There is a rumor about the Capitol—of course it is only a rumor —that you are going to do so-and-so. I wish you would hold this matter in abeyance until I have an opportunity to see you. Very truly yours.' Then Mr. Platt would turn to Miss Lawler and say, 'Send it by mounted messenger.' Within a trice the reply from Roosevelt would come, 'My dear Friend: Of course I will withhold action. When can I see you? Sincerely.' " [8]

Despite all the sharp political clashes that took place in the Senate, the Indian Summer in the main was a period of delightful personal cordiality. Mr. Aldrich particularly was superior to the rancors of debate. He was always ready to do legislative favors to senators on the opposite side.

Once when Senator Tillman was—or thought himself—in danger of missing re-election because of his failure to secure an appropriation for the Charleston Navy Yard, it was Senator Aldrich who saved his place for him by pushing through the desired appropriation.[9]

Innumerable stories are told of his graciousness—as when a blundering visitor pushed into his committee room, waking him out of a nap, and Aldrich treated him exactly as if he had been. an expected visitor. Naps in his committee room were part of his mode of bearing the strain of debate. It was not always understood. Opponents sometimes derided his "cowardice" because he was not in his place during some fiery attack upon his policies. What he was really doing was quietly dozing, preparing for a later moment when again there would be talk in the Senate that, in his judgment, was worth listening to.

The Indian Summer for all its appearance of serenity, contained some profound sources of future unhappiness both personal and political. Twice in the course of it Mr. Aldrich suffered the loss of a comrade whom he loved. Mr. Hanna's death was not the only one. Just as the period opened, Mr. McMillan died. Mr. Aldrich spoke characteristically on the day when eulogies over the dead senator were pronounced by his associates.

It was my good fortune to have known Mr. McMillan well through all the years of his senatorial service. . . . He was essentially a man of affairs and in a material age, in an era of wonderful commercial and industrial development, he was a pre-eminently successful business man; yet his spirit and nature must have come down to him from some ancestral knight of the romantic age. He was always gentle, chivalrous and genial. . . . The wisdom of his advice in the councils of his party was always acknowledged. . . . In that intimate companionship which forms the principal charm of our life here the vacancy occasioned by the death of Senator McMillan can never be filled; even the grateful and fragrant memories of the past cannot break the force of the ever-present consciousness of irreparable loss.[10]

II

The quick eye of Mr. Aldrich ranged far. He was in close and frequent communication with political managers in various localities. It was his shrewd advice that at times determined where campaign funds should be placed. "Again I am under obligations to you," wrote General Grosvenor who was fighting for his seat as an Ohio representative, "I have a letter from the Congressional Committee signed by Mr. Babcock with a contribution of two thousand dollars ($2,000.00) to my campaign. I will pull through and hope to have a complimentary majority. I thank you very much." [11]

Though the Republicans saved their skins and got a good working majority in the House, there were signs clear enough of skeletons in the closet. To those who could read political symptoms, there were hints of a coming battle within the fold. Just when the Conservative party had declared itself, a considerable number of seats while not changing their party label had definitely changed their complexion. What had so irritated Mr. Henderson—the appearance in office of Republicans who called themselves "progressives" who were enemies of the Four and all their works—was ominously conspicuous.

Mr. Aldrich would not have been himself if he had allowed his equanimity to be clouded in any way by the shadows of things to come. In the pause of that autumn, his thoughts ranged as far afield as China and its possibilities as a field for the expansion of American banking, an idea that wandered in and out of his thoughts a number of times but never apparently came to anything.[12]

His impatience with the fickleness of the crowd, and with those who purvey to the crowd, flashed out in a protesting letter to the President. Senator Jones of Arkansas, a Democrat, had received from his party managers what Aldrich considered unfair and ungrateful usage. Merely personal politics, as well as any form of cowardice, always filled him with contempt. He asked the President to appoint Jones to a place in the Isthmian Canal Commission. "I know, of course, that the position is one of great responsibility requiring character, courage, capacity and integrity. I think the Senator has all these. I have the greatest sympathy for him on account of the treatment he has received from members of his own party in Arkansas. His defeat by the men, and the methods by which it was accomplished was one of the most cruel things to be found in the history of American politics. I shall be gratified if you find you can give him a place and I am sure his appointment would be most satisfactory to senators of both parties." [13]

The Elder Statesmen still appeared to dominate both Senate and the House. When an ambitious Representative aspired to a place on the Ways and Means Committee it still seemed quite the thing for him to write a begging letter to Senator Aldrich and to be overjoyed when Aldrich consented to use his influence with the Speaker.

The session was one of those—so unfortunately frequent in the American Congress!—in which the acknowledged subjects of debate and the real subjects are quite different. The subjects that were acknowledged were such things as Cuban reciprocity which at the start Senator Foraker prophesied would certainly be accomplished, the beet sugar people to be "amply protected" by changes in the tariff; Foraker was also confident that the Philippine tariff would be promptly revised. He proved to be a false prophet. A more accurate forecaster was Secretary Hay who grumbled that he "anticipated a series of defeats for the state department," meaning that the administration would fail both as to Cuba and the Philippines and adding that "nothing will pass that anybody is opposed to." [14]

In other words, Congress was full of cross purposes, of secret factions, of enmities that were not ready to avow their own existence. The subterranean division in the dominant party was the clew to most things. The Conservative leaders had to be careful not to push their intentions too far; they had to be quick to shy off when an issue threatened danger within the Republican ranks.

Something was accomplished. The Elkins Act freed the railways of a certain embarrassment by forbidding them to grant rebates. The Department of Commerce and Labor was created. Provision was made for arbitrating a sharp international controversy over the boundary of Alaska. A satisfactory monetary arrangement was effected for the Philippines.

"Aldrich and I put through the Philippine currency bill," wrote Mr. Lodge to the President, "I think it did credit to our heads and hearts." [15]

And there was high talk on a possible change of the Philippine duties. "In the Philippine matter," the President wrote to Governor Taft, Mr. Aldrich "made a strong and loyal fight for the reduction of the Philippine tariff. On the latter point we were beaten purely by the resolute opposition of some of the Democratic Senators, notably those from the Rocky Mountain States, who filibustered so that in the closing days of the session it was impossible to get the measure through. That we will pass it next year I have little question. I am exceedingly sorry for the failure and appreciate the gravity of the situation thus created, but the blame must rest primarily on the little group of Democratic senators who all along posed as the special champions of the Filipinos and yet were willing to go any length to prevent their having the economic legislation necessary to put them on their feet." [16]

The President but scratched the surface of what was really taking place in Congress that session. Again the unacknowledged issues. Back of a hurricane of talk, the Four were striving to hold the Republican majority together and to close the fissures that were threatening to appear. The Democrats, in quite the orthodox way, were trying to get their feet in those fissures and to sow them thick with the dragon's teeth, setting Republican Radical against Republican Conservative. And still farther in the back of things, was the necessity of each party to put itself in a strategic position before the country. The money question was not dead. It was taking on new forms and Aldrich in his own mind was

casting about, not very successfully, for some financial programme that should once more persuade the country that
the Conservatives were its salvation. The Democrats were
determined to prevent him—as, of course, in the rôle of true
party men, it was their duty to do.

For the moment it seemed as if the success of the Four,
the previous session, were vanishing into air. Hay's prophecy about the defeats of the State Department was coming
true. Not one of the overseas issues was being decided on
its merits. The promptness of the Democrats in throwing
over their free trade principles in order to frustrate the designs of the administration, or to further the interests of
their comrades who dealt in sugar, was typical of the hour.
And chicanery, at times, was matched by frivolity—intellectual frivolity, that is. One can imagine the wicked
amusement Hay took writing to Roosevelt of the temper of
various senators and vengefully describing Senator Hale,
to whom he imputed a desire for war with England.

"He informed me not necessarily for publication but as
guarantee of bad faith that God intended to punish England for the Boer War—a statement that impressed me considerably, as of course he would not have made it without
authority." [17] Hay and Aldrich had this much in common,
neither ever was impressed by poses.

But what was making the deepest trouble for Aldrich
was brutally free from pose. It involved concealed motives
of still another sort harder to be sure about and far more
difficult to meet than was the separation upon principles
which was working its way through the Republican ranks.
A group of Republicans, not bound together by any principle that history has been able to discover, were willing to
make a deal with the Democrats and bring in as States the
territories of New Mexico and Arizona. Aldrich was unwilling to go along with them. This contention was at the heart
of the talk hurricane of the session. In the scornful words
of Secretary Root:

The Statehood Bill is the continuing order of every day at
two o'clock and pushes everything else aside. Almost every sena-

tor is more desirous of preventing something from passing than
he is of getting anything passed. The result is that they adjourn
from Thursday to Monday and talk against time and do nothing.
Bad feeling is being awakened and Bailey is objecting regularly
to letting bills come up by unanimous consent.[18]

Why the Republican schemers wanted the new States is
one of those problems of historical motive that are seldom
solved. Of course, the motives given were all lofty. The
imputed motives, malignantly whispered by their enemies,
were of a different sort, including real estate speculation
and the belief that land values would go higher in a State
than in a territory. The dissenting Republicans professed
to believe that the proposed States would not certainly be
Democratic, that their admission would not repeat the Republican mishap of 1890. But Aldrich had no such illusion. He had burnt his fingers once admitting States that
proved a danger to his party, and he did not propose to do
it again.

Opposed to him, leading the Statehood Republicans, was
the grim figure of Matthew Quay. Whatever Quay's motive, he was determined to bring in the new States or know
the reason why. He had a club over Aldrich that he would
not scruple to use. Aldrich had drawn up a bank bill. It was
his one distinctive measure of this season. He was offering
it to the country as the Conservative reply to the growing
demand for new financial legislation. Quay, the consummate political plunger, was sufficiently daring, if Aldrich
blocked his Statehood programme, to take revenge by blocking Aldrich's financial programme.

Here we turn a lost page of history. These two bold men,
each claiming to be a Republican of the Republicans, killed
each other's measures. Why? What was it that led Aldrich
to stand firm in rejecting the Statehood scheme when he
knew it meant a duel with so powerful a man as Quay?
What made the risk worth while? Was his course altogether party strategy? Was it a combat between those two
for senatorial leadership? The secret is hidden. What happened was that Aldrich threw down the glove to Quay and

Quay took it up. In the last week of the session, on Aldrich's motion, the Statehood Bill was set aside.[19]

Then followed the final debate on the bank bill. It was really an academic discussion for every one knew what was going to happen—that talk would be kept going until it was too late to vote on the bill—and no one was deceived as to why it had to happen.

Aldrich took a defiant note. At the same time, very characteristically, he said nothing to the discredit of his own party. Though the actual battle was between him and Quay, no one would have guessed from the form of his language that it was not between him and the Democrats. No situation was ever so irritating that it could jostle him out of his firm rôle as leader of the party. If he could not save his measure, the next best thing was to fasten the blame for its failure on the Democrats.

"The Senator from Colorado and his associates," said Aldrich, as bland as if Quay did not exist, "intend to talk this bill to death, and I am quite willing, so long as the country knows who is responsible for its defeat." [20]

III

This unsuccessful bank bill of Aldrich's is not an important monument in the history of American finance. Perhaps it was just as well, considering only the fortunes of the author, that it failed. Aldrich's mental progression was in definite strata. He had his periods of hard thinking and readjustment, followed in each instance by a period of reflection and observation, with action as his chief concern, the work of his mind going on subconsciously. The Indian Summer was, in the main, of the latter sort. Following the creative effort of 1902, he fell back for a time upon the lines of least resistance mentally, upon observation of the political currents of the hour, upon feeling his way while new thoughts germinated deep, while he waited to see what would happen next.

All the Four sensed the importance of a rising demand

for some new system of currency. But as yet neither Aldrich nor the others had ideas upon the subject. Far more portentous than the failure of the bank bill was an event which took place about the same time in the House. While the quarrels of the session were running their foolish course, a new star entered the political ascendant. It boded the passing of the undisputed power of the Four.

The session was Mr. Henderson's last, both as Speaker and as Representative. Who was to succeed him was a question of great moment. Would the Elder Statesmen be able once more to dictate the choice? Before the session had ended it was plain that they were less powerful than they had been; it became practically certain that the only man who could command a majority vote in the new House was Joseph Cannon.

Already he was a Congressional veteran, and though naturally a Conservative, predestined to a place in the party that was organizing this winter—the party of the Four— he had no mind to play second fiddle. In a narrow sense that borders upon craft, he had political acumen. He saw, this winter, how deep and far-reaching were the dangers within the Republican alliance. He looked afield and saw, rather sooner than most men saw, that there was a crisis gathering in the country—a crisis which now all the world can see. The Republicans had to keep a close front or go to the wall. The little rift that had proved to be hard fact was just wide enough to let in the thin end of the Democratic wedge.

In such a situation, who could expect any American party to think much about principles? The Democrats, if they were practical men—and "Uncle Joe" Cannon thought he knew what "practical" men are like—would take up or drop any principle, any idea, any programme, according as it would or would not serve to widen the Republican rift. Witness, how they had played their cards, recanting their own principles, over Philippine tariff. The Conservatives— specifically the Four—understood this as well as he, understood the necessity at all cost to keep the party united.

Therefore, any shrewd Republican, boldly on the make, could count upon the dread of giving the Democrats an opening as a restraining force in all Conservative councils.

Mr. Cannon's motives are guess work. In his later career —as when he sent up to the Senate the rate bill of 1906 with a House majority fit to shake the courage of most men —there is plenty that leads one to shrug one's shoulders. But in 1903 one may guess what he was after with tolerable confidence. Surely, he saw three things: that the Senatorial directors of the Republican machine were in a position that could easily be rendered desperate; that the country was more nearly in revolt against them than they realized; that those Representatives who were going to hold over into the next Congress, and a large proportion of the new men who were going to appear for the first time at Washington in that Congress, were catching—perhaps as yet in a mild form but unmistakably—that contagion of excitability which had been astir in America since 1897.

The psychological conditions were ripe for a revolt of the House against the domination of the Senate. The man who should engineer such a revolt, who should do it without letting slip his party label, might at one stride become a power inside the apparently omnipotent Republican organization. By playing upon the dread of the Elder Statesmen that the Democratic wedge might be driven deeper into the rift, he might be able to push them into a corner, force them to make terms, acquire recognition for himself as one of the prime factors in the party leadership.

It is a long and intricate story, all the various influences that came to a head in the winter of 1902–03 and here, there, the otherwhere, delivered this representative, or that, from fear of his senators. Still more intricate is the psychology of the mastery and the utilization of all this for his own daring ends by Mr. Cannon.

If we accept the familiar view—borne out by many, though not by all his later measures—that at bottom he was wholly in sympathy with Aldrich, wholly a Conservative, his rise to power is oddly ironical. It would not have

been possible, if, for example, a tempestuous young man
by the name of La Follette had not been elected, two years
before, Governor of Wisconsin and had not started on that
career of opposition to Senator Spooner which was to become more and more bitter with each succeeding year, was
to reduce steadily Senator Spooner's hold on the Wisconsin
congressmen.

The revolt of the House cannot be fully accounted for
without the fact that Iowa was breaking from the hand of
Mr. Allison, nor without taking note of another new man,
that Albert Cummins who had become Iowa's Governor a
little over a year before. It was by a wizard's use of these
Radical forces that a scheming Conservative caught his fellows at a disadvantage and snatched a portion of their
power.

Fate played into his hands. He was just on the verge
of securing his position as virtual Speaker-elect for the next
Congress when Senator Tillman made one of those amiable
moves which were quite orthodox according to the views
of the time, which ought not ordinarily to have produced
trouble. The Sundry Civil Appropriations Bill had been
sent up from the House to the Senate. It is common knowledge—common scandal, if you will!—that this bill is little
else than the pooling of the graft of all the members of
Congress, the payroll of their constituencies for the majorities that have elected them. Mr. Tillman was but
doing the usual thing when he held up the bill in order to
force into it, in the vigorous if inelegant language of politics, "a generous appropriation for South Caroline appe-
tites, a nice dish of pork." [21]

What an opportunity for Mr. Cannon! How easy, now,
to defy the masters of the Senate and yet keep wholly free
of any charge of disloyalty to the Republican party. A
Democrat had taken advantage of the Senate's rule allowing unlimited debate, the rule that made it practically impossible to consider a bill without unanimous consent. The
House was furious. Here was the very nick of time for a
coup de theatre that should become historic.

Mr. Cannon, who always calculated his effects, saw that for the moment the House of Representatives was in the temper of a cross-roads village. He played to that temper. He leaped to his feet, waved his arms—long, lean arms, topped by a face of sardonic angularity—and called upon the House to assert its independence, to put an end to the "legislative blackmail" of the Senate.

"Gentlemen," he concluded, "I have made my protest. I do it in sorrow and humiliation, but there it is. . . . Another body under these methods must change its methods of procedure, or our body, backed up by the people, will compel that change; else, this body, close to the people, shall become a mere tender, a mere bender of the pregnant hinges of the knee, to submit to what any one member of another body may demand of this body as a price for legislation." [22]

That night he was a made man. And never again were the Elder Statesmen to have their old-time domination over the House. The Four had a rival whom they could not choose but convert into an ally—on his own terms.

IV

There was no European wander for Mr. Aldrich this year. Instead the state of the Republican parties—for it was fast becoming plain that there were two, Conservative and Radical, uncertainly yoked together—and the new financial problem that was dimly in most men's minds, and the temperamental epidemic that was sweeping the land, were to engross his thoughts. It was never his way to dramatize himself. Though after time can see that he was entering a crisis in 1903—just as his country was entering a crisis— he doubtless, had any one said as much to him, would have laughed it aside adding some blithe remark to the effect that he had too much to do to think about such things. He wasted no time deploring the irony of fate and Cannon's rise to power. It was done. And now, as always with him, what is done is done. If the Four cannot any longer dictate to the House, at least they know Joe Cannon and they can come to terms with him. That was ever his way: not a moment of vain regret, instead swift but always perfectly serene rearrangement of the lines of advance.

Turning to the question of party policy there can be little doubt that he was not sure just what to do. His currency bill was an attempt—rather a feeble attempt—to get his thoughts on a new track.

It will not do to accuse many Americans in 1903 of knowing their own minds in finance. But most people had a dim notion that something was wrong. Very little attention was paid to financial experts or their theories. The term "elastic currency," later to become every man's shibboleth whether he understood it or not, was as yet a mysterious phrase. Nevertheless there was a general feel in the air that the money of the nation had a way of running short when it was most needed, and that statesmen somehow should be clever enough to prevent this.

The cool minds of the Four were stepping out cautiously into this dangerous field, stepping with extreme circumspection. The Aldrich Banking Bill had gone no farther than to propose allowing the secretary of the treasury to accept as "security for safekeeping of public money" bonds which were not bonds of the national government. The Democrats had pounced upon it and had torn it to pieces not because of its genuine faults but on the ground that it was class legislation, that it was devised as a benefit to the rich. This year we find Mr. Aldrich buckling down to the task of learning something about the theories of banking and currency. It was a new task for him, a difficult one, and the year passed without his getting anywhere.

But there was steady contemplation of the problem in the calm unhastening way that was Aldrich's only way. He corresponded with bankers and wrote letters to financial experts for "references on the note issue question." [23]

As yet he had no faith in that mysterious "elastic currency," but in his own way in his own time he would think the problem out. Aldrich had constituted the Four a sub-

committee of the Finance Committee. Twice he got the
sub-committee together on this particular subject. Three
of the Four were at Hot Springs in April,[24] and all of them
at Warwick in August.

The first meeting of the sub-committee formed a short
holiday for Mr. Aldrich soon after Congress rose. With a
few of his family he sought the delightful old Virginia
resort where many senators have foregathered, first and
last, and great affairs of state have been settled over tall
glasses, among the breezy, open-spaces rimmed by the pleasant Virginia mountains. The meeting had been elaborately
prepared for. Mr. Shelton, doubtless at Aldrich's direction,
had written Allison that he was having bound for his use
"a set of bills on banking of the fifty-fifth, fifty-sixth, and
fifty-seventh Congresses." Charles N. Fowler—one of the
few sound financiers in Congress—heard of the meeting at
Hot Springs and wrote Aldrich a modest note enclosing
bills of his own devising "not intended to obtrude" but hoping that his researches might be useful.[25] There is no evidence that his views, at this time, made any impression.
Nothing came of the Hot Springs meeting except the agreement to meet again at Warwick.[26]

V

Finance was not the only question to which the Four
gave attention that spring. Their relations with the President were as vital to the success of the Conservative party
as was their thinking on any public question. They watched
him well. As yet he gave no signs of not being with them
whole-heartedly. But there were two or three little matters that might be ominous—and might not. In the course
of the winter there was sharp discussion between himself
and Aldrich—in his own picturesque words, "a regular
stand-up fight"—as to whether the party should go in for
a programme of antitrust legislation.

Aldrich stood firm on the policy of the autumn of 1902.
The salvation of the party, in his view, depended this while,
on no innovations. Property—all sorts, big property and

little property, the millionaire and the corner grocer—must be solidly regimented in the Conservative ranks.

Republican Radicals in the House—notably Mr. Littlefield, who had found the ear of the President, with whom for a moment Roosevelt seemed inclined to agree—yearned for a programme of "trust busting." Mr. Littlefield was the sponsor of an antitrust bill that Aldrich was determined should not come to anything—and that did not.

There was a great pow-wow over the uses of a Bureau of Corporations that was provided for in the Act creating the new Department of Commerce and Labor. On all these points the President and Aldrich had at last formed a working accord. Reviewing the incident, in that letter to Governor Taft upon Aldrich's effort to reduce the Philippine tariff, Roosevelt said:

My experience for the last year and a half . . . has made me feel respect and regard for Aldrich as one of that group of senators, including Allison, Hanna, Spooner, Platt of Connecticut, Lodge and one or two others, who, together with the next Speaker of the House, Joe Cannon, are the most powerful factors in Congress. With every one of these men I at times differ radically on important questions; but they are the leaders, and their great intelligence and power and their desire in the last resort to do what is best for the government, make them not only essential to work with but desirable to work with. Several of the leaders have special friends whom they desire to favor, or special interests with which they are connected and which they hope to serve. But, taken as a body, they are broadminded and patriotic as well as sagacious, skilful and resolute. Each of them is set in his ways on certain points. Thus, with both Hanna and Aldrich, I had to have a regular stand-up fight before I could get them to accept any trust legislation; but once I got them to say they would give in, they kept their promise in good faith, and it was far more satisfactory to work with them than to try to work with the alleged radical reformers like Littlefield. Aldrich, for instance, has shied off from a number of propositions in which I was interested, but if I thought the matter vital and brought it before him fair and square, I have always found him a reasonable man, open to conviction and a tower of strength when thus convinced.[27]*

* This letter has been used more than once in a way that does not fairly represent it. See Rhodes "History," IX, p. 279.

Perfectly cordial were the relations of the Four with the President all this while. Nevertheless, there were curious rumors which, if believed, might have contradicted their personal experience. Part of the richness of Mr. Roosevelt's character was the power he had to be all things to all men. He drew out the people who called upon him, led them to exhibit their inner thoughts, and in so doing often gave them the impression that he was in full accord with them.

In the spring of 1903 there were talks at the White House —especially a conversation between the President and Governor Cummins—which were promptly reported in such a way that Cummins appeared to be "talking for the repeal of certain protection duties as a means of opposing the trusts" and implying that the President was on his side.[28] These reports led Roosevelt to write to Allison, "I do not like the appearance of some interviews which seem to be inspired by certain of Governor Cummins ill-advised friends to the effect that you and I have surrendered to him on the tariff business." [29]

The President was getting ready to go speech-making to the Pacific Coast. With the Cummins reports afloat in the air it was highly satisfactory to the Conservative leaders to receive from him such notes as this to Aldrich: "I would like to read over to you a couple of my speeches in which I shall touch on the trusts and the tariff. Can you come in Thursday evening at nine o'clock? I want to be sure to get what I say on these two subjects along lines upon which all of us can agree." [30]

Similar notes were sent to other Conservative leaders.

Oyster Bay over again!

Away went the President to the Pacific Coast. This was in April. Mr. Aldrich turned back into his financial problem and had his cheerful little outing at Hot Springs. He felt that the President, on finance, was in a safe mood.

"I do not intend to speak," Roosevelt had said, "save generally, on the financial question because I am not clear what to say, and I have endeavored to say nothing

where I was not perfectly sure of my ground. . . . The
Senate seems to be red hot for the Aldrich bill." [31]

The meeting at Hot Springs broke up. The Four were
scattered into distant places. The President roved the West
speaking frequently and carrying with him everywhere that
aroma of valiant cameraderie which was one of his trump
cards. From Seattle late in May he sent a famous telegram to Mr. Hanna. A few days later he was Mr. Allison's
guest for a night. It was a vivid, wonderful, somewhat
changed young man—he was not yet forty-five—who slept
that night under the Allison roof. The Seattle telegram was
ringing in every ear from ocean to ocean. Unnumbered
eyes from every quarter were turned toward him, questioning what next. Some were startled, some were glum, some
amused. The suave host has left no record of his own emotions. He had so many friends of so many different sorts
and he knew so well how to be benign with them all! One
of them—who was not just then a friend of the President
—was among those who laughed that day. He wrote to the
Wise Old Man,

Today, I suppose, you are taking care of the Pres. & I see by
the papers he is to sleep at your house—perhaps in my bed! You
won't tell him who last occupied it—any more than Mr. Forbes
told Gov. Stewart of Missouri, who spent a night with him in
Milton in 1858, that old John Brown slept in the bed the night
before.[32]

Indeed, no. One may risk it that the President never
had a more bland and genial host nor was ever more inspired to talk his best. It is as certain as two and two that
Mr. Allison was thanking inwardly all the kindly gods because the Four had had sense enough to steer clear of the
rumpus which had amused the writer of that diverting
letter.

It harked back to the election of 1900, when Theodore
Roosevelt was but a detail near the edge of the political
picture, and rash newspapers were talking of Mr. Hanna
as the logical successor of McKinley in 1904. But that had

seemed to have been snuffed out by the events of 1902, by the formation of the Conservative party. Later, beneath the surface of Republicanism, some deep plans were laid which to this day are not unearthed. The Western Radicals were not the only opponents of the new Conservatism —of Conservatism, that is, as represented by the Four, by Oyster Bay, by the President. Others besides Cummins and his fellows dreamed of splitting the Conservative ranks, of finding somewhere their man on horseback—even if on a tame horse.

Governor Taft had written to the President a frank letter, full of his delightful personality, warning him that there was an attempt to bring forward a rival to be groomed for the next presidential election. It was being engineered by "the trust people and possibly some of the machine politicians" that had "honored with their consideration your humble servant" who, of course, would not listen to the voice of the tempter.[33]

The evil ones looked elsewhere. In a sad hour for their cause and for Senator Hanna they decided that he was the man on the tame horse. Whether definite overtures were made to Mr. Hanna—whether he was rash enough to consider breaking away from the Four and from Roosevelt— is an historical secret which the few people who share it insist on keeping. There was a mistake in generalship somewhere, and on the part of a sworn enemy of Mr. Hanna, Senator Foraker—his rival for control of the party in Ohio —a lynx-eyed perception of it.

The Four must have smiled to themselves, but also must have shaken their heads in regret, when Mr. Hanna was caught napping by Senator Foraker and manœuvred into a position that seemed to be confessed opposition to the President. It was reported that he would compete with Roosevelt for the next presidential nomination.

Mr. Roosevelt had travelled a long way temperamentally since those delightful conferences of the autumn of 1901, when he was the affable youth suddenly elevated—Prince Hal become King Henry but not yet changed. Since then he had discovered himself. He had found how illimitable was his courage in the coal strike; he had seen the vision of the world and all the glory that might be when he turned the course of history in that amazing diplomatic victory of the previous winter, and bluffed the German Emperor over Venezuela; he had glimpsed, perhaps with eyes slightly dazzled, the domestic possibilities in the universal desire of the Radicals to acclaim him their man on horseback—on a real horse shod with iron and champing at the bit.

Nevertheless, as late as his departure for the West he had not taken the high hand with any of the Conservative leaders. Now for the first time, out of a blue sky, Jove thundered. The Seattle telegram in effect demanded of Hanna a statement of his purpose. It was a paraphrase of Shakespeare, "Under which King Bezonian, speak or die" —are you with me or against me.

Hanna's prompt collapse into meekness is still remembered. The President had notified the country that he intended to be master in the Republican party. There was no one who had the courage to be his rival.

On the surface, harmony was instantly restored. Roosevelt wrote to Hanna promising to attend his daughter's wedding, assuring him that he had consulted him and relied on his judgment more than he had done with any other man and that they must "have a real talk—not just a half hour's chat—about the Panama Canal in particular and financial legislation and then about the political situation." [34]

The Four took the outcome as a matter of course. Mr. Platt had a good chuckle over Hanna's "back-action-double-spring feat" by means of which he "got back into line very quickly." [35] He prophesied that there would be no cooling of the enthusiasm for Roosevelt at the next election.

The President kept his word and was at the Hanna wedding at Cleveland, June 10. Allison did not come East with him. The Wise Old Man was too busy keeping his eye on the situation in Iowa where the Radicals were steadily growing in strength. The Four were represented at Cleveland by Aldrich alone. A telegram was sent to Allison signed Hanna, Hale, Aldrich, Wetmore, Kean: "We are all here where you ought to be but retribution next winter."[36]

There is a curious little prophecy, all unaware, in that group of names, with three of the Four missing and including Hale. It was on the knees of the gods that a shift was soon to come about in the Aldrich alliances. The Four, little as they suspected it, were within two years of their disruption, within four years of the disappearance from history of all but Aldrich. From this time forward—eight stormy years—the relations with Hale become increasingly significant. We shall walk beside him later, fierce, old, dominant, Aldrich's chief lieutenant.

Much political talk occurred at Cleveland especially upon the abominably vague subject—*what the deuce did the country want in the way of financial legislation?* Aldrich was getting his eyes open upon the subject but he was still without a plan and he was keenly aware how vast were the difficulties in the way of any sort of departure from financial tradition in American affairs. He was for letting sleeping dogs lie; and this was to be his policy, for several years thereafter.[37]

The President was equally cautious. During the summer, the Warwick conference had a place in his thoughts. He wrote Aldrich mentioning men whom the Four ought to consult and saying that "Uncle Joe Cannon" was "very obdurate as regards anything being done but I think if we take the old boy the right way he will stand with us. Is there anything for me to do now?"[38]

The meeting of the Four at Indian Oaks in August was another futility—except for the pleasure it gave these faithful comrades meeting together in what seemed to be pleasant weather, politically speaking, in what was certainly a beautiful place where their most imaginative member was planting, building, and in his mind's eye seeing a noble landed estate arising out of the ground. They were photographed sitting together in the piazza of the boat house. But as to policy—they could agree upon nothing except that there was nothing to agree upon. The sleeping dogs must lie for a while longer.

The conference resolved itself into a discussion of the advisability of a special session to deal with the persistent Cuban question. At the moment this seemed to be their really serious concern. The President had gone ahead with his effort for Cuban reciprocity; a treaty had been negotiated with a reduction of duties; the Senate had agreed to it tentatively but had thrown responsibility upon the House by requiring its assent. For that purpose a special session was to be called. But what was a practicable date for calling it?[39]

Six days later, the Four dined, and spent the night following at Oyster Bay.[40] The President promptly reported their deliberations to Cannon. "Last night, Aldrich, Spooner, Allison and Platt came out here to discuss the proposed financial legislation. They have no definite plan, of course, as they wish to find out what your views are before even formulating their own and as they also wish to sound out certain of their colleagues and to find out, probably through you, what your lieutenants in the House feel about this financial matter. I earnestly hope we can get some legislation not of a radical or revolutionary sort which will provide a certain amount of elasticity, that is, will provide not merely for expansion in time of stringency, but for contraction when the stringency is over. . . . Now what are your views on the subject? We all decided that of course we would not make up our own minds in any way until we found what your judgment was." [41]*

Straws in the wind are these apparently amiable consultations of August, 1903, but they mark a new shifting of the

---

* In contrast with this letter there is an account of the incident by one of the ornaments of the literature of protest that is highly characteristic. C. W. Danforth, in *Human Life*, April, 1911, described his attempt to find out what happened at the Warwick Conference, which according to Mr. Danforth lasted "the better part of a week." Passing over a number of picturesque details, including an interview with Mr. Aldrich while he supervised the planting of a tree, an interview in which the writer believed that he was purposely led astray, one reaches a moment when Mr. Danforth happening "to meet a powerful friend who usually knew what was going on in big politics, I asked him if he could throw any light on the mystery. He smiled—he did the Aldrich

centre of gravity of Republican power. Had Mr. Henderson been the speaker, the Four might have sent him a mandate instead of an invitation to confer. But Cannon with a rebellious House behind him—that was another story! And the President—was he quite a known quantity? Again, the underlying question, was it quite certain he and the Four could permanently get on together. Mr. Platt, with his keen disillusioned old eyes searched sharply the conduct of the President. It did not altogether please him.

"In my last letter," he wrote Aldrich two days later, "I said as a postscript that the President appeared to be talking a good deal. Evidently he is inquiring of every one who goes to see him from Secretary Shaw down to Carlisle, what they think of certain things, meaning the matters which we talked to him about. I do not know that he tells them that we suggested them—I think more likely he would not—but he speaks of them as things which he thought of himself, and apparently he is not helping the situation very much. When we were there he seemed to fall in love with our opinions, but when Shaw and Carlisle and Cullom ventilate their ideas he is just as apt to side with them. He will mix and muddle this thing all up, I fear. He wants it understood that he is suggesting the particular kind of legislation which ought to be adopted, and that he expects every one to take hold, and carry out his ideas, all of which leads up to what I started to say, that I believe you ought to keep in pretty close touch with him. If you do this, he may accept your ideas as his own, and push them. If you do not, he will be filled up with others from various parties, and be working against what we think is the right thing." [42]

---

bidding as did most every one else in Rhode Island but he did not pretend to love the Senator—and said quietly: 'There is a man over at Oyster Bay with shining teeth and a devil of a temper. It seems he found something was going to be put over and sent for certain people. Then he told them they might as well stop the game right now, as he would fight them if they tried to jam the scheme through. So they tried to look pleasant—and went home.' It is a matter of history that thereafter Senator Aldrich did not call at the White House any more frequently than strict etiquette demanded during its occupancy by the man from Oyster Bay."

Here is a bit of writing where more is meant than meets the ear. Mr. Platt was a sincere and devoted partisan of the President. He was honestly troubled over the President's openness to counsel in these anxious days when the sudden rise of Cannon had introduced a new element into the problem of Conservative control. However, as we shall see, his loyalty to the President, for all his anxiety, did not waver. Whether the others of the Four shared his vague fears, whether at the back of their heads they saw an approaching break, we do not know. All of them stood shoulder to shoulder, in Roosevelt's especial body guard, as long as he remained the Conservative leader. Nevertheless the cloud the size of a man's hand had appeared on the horizon, and out of it great things were to come.

It was the new power, Cannon, that was ruling the ascendant in the summer of 1903. Mr. Allison had been deputed to confer with him. Soon after this second Oyster Bay Conference, they met at Chicago and talked together very pleasantly.[43] The question of an extra session had had no end of discussion among all the leading politicians. Who spoke the decisive word is made plain by a letter from Roosevelt to the coming Speaker. "Most of the Senators to whom I have talked, and one or two members of the House, have expressed the hope for an October session. On the other hand, Hanna and Frye, as well as Allison and also Secretaries Shaw and Root feel that it would be unwise to have this session until November 9. I gather from Senator Allison's letter that this is your opinion also. Unless there is some great change in the situation I shall treat this opinion of yours as conclusive." [44]

Congress was summoned to meet in extra session November 9, 1903. Before that happened astonishing things took place. By a sudden turn of events, the Senate, once more, became the heart of the matter.

CHAPTER XV

HOW THE REPUBLICANS UNDID THEMSELVES

I

AT many times in the careers of the two strong men, Aldrich and Roosevelt, their basic contrast is dramatically evident. The autumn of 1903 and the early part of the following winter was 'one of these periods of contrast. The glorious tempest that was Roosevelt, the sphinx that was Aldrich, were for a season arrayed in opposition.

The furies which the Panama revolution, in the autumn of 1903, sent on fierce wing across America roused the President in a transport of enraged energy. At first he found in Aldrich a support to his mood. But presently another vein in him came to the surface. A move of Aldrich's that was altogether in character was so foreign to the nature of Mr. Roosevelt, that he could not gauge it correctly. A brief space of estrangement ensued.

In the Panama episode Aldrich stood by the Administration. Whether Panama was a subject of discussion, that August night when the Four were at Oyster Bay, is guesswork. The Four were too busy with widely different matters that summer to give Panama much attention. That they approved the main drift of Roosevelt's foreign policy is beyond a doubt. We may assume that they looked upon the outcome as a foregone conclusion.

Mr. Hay negotiated his treaty with the United States of Colombia giving the United States of America control of the coveted canal strip across the Isthmus of Panama. The Senate of Columbia attempted to block the treaty. Its purposes do not matter. The result was an international crisis. The State of Panama seceded from the Colombian Confederation.

This mysterious episode—the Panama Revolution and the instantaneous recognition of the new republic by the

United States—is not illuminated in the slightest way by the private papers of any of the Four. There is no evidence that they were moved by the storm of vituperation that was loosed upon the President, that was given voice in such letters as this to Platt: "The recognition of Panama seems to me an unfriendly act against Colombia. . . . Such hasty action makes conservatives afraid of Roosevelt for another term and furnishes arms to our friends, the enemy." [1]

The day after this letter was written, Aldrich had a conference with the President at the White House.[2] The special session was to begin the next day. The situation now surrounding Congress was very different from that which had been expected when this date was set following the President's letter to Cannon in August. The country was all in a hubbub over Panama. A din of applause and condemnation blended in an unintelligible uproar with party lines threatening to disappear.

On the second day of the session the President began his official day with another conference with Mr. Aldrich.[3] What they talked about no one knows. Both were men who were at their best in the face of the enemy, and at their very best when there was nothing but their own wills to guide them. Confronted by a roaring opposition, Roosevelt became angrily resolute to crush it, Aldrich smilingly convinced that it was nonsense. And neither, ever, had a tremor of fear. If one had a courage that was epical, the other had that courage still more disconcerting, the courage of supreme humor. Had they been Greeks, Roosevelt might have quoted Homer, Aldrich, Aristophanes.

After the early conference with Aldrich on November 10, the President held a cabinet meeting. To the astonishment of Washington, two senators were present. They were Aldrich and Hanna. A little later when Senator Aldrich was leaving the White House, and the eager newspaper men tried to extract news from him, he put them by in his usual good-natured, imperturbable way. But Senator Hanna was built on another model. He could never attain that Olympian indifference to the stormy moods of the Public. He had to tell the Press that the subjects of discussion that morning were "The Panama Revolution and the prospect of building the Canal." [4]

The pale issues of finance vanished ghostlike in a tempest of what is popularly labelled human interest. Mr. Cannon had prophesied that no financial legislation would be reached during the special session. Perhaps it was with downright self-satisfaction that he beheld the sentimental tempest blowing this way and that and making it easy for his prophecy to be fulfilled. It is possible that the Elder Statesmen themselves were not grieved because problems which the Senate alone could solve, were thus unexpectedly given the centre of the stage. At any rate the two events of the special session were both in the province of foreign affairs. The incorrigible talkativeness of Congress could not be headed off before the end of that session, but sailed on in full career into the regular session. There was no interval between the two. Upon Cuba, talk was at last checked about Christmas time and the treaty was put into effect.

A treaty with the new Republic of Panama was even more troublesome. The Democratic leaders had thought at first that there was profit in opposing it. Their ears were attuned by hope rather than by understanding. They thought that in the popular clamor—of which a great deal came from Republicans—the note of protest was the dominant. But their hopes were deceiving them. The rank and file of the party had better ears. They recognized the real dominant in the roaring of the hour—the deep hoarse cry to possess. The country wanted Panama. Colombia might go hang. Within a week of the meeting of Congress the astute correspondent of *The Tribune* prophesied that there would be no real fight against this agreement with the new "republic," which was yesterday the seceded state, of Panama.[5]

This forecast was fulfilled, but slowly. Not until February was a vote obtained. Meanwhile Aldrich kept a watchful eye upon every stage of the tortuous debate. He continued to hold conferences with the President.[6] Platt took charge of the treaty on the floor of the Senate in order "to defend the Administration and party against all comers," and made a speech that delighted Roosevelt.[7]

In the midst of this clamor the President thought that the time had come to review his personal forces preparatory to his campaign for renomination. He wanted to be quite sure that the Hanna boom was a dead dog, that his future was well in his own hands.

He had asked Mr. Hill to obtain interviews with prominent senators committing them to his cause. "Mr. Hill told the President he would try to get them but he did not think he would find that Mr. Aldrich thought the plan wise in his case. Sure enough when approached in the matter, the Senator stated that he was in favor of the Roosevelt candidacy and would endorse it in practical quiet way; but that he did not think it would be to the advantage of Roosevelt for him to give out an interview endorsing him. So the others, Spooner, Allison, and Platt, gave out endorsements but Aldrich did not." He said to Hill: "The President may think my public endorsement would help him but I know it would do him more harm than good." [8]

If Aldrich could be utterly free of illusions about himself, could accept the rôle of Bogey Man and make no bones about it, the President was more human. He jumped to the conclusion of bad faith—at heart Aldrich must be in league with his enemies!—he was angry.

II

The character quality that separated Aldrich from Roosevelt comes out in the reasons why Aldrich refused to endorse the President. He was accustomed to the rôle of Bogey Man. It made no impression upon him. But never was a man more clearly judicial in estimating the strategic value of his own name. When he told Hill that his support would injure the President he had two things in mind.

The previous year Rhode Island politics, always bitter enough, were exceptionally bitter.

There was a street-railway strike that year and Aldrich as president of the Traction Company came in for his full share of abuse. Despite the appeals made to the labor vote, the Conservatives lost ground in the elections. The district which Aldrich had once represented went Democratic. A vigorous stir among all the element of discontent took the governorship away from the Republicans.

In 1903 the literature of protest was in full flood. It caught up and absorbed into its vociferous tide the less sophisticated minds that had found their function in the newspapers as professional informers. As if to rival the success of *McClure,* whose circulation had risen by leaps and bounds, and to recover the field for the newspapers, the New York *Evening Post* contributed a classic to the literature of the professional informer. It fixed upon Rhode Island as a field of exploitation.

A corrupt State. Analysis of Conditions in Rhode Island. Review of the venal towns. A shocking picture of political and social immorality. Causes that underlie the present system of boss rule. Indifference and Apathy of the electorate explained. Many villages sunk in poverty. Ignorance and Depravity. Decreases in population and Decay of Intelligence and Character. The work that lies before the reformers of a New England Commonwealth.

Such were the terrifying headlines on the first page of *The Post* one day in May, 1903. The professional informer —or if you will, the literature of protest—had found Brayton out and was after him hot foot. There was instant response. Before the month was out the Bishop of Rhode Island had referred to *The Post* article before the annual convention of the Episcopal Church; he had preached, virtually, with the article as a text: "That the political machinery by which we are governed is corrupt to rottenness is not too much to say." [9]

At first the newspapers were careful to avoid the implication that they were hitting at Aldrich. *The Post* on the day it unmasked its batteries, remarked editorially, "We do not for a moment mean to say that the shortcomings of

the Rhode Island leaders have been intentional or deliberate . . . These men have gone their way happily unconscious of the filth in their own back yards. But their eyes
are now open."

Later in the year, when the financial conferences of the
Four had come and gone, the tension of election time made
men less polite. The Providence *Journal* became indiscreet.
In spite of it—or because of it—the Republicans lost. Aldrich had taken no active part in the campaign. Probably
he looked upon the governorship as a matter of no importance and was reserving his whole strength for the great fight
that would come the next year. But by this time all his
enemies were in bad humor, ready to hold him personally
responsible for all the evil that had been laid bare in Rhode
Island. *The Journal* had incensed them.

Voice was given to their ruthless mood by a very grim
enemy. In a vein of heavy irony *The Nation* took up the
cudgels. "Governor Garvin's re-election has excited virtuous rage in Rhode Island. The Democrats and the Independent Republicans who supported Mr. Garvin were
very unfeeling in their treatment of the Republican machine. They actually ventured to hire detectives to stop
bribery at the polls. As a committee headed by Bishop
McVickar had already been circulating in pamphlet form
the *Evening Post* articles on corruption in Rhode Island,
and had been agitating for an honest election, the employment of detectives was obviously the culmination of a
dastardly attack upon the right of a freeman to sell his vote
to whom he pleases for whatever price he pleases." And
then with that subtle use of a paranthetical remark so
familiar to all crafty propagandists, the whole attack was
focussed on one man without confessing it in the sentence:
"The Providence *Journal,* mouthpiece of the machine and
of the traction interests of Senator Aldrich, has flown to
the defense of Rhode Island liberties." [10]

There was another attack upon him that was animated
by a variety of motives—as is always the case politically—
but that took its significance from the inclusion among its

supporters of a group of people whom everybody respected. The doctors of America and certain philanthropists of unquestioned purity of intention were clamoring for legislation that would prevent the adulteration of foodstuffs. Their watchword was "pure food." There was a Pure Food Lobby at Washington. A Pure Food Bill had appeared in Congress.

It was a curious bill; part of its political significance has generally been missed because the perspective of its proposals has been ignored. Clever manipulation of political method had taught the American people how to remove from the shoulders of the government the burden of enforcing a law. Their principle was in substance: so frame the law that it will automatically force a large body of citizens to see to its execution in self defense. This thinking was applied conspicuously in the arguments over the restriction of the liquor traffic: so legislate, was the cry, that reputable liquor sellers, for their own profit, will form themselves inevitably into a police to exterminate the disreputable ones. This principle had been taken up by advisers of the Pure Food Lobby. The result was a bill decreeing fine and imprisonment for every corner grocer who offered for sale a sealed tin that contained adulterated food. Thus the whole body of grocers was to be formed into a private police to detect and expose adulteration with the alternative of going to prison if they did not.

Aldrich was uncompromisingly opposed to the bill. He did not explain his motives, and he suffered in reputation because of the company in which he found himself. The bill covered liquor as well as food and the distillers' lobby was fighting it. Corrupt manufacturers of food were with them. All this gave a new handle to his enemies: he could not be inspired by any good motive; he must be aiming to protect the makers of impure food or those who intentionally dealt in it; he had personal interests in the grocery business; he wanted to be free to sell the American people poison in the guise of food. There was no recognition of his having sold out his grocery business long before.

In the popular discussion, the constitutional principles involved were buried in silence. The hue and cry was in the key easily imagined. When Spooner said in the Senate, "the honor of the citizen and exemption from prosecution and punishment throughout the whole country are perhaps of quite as much consequence as this matter of adulteration," obviously he was but a Machiavellian lawyer trying to play into the hands of poisoners. Aldrich stated his attitude with his usual boldness:

Is there anything in the existing condition of affairs that makes it the duty of Congress to put the liberty of all the people of the United States in jeopardy because some man thinks that at some time some imported article contains certain substances which ought not to be there? Take this question of [olive] oil, are we to pass a sumptuary law that will prevent people all over the United States from using or selling or receiving or transporting articles which, in the opinion of some of the people of North Dakota, may be injurious to their health? Are we going to decide that question here? Are we going to take up the question as to what a man shall eat and what a man shall drink, and put him under severe penalties if he is eating or drinking something different from what the chemists of the Agricultural Department think it is desirable for him to eat or drink?[11]

Aldrich was looking ahead, with his eyes on the election of the next year. A purely politic reason for preventing the passage of the Pure Food Bill, in December, 1903, was the effect such a law might have on the electorate in 1904. Aldrich had a long memory. He had not forgotten what happened in 1890—how fickle the electorate had proved, how easy it had been to bring home to the small purchaser a hardship created by Republican legislation. He knew that whatever the Democrats might be saying aloud, in 1903, they were in their closets sacrificing to Fortune praying that the Republicans might be trapped into passing a law under which their pious enemies might send a dozen small grocers to prison—and repeat the landslide of 1890.

Utterly free from illusion, as carefully analytical in observing himself as in observing others, Aldrich served the President well by refusing to talk. Presently Mr. Roosevelt got himself in hand. He reconsidered; he listened to the others of the Four; he began to see things as they were. But he had to have time in which to come round.[12]

There is a very famous passage that cannot be quoted too often.

> Deep in the man sits fast his fate.
> Unknown to Cromwell as to me
> Was Cromwell's measure and degree.

And so of these two men of genius—the two gigantic figures of their day. That unknown fate within neither ever successfully allowed for. Aldrich could never appreciate the effect on others of his own incredible detachment, his superiority to his sensibilities. He had something of that strange power to be intensely in earnest and yet to be passionless about it, even amused—to play the game with his whole strength but at the same minute to be the critical observer taking it all as an entertainment—that Lincoln had. Herein was his basic contrast with the fiery and exalted spirit which by some oversight of destiny had been born too late to be the central figure of the Crusades.

III

A real disaster overtook Mr. Aldrich in the period of the interval. There is indeed a strange solemnity about the time in any great career when death begins to confuse the game. Hitherto, except for the death of Mr. McMillan, which did not occur at a strategic moment, there had been little in the career of Aldrich to remind him of the eternal scythe swinging over him by which eventually all the poppies even in the field of statecraft would be mown. That group of astonishing old men, so brilliantly self-contained, who had controlled the Senate since 1897, now began to disappear. Mr. Hanna who in spite of failing health had struggled to keep up with all his many affairs broke down. Typhoid appeared. The end came quickly.

It was a severe shock to Mr. Aldrich. Almost the only

instance of his giving way to his feelings in public occurred
the day Mr. Hanna died. "Senator Aldrich," writes Miss
Lawler, "was capable of deep feeling though he rarely manifested it outwardly. He, as well as Senator Platt, were devoted to the genial Ohio senator and both, during Senator
Hanna's last illness, remained in close attendance on the
sickroom. The Sunday before Senator Hanna died he rallied sufficiently to give hope, and this was reflected in the
appearance of both these senators, particularly Senator
Platt, who with Mrs. Platt spent much of the time in the
Hanna apartment and was there when the Senator died.
Soon after the death, Senator Aldrich with Mrs. Aldrich,
came to the apartment and when they left Senator Aldrich
was crying, though struggling hard to overcome his emotion. As he passed, sadly and solemnly to the elevator,
the tears coursed down his face, much increasing its usual
floridness. In the effort to suppress his emotion, his face
took on a fierce expression as he stalked away, sullen and
rebellious. His agony was very genuine." [13]

IV

In March when the temporary estrangement had blown
over and was forgotten[14]—with Aldrich, such things vanished the moment they came to an end—the New England
Manufacturing Jewellers and Silversmiths Association gave
a banquet. Mr. Aldrich was their guest and made a brief
address. "The prosperity of your ancient trade—for it is
older than civilization—depends to a greater degree than
any other upon the general prosperity of the country; and
in wishing you every success for the future, as I heartily do,
I feel that I am expressing a patriotic solicitude for the
general welfare of the American people." [15]

This implied a more easy going—if you will, a more
aristocratic—conception of "welfare" than was professed by
those enemies of his whom he had had in mind when he
insisted that it would hurt rather than help the President
if he pushed himself into the foreground as his advocate.

With them welfare hung upon such questions as—who gets the profits of excess production? does legislation favor the large or the small producer? do the middle class or the rich control Congress?

Back of Aldrich's generalization—so far into the background that literally minded people could not see it—lay the hierarchal conception of industrial society, with its small apex of organized intelligence and its broad base of trustful labor. Back of the formulations of the literature of protest lay the passionate terror of a reviving middle class that feared it would be ground to death between an upper and a nether millstone. And entangled with all the deep confusion of the time was that restless discontent which was rumbling in a subterranean mutter through the West.

Again, as so often in this period, local politics in Iowa formed the weather vane. It was increasingly doubtful whether Mr. Allison could remain much longer the lord of that manor. An Iowa Republican convention, though not quite anti-Allison, nor antiprotection, had been sufficiently tinctured with Cumminsism, so to speak, to lead Mr. Allison to urge the greatest caution in framing the national platform. It was a time for walking over eggs.

One of the most fateful moments in the history of the Four did not, when it occurred, seem to any of them to be fateful. Crisis—real crisis—has such a curious way of disguising itself as commonplace! In the first week of May there were conferences with the President on the subject of the platform, and following these a meeting of Conservative leaders in Mr. Aldrich's committee room. A platform was drafted. It was designed to propitiate Iowa without a surrender to Cummins.

"We insist," read this preliminary draft, "upon the maintenance of (protective) principle but we recognize that particular tariff schedules are neither sacred nor immutable. Rates of duty must be altered when changed conditions and the public interest demand their alteration but this work cannot safely be committed to any other hands than those of the party of protection." [16] The draft also made an appeal to labor through a demand for immigrant restriction. Practically all the rest of it was verbiage.

Mr. Aldrich seldom took part in the framing of platforms. In the year previous to this fateful May meeting, he made a bland confession to the Senate. Mr. Clay, irritated by one of Aldrich's cool moods, had demanded of him "whether the Republican party had carried out any part of the platform that it provided in 1900." "I answer," said Aldrich, perfectly unruffled, "that I have never read the Republican platform of 1900." [17]

Still, that persistent limitation which eventually cost him dear—his undervaluation of the power of the crowd, his contempt for all the devices that purveyed to the crowd. He could never get over his impulse to regard verbiage as nothing but verbiage, to ignore its magic. And there was always the genial impulse to let dear Mr. Allison be at ease in his own mind if possible. What Aldrich himself thought will appear presently in the cool words with which he opened his personal campaign when he went the whole length of the new Conservatism, facing the most powerful opposition he ever faced.

If it was Mr. Allison whose genius for diplomacy dominated the Elder Statesmen that day in Aldrich's committee room, he had made the mistake of his life. It was precisely the wrong time to walk over eggs. The country was really interested not in generalities about the record of the Republican party, not even in the cautious admission that protection might be modified as conditions changed, but in searching questions upon the relative objectives of Conservatives and Radicals, upon the place of wealth in a commercial civilization, upon a re-definition of classes.

What counted that moment, in political strategy, was first of all temper. The significant issue in that inner council of the Conservatives was what temper should prevail— the temper of Aldrich, the defiant conservative, or of Allison, the conservative opportunist? Mr. Allison was in tune with most of the Elder Statesmen and they with him. Just how the Four divided that morning we do not know—

though one could make a shrewd guess! All of them áccepted the conclusion of the Conference. As a consequence the Republicans officially went before the country totally uncommitted upon all the vital interests of the hour. And out of this, as will be tragically apparent, came at last the ruin of the Conservatives.

Aldrich at once took a bolder attitude than the Conference seemed to warrant. While there can be little doubt that he and Allison were drifting apart politically, it is equally plain that he and Platt were closer than ever. And thus the cleavage among the Elder Statesmen is revealed. Aldrich and Platt stood frankly for confessed opposition to the Radicals, and they had no fear. They were willing to take what came. The West did not terrify them. The demand for economic democracy did not terrify them. The day following the Conservative conference, Aldrich gave interviews both to *The Herald* and *The Tribune*. Besides stating the conclusions of the conference he recognized the real nature of the opposition which was gathering against the Conservatives and set it at defiance.

They (the Democrats) may attempt to show that the tariff favors the establishment of trusts, but that proposition was ably disposed of by President Roosevelt in his speeches of last summer, in which he showed that any reduction of the tariff which would drive the trusts out of business would entirely destroy every industry in which they were engaged.[18]

The Tribune—Mr. Hill's paper, the particular champion of the President—recognized the importance of the Aldrich interview by saying it "will probably be quoted again and again by speakers until the end of the presidential campaign."

Aldrich had a personal stake in this election. Again he was a candidate for senator—the sixth time. Had he accepted the temper along with the formal conclusions of the May conference, his cue would have been to deal in generalities, to trust to his standing arrangement with Brayton, to rely upon deep and silent work by the ma-

chine. His personal campaign would be a hard fight. All
the forces represented by *The World* and *The Post* and the
literature of protest would make a test case of Rhode Island.
Their cry, once more, would be the familiar indictment of
the new Conservatism. The country was to be rallied
against the idea of the economic hierarchy as the basis of
society. Aldrich opened his personal campaign with a
speech to the Young Men's Republican Club of Providence.
He told them that the tariff did not foster monopoly, but
that virtual monopoly was "an incident of our industrial
development." He praised Roosevelt for his "zealous and
constant devotion to the highest interests of the public." [19]

This last campaign for the senatorship was hotly contested. Brayton was in ill health and Aldrich for the first
time as senator was practically his own manager. He does
not appear to have done particularly well. Again, his constant bias was for direct personal management rather than
mass management. But it is possible that keeping Brayton in the background was fortunate—even that it was designed—as all the furies of the previous year were out to
defeat Aldrich. It was a duel to the death. Though now
as formerly every effort was made by the Conservatives to
persuade the labor vote, there was no thought of conciliating
it. When Aldrich got control of the Providence *Journal* for
campaign purposes, he wrote to the managing editor that
he was "to be independent in politics and news but . . . to
oppose by all proper means the socialistic and anarchical
tendencies of the labor unions and similar organizations." [20]

In his *Herald* interview Aldrich made a false prophecy.
"No new elements will be introduced in this campaign. The
contest will be along familiar lines." The forces of politics,
like the ways of God in the hymn, move mysteriously. Aldrich's prophecy was brought to nought by singular events
which, even as he made it, were brewing in the State of
Wisconsin—Senator Spooner's state.

The fact opens up the strange character of the election of
1904. As so often, what really mattered lay far behind the
ostensible issues that display themselves on the broad page

of history and impose upon the credulous. Seldom if ever
has the support of a presidential candidate been so much of
a gamble. Never were political leaders bound together in
a more singular fashion, by agreements that enabled every
one with honesty to have a mental reservation out of which
—as out of the fisherman's pot in the Arabian Nights—
incalculable results might come.

A storm centre full danger to Aldrich was Wisconsin. Its
Radical governor, Mr. La Follette, had made longer strides
toward power than had his rival, Mr. Cummins, in Iowa. A
born and inveterate reformer he had flung himself heart
and soul into a fight against the Wisconsin railroads. He
was one of those in whom the new temper that had infected
so many since 1897, that was building up the literature of
protest, was furiously directed against organized money,
especially against money in corporate form, specifically
against railroads. To stem the tide of his radical example
Senator Spooner was exerting all his influence. The result
was civil war inside the Republican party in Wisconsin.

And now the adroit evasion by the conference in Aldrich's room began to bear fruit. Neither faction in Wisconsin was at odds with anything laid down that day as
party orthodoxy. Their furious antagonism was over the
things that had been evaded, the things upon which the
President was not as yet committed in so many words. Here
it was that the great gamble of the campaign revealed itself. Each faction was taking its chances on being able to
bind the President to itself on issues that were not ostensibly before the country, but that were in fact at the back
of every mind. Each side was plunging boldly on the
strength of its guess what the future might bring forth.

An absurd situation but very characteristic of American
politics. Its absurdity culminated when two rival Wisconsin delegations—a La Follette delegation and a Spooner
delegation—both applied to the Republican National Convention, demanding to be seated as official representatives
of the party; two delegations, hating each other like poison,
with principles that were almost antithetical, clamored to

be admitted to the convention in order to vote for the same man for president. Each delegation posed as true blue followers of Mr. Roosevelt.

It is a curious—and like so many similar cases—rather a discreditable story. There was a fruitless attempt to induce the factions to compromise and split the delegation between them. Aldrich did not believe in Mr. La Follette and doubtless agreed with Mr. Platt who wrote to Mr. Spooner to stand firm. "I have a kind of an idea that when La Follette is once whipped thoroughly the trouble will be largely over." [21]

Spooner replied bitterly deploring the contest forced upon him, saying, "He is not a Republican, cares nothing about the party or its principles, but will to the extent of his ability rule or ruin." [22]

The La Follette forces threw out an ominous hint. "We are sincerely anxious for the re-election of President Roosevelt, for we realize that he and Governor La Follette stand squarely on the same platform. . . . We ask no favors. If justice is done, there need be no fears of the result in Wisconsin as to President Roosevelt." [23]

This singular situation naturally troubled the President. Though the subjects at issue in the Wisconsin civil war had all been ruled out of the platform, this fierce young man La Follette, was successfully conjuring back these traditional spectres out of the froth of the Western cauldron. And he had so manœuvred that the national convention would have to appear, at least, to take sides for or against "trustbusting"—and all the rest! The contention of Mr. Lodge that it was a question not of politics but of legality, that the convention would not have wishes in the matter,[24] had been called forth by the irritated remark of Mr. Chandler: "The reasoning of the people next November is very likely to be utterly illogical. More great political changes have taken place in this country illogically than were caused by pure reason or right thinking." [25] Meanwhile the President was painfully deliberating upon the merits of the question and at last accepted the view of Senator Lodge and decided that strict legality required the recognition of the Spooner delegation. He threw his influence on the Spooner side and Spooner's men were seated. [26]

In the illogical popular mind the President stood committed to the Conservatives.

Throughout the summer the Conservatives worked quietly, steadily for his election. He kept close in touch with them. Now it was through a line to Allison. "Many people have been good enough to say kind things of my speech of acceptance but no one of them has said anything that I appreciate quite as much as I appreciate your letter." [27] To Spooner: "Next to Root it is you who have given me the best suggestions for changes in my letter (of acceptance)." [28] To Platt: "No one has worked harder to make my administration a success than you have done, and I am indeed keenly appreciative of that work; and still more of the friendship lying behind it, my dear Senator." [29] To Aldrich: "How are affairs in Rhode Island? Is there any chance of seeing you some time this month, either here (Washington) or at Oyster Bay? There are a number of things I would like to talk over with you." [30]

The Conservative leaders had their hands full persuading their followers that the President was "sound." The possibility of a national eight-hour law especially troubled the manufacturers. Platt kept himself busy allaying such fears. It was in this connection that the Bureau of Corporations threatened for a moment to justify the fears of those who had opposed its creation. Word went around that it was preparing to launch a campaign in favor of the eight-hour day. So great was the alarm of the manufacturers that an arch conservative, Mr. Brooker, had an interview with the President and received "all the assurance that any reasonable man ought to ask for in regard to . . . the attitude of the Administration toward Corporations like our own who are interested in various kinds of pools, and the Department of Commerce and Labor in regard to the investigation referred to in your letter." [31]

The Conservatives did not hesitate to ground their position on a repetition of the promises of the first Oyster Bay Conference—continuity, only gradual changes, the protection of property. When the Democrats, catching up a watchword of the hour, declared that "the most dangerous trust was the Senatorial trust," the Four were not disturbed. Platt defined their position by saying that the Republicans stood for the regulation of trusts, the Democrats for their abolition.

A very different tune was sung by that group of Republicans who presently gained the upper hand in Wisconsin. Two State tickets had been put into the field—one backed by Spooner, one by La Follette—and each faction claimed to have the sole legal right to use the label "Republican." The matter had been taken into the courts. Meanwhile the President watched with anxious eye the growing bitterness within the party in the Northwest. And then came a fateful decision of the Supreme Court of Wisconsin. The La Follette ticket was pronounced the legitimate Republican ticket; the Spooner people were not the genuine Republican organization.

This settled things for the President. Again, he asserted that principle of legitimacy—otherwise legality—which Senator Lodge had advocated at the National Convention. He let it be known that in his opinion "any weakening of the La Follette ticket was a weakening of the national ticket." He felt that the Spooner faction "have acted badly from the beginning"; he would not be "implicated in supporting" them.[32]

In the illogical popular mind the President had committed himself to the Radicals.

While this criss-cross of misapprehension was drifting this way and that, and the electorate was preparing to act as Mr. Chandler had prophesied it would act, Mr. Aldrich interested himself in a few things besides politics. In an address to the alumni of Brown University he expressed both his momentary and his permanent feelings. He thought that education should enable men "to bring to the consideration of public affairs the calm intelligent judgment of the student, and prevent their being misled by the noisy clamor of the self-seeking demagogue." [33]

Toward the end of August when the political situation was growing tense, his unruffled humor glinted through a note to Hale in response to a request to make speeches in Maine. "I can say to you very frankly that I am not a success as a stump speaker but will try not to do you any harm." [34]

Amidst a clamor of flag raisings and torch light parades, and appeals for money, and furious crimination and re-crimination, he found time to take a day off and attend "old home week" in the town where he was born. The great man, on his return to Foster, made a few graceful remarks with especial emphasis on the integrity of the rural communities.[35]

Throughout all this anxious and persistent effort Aldrich the politician never let go Aldrich the humanist. His political conferences generally took place on his beautiful estate at Indian Oaks, frequently in his "office" in the boat house beside the shining sea—where the Four had held such momentous councils. A note from Platt to one of Aldrich's visitors this summer has a pathetic significance which, in the light of after events, sets it apart among the unconscious sadnesses of history. The eternal shadow that had fallen so deeply over Aldrich the previous winter was to return early the following year. Though without premonition of the final curtain, Mr. Platt was within six months of his own end.

"I do not know where to address you," he wrote, "but I think you will get this from Boston. You are probably at Warwick, which place with all its beauties I can just see as I write—the bay and the sails and yachts, the shrubs and the flowers and the garden, and the house and the porch—it is a beautiful picture!" [36]

As the campaigns—both senatorial and presidential—drew to a close the cry everywhere was for money.[37] Expenses were piling up mountain high. At times the financial shrift was well-nigh desperate. Clerical forces proved inadequate for emergencies.

Mr. Aldrich was tided over, at least once, by one of those pleasant little instances of returning legislative favors which give an ironical cast to so much of politics. There had arisen a swift need for distributing a new flood of campaign literature. Mr. Aldrich, who was then at Washington, wired the chairman of his literary bureau of Providence, only to find that it was physically impossible for him to put 5,000 pamphlets into the mails in the time desired. His clerical force was inadequate. To the amazement of the chairman the pamphlets came to him in good season, addressed for mailing in unformed childish hands. They had been addressed by children of the parochial schools of Washington. This was by way of grateful return for the activities of Senator Aldrich the previous winter, when he had secured legislation friendly to the Indian Mission Schools of the Roman Church.[38]

The problem of money was constantly in Aldrich's mind as a national, no less than as a local, manager. With Governor Crane he was the mainstay of the National Committee getting funds from Conservative sources.[39] In the closing weeks of the campaign he was the chief reassurance, says his secretary, of the timid among the New York Republicans.

At the same moment his very opposite, La Follette, was working for Roosevelt's election with equal zeal. He had the same personal interest that Aldrich had. It was a foregone conclusion that if La Follette carried Wisconsin, he would go to the Senate the following year.

At last November came. Mr. Aldrich carried Rhode Island for the Conservatives as a Republican. Mr. La Follette carried Wisconsin for the Radicals as a Republican. Mr. Roosevelt, whom both sides claimed as their firm hope and reliance, was elected President as a Republican.

A pretty kettle of fish!

CHAPTER XVI

COUP D'ETAT

Why had not Aldrich foreseen the dangerous situation in which the Conservatives now found themselves? Why had he not opposed more strenuously the fatuous decisions of the Elder Statesmen that May day in his committee room?

One of his main characteristics resists the elusive medium of words. The closer one gets to this veiled statesman of the background, who for all his mystery was so great a power, the more one is conscious of his difference from his fellows. His utter disregard of verbiage is but the starting point of difference. His disregard of the crowd is also relatively a superficial matter. Deeper, far deeper, than those things lie the real distinctions.

Observing the surface qualities, shallow people might call him cynical. But cynicism is just the note that closer observers never find in him. His geniality was a spiritual feature. It was also a constant. One day when the Senate had listened to a very able but vindictive speech, Aldrich said to the speaker, "That was very fine, Senator, but it was a pity to put any bitterness into it."

He never laid up resentment. If a man betrayed him, he put him out of his mind, sponged out the image of him as if it never had existed. He told his children, time and again, that malice and revenge are futile things which never justify their existence.

His lack of malice, his geniality, his inability to remember antagonism after it had ceased, these three characteristics always are his distinguishing marks. The trio take so many forms, they are so obviously derived from the very bases of his nature, that one seeks a unifying source.

Destiny still had in store for Aldrich three political combats of first magnitude. One is directly traceable to the equivocation of the May conference, to the ambiguous situation in which as a consequence the Republican party was now placed. The other two present the same problem with regard to Aldrich's make-up that the first presents—always the same disregard of certain elements of danger by which lesser characters were thrown into dismay!

The deepest difference between him and the others is in what might be called the spiritual aspect of the belief that the mass of the people are not the final sovereign. Those others wanted to accept it but were a little afraid to do so because they had no faith in anything but their own abilities as the means of compelling the people. There was lacking in them, in spite of superficial appearances, that reminiscence of the seventeenth century, and of the Lord General and his proud superiority to the popular will, which was in Aldrich. The clew that unifies Aldrich and makes him explicable, is the idea that his perfect composure in the face of an adverse multitude is due to the belief that there are forces mightier than the people, mightier than himself, dim but irresistible compulsions, which in the long run shape this world. Politically, economically, in the condition of the United States at the opening of the twentieth century, he thought he knew what those powers had decreed. The temper of the evolutionist, the temper of the late Victorian rationalist, was shot through—as so often in that brilliant age—by a long descended Puritanism, which had passed into solution, which was recognizable only in its effects, in the color it gave to a mental compound.

Aldrich read widely in the literature of his day, but was not much given to poetry. It was a pity. He would have enjoyed Matthew Arnold—his serenity, his relentlessness, his disbelief in the crowd, his Puritanism (never more real than when he was denying it), his faith in a destiny "Man did not make and cannot mar."

A frame of mind that produces great powers of endurance, that is incomparable in attack (assuming that it is permeated with energy as in the case of Aldrich), but that sometimes takes too lightly the problems of the council board.

And this brings us back to the moment and to the question—

Who had gambled well, the Radicals or the Conservatives?

All eyes were fixed on the President seeking an answer.

Mr. Platt was deeply worried. His voluminous correspondence is a sure reflection of the varying points of view of the whole conservative and semi-conservative world of his day. In November and December 1904, it abounds in startled warnings that something is going to happen, that the country is hysterical, that all sorts of hopes are centring rather wildly on the President.

While Mr. Aldrich was the general of his party, Mr. Platt was its father confessor. These confessional letters of the close of 1904 range all the way from mere party strategy, on the one hand, to blunt self interest on the other. "I look forward with a great deal of apprehension to the action of the fifty-ninth Congress with more than one hundred Republican majority in the House of Representatives, for you and I are both aware it will be extremely difficult to satisfy so large a majority, for every one of the members from hitherto Democratic districts will feel the need of appropriations for their districts as a means of holding them Republican."[1]

One of the frankest of these letters had been sent to the President and by him was sent to Platt. By way of exhibiting the strange complex of interests animating large groups of Americans at that critical moment, nothing could be better. Having visited the West, especially the tanners and the leather manufacturers of Chicago, a belt maker wrote:

The Shoe and Leather Trade stood loyally by the administration at the last election believing that the friends of protection for American labor will understand best how to adjust the schedules of the tariff without injury to the general prosperous condition of the country, but they are indignant at the claim made by some protectionists, that the result of the last election was an indorsement of the "stand pat" policy of the Republican party. This is not true and these gentlemen deceive themselves. They should understand that the last election was an indorsement of the efficient administration and its Executive by the whole American people.

Already extensive plans are being made for a vigorous campaign on the tariff question. These western men are in dead earnest, they express most implicit confidence in the President and believe they will receive fair treatment at his hands. Tariff revision is the prevailing sentiment in the West at this time.[2]

This letter with its shrewd mixture of industrial self-interest and sectional feeling pointed the way the Republicans were doomed to go until at last East and West fought it out and tore the party to pieces in the fury of 1909.

Mr. Platt was fully aware of the unstable equilibrium of the hour. His clear old eyes, for all the petulance that was gathering behind them, saw things as they were. Like his friend Aldrich he had no illusions and no fear, but unlike Aldrich he could not accept danger with a jaunty delight in it. He could not have quoted honestly as Aldrich could have done:

> And if the path be dangerous known,
> The danger's self is lure alone.

He summed up the problem of the moment, saying: "What is to be done now with our victory is a pretty serious question. It was a tremendous plurality for Roosevelt, but it does not mean that it can always be depended upon in future elections. When Massachusetts could elect a Democratic governor, Rhode Island come near to it, two or three Western States could do it, and when other Republican governors had to get in by the skin of their teeth, it shows the votes that were given to us this time may not be held always, so, what we are to do is a very serious problem."[3]

This acknowledgment of the personal character of Roosevelt's success might have been further demonstrated by quoting the figures of the Rhode Island vote. While the President's majority was 16,706, the majority for Governor Utter, the Aldrich candidate, was only 856.[4]

In the anxious mood that was becoming chronic with Mr.

Platt it was natural enough for him to write to Aldrich: "The Rhode Island election came out all right, thanks to your taking charge of the job, I think. That must be true so far as Utter is concerned. If you had not, Garvin would have beaten him. The drift to Roosevelt was so great that we would have carried the (presidential) election anyway —committees or no committees: but the question is, what are we going to do with our victory! It worries me. I think I shall go down to Washington the last of the week for a day or two. Shall probably see the President. I wish you could see him with me. I am beginning now to ask the opposition question, 'What will we do next?'" [5]

The Allisonian chickens were coming home to roost. That evasive temper which had prevailed the previous May, at the meeting in Aldrich's committee room, which had freed the President's hands on every essential matter—the temper which contrasted so sharply with the temper of Aldrich's speech to the young Republicans—that temper was now to reap its sowing. Whatever Mr. Platt had thought about it, then, he now saw what had happened. Despite the menacing voices out of the West, he was for standing firm and taking plenty of time. Between the lines of this letter to Aldrich we can see that he is afraid the President may lose his head; but not as yet has he any suspicion that he may be going to change sides. His letter closes with an amusing little detail of his powerful friend.

Are you going to Europe? I rather hope not, because we want you pretty badly now. If you are not going, where can you and I meet for a little talk about the situation?

You never do answer letters, but I wish you would sit right down and answer this.

Before this letter reached him, Aldrich, passing through Washington called on the President.[6] Who can doubt that Mr. Roosevelt in the full glory of his tremendous personal victory, was delightful. He was so eager to have the Conservative leader on his side that he did not observe how coolly guarded were his visitor's remarks. To the President's buoyant declaration that "Some tariff legislation was necessary during his second term," Aldrich answered, "Possibly." Writing of this interview to Platt, Aldrich said "I agree fully with you that if there is to be any legislation it should be done in the regular way with only an informal agreement as to the subjects to be considered. 'Possibly' in this way we may secure action along certain lines that would be beneficial." [7] This remark was an allusion to the possibility of a special session the following spring which Aldrich had advised the President not to consider.

Apparently, in their interview, each man slightly misunderstood the other. On reaching home Aldrich found there Platt's letter; wired to him "I sympathize fully with your wishes and fears";[8] and the next day wrote him at length.

I am going to obey your injunction and answer your letter, although I realize I am a very poor correspondent. I was obliged to go South right after election to look after a railroad in North Carolina that some friends of mine are interested in. I stopped at Washington for a few hours on my way North and made a hurried and unsatisfactory call on the President. He told me that he was thinking about an extra session but that nothing would be done about matters of importance until we were all together.

Aldrich wanted a meeting of the Four at Washington before the meeting of Congress. "I have postponed my trip to Europe until a more convenient season later on." [9]

Two days passed. He was surprised to hear from Platt that the President understood "that you had indicated that you thought something would have to be done in the way of changes" in the tariff.[10]

It was this letter which called forth Aldrich's account of his interview with the President. His reply also revealed that he had closed his mind against the outcry from the West—an attitude which he maintained with disastrous result throughout the gathering of the sectional-economic storm, even until his last parliamentary victory in 1909.

I should have said off hand that there was absolutely *no demand* for tariff revision and was greatly surprised at the President's feeling and I am yet at a great loss to know where the pressure comes from.[11]

If Aldrich could have read the President's Engagement Book, or had paid more attention to the newspapers, or had waded through Platt's correspondence, he would not have changed his course but he might not have been at a loss to know where the pressure came from. The day Platt wrote him upon the President's interpretation of their interview, Mr. Roosevelt was closeted with "Governors La Follette, Van Sant, and Cummins." [12]

Some day, when some very daring biographer attacks the great subject of Roosevelt, his most brilliant chapter will account for the inner life of this extraordinary man, during the ten months between his interval of distrust of Aldrich and his annual message of December, 1904. That curious official life by Mr. Bishop—which ought to be called *The Concealment of Theodore Roosevelt*—is silent. The *Autobiography* for obvious reasons, lifts no veils. It was written too soon after the event. One has nothing for it but to guess. Why, at this particular moment, did he choose to surprise the world by making the bold move which established him at one stroke as the Roosevelt of History? Hitherto, except for his courage and his marvellous personal influence, his genius had not disclosed itself. Now, suddenly, by means of the message, he revealed his insight as a political strategist. A great captain had spoken—suddenly, without warning, in trumpet tones.

It has been vehemently asserted that Mr. Roosevelt in this famous message boldly attacked the whole system of capitalism as it then existed in America. It has been asserted with equal vehemence that this interpretation is mere Roosevelt propaganda, and he and the Conservatives at the end as at the beginning and at all other times occupied the same ground.

Both views are fallacious. Mr. Roosevelt had watched with keen eyes the rising tide of discontent. He was fully conscious that his amazing personal victory was due in part to the "independent Democrats." [13] He must have calcu-

lated that the radical Republicans and the independent
Democrats, if somehow they could be yoked together,
would far outweigh the Conservatives and would render the
regular Democrats ineffective.

He saw—who could not help seeing!—that there was in
the country a passion of animosity toward wealth. La Follette, Cummins, the independent Democrats, all had the
same shibboleths, all talked of trusts as iniquities and of
corporations as their instruments. All were for making the
railroads—interstate commerce legislation—a test case.
Very well! But none of them had formulated any issue that
brought things to a head nationally. All they had been able
to think of by way of a programme was somewhat hysterical denunciation of the favoritism shown by the railroads to
the rich in the way of rebates and special agreements. But
the Elkins Act, forbidding rebates, was supposed to have
put an end to all that. And the Elkins Act was a Conservative measure. The railways themselves had backed it—
weary as they were of playing into the hands of the great
merchants.

When and how the last feather was dropped upon the
trembling scale of the President's resolution has not been
disclosed. Was it such a trifle as a paragraph in that letter
from the leather manufacturer, a Republican elector in the
State of New York, who appealed to him—or did he threat-
en him?—in the name of the Shoe and Leather Trade?
"The Shoe and Leather Trade suffers severely from the
duty placed on hides in the Dingley tariff. Tanners and
leather manufacturers in general complain that the price of
hides is entirely controlled by the Chicago packers, and that
the duty of 15 per cent has operated for the benefit of
the packers alone." [14]

For reasons not altogether clear Mr. Roosevelt decided to
cut the tariff out of his message[15] and to that extent disappointed the worthy manufacturer who wished to teach him
his business. But he was far too astute to rest there. The
real heart of the leather makers' protest was a class distinction; the small manufacturers were not getting their share

of protection. Generalizing this idea, he had the clew to the particular sort of discontent that lay back of the literature of protest, back of La Follette in Wisconsin, back of Cummins in Iowa, back of the independent Democrats everywhere. If he could focus this generality on a specific proposition that would draw a line sharply between the interests of the rich and the interests of the merely well-to-do, all the new forces of politics would be his to command.

When the message appeared, silent on the subject of the tariff, it blew a clarion peal on the subject of interstate commerce. But the peal was something totally new. Hitherto, when a railway rate was challenged before the Interstate Commerce Commission the old rate remained in force during all the long and tortuous process of the litigation to determine its "reasonableness." Thus the burden of the situation had been thrown upon the shippers—a numerous class among whom the small merchants formed the vast majority. These shippers might be assumed to represent the same great class that the Shoe and Leather Trade at Chicago represented while the railroads represented the class symbolized by the great packers. By a stroke of genius Mr. Roosevelt had seen how to proclaim himself the champion of the well-to-do against the rich, and to do so in the most effective way possible—by means of a concrete proposal. His message called for the restoration to the Interstate Commerce Commission of powers that had been granted in the original act but that since had been taken from it by the courts. That is, the commission should be given power "To decide, subject to judicial review, what shall be a reasonable rate" but also—and this was the great thing!— "the ruling of the Commission to take effect immediately and to obtain unless and until it is reversed by the court of review." [16]

To take effect immediately! To shift the burden of the situation from the well-to-do to the rich. To proclaim to the country that with the Shoe and Leather Trade and with the small shipper and with the literature of protest, lay the President's heart. The significance of this surprising move was at once perceived. The Radicals greeted it with cries of joy. Mr. Chandler, now wholly the Radical, who was begging Mr. La Follette to come East as a senator[17] wrote jubilantly to the President:

The railroad companies have no intention of submitting to your proposition. . . . They intend to fight it tooth and nail. It has been their contention for 25 years that the companies shall fix their rates of fare and freight and that the shippers shall pay them until at the end of long and costly litigations they procure decisions that shall change the rates. And the hope for that is futile. The shippers are not numerous enough, nor powerful enough, nor rich enough to obtain relief. . . . You proposed a crushing blow at railroad extortion and a triumphant blow for the people.[18]

According to the melodramatic views of the literary reformers of the time, there should have followed a ruthless political war, the President on the one side and the Conservatives on the other. But nothing of the sort occurred. And yet one can forgive the literary people—the *McClure* coterie and the others—for being confused, for getting things somewhat mixed.

American politics that winter had three mysteries, Roosevelt, Cannon, and Aldrich.

What was Roosevelt's ultimate purpose? The more we know of his course, the less explicit it appears. Though he had thrown his great bomb into the Conservative camp, he had not bowed down before the threats of the Wisconsin Radicals. He made appointments there which were in the interests of Senator Spooner. Presently a furious Radical sounded a warning.

It seems wonderfully strange to me that President Roosevelt cannot see the hand writing on the wall, and fails to recognize what we have done up here in Wisconsin. He is not popular here to-day; except for the fact that he has taken a stand on the rate question which is too moderate to suit us.[19]

Was it that he had some other phase of policy still closer to his heart than trust busting? Was his one true love, after all, international affairs?—in which already, secretly, he had played so great a part! And did he, while seizing the full power of a Tribune of the People, aim nevertheless to propitiate the Senate, to hold out an olive branch preparatory to thrusting upon the Senate and on the Nation a vigorous foreign policy? These are the questions that make his course a mystery, these and the fact that he had negotiated a batch of arbitration treaties that were about to be sent to the Senate for ratification, and the further fact that he was deep in curious and somewhat domineering negotiations with San Domingo.

That olive branches in this connection were not mere words was shown by the conference which he called at the White House in the first week of the new year. It was a Conservative Conference. Present, the Four, also Cannon, and others.[20] He told them that he wanted a great navy, that he would "not oppose the views of a majority of both houses on the tariff," but that he would "continue to urge Interstate Commerce legislation." [21]   Again the question, why?

And Cannon—what game was he playing? A bill had appeared in the House—the Esch-Townshend Bill—embodying the President's recommendations on Interstate Commerce. In time it was to pass the House with but seventeen votes in opposition. Cannon, the sly Conservative, did not oppose it. And yet, he took good care that it did not reach the Senate until too late in the session for there to be a ghost of a chance of action upon it. One casts about, hither and yon, seeking in vain any evidence of an agreement between Aldrich and Cannon whereby the bill should be held back and Aldrich might free his mind of it for this winter. Such agreements, at Washington, are not recorded. But every one knows that they happen.

Last, most mysterious of the three, Aldrich. He was curiously cavalier in his political activities this winter. As to just where he stood he was frank enough. Another Pure Food Bill had been introduced, and Aldrich treated it with contempt. His attitude toward all the business of the season was—what did it matter?

In December he voted a few times. But after New Year he did not once participate in a vote. How difficult to suppress the idea that in taking things so lightly he knew—either through secret information or through his own matchless power of congressional analysis—that nothing was going to happen.

And yet such great things were toward. When, in middle January Aldrich was unable to attend a great political dinner given by the President[22] the country was ringing with the controversy over the Esch-Townshend Bill. The war of the classes was on. At the same time the new arbitration treaties were beginning to be sharply scrutinized. A little later, San Domingo became a subject of furious debate. Had the President exceeded his powers, negotiating for a settlement of the debt of the black republic? Watchful Democrats were quick to assert that he had. Many Republicans drew long faces and were afraid that their enemies had the better of the argument.

But Aldrich shrugged his shoulders. Twice, in later January, he had conferences with the President[23]—one, when the San Domingo contentions were in full swing—but what these conferences were about—who knows?

The one plausible conclusion is that he was convinced that the session was predestined to futility. Futile things were things he would not take seriously. He must have laughed gaily when his dear friend, Platt, grumbled that "the great victory in November has stirred up every fool crank in the United States, and we are going to have lots of trouble." [24]

Before the session was at an end, Aldrich had slipped away from Washington and had gone to Europe. For once, Platt felt that his friend had deserted him. A miserable farce of an impeachment trial had been forced upon the Senate, and Platt much against his will was drafted to preside.[25] Very tired, feeling his years, he gave rein to his irritability. "It was inexcusable for Aldrich to go off to Europe as he did, but he is always doing inexcusable things." [26]

In a way Mr. Platt's unhappiness had the force of premonition. For once, Mr. Aldrich had trusted his sense of things a point too far. Though his forecast as to the rate bill was fully justified by the event—the bill was buried in committee—the treaties produced a crisis.

The mystery of the President's purposes again shrouds the story. There were provisions in the arbitration treaties which placed in his hands wide freedom of international arrangement; and these treaties were proposed to the Senate at a moment when any one could see that the President was feeling out in various directions for extensions of the power of his office. The haunting question arose: was he aiming to subordinate the Senate to the Executive?

The question broke party ranks. It was at once plain that an overwhelming majority of senators irrespective of party were against extending the power of the Executive —or permitting what they thought was such an extension.

And then the President did a remarkable thing. He wrote a fierce letter to the chairman of the Committee on Foreign Relations commanding the Senate to pass the treaties. The reason governing his course? At the moment when the country was all agog over the class issues precipitated by the rate bill, when the literature of protest was successfully persuading the middle class that all the rich were heartless tyrants and that the Senate was their organ, was it strategy that led the Executive to manœuvre the Senate into an attitude of opposition? The question is inescapable; the answer, still to seek. The Senate rose to the President's challenge almost unanimously. It altered the treaties and the President refused to accept them.

But this was not all. The San Domingo snarl has been the subject of sage debate. Mr. Justice Gray at the request of Platt—who was trying manfully to save the President's face, while his enemies shouted that he meant to play the autocrat in the Caribbean—wrote learnedly upon the legal precedents by which the President's action might be justified.[27] So did another high authority, Doctor John Bassett Moore. Both of them missed the heart of the matter. It was threefold.

First: the President had intended to make this country a

receiver, so to speak, for the liquidation of the debt of San Domingo, without asking leave of the Senate and had been forced by the outcry of the Democrats led by Senator Bacon[28] to alter his course and to ask the Senate to approve a treaty empowering him to do what he wished.

Second: this was not, as the learned authors seemed to think, merely a speculative question of constitutional right to be considered *in vacuo,* but also a specific question of political strategy conditioned in every detail by the other movements of the hour.

Third: whatever were the President's obligations before he had evoked the co-operation of the Senate, he lost control of the situation and put his conduct in a new perspective the moment he encased it in a treaty and submitted the treaty to the Senate for ratification.

The curious and diverting experiences of the San Domingo Improvement Company which had been organized in the United States to "run" the black republic financially, its failure to make the job pay, the entanglement of American interests with those European creditors who were trying to do the same thing, had produced a San Domingo crisis two years before, and had led President Roosevelt to intervene informally. After an unsatisfactory arbitration in 1904, came his more formal intervention at the opening of 1905.

Senator Bacon now demanded a general inquiry into what the President had done these two years past. His resolution amounted to asking the Senate for a vote of lack of confidence in the government. Hence, the Conservative senators were put in a difficult position. Most, if not all, of them agreed with Bacon that there had arisen "very grave questions which involve in the highest degree the most serious and fundamental prerogatives of the Senate," its right to participate in the making of treaties. At the same time they saw the danger of playing into the hands of the Democrats in so intricate a political moment. They could not make up their minds just what to do. Spooner took one view, Platt took another.

The feebleness and uncertainty of their course was further evidence that their general was not on the field. During the period we are now entering, Aldrich and Bacon are foemen worthy of each other's steel. As sheer skill in parliamentary tactics, we shall applaud what is done by both when we come to the subtle deftness of Bacon and the invincible audacity of Aldrich in the last battle over the famous Rate Bill of 1906.

The Senate refused to ratify but neither did it vote want of confidence and the session came to an end.

And now, the unbelievable—from the political, not the legal, point of view—came to pass. Ignoring the refusal of the Senate, the Tribune of the People, on his own authority, put the treaty which the Senate would not ratify into force. *The Review of Reviews,* edited by his friend, Doctor Albert Shaw, sang a pæan of praise and denounced the Senate because of its "refusal to do what was expected of it." [29]

CHAPTER XVII

THE MAN ALDRICH

I

MR. ALDRICH was having a delightful time in Italy. The hill towns were his happy hunting-ground. With grown daughters who had something of their father's joy in the lark, he wandered the unusual paths, spending many hours in little shops, anywhere, everywhere, hunting for objects of art that might catch his fancy and making friends with the shopkeepers. He was an adept in such adventures because he had no condescension toward these chance acquaintances. A shopkeeper to him was always a human being—just as interesting as most senators of the United States, and always more interesting than some.

It was a pleasant wander that filled the months from late February to the end of June. His health was not what it had been and the Senate was beginning to wear on him. But he was still elastic, with an enormous reserve of spirits. This journey gave him back his strength. With the serenity that was his forte he passed from such occupations as occurred in the hill towns to others of a vastly different sort. Easter was spent at Rome—and Rome at Easter was one of his delights. He saw much of his friend Pierrepont Morgan. Both of them had audiences with the King of Italy. One of the unfailing characteristics of Aldrich was his inability to be impressed by mere station. Previous to his audience, a member of the American embassy had grown solicitous lest the Senator break some of the rules of the occasion. He begged Mr. Aldrich to remember that he must not ask questions of His Majesty, he must not forget to leave the room backward. With sympathetic attention the Senator listened and promised. You would have thought that he had his lesson by heart.

When he returned from the audience his family were curious. Perhaps they suspected. Had he remembered his instructions?

His eyes gleamed with mischief. "I asked him as many questions as I wanted, mainly about strikes in Italy."

What about leaving the room?

"I walked out without any concern just as I would from any gentleman's room."

He greatly admired the King because of his "poise."

An audience with the Pope was an incident of the same visit. Mr. Aldrich was deeply interested in the feelings revealed upon the faces of the Catholics present; he received His Holiness's blessing as reverently as if he were one of them.

The services at St. Peter's, now as whenever he was in Rome, delighted him.[1]

Apparently, a semi-official undercurrent in this visit to Rome has escaped history. Interesting lost thoughts undoubtedly filled the historical silences of that spring when the devil and all was getting ready to break loose all over the world, when Germany and the other powers were fencing sharply in Morocco. Some of these unrecorded matters may be guessed from a letter of the American ambassador, Henry A. White, thanking Aldrich for having brought about an interview with the papal secretary of state, Cardinal Merry del Val. It was desirable that the interview should escape publicity.

Why it should happen at all, and why it should interest Mr. Aldrich—except as a favor to Mr. White—becomes plain enough as the ambassador in a rambling delightful letter tells Aldrich what he and the cardinal talked about, how he said to him that "while it might be irregular and impossible for European ambassadors to the Quirinal with their international complications to meet him, it was not only proper but very desirable in view of the large and important section of our people belonging to his faith who are unanimously in favor of the friendly relations now subsisting, that the American ambassador and he should know each other and meet occasionally, to which he cordially assented." Altogether he thinks Aldrich "will feel that the meeting was a success." [2]

Many reports came to the roving Senator that spring, when there was such bitter excitement in his own country, and when Japan and Russia were at the cannon's mouth in Siberia. It may be assumed that he did not trouble himself to read a furious article by Mr. Lincoln Steffens on "What Aldrich Represents." Though Mr. Steffens was once among the chief apostles of the literature of protest, it is not certain that his writings have found a permanent place in English literature and perhaps an ungrateful country no longer remembers him. But there was a time when his name was one to conjure with. He was a violent partisan of Mr. La Follette. In the fury of the Wisconsin civil war, the previous year, he had taken part enthusiastically with his hero. It was his fixed belief that Mr. Aldrich was the devil. He elaborated this vigorous conception in the essay on "What Aldrich Represents." [3]

Mr. Steffens, with his ardent excitability was not the sort that would have impressed Mr. Aldrich one way or the other. But Aldrich would have been much amused could he have seen, the next month, a letter from Mr. Bryan to Mr. Chandler thanking him for renewing his subscription to Mr. Bryan's paper, *The Commoner,* and exhibiting that delightful vein of humor with which the lovers of melodrama have not been able to credit Mr. Bryan.

For the last eight years our party fights have furnished about all the excitement we have had in politics, but if I mistake not, your party is entering upon a struggle by the side of which our contest will seem a love-feast.[4]

There is grim dramatic propriety in the re-entrance into the Aldrich story, even in this casual way, of that great figure which had once been the chief adversary, which was destined to come slowly, but irresistibly back into the central position, which was at last to play the rôle of the destroying Fate. As to Mr. Bryan's thought this spring, watching from afar the gathering of the enemies around his great opponent, with its note of other-worldly amusement, as if he were murmuring to himself, the Kingdom of God and His Saints is not of this world—how delightful it would be to know something of all that!

Considering the value in human life of sheer amusement, it is a pity that Mr. Aldrich did not see another letter which he would have relished, but which went to its rest deep among the Chandler papers. La Follette, now chosen as the junior Senator from Wisconsin wrote:

I have been repeatedly warned that I have already been disposed of; that the "hole is prepared" for me, and the cover ready; that at the end of four years of Senatorial suppression—already arranged for—the Senior Senator (Spooner) will come back for his reelection and convince the people of Wisconsin that the State has "one Senator and a vacancy." [5]

But nothing of this sort could break the gaiety of Mr. Aldrich's mood when, like a boy out of school, he had escaped from Washington for a holiday. It is possible that negotiations with Germany over tariff adjustments may have broken in upon his free time but no direct evidence that they did has been found. Possibly too, he had some roundabout influence upon the confidential conversations that at last produced the conference at Algeciras.[6] If these things occurred he took them lightly. He could not take lightly the news which he received toward the end of April. Mr. Platt, tired and in low spirits, had attended the funeral of Senator Hawley, had stood too long bare headed in bleak air, and had gone home to develop a cold which quickly became serious. He was not able to rally and in a few days the end came. From Rome Mr. Aldrich cabled "We are shocked and pained by the sad news. I have lost a dear friend, the best man I ever knew." [7]

II

Aldrich had passed a dividing line. The inner party within the Republican party had done the same. But neither of them knew it. Aldrich was not the sort that dramatizes himself, that gave any thought to his own stages of development. He took himself as simply as he took events and the weather. Here they were; he had not made them— neither himself, nor the clouds, nor the sunshine—but he knew how to get something out of them: why do any prating or attitudinizing?

The generation to which he belonged, when it was not weak, was not given to self-analysis, still less to self-revelation. The age of the diarists had gone by. None of the Four have left a record of the last stage of their fraternity. But, reasoning back from what took place in the twelve months following Platt's death, it is plain that even before his death their association had been getting ready to dissolve. A question insists on arising—was it the peculiar nature of Mr. Platt that was the cement in their combination? The quickness with which, following his death, a cleft in their organization appeared moves one to ask— what do you make of that? Within the twelve months, Aldrich and Allison were on opposite sides of the greatest dispute in which both were ever involved at the same time.

When the fight came, over the railroad policy of the President, they parted company. The lower stratum of the Conservative party was also divided. The breach opened slowly. Mr. Dolliver, that same Dolliver of Iowa who had attracted Blaine's notice, who had become the loyal follower of Mr. Allison, went over to the President at once. Mr. Beveridge and others on whom Aldrich hitherto had relied shifted their allegiance more gradually. In connection with Mr. Beveridge, when he had finally declared himself, there is one of the few flashes of temper recorded of Aldrich. Under his breath, on the floor of the Senate, he snapped at his former lieutenant, "We'll get you for this." [8]

Subsequent writings, especially the autobiography of Mr. La Follette, make it appear that Mr. Allison had been drifting away from his old friends for a considerable time. Sadly, he had concluded that the new forces were irresistible; sadly, in his heart, he recanted; he forswore his old allegiance. He turned his face to the wall, though no one, probably except his devoted disciple, Dolliver, knew the depth of his loss of faith in Aldrich, nor the completeness of his silent apostasy.

The Wise Old Man read the handwriting on the wall with tragic accuracy. He gauged the strength of the new forces of popular wrath. To use another biblical image, the cloud the size of a man's hand was visible on the horizon; it was the size of a huge hand and might have suggested a big stick. In literal speech, a renaissance of democracy was the coming note. It was to be the counter revolution after the renaissance of aristocracy. And Allison, so wise, so deep, so responsive to popular influences, felt in his bones that the powers which had created his own day, of which the Four had been the interpreters, were no longer in the ascendant. For him, for his lieutenant Dolliver, for many another cautious soul, the cry to them out of the rising wind was to shorten sail, very soon to be prepared to go upon a new tack, to change their whole course.

Mr. Allison had none of Aldrich's quiet enjoyment of a fight. Neither had he the Cromwellian temper that was ever Aldrich's temper: " 'Tis the general good of the kingdom we ought to consult. That's the question, what's for their good, not what pleases them." The new turns of event, the mandates of *vox populi*, were, for him, clear as the roll of thunder on a near horizon, *vox Dei*.

Aldrich was precisely the opposite. What did it matter to him whether the forces that had once sustained him would continue to sustain him? There are more things in heaven and earth, Horatio. Aldrich existed not to express those forces but to use them. The artist in politics! What he would express came out of his own thoughts. It had its validity because his mind approved. The very seal of Cromwell was upon it all. Not what pleases the audience but what fulfils the vision of the maker of new things, the artist.

Consummate strategist, he would turn and double, advance or retreat, as the exigencies of battle might dictate.

But it was only strategy. The goal was fixed. To break the enemy's line, never to surrender; to fall back if necessary, but only with a view to keeping his forces intact; or, if driven to the wall, to take his last position in such a way as to enable him to make terms—these were the tactics of Aldrich, the political general.

If it be a true guess that the personality of Platt had made possible the conjunction of two such different characters as Aldrich and Allison, the passing of that apparently simple but really subtle nature grows in significance the more one reflects. Was it Platt who had kept Aldrich from going too far, who had tempered his disdain of the crowd, who had reconciled aristocracy with the middle class? Was it Platt who had inspired Allison to hold out as long as he did against the changing winds in Iowa, who had kept him year after year from cutting his cables of Conservatism and going adrift upon the new currents that were revealing the inaccuracy of the old chart of the political seas?

Be that as it may, Platt's death marks the end of a chapter. It is the end of the period of the Four in more than a literal sense. It terminates the period when Aldrich is one of a group; it opens the period when he stands alone, a great and defiant figure, over-shadowing all his associates, the exponent of a political philosophy which now has the cards against it. The coming period was not destined to be long. Seven years, from 1905 to 1912, embraced it. But it includes three episodes of first importance. It rounds out and completely exhibits his character.

No statesman, in all his policies, ever issued from his inner self with more unfaltering certainty than did Aldrich. His distinction among statesmen—especially American statesmen—is right there. It is a distinction that Democracy generally lacks. The limited experience and the scant education of the bulk of mankind make them seldom appreciative of the true issues in government, the ones that are atmospheric and pervasive, that are not susceptible of dogmatic statement. This is but natural. It is the defect of the qualities of government of the people and by the people—

at least, as that form of government has operated in modern times. Democracy thinks in terms of specific issues. Aristocracy, when it is vital and enlightened, thinks in terms of atmospheric issues—the temper of society; the quality of the human product; the tendency of institutions to bring forth this type or that; whether the right of initiative belongs inherently to one sort of human or to another. The defects of aristocracy are of course obvious. Aldrich did not escape them. The hierarchical conception of society is defensible only on certain assumptions and these assumptions constitute a class point of view. What distinguishes Aldrich is the perfect honesty of his convictions, his refusal to play tricks with them; his boldness in nailing his colors when strategy was no longer available; the completeness and logicality of his deliberate trains of thought.

The very appearance of the man asserted both his independence and his subtlety. The powerful figure, the air of complete self-reliance, but with it the absence of anything like self-assertion; the freedom from egoism in the ordinary sense of the word. He was so much the man of power that he never thought about his power; it was natural to him, like breathing. People who watched him in action felt this. In the high tide of senatorial debate he radiated strength. But he also radiated an influence that is not so easily described. His affability—recorded in a crowd of anecdotes—his humor equally well recorded, the gaiety of his fighting mood, the power to hold his ideas lightly, the general effect which he made of being too securely placed even to be troubled by his own defeat—an effect that was emphasized by contrast when once in a blue moon he glowed with anger: all this was part of the mystery of the man; because of it he stands out among the drab souls that were so conspicuous in the politics of his day, like a tall flame in a windless air. It was this immeasurable reserve, which every one about him felt but could not describe, that led the painter, Zorn, to say to one of Aldrich's close associates: "Of all the sitters I ever had Senator Aldrich is the most difficult because of the expression of his eyes—it is so hard to get." Virtually, the same comment was made by another gifted painter, Cecilia Beaux, who did not attempt his portrait. A clever newspaper man who interviewed him compared the atmosphere about him to the tense alertness of a thoroughbred race horse.

It was his subtlety behind his strength that inspired an expression of opinion made to the same friend, Mr. W. A. Slade, sometime secretary of the Monetary Commission, in whom Zorn confided. Mr. Slade had read to Aldrich these sentences from Cardinal Newman: "In public life a man of elevated mind does not make his own self tell upon others, simply or entirely. He must act with other men; he cannot select his objects or pursue them by the methods and practices of minds less elevated than his own. He can only do what he feels to be second best. He labours at a venture, prosecuting measures so large or so complicated that their ultimate issue is uncertain." Mr. Slade says that "Aldrich affirmed his assent to Newman's statement, less with a phrase than with a look on his face that I can still see, these sixteen or seventeen years later. I felt as though I had Aldrich's own view, not Newman's." [9]

But this, to repeat, is incidental. It is abundantly evident in all he does. He believes in the reign of the enlightened few—Cromwell again—but he is so much the realist that he is willing to accept whatever terms circumstances impose upon him, to get his end in roundabout ways, whenever the clarity of his insight forbids the smashing blow. Nevertheless, he is happier when he can sweep aside all the views of the populace. There are times when he does so with a ruthlessness which the crowd calls despotic.

Never did a statesman have more unhesitating faith in natural selection. Part of his distinction, part of his significance in American history, is in this fact. In him, out of the very heart of democracy the impregnation of the evolutionary idea has given birth to a peculiar form of the aristocrat. Emerson—own brother in the speculative field to this typical American of the practical field—talked of "aristocracy with the doors open," of a social system in which it could be said of whomever had talent, *let him come in.* Emerson, the dreamer and optimist, thought only of the glorious opportunity in such a vision. His thought derived, in part, from the Romantic Movement and the Rights of Man. He had not encountered Darwin. Aldrich came a generation later. The romanticism of his inherited politics had received into its bosom the new precipitant, the terrible relentlessness of the doctrine of evolution. He held on to all that Emerson believed but added what Emerson temperamentally was estopped from contemplating. With him, it was not only, let talent come in, it was also, with equal firmness, let mediocrity stay out.

Perhaps there is no phase of statesmanship in democratic conditions that is more often at the root of things—though so often denied—than the question how rewards are to be distributed. One interpretation of Aldrich turns on this question. There are some who would have us believe that the clew to him was the acceptance of tradition in apportioning the rewards of our social-economic life, and that Roosevelt was a revolutionary in demanding a great part of those rewards for types of people who hitherto had scarcely shared in them. I insist that there is a confusion here between kind and degree. We are told that Roosevelt recognized intellect, originality, every sort of public virtue—that an inventor or a consumer, was as dear to him as a capitalist, and in politics more dear. But was Aldrich the man of many interests, the collector of art, the omnivorous reader, the respecter of intellect in every form, was he unresponsive to the demands of sheer mind? Surely not. The kinds of persons who were to share in the rewards of our economic system were the same in his mind as in Roosevelt's. There was where he differed from old-style aristocracy. Where he and Roosevelt differed was in the degree of the excellence they would recognize. Roosevelt, the aristocrat who had gone over to the plebs, was for recognizing in his distribution of economic spoil the less distinguished specimens of

each type as well as the highly gifted ones. Aldrich, the
evolutionary aristocrat, was for recognizing in a large way
only the large products, the men of talent, the men of
genius.

And back of this difference between these two great men
—each so truly a prodigy of the time, each so delightful to
the dispassionate observer because of the way he illumi-
nates the other by contrast—back of the difference in the
application of their beliefs lies the most fundamental of all
the issues of political science. What title has a given sort
of man to the share he demands in the control of society?
To this basic question, each of those political poles gave a
definite answer. Roosevelt, the untrammelled Romanticist,
was still the champion of the Rights of Man, could still
read Rousseau with a thrill, politically was untroubled by
Darwin. To him the title to social control was partly in the
mere fact of being a human soul, of being alive. Aldrich,
his Romanticism so profoundly transformed by the doctrine of natural selection, admitted no title to power except
achievement. With what measure ye mete it shall be mea-
sured to you again. By just the proportion in which you
lift yourself above the general level you are entitled to economic reward and to political power, but only by that proportion.

It is in this contrast of basic ideas—their atmospheric
qualities—far more than in any specific clash, any easily
formulated issue, that the significance of these bold men
and their historic duel really lies. So it is, often, in history.
Shallow people see a definite issue, or the lack of a definite
issue, and fancy that therein is a great battle, or no battle
at all. The atmospheric significance escapes them. But in
that significance the actual heart of the matter is generally
to be found.

In the first decade of the twentieth century, America
reached a parting of the ways. An inevitable conflict was
embodied in two of the most interesting figures our country
has produced. We are too close to them to anticipate the
verdict of history, to say which, in the light of after events,

will stand revealed as the true incarnation of the most potent force of his time.

To-day, interpreters of the era disagree. There are those who hold that the renaissance of arithmocratic democracy was not checked, that its temper, its atmosphere, will color the next chapter of our development. If this be so, Roosevelt was the victor.

There are others, equally keen, who say that the conservative renaissance was the real thing, that it has cleared the way for a reorganization of our social life, for new forms of rule based on economic realignment and the investiture of economic groups with governmental functions. If this be so, Aldrich was the victor.

To the disinterested lover of human life, the duel of those titans was a beautiful counterpoint of personalities, a splendid episode in the game of political war.

CHAPTER XVIII

CLEARING THE DECKS

ALDRICH was back in America at the opening of July and found much to think about. The Interstate Commerce Committee of the Senate had been conducting hearings on the rate problem. It was sharply divided in its views.[1] Mr. Tillman, one of the minority members of that committee, had written the chairman, Senator Elkins, very characteristically, that he was "not ready to participate in the farce of attending the meetings of the Interstate Commerce Committee and . . . watching the manœuvres of himself and his followers in the game of how not to do it." He was "with Roosevelt in the fight" and was watching "with keen interest and enjoyment to see the first round in the great contest of the President and the people against the Senate and the railroads next winter. . . ."[2] Hardly was Aldrich in the country again, when a letter from Elkins reviewed the situation forecasting a battle over a new rate bill, first in the committee, and then in the Senate. The people were behind the President in desiring to confer rate-making power on the commission.[3] From the Conservative point of view the situation was very grave. Active lobbying had begun. The railroads were trying to convince the public that honest enforcement of present laws was all that was needed while the American Anti-Trust League had assailed the committee with great earnestness.[4] The authors of the Esch-Townshend Bill were hard at work spreading their gospel in the West and in the magazines.[5] All the country was reading with bated breath two classics of the literature of protest—"Frenzied Finance," the confession of that superb financial plunger, Mr. Lawson; and the completed form of Miss Tarbell's "History of the Standard Oil Company." Both, doubtless, had helped to make it good politics for the Department of Justice to enter upon a season of "trust busting," which reached its peak in July when the Chicago Grand Jury indicted five corporations and seventeen individuals for participation in obnoxious practices connected with the beef traffic. So intense was the general fury against corporations that the railroads began to change their tactics. In the words of one of the shrewdest of Republican observers, "The railroad people have almost all changed over from the view of accepting action by the commission on a reasonable rate to a determination to fight it. . . ." He held the committee indirectly responsible for the present fury because it had allowed the impression to get abroad that the Senate did not intend to take any action at all. He thought the trouble could all be quieted, if it could be known that the Senate would consent to investing the commission with the rate-making power "and then have the courts decide within sixty days whether it is a reasonable or unreasonable rate." [6]

These were the views of Mr. Dodge expressed to Mr. Allison. Judging from subsequent events they were substantially the views of Mr. Aldrich. Whether Mr. Allison shared them is—as we shall see—a very different question. Again, one is thrown into the poetical vein and is reminded of the little rift within the lute. But of all that hereafter. The crucial matter in the late summer and early autumn of 1905 was the new form that the issue had taken as an outcome of the furious propaganda of the previous spring.

Again, Mr. Roosevelt and his undisclosed purposes form the heart of an enigma. Between the time when he sent to Congress the message of 1904 and the spring of 1905, a great change came over his thoughts.

Politics so often are a matter of words, not so much of their exact meanings as of their floating associations, their popular interpretation. The revolutionary controversy over setting up a new sort of railway commission had three stages ruled successively by three words—"reasonable," "confiscatory," and "constitutional." The "reasonable" stage of the controversy lifted its curtain with the President's proposal to vest in the commission the power to initiate a "reasonable" rate. He did not suggest—at that moment very few if any Americans were ready to suggest—that the commission should be the judge of its own reasonableness. In December, 1904, it was still generally assumed that even if the commission were given the great power asked for it, its judgment should be subject to review by another, by a presumably just and impartial power, by the courts. Therefore, Mr. Roosevelt's proposal had the strictly class significance which has been indicated. It was in the provision for putting the rate into immediate effect—the shifting of the burden from the middle class to the upper class—that he showed himself a political strategist of rare insight. That proposal created for him a personal party. In the eyes of many people that proposal remained to the end "the crux of the whole fight"—the new rate to be "defended by the whole power of the Attorney-General's department until a court destroys it." [7] "If we can carry that we can accomplish everything. If we do not carry that, substantially nothing will be accomplished." [8]

But sentiment moved fast in America between December, 1904, and May, 1905. In that interval when "Frenzied Finance" was but a symbol of the nation's mental pabulum, a much more extreme demand found voice. The bourgeoisie, narrowly speaking, found itself less impressive—or at least less domineering—than people of more extreme views. Most illuminating as a clew to the social-political distinctions of the time is the attitude of that very clever paper the New York *Nation*. At times *The Nation* could be as sharply antitrust as the most frenzied ornament of the literature of protest could desire. But it was very cool toward the President, and it searched with a relentless eye for the signs of revolutionary purpose in the literature of protest. The "History of the Standard Oil Company" had been promptly assailed by *The Nation* as being a partisan statement, purposely inflammatory. [9] In a word *The Nation* was pretty thoroughly the voice of the bourgeoisie in the old sense. It and all it stood for were a suggestive contrast to the new temper which swept a great part of the country in those months when Aldrich at Rome was amusing himself bringing about the meeting between Mr. White and the papal secretary of state.

Mr. Roosevelt, this while, decided to throw overboard the point of view represented by *The Nation*. He cast in his lot—temporarily, at least—with the extremists. He decided to advocate a new, and for people like the editors of *The Nation*, a startling reconception of the institution he was criticising. A commission that should have merely the first word in deciding what rates were "just and reasonable" was to be supplanted by a commission armed with absolute power to make any rates it pleased, with no restraint upon it but a single provision. The review of its actions by the courts, except for merely technical considerations, was to be limited to the one function of seeing that the property of the roads was not actually taken away. He made public his conversion to this view in a speech before the Iroquois Club of Chicago.[10]

The controversy had entered its second stage when the word "confiscatory" was the dominant. How far might the commission go in reducing the earning power of a railroad without the reduction becoming "confiscatory"? If invested money could make, say, six per cent—or what you will—in some other way, would it be a "confiscatory" action if the commission forced a railroad to fix rates so that its earnings would not pay a dividend of more than five per cent? If it could cut dividends to five per cent could it cut them to one per cent? These were lawyers' questions obviously involving infinite subtlety—not to say sophistry—in determining what might or might not be a "confiscatory" rate. But it did not require a legal mind to sense immediately the purpose of the revised programme. What the President intended to set up was a dictatorial commission with practically unlimited power. The court review by which alone it could be restrained was to concern itself no longer with deciding whether a rate was "just and reasonable," but only with whether it was "confiscatory." To the ordinary non-legal point of view this was much the same as arming a commission with power to do anything it pleased to an individual except actually to deprive him of his life.[11]

The instantaneous recognition that the proposed new institution would, for practical purposes, be a business despotism controlled by the party in power, took at least one amusing form. Might not this omnipotent commission prescribe rules and regulations for the seating of passengers in railroad-cars? In Southern States there had long been a fear that some turn of Fortune's wheel would enable the ruthless Northerners to enforce railroad equality of the blacks and whites. An appeal to race feeling in the South was one of the devices which the railroads now did not disdain to use.

Fortunately for the credit of the strong men among the Conservatives they made no such frivolous appeals. Their position was that of Senator Lodge who was "thoroughly in favor of government regulation and supervision," who favored wide power in the commission "to abrogate an unreasonable rate," who was willing to have "that abrogation take effect immediately" but who when it came to giving the commission "power to fix a specific rate" considered the remedy "far worse than the disease." [12]

However, despite all the outcry of the Radicals and the professional informers—who were busier than ever in all the sensational sheets that year—both the President and the Conservative leader kept their tempers, and when they met talked of other things besides the irreconcilable issue. Mr. Aldrich lunched with the President at the end of August,[13] and it may be fairly assumed they did not talk about rate legislation. They understood each other too well. Though a great fight was on, it was all in the rhythm of life, not as the hysterical people and the professional informers would have us believe in the rhythm of melodrama.

The President was then deep in manœuvring the settlement at Portsmouth between Russia and Japan. He was also trying to effect a reciprocal trade agreement with Germany. It was the latter subject that he discussed with Mr. Aldrich.[14] There was also general discussion in the early autumn of the tariff. The President was very gracious; he would be guided by Mr. Aldrich and Mr. Allison.[15] Because of their attitude he reluctantly dropped the matter.[16] In these incidental concerns there was nothing that was really significant. One great subject over-shadowed all others. As Mr. Tillman put it: "The coming session of Congress promises to be interesting and perhaps fruitful of surprises. It all depends on your man Teddy. If he means business on the rate-making programme he laid down last year, we Democrats—all the patriots who are left—will have an opportunity to help him use the big stick on recalcitrant Republican heads." [17]

CHAPTER XIX

THE SENATE WINS

I

IT is a pity that the two great sportsmen who were trying their rapiers for such a handsome duel that autumn, have not left more record of what they felt. Three years later—long after they had fought their fight out and had shaken hands, metaphorically, and had started over—each made a parting bow to the other which luckily has been recorded. Aldrich said of Roosevelt, "He is the greatest politician we have had," while Roosevelt said, "My intercourse with Aldrich gave me a steadily higher opinion of him." [1] When those fine compliments were passed, their duel, in both their minds, had faded into memory's haze. Aldrich had resumed his rôle of administration leader, and Roosevelt had gone to Africa. And each, though he did not suspect it, had prepared for the other, the disappointment that was perhaps the bitterest of his life.

The episode opens with another mysterious move on the part of the President. For the third time, one has to guess why he changed his tactics. He made no public explanation, and whatever private explanation he made to his lieutenants is still an undiscovered secret. It might have been expected that the message of December, 1905, would have capped the climax of the speech before the Iroquois Club. Dramatically, as well as logically, the audience had a right to expect a fanfare as the curtain rose on a splendid final act. Instead, the spectators took their breath and batted their eyes at the tameness of what happened. The message abandoned the position of the Iroquois speech and fell back on the much safer ground of the message of 1904. The language was even milder than the language of the previous year. "In my judgment the most im-

portant provision which such a law should contain is that
conferring upon some competent administrative body the
power to decide upon the case being brought before it,
whether a given rate prescribed by a railroad is reasonable
and just, and if it is found to be unreasonable and unjust,
then, after full investigation of the complaint, to prescribe
the limit of rate beyond which it shall not be lawful to go—
the maximum reasonable rate, as it is commonly called—
this decision to go into effect within a reasonable time and
to obtain from thence onward, subject to review by the
Courts."

There will be nothing more interesting in the ultimate
biography of Mr. Roosevelt than the explanation why he
wrote that long sentence. *The Concealment of Theodore
Roosevelt* is, on this subject silent as the grave, the grave of
historical fact. Was it a strategic retreat? Did he see, or
think he saw, a way to turn the enemy's flank by a ruse?
Or, had he some other, subtler reason?

In the early days of the new session, though the atmosphere was charged with the consciousness that things were
about to arrive, the surface of life in the Senate was not
seriously ruffled. The chronic issues, Philippine Tariff, Pure
Food Bill, Reciprocity, Statehood for the territories, etc.,
continued to be chronic, and were talked about intermittently with that easy freedom from any serious purpose
that has always characterized American legislative controversy. Not until the great subject of the hour was got out
of the way were these incidental subjects given genuine attention.

In December and January, with every one aware that a
battle was impending between the Senate and the Executive, the Senate's general was as bland as ever. He observed
with quiet eye several little clashes which in his cool detachment he left to take care of themselves. Chief among
these was the debate over a chastened Pure Food Bill that
had been pulled into a form which the Conservatives might
approve. Aldrich took no part in its discussion and was absent unpaired when at last it was voted upon. Doubtless

the controversy was settled off the floor, and the voting was
mere gesture, about which characteristically, Aldrich cared
not a straw.[2] It is likely that he got some amusement late
in January when a bill to reform the Consular Service was
robbed of a significant provision. The service was to have
been reorganized as provided in the bill, "and under such
rules . . . as shall be prescribed by the President." These
words were struck out on amendment without debate.[3]

A bill to subsidize shipping called forth an expression of
opinion and revealed also that he did not perceive the true
nature of a menace to his own leadership which was steadily
gathering. Once more the useful quotation about the rift
and the lute. The policies of the Four had threatened so
long to go to pieces on the rock of economic sectionalism,
but had escaped the rock so often, that Aldrich had ceased
to give heed to it. After a while, looking backward, we
shall be tempted to call this disregard of sectionalism the
one strategic mistake of his career. At this very moment,
at the opening of 1906, he and Mr. Allison are already further apart than they realized. But who ever saw things at
the beginning as he saw them at the end! Only closet philosophers cling to the delusion that life happens that way.
Hence the usefulness of the little rift as a refrain. The significant part of what Aldrich said upon the Ship Subsidy
Bill was his silences. He criticised the bill because it did
not face squarely the economic difficulties which America
had to overcome "in order to contest on equal terms for the
supremacy of, or for equal status upon the sea." He hoped
that ten years thereafter, when he would not be in the Senate, his successor would have occasion to vote for much
larger subsidies than were contemplated by this bill.[4] He
was curiously silent when his friend Hale put his finger on
the threat of discord latent in the debate over the ships.
Easterners favored subsidy; Westerners opposed. Hale
pointed out that the proposed subsidies were a trifle in comparison with what the West was getting from the public
purse for reclamation.[5]

Another step had been taken toward the deadly sectional

battle of 1909. Hale made no impression upon the determined Westerners who were grimly biding their time.

Strangely remote Aldrich seems on this one point—only this one—while the House is at work on a new rate bill and all the excitements of 1905 are filling the air with pulsations of hostility toward the moneyed interests. Why he did not perceive that the West was the fallow field for this bitter propaganda is the mystery of his inner life. Mr. Allison saw and was troubled. His acute ear heard again the deep murmur of the Iowa ground-song. A new note in it told him to look out for squalls, warned him that the great Western cauldron might at any moment bubble over. All the prophetic witches of the stricken heath inhabited the back of the head of this wonderful man. There had been a time when Mr. Aldrich paid scrupulous heed to his advice. That time was passing. In this year, 1906, temporarily they part company. Again, the question insists on arising —Was it the peculiar coherency of the mind of Mr. Platt that had held them together so long?

The rift between Mr. Aldrich and Mr. Allison had reached the stage when it was clearly perceptible. Mr. Allison knew that the upper Middle West had turned a corner; he knew that it meant business; he saw with political prescience which was almost second sight what it signified at this moment having in the White House an Eastern man with Western principles—as the whole country was soon to see—and he was eager to anticipate the storm which he feared was coming.

Mr. Allison had an understudy in the man who now steps forward and takes briefly the centre of the stage. Mr. Dolliver adored him. Mr. Dolliver had learned from him the art of politics. But he was far more ardent, much more in danger of being ensnared by a dramatic situation, than was his beloved mentor. He was entirely devoted to Mr. Allison's fortunes. The fact that Mr. Dolliver presently took the rash course he did, the fact that Mr. Allison was drifting toward the President and away from Aldrich, the fact that the President needed at the moment every ally he could find—

What is the good in speculating upon subjects that are shrouded in perfect secrecy!

All that is certain is that on every hand dangers were gathering around the leadership of Mr. Aldrich.

The advent of Mr. La Follette had brought into the Senate a man of genius who was to serve hereafter as the rallying point of all the anti-Aldrich forces. At the same time there was a change of mood, or what appears to be that, in Mr. Spooner. He was growing sick of politics. Mr. La Follette had beaten him in the struggle to control his own State. It may be inferred also that he was deeply hurt by the course of the President in not standing by him against all comers in his fight with La Follette. He had a sensitive nature and his disappointment took the course of desiring to be rid of the whole business. Notwithstanding all this, his old-time affection for the President, the strong, personal hold which the President had upon him, made it hard for Mr. Spooner to go squarely against him and remain happy. In the controversy that now begins, he reminds one of those noble generals of the Parliament whom Cromwell charged with a terror of defeating the King. To be sure, he stood manfully by the Senate's commander while the battle was on, but one may risk the guess that fear of another clash with Mr. Roosevelt was part of the explanation of his retirement the next year. Surely it is significant that at no time in the battle of 1906 is Spooner the corps commander, so to speak, upon whom Aldrich chiefly relies. He finds a new corps commander. If Aldrich is the Senate's Lee, in its battle with the President, Knox now becomes its Stonewall Jackson. It is Knox who delivers the smashing attack on the wavering flank of the enemy just at the critical moment. Spooner merely brings up the reserves.

But the key to it all is Mr. Allison—though never in his life was he more mysterious, more evasive, more suggestively in the background. With his traditional prestige he still had his own senatorship pretty securely in his pocket. But his influence, his power to do more than save himself, was doubtful. He could no longer think in the same terms in which Aldrich thought. Temperamentally, he had never been quite able to do that. He could approach doing it only when he had behind him a sure constituency, when he had no personal reason to be afraid of Aldrich's boldness. And now, the ground was singing beneath his feet, calling to him like a harp-string of the gods—*vox populi, vox Dei!* It will be very strange if it is ever proved that Mr. Allison was not unhappy in the winter of 1906, was not deeply disturbed by the course his old friend Aldrich had marked out.[6]

But it is the younger Iowan who, in all this, as it bears upon Aldrich, is the immediate instrument of the ironic fates. Every now and then a bold man has staked his head on the belief that his country, or his leader, would stand by him if he dared the uttermost and took the whole responsibility for bringing about a crisis. This risking one's head is such a grandiose gesture, it is likely to have its reward. But the condition of success is in the audacity of the risk. If one asks to be authorized to take it, one is lost. A certain Shakespeare who knew life tolerably well, including political life, has poetized delightfully the failure of a noble Roman—that Menas who was lieutenant to the younger Pompey—who was willing to risk everything for his master but who had to be told to do it. If Mr. Roosevelt was the Pompey of this episode, Mr. Dolliver was its Menas, but a shrewder and bolder Menas than the original, one who might be trusted not to make his fundamental mistake.

And this brings us back to the singular ambiguity—so far as the world knew—in Mr. Roosevelt's position at the opening of the session of 1906. What Mr. Dolliver knew of his real intentions has not been divulged; what he thought about them is plain. His actions show that he believed the President to be at heart willing to go a long way beyond his message. He was determined to make the President's cause his own. Unless all signs have failed, he made up his mind in January, 1906, that a golden laurel was in store for Mr. Roosevelt if only he dared go unconditionally with the revolutionary movement, and a silver laurel, to say the least, for whomsoever should force his hand—or appear to force his hand—in that direction, create an extreme situation in which there should be no choice but to go still further or to retreat.[7]

Mr. Dolliver found his opportunity when the House sent up to the Senate the Hepburn Rate Bill.[8] This famous measure arrived in the Senate amid a roar of applause. Its extreme proposals were hailed as the beginning of a new day. Only seven members in all the House of Representatives had had courage to vote against it. But this fact must not deceive us. No bill was ever a more disturbing challenge to the mere politician than was this one. There can be little doubt that many votes had been cast in its favor through sheer cowardice, the representative thanking his stars that there were men in the Senate brave enough to do what he did not dare to do, pull the bill to pieces.[9]

This extraordinary measure was not exactly what any one outside the inner circle of its sponsors had expected. First of all, it was ambiguous. Was its ambiguity accidental or strategic, stupid or sly? The bill was conspicuous for its silences. Perhaps—as some able lawyers insisted—it contradicted itself. Again, stupid or sly? To be sure, it was definite enough on the one point which almost everybody —Senator Foraker excepted—took for granted, the conclusion which the President had asserted so vehemently, that the time had come to give the commission the power to initiate rates. It was also clearly at one with the purposes of the bourgeoisie; it was out to turn the tables—as Mr. Chandler would have said—and to penalize the railroads to the very limit. It clearly affirmed the principle that the railroads must be made to suffer whenever possible; that as corporations they must, in the slang of the day "pay the freight." Therefore, it provided that a rate initiated by the commission should not be suspended in case any sort of reconsideration might be brought about, even reconsideration by the commission itself. There was no provision whatever for any reimbursement of the roads should the commission whether by choice or under compulsion, ever confess itself mistaken and restore the old rate.

Clear and dictatorial on all these points, the bill became evasive when it touched the subject of court review. It contained three sentences which were interpreted so differently, that for practical purposes, one might say—in the absence of a judicial interpretation—they meant anything you pleased. Herein lay the mystery of the bill; also the mystery in the attitude of some of its defenders, Mr. Dolliver and others, who stubbornly evaded the questions—is the bill in sympathy with any sort of court review? If with any sort, what sort?

Two terms had come into use that were to be on all men's lips until the controversy reached its end. These were, "broad review" and "narrow review." A broad review senator held to the old belief that "just and reasonable" was a legal idea involving the ancient heritage of the Common Law, and therefore an idea that rightfully should have its final definition not in a legislative but in a judicial body, not in Congress, or a commission, but in the courts. A narrow review senator believed that the Constitution of the United States had released the Congress of the United States from all regard to inalienable hereditary legal privileges and that Congress as things stood in the year 1906 had no limit to its powers over property except the one recognized by the President in the Iroquois speech, the obligation not to confiscate.

Mr. Dolliver and his friends obviously were not broad reviewers. Were they even narrow reviewers? Did the bill they championed contemplate any sort of review at all? Their refusal to explain themselves caused the emphasis upon "constitutional" which characterized the third, the final, stage of the controversy.

This third stage had two distinct periods. In the first which extends until March 31, Mr. Dolliver is the ostensible captain of the revolutionary forces; Mr. Roosevelt is in the background; his position is obscure; the outside world is not certain just where he stands, just what is the relation between him and the man who appears to be playing his hand. In the second period, the relations are reversed.

Mr. Roosevelt emerges from his silences; Mr. Dolliver is suddenly reduced to the ranks—or nearly that—the President defines his position and himself becomes the confessed commander of the revolutionaries.

The first period is the strange and problematical one. Mr. Dolliver is the centre of the problem. His strategy is not explicit. The one thing certain in it is that he is aiming to seize for the commission the greatest measure of power which by hook or by crook can be got into its hands. Though he and his immediate group fought desperately against clearing up the bill's ambiguity, they also took the position that their motive was merely a refusal to assert the obvious, that the bill conceded all the court review that any one ought to demand. But what was that? They would not say. This extraordinary position was interpreted by the Conservatives as deeply lacking in candor. Because of it we shall listen to a severely ironical attack by Senator Knox. At a crucial moment he will taunt Senator Dolliver and his comrades with their appearance of inconsistency. Professing to take them at their word, he will say "But for the seriousness of the situation the matter would be most ludicrous. Both sides agree that the right (of court review) should exist; one holds that it is in the bill, or exists independently; the other that it is not in the bill but should be; and yet the former for some mysterious and unaccountable reason object to an amendment which would place the matter beyond doubt." [10]

Hard-headed people the country over perceived the heart of the matter. There was no clearer-sighted observer of railway problems than Arthur T. Hadley, president of Yale University. Writing of the bill, comparing it with the Esch-Townshend Bill which had provided for a special court to which appeals might be taken, Mr. Hadley pointed out that the Hepburn Bill attempted to limit rather than facilitate the right of appeals by making the decisions of the commission itself final in all questions of fact. . . . "Mr. Hepburn's committee desires to avoid the double hearing, but it does so by eliminating the court instead of the commission." [11]

Aldrich with his usual directness put the issue without reserve: "the heart of this controversy is, Shall we give the commission power to fix a maximum rate of charges or to prescribe a just and reasonable rule when it finds that the one in force by the railroads is unjust and unreasonable?" [12]*

To follow this controversy through all of its ramifications and not to lose oneself among legal niceties, among distinctions that appear to be wire drawn—though in fact they are not—would be something of a feat. The main issues, in the course of a downpour of proposals to amend, frequently threaten to disappear. But just as they are about to do so their basic simplicity, their inherent vitality, break through all the complications, push the incidentals aside, and again lay bare the essentials: the two questions—What body shall be empowered to define "just and reasonable"? Who shall bear the burden while rates are in dispute?

The enemies of the bill objected that it proposed to delegate to the commission the full legislative control possessed by Congress over the earning power of the railroads. Even granting that Congress had the right constitutionally to delegate this function, was it safe to do so? In the conservative mind this was questionable. The commission once created would not be answerable to Congress. It might set up rates that Congress disapproved. But there would be no way of restraining it except by sudden repeal of the statute under which it had been created. As such repeal would necessitate the concord of the President and both the Houses, on intricate questions of commercial justice, was it likely ever to happen? The practical argument of the enemies of the bill was that Congress was rashly giving away a power that it would be difficult to recover.

Still another objection grew out of the constitutional debate. Since the commission would be part of the administrative system of the country, the bill would remove certain far-reaching powers from the field of legislation to the field

*It must be remembered that Aldrich uses words with precision. When he uses "fix" it is with the true meaning of *make permanent* not in the loose popular sense of initiate. He was quite willing to allow the commission to initiate rates; he was not willing to allow it to fix rates.

of administration. It was also contended—and Aldrich
made very skilful use of the contention—that the functions
of the proposed commission would be in part judicial. In
the course of debate the changes were rung on the idea that
what was really proposed was the creation of a new type of
institution, a blend in one body of all the three functions
which our governmental tradition requires to be kept separate—the legislative, the administrative, and the judicial.
Stating it colloquially, Aldrich charged the Radicals with
aiming to create an institution that should be judge, jury,
and prosecution, all in one.

To sum up: The original unchastened Hepburn Bill proposed to put both legislative and judicial power in the hands
of a commission that represented the President and was
beyond the control of Congress. It assumed the right of an
administrative commission to regulate a man's business—
or we may say, a corporation's business—or at least the
business of a "public" corporation—without assuming responsibility for the losses it might inflict, and without
allowing him, or it, an appeal to any judicial body except
upon the one issue of the violation of a constitutional right
in the narrowest interpretation of the term; the idea of
"just and reasonable" was to be kept within the scope of
administration and to have no protection from the courts.

Whether this was all that was contemplated by its sponsors when it passed the House, or at least after Mr. Dolliver
took it up, is a question. There are a few dark hints that
behind the bill lay some larger purpose. Perhaps its true
significance was not after all as a proposed statute but
rather as the introductory article in a programme, the inauguration of a new stream of tendency social and political.
Early in this first stage of the controversy, when the President was a mysterious figure in the background, he gave
the country a broad hint that something momentous was
germinating in his thoughts. He did so by means of an
inspired interview—"Much has been said about the constitutionality of the proposed rate legislation. The President
would be in no wise deterred from pressing the proposed

legislation even though he knew it was practically certain to be declared unconstitutional. He is not wedded to any particular form. His object is to obtain relief from existing conditions, and if the proposed legislation shall turn out to be unconstitutional, he will make an effort to attain the object through other legal means." [13]

Did he have in mind an amendment to the Constitution making possible the consolidation of powers in defiance of our three-fold tradition?

II

The bill was referred at once to the Interstate Commerce Committee of which Mr. Dolliver was a member.*

At the second session of the committee, the deep antagonism over the bill was sharply even rudely manifested. One of the few instances of Aldrich losing his temper occurred at this meeting. Dolliver protested that the committee by receiving for discussion a flood of proposed amendments was treating the subject of rate legislation with "levity." Aldrich flashed fire saying that he was perfectly serious in the matter and would not be called to account by Senator Dolliver. The latter struck back with heat. He "would choose his own language and characterize as he chose, the methods that he said had been resorted to." The chairman, Senator Elkins, rapped for order.[14]

A week later the floating sentiment at Washington as reflected by the newspaper men was that Aldrich would have his way, and that the committee would amend the bill so as to bring all its provisions within the authoritative

*In entering upon the controversy which now ensued—one of the most distinguished in the modern history of the Senate—it must be borne in mind that the Hepburn Bill, despite its crucial importance, has had hitherto almost no treatment genuinely historical. Economists have discussed it as a problem in efficiency; lawyers, as a technical question in constitutional law; the literature of protest as a manifestation of creative righteousness; alarmed conservatives as a first step toward bolshevism; politicians as party tactics; but none has discussed it in the true way as a class measure in the perspective of American tradition and against the immediate background of the literature of protest. Only by so doing can the color of the bill in the picture of the time—as a painter might say—be accurately seen. The two cardinal mistakes with regard to it are, on the one hand, a total disregard of perspective and juxtaposition, and on the other hand, a total disregard of everything else.

scrutiny of the courts.[15] Mr. Dolliver nailed his colors and took his crucial risk by announcing that he would not allow the inclusion in the bill of any specific statement upon court review.[16] His opponents replied that they would put in such a statement and that it would be made possible by Democratic votes.[17] At the same time it was known that there was an anxious stir among the Democrats generally lest their representatives in the committee fail to play politics with the full rigor of the game. Two Democrats held the votes that might settle things. Were they to be allowed to follow their judgment upon the merits of the bill, or were they to think only of "putting the Republicans in a hole," supporting that form of the bill which if put over as a Republican measure would be least advantageous to the party in the next election.

The 15th of February was the first turning point. That day Aldrich went to see the President with a proposal.[18] The President declined to commit himself. Evidently Aldrich had expected a different reply. Like the newspaper men he seems to have thought that he had the situation in his hands, that the President would promptly come to terms. After their interview he told the press that he had expected to have a statement to give out but found that he had none.[19]

Mr. Dolliver took fresh courage. Also, he had an instant reward. It was at once reported that the two Democrats who could turn the scale—Senators Foster and McLaurin—had become equivocal; furthermore, that both sides were now afraid of a vote, were willing to procrastinate and intrigue.[20] An absent member of the committee, Senator Cullom who was recuperating "somewhere among the magnolias and orange blossoms" now became of vital interest to each faction.[21] Aldrich told the press that his programme would go through the next day.[22]

He had made a slip in his calculations. The next day a telegram from Cullom came, not to Aldrich but to Dolliver who communicated it to the committee. Cullom wished his vote recorded either for an earlier bill now pigeon-holed or for the Hepburn Bill unamended.[23] That Mr. Dolliver appeared to the world to be the true champion of the President, and was assiduously giving out that the President was behind him, cannot be doubted. His attitude led to the description of himself and Senator Clapp of the committee as "the White House reformers of the Senate." [24] *The Tribune*, though it avoided any analysis of the Dolliver strategy insisted on the President's devotion to the narrowest sort of narrow review.[25]

Mr. Foster and Mr. McLaurin, though good friends of Aldrich and quite eager to repay many political favors, were weakening. It would never do to back the wrong horse! Aldrich's quick strategic sense told him that for this while the tide had turned against him. He must play for time. A letter from another member of the committee gave him his chance. Senator Tillman was ill and hoped that the committee would delay its action. The considerate committee at once took a recess.[26] It was a tense moment. As *The Journal of Commerce* truthfully remarked, the situation was emphatically in the hands of the Democrats.

The recess lasted a week during which both sides redressed their lines. Aldrich made one of his subtlest strokes in fixing upon a new corps commander. Senator Knox had a great reputation as a constitutional lawyer. Hitherto he had stood close to the President. Like Spooner, Knox was a devoted friend of Mr. Roosevelt, personally, but like Aldrich he could forget the man in the official. This was not an issue between himself and Theodore Roosevelt, but between the Senate of the United States and the President of the United States. More than that, it was between what Knox considered a necessary constitutional right and what, in his mind, was a temporary aberration in a large part of the American people.

Few weeks in Mr. Roosevelt's life are more interesting or less obvious than the week of the committee's recess. In the course of it there were conferences at the White House which Dolliver attended, the purport of which is unknown.[27] At the end of the week, Aldrich and Knox had formulated an ultimatum. Knox presented it to the President who rejected it—at least, he refused to accept it.[28]

Aldrich had been out of town during a considerable part of the recess. One of his daughters was seriously ill. Throughout the rate bill fight whenever possible, he made visits to her bedside. Business interests were also insistent. There were new investments in rubber that had to be watched. But he was always in his place in the Senate at every moment of strategic importance. He was there on February 22. On this day he and Knox published to the world the closeness of their concerted action. Knox rose and said that he had prepared an experimental bill dealing with the problems which the Hepburn Bill had tried to solve and he would like to send it to the committee as a mere suggestion. Instantly, Aldrich was on his feet asking that the bill be read in full to the assembled Senate. The request was granted. Knox read the bill. It was a clearcut announcement of the position of the Aldrich forces: it granted the power to initiate rates but established broad review by giving an aggrieved party full liberty to bring suit in the courts, to test the validity of the commission's judgment; it protected both shipper and railroad by providing for suspension of rates pending review but also for the reimbursement of the railroad, in case a lowered rate should be cancelled and the former rate restored. This bill permitted the commission to decide what rates were "just and reasonable" but also permitted the submission to the courts of all the facts involved by way of argument to impugn the conclusion reached by the commission.[29]

It was in keeping with Aldrich's astute frankness as a campaigner to make all this so entirely clear the day before the final struggle in the committee. But Mr. Dolliver was not dismayed. Again, he assured the world that the President was on his side. He was in high good humor.[30] He thought he had persuaded the two Democrats who with the radical Republicans in the committee could give him a majority. By means of them he expected, that day, to see the bill sent to the Senate unaltered, and himself given the conspicuous rôle of taking charge of it.[31]

The committee met only to adjourn for two hours. There was much confabbing during that last pause. If Dolliver knew that Aldrich and the shrewd old Democratic leader Senator Bailey had their heads together, that while, it did not duly impress him. He forgot for the moment that he was in Belshazzar's palace where strange things happen quite naturally. Directly the committee reassembled he moved that the bill be reported without amendment. The words were hardly out of his mouth when Aldrich, in his casual way, moved that it be understood that every member of the committee reserved full right to amend the bill as he saw fit on the floor of the Senate.

In this motion came the beginning of the end. In another moment Mr. Dolliver saw that his position had been turned. The two doubtful senators voted to sustain Aldrich—in other words to throw the whole discussion into the Senate preventing either side from claiming a victory in the committee. Mr. Dolliver saw that something had happened during the recess; that his enemy was more astute than he. But worse was in store. In his best ironical vein Aldrich who had made so entirely clear just what he was fighting in the bill, remarked that as it stood, it was more of a Democratic measure than a Republican measure, that mere justice required it to go before the Senate in the charge of a Democrat. He moved that Senator Tillman be instructed to report the bill to the Senate without any indorsement from the committee. Here was a terrible disappointment for Mr. Dolliver. Kind-hearted Mr. Elkins, though firmly with Aldrich on the issue, could not help pitying him. He nominated him to be sponsor to the bill. But Aldrich, the parliamentary strategist, was not to be side-tracked. He intended the bill to go before the Senate in a way that should throw all its issues upon their naked merits, that should prevent Mr. Dolliver or any one else claiming for it the sanctity of an approved party measure. Furthermore, he did not intend, should it happen that his own party bungled this bill, to let the Democrats make capital out of it, "put the Republicans in a hole." Doubt-

less also, behind all else was some agreement reached with
Bailey during the recess, and now forever lost. Ruthlessly,
Aldrich stood to his guns. When the vote was taken be-
tween Dolliver and Tillman, the latter was the choice.[32]

A tale is told of the last moment of this meeting. Aldrich and two other senators were standing apart, laughing
among themselves. Dolliver came up to them. He was
very angry. "That was too shabby a trick for a gentleman
to participate in," said he, and strode out of the room.[33]

III

Aldrich had scored his first victory. He had got the bill
into such a position before the Senate and before the country that the Democrats would find great difficulty making
party capital out of whatever attitude the Republicans
might now assume. The better heads among the Democrats recognized this fact. Perhaps they were glad. To an
unusual degree the rate-bill controversy broke through the
crust of party politics and grounded itself on the merits of
the question. To reverse the image it transcended chicanery
and rose into the pure air of conviction. This was especially ,
true of Mr. Tillman. A rash man, he was none the less
honest and without fear. The position in which Aldrich had
put him came as a surprise and was not altogether pleasant. He accepted it as imposed by circumstance and entail-
ing upon him an obligation to do all he could for a measure
which in his eyes had been accurately described by Aldrich
as more Democratic than Republican. Both of them, of
course, had in mind when they said this, the unaltered bill
with its class animus against the railroads and its distrust,
to say the least, of the courts. Tillman frankly regarded the
bill as heralding a general attack on "the great accumulations of wealth in the hands of the few" before which "the
honest patriot stands appalled." [34]

Just the same the bill presented to the Democrats a difficult problem as Mr. Tillman promptly discovered.[35] He
represented an advanced wing of his party among whom
class feeling had broken away from some of their most

cherished party traditions. Among the latter was the fear of administrative autocracy. That this fear was not dead was quickly demonstrated by Senator Bailey. He submitted amendments. They went the whole length of the class discrimination in the bill by forbidding the lower Federal Court to issue injunctions to stay the execution of the commission's orders, but then wheeled about and gave rein to the traditional Democratic fear by asserting the full right of appeal from the commission to the courts. In other words, Bailey was willing to let the railroads suffer by having to lose charges while a case on appeal was being argued, but he could not at this time overcome his traditional Jeffersonian dread of investing any presidential commission with dictatorial power. To him, at first, quite as much as to Aldrich, the unpardonable sin of the bill was in putting this enormous power into the hands of a commission not answerable to Congress and beyond the reach of the courts.[36]

Throughout the debate, Aldrich refrained from speechmaking. Plainly his policy was to make it a lawyer's controversy.[37] But he kept his finger on the pulse of the Senate none the less. His mind hovered, as it were, over every argument, pouncing hawklike whenever an opponent made a slip in reasoning, or afforded him an opportunity to draw out to full strength a point that he wished to stress. In this way he seized upon the part of Bailey's position that coincided with his own. He interrupted him to ask, "As I understand the views of the Senator from Texas, he is in favor of having a full and fair judicial determination finally of the question whether the rates fixed furnish just compensation or not?"

And Bailey replied, "I am. I have never seen the hour, and I sincerely trust I will never see the time when I can be clamored into closing the doors of the courts against any person natural or corporate. . . . The Senator from Rhode Island and every other senator in this chamber, I trust, credits me with a proper respect for the law." [38]

A bit grandiloquent, but—enough said! No wonder the

President wrote in a private letter, "I was entirely opposed to Bailey's broad court review amendment." [39]

It was a battle of phrases. While the Radicals wished to word the law so that the commission should have power to determine "in its judgment" what were "just and reasonable" rates, the Conservatives wished to strike out "in its judgment" and to require that rates should also be "fairly remunerative." No one had the courage to propose abandoning altogether the hallowed words "just and reasonable."

Aldrich, in his keen manipulation of the debate, was always centring the question upon "just and reasonable." These words implied a standard. If Congress did not intend to make such implication, why did it not say so? Why not say that the commission might impose on the railroads whatever rates it liked? Since, as he assumed, nothing of the sort was proposed, how was the standard of "just and reasonable" to be determined? He demanded a clear answer whether senators wanted it determined by a political body appointed by the President, or by an impartial court.

When Senator Fulton grew a trifle careless and appeared to confuse the legislative power to establish rates with the judicial power to pass upon their reasonableness, Aldrich was upon him in an instant. Before Fulton realized what he was about he had been trapped into contradicting the Supreme Court as to the nature of the power to declare a rate unreasonable. Fulton was nagged into losing his temper when Aldrich asked, "Suppose the rate (fixed by the commission) is unreasonably high? Suppose it is extortionate?" Fulton snapped out what amounted to a confession that the commission would always look after the interests of the shipper. Of course, this was just what Aldrich wanted him to say and he made the most of it, rising to a controversial climax in the warning, "If the commission should become favorable in the course of time to the railroads and the right of the shippers be invaded by their action . . . the shipper would be absolutely powerless to have the rate set aside as extortionate and unreasonably high. In such a case you propose to leave the shipper without remedy?" Fulton could only flounder in the trap reiterating, "I still insist that the shipper is not worried. . . ." [40]

Senator Long in an elaborate argument for narrow review entangled himself in an attempt to define the true field of the commission's activity as lying between "confiscatory" rates on the one hand and "extortionate" rates on the other. Aldrich at once closed with him insisting that he implied distinctions and mental boundaries which only the impartial courts could be trusted to determine.[41] He never allowed the debate to get far from one or other of the two questions—Whom will you trust to determine what is just and reasonable? Do you want to create a new type of institution that shall combine all three functions, to legislate, to administer, and to judge?

Near the close of the controversy, Senator Clarke rashly involved himself in a "colloquy"—the pompous senatorial term for informal discussion—which he opened by the rash device of quoting Aldrich not quite fairly. "I said," Aldrich replied, "the proposition to make the decision of the commission final, without any possible chance to have the rights of the parties litigated or maintained by the courts was an infamous proposition." Clarke cited judges who held that the commission rate "should be entirely free from judicial interference or control"; to which Aldrich replied, "that is from the legal standpoint. I was not discussing it from the legal standpoint but from the ethical standpoint. I understand the Senator would be glad to make the decision of a political body upon the question of rates throughout the United States final if he could." Clarke tried to veil himself in a cloud of words. Aldrich blew the cloud away. Eager as Clarke was to score a point for the bill, he could not conceal under Aldrich's inquisition the fact that he did so with mental reservations. "Then the Senator is not entirely pleased," was Aldrich's parting shot, "with the proposition to make this commission prosecutors and judges and executors." [42]

Thus the battle raged over the three phrases. Eventually, "in its judgment" on the one hand, and "fairly remunerative" on the other, dropped out. The Conservatives staked their cause on "just and reasonable" conceived as a matter of fact, not as a matter of opinion.

Meanwhile the Democrats had a long and unhappy dispute among themselves. One wing under Mr. Tillman were for the bill as it stood, with both its revolutionary provisions—narrow court review and penalization of the railroads. The other wing were half and half.

During the month of March the Aldrich strategy had one main objective: to hammer in the challenge—Is the bill however interpreted, constitutional? The appeal was to the legal conscience of the Senate. This aim was served by keeping the lawyers constantly in the foreground, by giving to the debate as remote and objective a tone as possible. It was at this time that the President published his intimation about "other legal means" and probably did not help matters for his lieutenant in the Senate. At this time also Mr. Dolliver made his refusal to accept any amendment that would clear up the bill's ambiguity while at the same time admitting that court review of some sort was inescapable. While skilful lawyers of the opposition—Knox, Spooner, Foraker—drove home the constitutional argument from a dozen points of view, Mr. Dolliver finally committed himself to this inexplicable contradiction. It was seized upon as evidence of a concealed ulterior purpose in the administration party.

The moment this had sunk into the minds of all the senators, and had made its full impression, was the psychological moment for the first great attack on the President's outer line—if the military metaphor may be used. The moment came on March 28. It was then that Knox delivered his blow declaring that "but for the seriousness of the situation the matter would be most ludicrous"; skilfully underscoring the "mysterious and unaccountable reason" which led the friends of the bill to refuse to safeguard their own admissions. After a close technical argument designed to show that the bill was either self-contradictory or worse, he turned all the batteries of a rich legal mind upon the general principles involved. His peroration may be taken as expressing Aldrich quite as much as it expressed himself.

Mr. President, men of our inheritances repel summary and arbitrary methods and none the less if these methods proceed from acknowledged power accompanied by the mere empty professions and forms of law. Judicial review of every substantial controversy affecting persons and property is a right. This right was painfully won from tyrannies of the past and is established now beyond the power of any present tyrannies to destroy, in whatever guise they may come, and even if masquerading in the name of the people.

This right is to have the rights of the parties in every controversy determined by the courts. Why then should there be any doubt on that point in this bill; why should the relative provisions not be clear and explicit? I have heard that doubt suggested in and out of this chamber, and I now take leave to raise my voice in protest against the shallow and dangerous notion. . . .

It is the sober truth that the courts are the guardians of our rights and liberties. . . .

Mr. President, this great subject should be discussed and considered in a spirit of sincerity and courage, far removed from political expediency, or levity, or passion. It is a question affecting the entire country and every section. It concerns vitally great aggregates of the people and each individual citizen. It touches at all points the interests of capital and the interests of labor. It is a question of constitutionality, of fundamental rights, of law. It is therefore a question which peculiarly concerns the lawyers of this chamber. It would be . . . a reproach to those of us who are lawyers if for lack of intellectual integrity, for want of courage, because of expediency—for any reason short of absolute conviction—we should urge this bill, or sitting silent should supinely permit it to become law although believing it to be unconstitutional or illegal and unjust on any ground. . . .[43]

IV

During the last few days of March, each side got what athletes would call its second wind. There was pretty general agreement that the administration tactics had failed.

Evidently the President was dissatisfied with Mr. Dolliver's course.[44] Whatever else one may think of the situation at the end of March, it is impossible to escape the conclusion that the President thought that his forces had got out of hand. He resolved to bring them sharply back. On March 31, he took direct control of his campaign. It was high time he did so. Knox in his great speech had assumed that the effort to prevent a specific statement on the subject of court review was no longer worth considering, that the only question now was, What sort of statement was to be made— whether broad or narrow—and what was to be done upon the class issue, the suspension or enforcement of rates pending review. He went even further than that. He threw down the glove by implying that broad review was as good as certain; that the real battle now was upon the power of the courts to suspend orders of the commission pending review.

It is probable that Aldrich and his comrades, in the closing days of March, felt that they had carried the enemy's first line of defense and were about to begin an enveloping movement—if one may continue the military metaphor— that would destroy him altogether. The press, even the administration press, inclined to the same view.[45]

It is very curious that at this moment of crisis there was so much misapprehension both of the character and the general aim of the President. If the opposition thought they had driven his forces from the field, the President now proposed to open their eyes. He would call up all his reserves and lead them personally to the recovery of the lost ground. Whenever Theodore Roosevelt made a decision like that the rest of the world was sure to see something worth enjoying. There is the rousing old line, "For Rupert never charges but to conquer or to fall."

He called a conference at the White House. Mr. Dolliver came and also Mr. Clapp; also two members of the Interstate Commerce Commission; and the attorney-general. There were others, including—above all—Mr. Allison.[46] What better evidence that he was a Roosevelt man rather than an Aldrich man. Indeed, the Four were ancient history.

The President laid his cards on the table. He had made up his mind. He meant business and no mistake. An amendment to the bill which he had had prepared was to be introduced into the Senate by Mr. Long. It aimed to do three things. It would put a full stop to the previous strategy by making a specific statement upon court review. This statement would meet the opposition demand for broad review by reasserting the President's position in the Iroquois speech and writing into the bill a provision for court review of the very narrowest sort. As the opposition had served notice that it would insist on the virtual suspension of commission rates pending review, the President burned his bridges declaring that such rates should not be suspended.

To effect all this, "the Long Amendment"—as it was later known—proposed to strike out of the bill those questionable sentences behind which Mr. Dolliver had taken position and to replace them by clear-cut statements which in Knox's phrase would "place the matter beyond doubt" and in a way that drew the line between the factions hard and fast.[47]

Such was the first move in the President's counter-attack. But there was more to come. It was not for nothing that Aldrich called him our greatest politician. On the night of March 31 he sent for Mr. Chandler. No Republican stood closer to the Democratic leaders, especially Mr. Tillman. The President hoped that he could bring the Democrats, or enough of them to make a majority of the Senate, into line behind the programme of a narrow review and no suspension of rates. Mr. Chandler was confident that a coalition could be effected and was eager to bring it about. He left the White House to go in search of Mr. Tillman.[48]

Of course the President, like every one else, knew that he was taking a chance. Everything depended on the relative numbers of the two sorts of Democrats. He knew, everybody knew, that practically all the Democrats, that moment, were sufficiently class conscious to rally to his programme of no suspension of rates pending review. This was not the danger point. His other issue was the one on which he would stand or fall with the children of Thomas Jefferson. What of their great tradition of scrupulous restraint of administrative despotism, of scrupulous protection of minorities? To be sure, the new type of Democrat had only a theoretical reverence for the shade of Jefferson, and would be quick enough to use any power he could lay his hands on in what he regarded as the cause of "the People"—a phrase which in American politics had always meant ME.

Well, were there enough of these Democrats of the new sort to make possible an administration coalition that would carry the bill through the Senate just as a similar coalition in miniature had carried it through the committee? On that question hung victory or defeat.

As might have been expected, Mr. Chandler found that Tillman was willing.[49] Less explicable is the course of Mr. Bailey, who strangely enough, fell in line at Mr. Tillman's solicitation, and promised to support the policy of narrow review.[50] During the next two weeks Mr. Chandler and Mr. Tillman conferred several times. Mr. Tillman and Mr. Bailey had a conference with the attorney-general. Mr. Dolliver and Mr. Tillman encouraged each other to believe the coalition possible; finally, most significant of all!—Mr. Allison joined what Mr. Tillman playfully described as "the conspirators." What a difference from the high days of the united Four!

Putting this and that together the "conspirators" calculated that they could muster twenty, or possibly twenty-two Republican votes, and twenty-six, or possibly twenty-eight Democratic votes.[51] There were ninety senators. The coalition, if it did not run upon a snag, would be sure of a majority of two. It had hopes of a majority of ten. Pretty risky chances in the manipulation of a measure generally conceded to be revolutionary!

Having once taken command of his battle, the President threw himself into it with all that magnificent energy, that

special form of *esprit,* which made him the unique figure
he was. He had need of it all, for on the same day, April
2, when his new lieutenant, Long, laid the Roosevelt programme before the Senate, the Supreme Court rendered its
decision in the Michigan railroad rate cases. Just what that
decision signified as a matter of law is not germane to this
subject. What concerns us here is its effect on the controversy in the Senate. The enemies of the Hepburn Bill found
in the decision by implication a condemnation of the principle of narrow review. Whether the reasoning was sound
or false it had an immediate effect in strengthening their
influence with the weaker brethren of the Senate, the doubtful fellows not sure of their constituencies who were terribly afraid of the people at home. By the same token it
strengthened the resolution of the President. Those doubtful fellows must be whipped into line.

And now as if by common inspiration both sides resorted to the same tactics. After all, the Hepburn Bill was
not the only legislation before Congress. There were those
other measures in which the nation was interested—the
Pure Food Bill, the Philippine Tariff, and the rest. And
there were lesser measures, highly interesting to particular
constituencies, which the small fry of both Houses, those
same weaker brethren, were desperately solicitous to have
done into law before the session ended. Almost simultaneously, both the President and his enemies let it be known
that all these other measures would have to mark time until the duel upon the Rate Bill had been fought to a finish.[52]

All the while the negotiations with the Democrats went
on with Mr. Chandler as the chief intermediary, and the
signs of the times as seen from the White House were promising. Mr. Dolliver, though now so distinctly in eclipse,
stood bravely by his chief and published an article in *The
Independent* (April 12) defending the President's course.
There was suppressed passion in his article which cited the
Iroquois speech as the measure of what was demanded on
one side "the line of division in the Senate," and restated in

unmistakable terms the fixed intention to create "an impartial public tribunal administrative in character with authority to apply the standard of 'just and reasonable' to" railway rates.

In the second week of April the President was in high feather. That predominant interest in foreign affairs, always so near his heart, must have been freshly recharged by the news of the Treaty of Algeciras—that far-reaching international arrangement for which he was himself so largely responsible—the last bold projection of his shadow upon the nations.

It was in a very confident mood that he now delivered one of the most resounding blows of the campaign. He chose this dramatic moment in which to let the world know that the Rate Bill, for all its deep significance, was but one step in a contemplated triumphal progress. This was done in the oration which he delivered April 14 at the laying of the corner-stone of the new House of Representatives office building. Besides reiterating his position on the issue of the moment he announced what for that day was a startlingly radical programme—his advocacy of a tax on inheritances. As Knox, two weeks before, had formulated the conservative position in ringing words, so now, the opposing general, the giant who still appeared to dominate the field, gave back in trumpet tones the valiant war cry of the advancing enemy.[53]

V

While the President was thus moving to the attack, Aldrich's strategy was delay. It used to be said that the House of Commons represented England's variable moods and the House of Lords her settled purposes. Aldrich had a similar idea about the Senate. One of his maxims was that most people did not know what they wanted.[54] The function of the Senate was to make them known to themselves. A bold theory of legislative leadership which few men—hardly any from the variable States—ever dared to put into practice except when shaken out of themselves by a spasm of genuine conviction, a political pentecost. It was because he believed that the Senate when sufficiently stirred was capable of striking down beneath the eddies of the surface and grounding itself on its own fundamentals—whatever they might be!—that he could hold on so firmly, so serenely, waiting for it to find itself. Not often had this faith of his been justified. Perhaps it would be safer to say that even he did not often risk putting it to the test. He was taking that risk now, and despite considerable nervousness in his followers while the President was urging his forces on, cheering them lustily to the attack, Aldrich insisted on standing still.

Even earlier than this when Dolliver still appeared to be the general in the field, Aldrich had had to restrain the impatience of his friends.[55] They did not know men as well as he did, and they had not his power to endure a crisis interminably. In the changed state of things following the White House conference, Tillman said he would "like to suggest to the Senator from Rhode Island who seems by common consent in the control of those who are opposing this bill, or guiding, or managing it for that side, whether he is now prepared to offer any idea as to when we can get a vote."

Aldrich dextrously turned the question by suggesting that the Senator from South Carolina was not fully committed to the bill, and then drew him on into delicate distinctions as to just how far they disagreed, and the question of voting was dropped.[56]

A few days later Tillman tried again with no better result. He spoke of the "lagging character of the debate"—which was just what Aldrich, at this moment, wanted it to be, and got in reply a graceful sentence to the effect that Aldrich had never known "debate on a great question that was so well sustained and so continuous as this debate has been." These two always treated each other with marked respect, and generally could inject into their gravest "colloquies" a bit of fun or a bit of irony. Tillman illustrated on this occasion. With a mental shrug he spoke of his own "inexperience" in "caring for any babies"—his way of alluding to bills in the charge of senators—"or furnishing rations for them every day, and this one seems to be begging." He got a reply of the sort he must have expected which doubtless made him chuckle—an apparently grave admission that "the Senator perhaps ought to be forgiven in view of his inexperience." [57]

But all the while Aldrich was busily studying Tillman's followers. Among them, he knew, lay the President's only chance. Until they broke ranks—and Aldrich was sure that if he kept the game at a standstill sufficiently long, they would certainly break ranks—he did not propose to budge.

There was practically none of the petty bargaining, the "trading" that disgraces so much legislation. It was charged, of course. Newspapers with their customary recklessness gave out that the President was using all his influence to coerce senators—threatening to withhold patronage, or to block measures dear to their constituents. The authority for such statements was not produced. Though there was some gossip of deals among senators, this also evaporated into thin air. At last the Senate was meeting the crisis in a dignified and serious manner, fighting grimly on a basis of real belief.

April 14, with the President's trumpet call to the faithful, came and went. Four days later, the Democrats held a caucus. Even before it met Aldrich knew what the outcome would be. He told Bailey, now openly advocating the President's programme, that only twenty-five Democrats would stand by him. And twenty-six were absolutely necessary to success! Later, Bailey paid him ironical compliments before the Senate, attributing to him an understanding of the Democrats, superior to his own. [58]

What Aldrich was waiting to have demonstrated was the impossibility of securing for the coalition those twenty-six Democratic votes. He was confident that the President had missed his guess, that at the pinch the Democrats would not hold together; that Tillman, Bailey, Dolliver, Allison, could not among them command enough votes to produce the majority which was life or death for the administration programme. And this the caucus on April the 18th demonstrated. The Democrats broke ranks. They would not as a body follow either Tillman or Bailey; they were hopelessly divided among themselves. The President had missed his guess. The administration coalition would not arrive.[59]

Here, at last, was what Aldrich had waited for so stubbornly. For all the brilliancy of the President's counter-attack, despite the audacity of the clarion of April 14, the Aldrich lines had held at every point and the enemy's offensive was crumbling. Things had turned out exactly as he had promised they would. The time for his own counter-attack had come.

VI

His development of it was as deliberate as his cool and resolute defense. A little more time was needed in order to let the significance of the Democratic break-up take possession of the senators. Mr. Tillman, who was the last of all to admit that his cause was lost, tried to push him into consenting to a vote. Aldrich, bland as ever, put the question aside. In doing so, he had again to override the impatience of his own friends. Senator Hale—especially close to him now that Allison and Spooner were drifting away—showed a touch of petulance when Aldrich replied to Tillman, "I should not think it practicable at this time" to come to a vote. Hale felt "that there is a general feeling that we ought pretty soon to come to some agreement about" voting. Other senators put in their oars and Aldrich retorted that he was not aware of any disinclination "to fix the time for taking a vote when the discussion was exhausted." He added, "I can see no occasion for any suggestions or attempts to lecture the Senate as to what it ought to do in this matter." [60]

By this time everybody understood that he was not going to allow a vote until he was perfectly sure where he

stood. When at last on April 30, he consented to open the
final chapter on May 4, the veterans of the Senate knew
that the game was up. A great deal had been accomplished
quietly, almost silently. The Senate had been "polled" as
they say—that is, every nose had been counted and sufficient votes had been pledged. A new set of amendments
had been drawn up. By a subtle magic—which turns out
upon close examination to be an amusing sort of magic—
they reconciled temporarily what had seemed to be irreconcilable, the purpose of the two groups of Republicans, the
broad and narrow reviewers.

And now, since the presidential coalition had gone to
pieces, since it was obvious that the only way to get back
to the suspended legislation was to accept the Aldrich programme, a majority was assembled. Mr. Allison, the sure
barometer of this episode, registered the passing of stormy
weather by returning to co-operation with his old friend.
He consented to introduce the Aldrich Amendments which
therefore are known in history as the Allison Amendments.[61]

And what, pray, was the magic in these Aldrich Amendments?—it is fanciful to call them the Allison Amendments.
In this connection that factor which for a time had so
nearly disappeared, pure politics, reasserted itself. Fifteen
Republican senators were facing re-election. They came
from States where the revolutionary programme was in full
swing. To go home without a rate bill to their credit was to
take a serious risk. Furthermore, it must be one which as a
"talking point" would not betray to the average eye any
wide divergence from the original bill. *The Tribune* divined
their quandary when it stated bluntly: "Negotiations between the senators who favor a broad court review . . .
and those who are opposed to it are still on, and the hope is
expressed that a compromise may yet be reached whereby
the conservative Republicans may obtain all they desire in
the way of breadth of review, while the narrow review senators get radical concessions in the way of verbiage." *The
Tribune* also put its finger on another clew to Aldrich's
strategy—his determination now that this legislation was

coming his way, to take it back from the Democrats, to resume it as a Republican measure. Therefore, "now that the advocates of the Long Amendment foresee their inability to prevent the adoption of a broad review provision, they are disposed to agree on a compromise which will permit of the adoption of every amendment as well as the bill itself without the aid of Democratic votes." [62]

The "compromise" which *The Tribune* talked about was the subject of a great deal of speculation then and afterward. So far as the analysis of *The Tribune* went, it was correct. But it did not go the whole length.

The radical senators, for all their fear of their constituents—rather because of their fear of their constituents— were not to be caught as easily as *The Tribune* supposed. They demanded as the price of their surrender something a little more real than "verbiage." The astute lawyers who were behind Aldrich had seen how to give it to them. The amendments were so framed as to leave to the courts themselves the final decision as to whether it was or was not proper for the court to pass not only on the confiscatoriness but on the reasonableness of the orders of the commission. This was done so cleverly that each side could look confidently to the courts believing it knew what the final arbiter would do.

Upon the other of the two main contentions, Aldrich felt himself strong enough after this concession to stand firm. The circuit court was to be given jurisdiction to hear and determine suits "to enjoin, set aside, or suspend, orders of the commission."

In addition to all this there was a purely temperamental element in the "compromise"—if that loose word is to be retained!—which is the most interesting of all. No one can read *The Congressional Record* for the days when these amendments were debated, no one can do that, noting the silence of the great lawyers on the Aldrich side, the silence of Aldrich himself—no one can listen understandingly to the voluble credo of narrow reviewer after narrow reviewer —and not form a pretty shrewd guess at a bit of history that is deeply buried. The real heart of the "compromise" was Aldrich's promise "You may talk and we'll keep still." [63]

With his majority securely in hand Aldrich went to the President. Apparently it was their first interview since his ultimatum had been rejected two months before. On this occasion he was "so suave," says Senator Beveridge, who adds, "But he brought away Roosevelt's capitulation." [64]

One can easily imagine the sort of scene that took place. The President's sense of humor was equal to carrying off almost any situation, even his own defeat. Aldrich's sense of humor which delighted in giving everything a surface of the casual, rose from note to note of subtle enjoyment whenever it met humor in another—astute humor, that is. The man who could laugh at himself was the foeman worthy of his steel. With such a man his sense of the amenities of war was delightfully generous. Therefore, in imagination —reasoned imagination, which is more than impression, which is based on circumstantial evidence—the President flashes upon the screen (hear! hear!) with his familiar smile, his hand outstretched, and "the spoken title," as your movie men would say, "Well, Aldrich, you got me. Of course, you are all wrong. You don't represent more than ten per cent of the American people.[65] We'll beat you yet. But there's no denying, old man, you put up a lovely fight. Now, what are your terms? Between ourselves, I guess I know. But what are we going to tell the world? I am in this fight for keeps, but there's the party to consider as well as you and me and our personal convictions."

And Aldrich—he had in him none of the vulgar pride of victory, such as the morons have. Back to Pater again: to hold one's ideas lightly, to take one's victories as if they did not matter, to see life with the eye of an artist—there is the civilized man. Aldrich must have relished the moment immensely, but not as your vulgarian would have done. He was a connoisseur of men. He enjoyed a completely developed human type as he enjoyed a perfectly blended Persian rug. And whatever else one may think of Mr. Roosevelt, he was perfect of his kind. He had the terrible power that all perfection has, the power that Aldrich, the uncompromising Darwinian, respected most.

It is plain that he and Roosevelt reached a new understanding some time between the moment when Aldrich entered the White House, that day, and the end of the year. It is not at all unlikely—both men being what they were—that they came to terms at once, at this conference. The biographers of Mr. Roosevelt have failed to notice that his methods underwent a subtle change in the latter part of this year 1906. This, of course, is across the horizon of the present story. But it has obviously an incidental significance. A good argument could be made for the assumption that he and Aldrich recharted the field of politics and divided it between them, Roosevelt agreeing to keep certain activities outside Congress and Aldrich agreeing to support him inside Congress. Anyhow, that is what happened. Whether all this was tacit or clearly defined, whether it happened this day or some other, is all to seek. Done somehow, somewhere, it was.

The President was defeated, but he was still a terrible enemy that could make terms. His terms were that he should march out with the honors of war. He must be allowed to withdraw from the field with his army intact. The fight was not over. "To-day to thee; to-morrow to me."

This was the bargain on which he and Aldrich shook hands. For the moment, they would combine to effect the Aldrich compromise. The whole question of the definition of court review should be set aside. The President would cease to press narrow review, and the Conservatives would take their chances on the Supreme Court as a defender of broad review.

VII

Mr. Roosevelt with his usual faculty for swift rearrangement got his whole programme on a new basis almost immediately. He prepared a new blast of destructive criticism, a new call to his followers, in the message to Congress on the Standard Oil Company, ringing with denunciation

of the "malefactors of great wealth." It went to Congress
on the morning of the 4th of May.

All this was done so quietly that Mr. Tillman did not
know it was taking place. This remarkable man still awaits
historical appreciation. Rough and furious as he was, he
was also, in a way, the last American expression of the age of
the code of honor. He had its rigid notions of obligation,
its scrupulous ideas of what gentlemen committed themselves to when they agreed upon joint action. And with this
he had a die-hard faith in his causes that other brave men
instinctively salute even when they disagree. To his mind,
it was inconceivable that the coalition could be dissolved
without formal notice to all the participants; neither did he
yet admit that its cause was lost. He sent word to the attorney-general not to believe the reports in the newspapers, to keep faith that he would yet contrive to pledge the
twenty-six necessary votes. He was a man in a dream. Not
until May 4, after the Standard Oil message had been received and the final discussions had begun, were his eyes
suddenly opened.

It looks as if everything done that day was by pre-
arrangement. A dramatic scene occurred at the White
House. It has been described by one of the ablest of the
men who were present: "At the cabinet meeting Friday
morning (May 4) it (the Allison Amendment) was not
mentioned though Roosevelt had agreed to it. After the
cabinet meeting Roosevelt telephoned the Press Gallery
that he wanted a group there to come to the White House
at three. When they arrived he launched upon an elaborate
statement designed to present to the country the idea that
the Senate rather than he, had receded in the matter of
the much-mooted broad and narrow review. His explanation was quite labored, and after about eight minutes of it,
one of his warm admirers, Lindsay of the Kansas City *Star*,
interrupted him to ask, 'But, Mr. President, what we want
to know is why you surrendered.' This was a body blow
and quite took Roosevelt's breath away. But instead of
replying he went on to repeat the sort of explanation on

which he had set out, continued it for half an hour, and then the Press departed." [66]

No one since Napoleon has been more happy in the phrasing of bulletins than Mr. Roosevelt. The inspired statement in the papers next morning was a masterpiece. Its subtlest intimation revealed just enough—and not, for strategic purposes, a hair too much—of the "compromise." The country was told: "The President regards it as impossible to determine with any degree of certainty the breadth or narrowness of the review of the orders of the Interstate Commerce Commission which the courts assume they have authority to conduct. Personally, he believes that the courts will confine themselves to 'the two points' of the narrow review." [67]

We return to the senators. What the President had told the newspaper men was noised about Washington on the evening of the 4th. While Mr. Tillman was eating his dinner, Mr. Chandler came in very much excited. He had heard the news. Hastily, they sought Mr. Bailey. The three went in chase of the attorney-general. All were thunderstruck.

And then, the flood-gates of recrimination were opened. Mr. Tillman bitterly arraigned the President before the Senate for having "abandoned" his allies. It was an interesting display of an antique point of view, a voice from another age. The President with his intense modernity could not enter into the Southerner's mind; he said harsh things in reply.[68] But all that is beside the mark. The delicious part of this concluding episode is in Aldrich's sense of humor. He was never more ironical, never less intelligible to the morons. While the Press rang with the President's "surrender" echoing the Democratic senators, Aldrich with his tongue in his cheek did his share in the "compromise" helping the fifteen imperilled senators to save their faces.

Whether he kept his own face perfectly straight in this solemn farce may be questioned. There are moments that make one recall with a gasp those sprightly ancients and how they "winked at 'Omer down the road, And 'e winked back, the same as us."

After Senator Long had talked at length insisting that the narrow reviewers were not changing front, Aldrich had the effrontery to come to his aid, saying that the new amendment "simply confers in terms upon the courts jurisdiction which the Senator from Kansas (Mr. Long) and other senators who are in favor of this legislation"—how careful he is not to say narrow review!—"have always contended was accomplished by the bill." [69] Thereupon, Senator Bailey winked at him—metaphorically speaking—and harked back to some jesting remarks of Senator Raynor who had told the Senate he would not say that "any one," (that is, Aldrich), "has set a trap for the President of the United States," but who convulsed the senators by his humorous account of how the President had been caught in the trap that somebody had set, so that now "his party friends and his party enemies are vying with each other as to which one of them can get in first and participate with him in this gratuitous captivity," while his commands to the Senate are now, "authenticated in a manner that ought to give them absolute authenticity by the coat-of-arms of the Senator from Rhode Island." After Aldrich had protested that nothing was being put over upon his narrow review friends, Bailey picked up the note from Raynor, and the Senate was diverted with more of this Homeric banter. "I congratulate the Senator from Rhode Island who denies the soft impeachment of the Senator from Maryland and modestly disavows any part in this arrangement; and yet from the beginning of this long debate to this day the one insistence of the Senator from Rhode Island has been for a broad court review. He has at last obtained what he wants, and hence he is so well satisfied with this amendment. Some senators may not know what they have agreed to, but the senator from Rhode Island is not one of them." [70]

The debate which this playfulness opened, took very quickly a turn which must have taxed the sobriety of Aldrich who could see it as a joke, and of Knox and Spooner who were so differently constituted, to the uttermost. It

was the very peak of this ironic comedy. Except for that
bit of sparring at the start, Aldrich did not open his mouth
and neither did Knox until the roll was called on an amendment proposed by Raynor.

A sad strategic blunder was made by Mr. Allison, who
could not endure the sort of thing in which Aldrich and
Raynor and Bailey were indulging. He made a careful,
ponderous statement to the effect that the amendments
properly construed conceded nothing of the narrow review
position. Of course, this was for the benefit of Iowa and
not for the Senate. Senator Bacon pounced upon it like a
cat on a mouse. Senator Fulton came to the rescue and
even more irretrievably committed the narrow reviewers
to the idea that they were voting for this amendment because it granted only what they had always contended for.
And then Bacon had him. He called for a vote on an
amendment of Raynor's stating exactly what Allison and
Fulton had said they were trying to get: "But such order
(of the commission) shall not be set aside by any court unless it violates the Constitution of the United States or
exceeds the jurisdiction of the commission." Fulton who
was not a skilful debater failed to give an intelligible reason why he would not accept this phraseology. Senator
Cullom tried to help him out but floundered deep into inconsistency. Bacon thrust home the obvious fact of their
evasion by pressing the Raynor Amendment after asserting
that the wording of the other amendment left the courts
free to assume any jurisdiction they pleased. A vote was
called. Now Aldrich uttered his first word since Allison
began this unfortunate exposure of his thoughts. His one
word was "No." Fifty-four others voted the same way,
among them such devotees of narrow review as Mr. Dolliver and Mr. Clapp.

Was ever a man more blandly indifferent to the way the
crowd would understand him! He had his reward. They
did not understand him and they took Mr. Allison and Mr.
Dolliver and Mr. Long and Mr. Cullom at their word. And
of all that there were consequences—as we shall see.

But the Senate understood. It was only the next day that

Tillman in a furious lament over the break-down of the coalition, exclaimed, "I shall not pursue the argument; I presume it is useless. The Senator from Rhode Island has resumed control of the Republicans. He shakes his head. That may be due to his modesty or the fact that he has come nearer being unhorsed and thrown into the ditch in this struggle than ever before since I have been here. All the same, I repeat it."

Everything that followed until the Senate passed the bill with the Aldrich Amendments was a foregone conclusion— or very nearly that.[71] Aldrich was not in his place when the final vote was taken. He had remained in Washington just long enough to make sure the amendments would go safely through and then left the city on the 15th of the month to attend to private business. He did not remain for the final vote. On the 18th, the bill was passed by an overwhelming majority which included both Tillman and Bailey as well as Dolliver and Allison. Senator Teller announced that he was paired with Senator Aldrich who if he had been present would have voted for the bill.[72]

A period ended, a period began, May 24, when Senator Aldrich accepted the invitation of the President and Mrs. Roosevelt to dine with them.

CHAPTER XX

RESTORING REPUBLICAN HARMONY

I

ALDRICH was now in his sixty-fifth year. He was a fine specimen of mature vigor. The arduous public life that had worn out Hanna and had worn out Platt, though it had taken its toll of Aldrich had merely strengthened his will to live, to enjoy, to prevail. His interests were never more varied nor more keen. He turned with equal zest from the great game at Washington to the development of Indian Oaks. He was eager to build his new house. A great mansion was soon to arise and to be the delight of his last chapter—or chapters—for his powerful spirit, like the philosophers of the absolute, denied the existence of time. The mansion arose in the last year of his senatorial life. His seventy-second birthday was the first that he spent in it.

His most remarkable achievements occurred in the years between sixty-five and seventy—a change of intellectual view, his most daring parliamentary triumph, the invention of a financial policy, the conquest of immense opposition to financial change. The prelude to this extraordinary period was the two years following his reconciliation with Roosevelt—political reconciliation, that is, both men being too large to need private reconciliation—in which Aldrich was again the administration leader and, for the second time bent his whole energy to the formation of an administration bloc.

It was this achievement that wrote finis in the history of the Four. Mr. Spooner withdrew from public life before the re-establishment of the bloc was complete. Mr. Allison's death closed the story of the Four just when the harmony of the Republicans appeared to have been restored. That was in 1908. Mr. Aldrich, sole survivor of the Four was

left alone, the undisputed master of the Senate—at the age
of sixty-seven.

This last chapter in the history of the Four is not explicit.
The relations of Aldrich to Spooner and Allison were changing fast. Their fraternity, cracked by Platt's death, was a
thing of the past as early as the battle of the Rate Bill.
Whether the inner, unrecorded relationships of that trying event contributed to build up Mr. Spooner's resolve to
quit public life has not been told. His eclipse by Mr. Knox
may have been part of a tale unfolded. But there were
other reasons in plenty. He was intensely proud, intensely
sensitive. No one could doubt that his day had passed. In
Wisconsin, Mr. La Follette had the centre of the road.
Mortified by defeat, Mr. Spooner was being pushed to one
side. Then, too, the tone that was invading the Senate filled
him with disgust. He was one of those fastidious minds to
whom controversy when it permits itself to become insolent
becomes vulgar.

And the Senate was being invaded by the tone of the
street. Spooner, like Aldrich, could be indifferent to the
fury of the proletariat while it raged beyond the Senate
walls. When it broke fiercely in upon the courtesy of that
restrained body, in the speeches of radical senators, he felt
that life in the Senate was no longer worth living. Not
his, the power of Aldrich to lift his eyebrows, smile dangerously and try if his weapon was loose in the sheath. The session of 1906–1907 closed Mr. Spooner's career as a senator.
Afterward in the magnificent parliamentary battle of 1909,
Aldrich exclaimed, "If Spooner were only here!" [1]

With Mr. Allison the old pleasant relations continued as
before, at least on the surface. Again, as in the old days, he
and Aldrich were the President's advisers upon all such
matters as tariff and finance. Apparently there was an end
of the drifting apart of the two comrades in whom memory
overlapped at so many and at such thrilling points. But
one has merely to remember the Rate Bill, to feel sure that
their harmony now was superficial. Mr. Allison had found
his place, at the last, and it was not the same place that

Aldrich had found. The little rift within the lute that was the Fate in the tragedy of the Four had widened until destruction was the result, and the rest is silence.

Literally, in the last two years of his life, Mr. Allison as to his deepest purposes was a silent man. Casting back over the years since McKinley's death, one remembers how concerned he was in 1901 over the singing of the ground in Iowa; how sharply his mood of caution, that year, contrasted with Aldrich's mood of blunt frankness; and again, in the great error of party policy in 1904, how the evasive and temporizing spirit of Mr. Allison formed a contrast with Aldrich's bold confession of his fundamental point of view; in the Rate Bill fight, how Mr. Allison parted with his old friends, threw to the winds the traditions of the Four, and went over to the opposite camp taking with him his spiritual son, Mr. Dolliver, whose heart perhaps had gone before. But in all this his instinctive reticence kept him from any general pronouncement upon his views.

Meanwhile, in Iowa the rebellion against his leadership became formidable. At last, in 1908, Mr. Cummins came out openly in a campaign for possession of Mr. Allison's place in the Senate. Mr. Allison, with the ardent support of Mr. Dolliver, saved himself. But his heart was broken. Iowa was not quite ready to cast him off, but it was wholly ready to repudiate his principles—that is to say, the principles that were associated with him in the public mind. Virtually, he had repudiated them himself in the controversy of 1906. But he was unhappy about it; he could not bring himself to make a public recantation, to break openly with his old comrades, and to confess that the career of the Four had ended in fraternal tragedy. Mr. Dolliver, who had taken such a bold course in 1906, was for harsh measures. The Wise Old Man who had been Dolliver's mentor during so many years sadly urged him to hold back.

"Jonathan," said he, if certain remarks made subsequently by Mr. Dolliver have been correctly remembered, "don't do it; don't do it now; wait until I am gone, I know it (the traditional attitude of the Senate) is wrong. It has grown up here gradually in the last quarter of a century. I have gone along with it. These men are my associates. I have only a little while left, and I haven't the strength to break away. . . . It is a cancer; it's got to be cut out. But wait until I am gone, and then go into this new movement where you belong." [2]

In more ways than one the shadows were mantling all the great figures of the old day except one. As the light of purpose fell away from one after another it was concentrated—purpose blazing more clearly, more steadily than ever—on that one. Even Mr. Dolliver was held for a while longer by the indomitable resolution, the infectious confidence, of Aldrich. It was some time after Allison's passing, and not until quite new circumstances had developed, that he followed his advice. Before that happened, Allison's sudden death revealed how slight, how purely personal, his influence had become. The moment he was removed from the scene, Iowa reconsidered her choice for senator and selected the inveterate enemy, who had failed to dispossess him, Mr. Cummins.

Thus the Four passed.

II

In the two or three years following the great event of 1906, when the Four as a political unit disappeared, may be found another turning point in the Aldrich fortunes. Perhaps the largest single deal in the life of Aldrich the man of business was negotiated in 1906.

Mr. Mellon, the astute president of the New York, New Haven and Hartford Railway, had in mind a great scheme. He aimed at a virtual monopoly of the transportation of southern New England. He cast a covetous eye on the network of traction properties of which Aldrich had control.

The keenness of the traction magnate—for as such Mr. Aldrich may now be rated—saw the value of his holdings to the New Haven road. He called upon Mr. Mellon and offered to sell. But his price took the other man's breath. It struck him as enormous.

"Very good," was Mr. Aldrich's attitude, "take it or leave it. But that's the price."

He left Mr. Mellon to think it over. The more Mr. Mellon thought, the more convinced he was that he had to have the Aldrich traction properties. He accepted his terms.

Years afterward both the State of Massachusetts and the federal government investigated the New Haven policies. Mr. Mellon was required to testify. He did not disguise the fact that the price he had paid was extremely high. But he strongly defended himself on the ground that the potential value of the property was higher still and therefore that in point of fact he made a good purchase.[3]

The sale was the capstone—or almost the capstone—of the Aldrich fortune. He was never a multimillionaire. His enemies endeavored to convict him of great wealth. A famous sneer was to the effect that he had sold out his grocery business for $50,000, had never done anything since but be a senator of the United States, and was now worth fifty millions. But when a professional informer made a secret investigation in Rhode Island he came to the conclusion that Aldrich's whole fortune was less than ten millions.[4] The final appraisal of his estate was but little over seven millions.

The traction sale probably marks the date when Aldrich concluded he was rich enough to begin the realization of his life-long dream. At last he would build his house. For the rest of his days the estate and public affairs divided his interest between them.

A tribute to his judgment as an investor was the way he weathered the panic of 1907. When so many investors went to the wall, Aldrich appears to have had no losses. He had made no mistakes in the placing of his fortune.

In spite of all the public turmoil that filled the two years following the Hepburn Act they were pleasant years for the leader of the Senate. Again he was the bulwark of the administration. He played the President's hand putting through a number of Roosevelt measures that had been held up until the agreement was reached over the Rate Bill.[5]

When Senator Foraker made an attack on the President because of his attitude toward certain negro soldiers who were accused of shooting up the town of Brownsville, Aldrich was the captain of the President's defense.[6]

He was never more strikingly on the President's side than when the San Domingo issue reappeared in the Senate.

There was some anxiety lest the two-thirds vote necessary to the ratification of a treaty could not be obtained. But Aldrich had two trumps in his hand. The original treaty had been skilfully amended so as to save the faces both of the President and the Senate; also, several Democratic senators had troubles of their own which made them desperately afraid of an extra session. Bacon, the great antagonist of the President two years before, was one of these. Not only Congress but the whole country was given a broad hint that only expedition in ratifying the treaty would prevent an extra session. "It is the expectation of Senator Aldrich and others of the Senate leaders that the new treaty will be promptly reported and that its ratification can, despite the opposition of Senator Bacon, be accomplished in the immediate future." A further hint to every one that expedition was imperative was the unprecedented way in which the treaty was laid before the Senate. The moment it was signed at San Domingo the whole text was telegraphed to Washington, and this telegram was accepted by the Senate as if it were the actual document. About two weeks remained of the session. The treaty was ratified by the aid of four Democratic votes. Though Bacon did not join the administration forces he as good as did so by refraining from active opposition.[7]

III

During the year 1907, there were rumors on every side that the business of the country was not sound. Suddenly, in October, the Knickerbocker Trust Company closed its doors. Its failure cracked other concerns. The panic of

1907 had arrived. Interest on loaned money soared to ten per cent a month.

Here was a new complication for all the Republican leaders. A general business collapse in the classes on which especially the Republicans relied!—at all cost it must be prevented! But what was to be done about it?

Throughout this year both the President and Mr. Aldrich had been thinking upon finance. But neither was prepared for action when the panic came. To Mr. Roosevelt it presented immediately an extraordinary problem. No moment of his life is more certain to be remembered and to be discussed, forever, than his famous conference with Mr. Frick and Mr. Gary, November 4, 1907. They told him that the Steel Trust could avert a series of failures if it were allowed to take over the Tennessee Coal and Iron Company. As the Steel Trust controlled nearly sixty per cent of the industry in the United States, they wished to know whether he would regard their purchase of the Tennessee Company as a move toward monopoly, bringing them within the scope of the Sherman Anti-Trust Act.

In substance they said to him: here is a tottering concern whose funds are locked up in securities upon which in the present state of the market, it cannot raise money; for the general good, in order to avert further disaster, we will enable it to turn its securities into money. And then came the question, but if we do that, will the President prosecute us? The reply of Mr. Roosevelt, after consultation with Mr. Root, was one of the grand audacities of his career, one about which different temperaments will disagree till the crack of doom. He told them that while he had no power to suspend the law, they need not fear for anything he might do.[8]

The reasoning which lay back of this daring course lay back also of the course which Aldrich now adopted. His aim was to save the values of the securities of the country, and at the same time to get a fresh supply of money into circulation, thus to head off a storm of bankruptcies. By so doing he would recommit the prosperous classes to the Re-

publican party, and prevent a landslide toward the Democrats in the presidential elections. He introduced a bill providing for the issue of emergency currency to banks that
could secure it by deposit, with the National Treasury, of
ample security in the way of bonds issued by States, cities
or railroads.[9]

And now was revealed another instance of the strange
bed fellows of politics. There was prompt opposition to
the bill by a group of thorough-going Conservatives and by
another group of thorough-going Radicals. Both groups
were Western. There was the rub—the old story, growing
each year more threatening, the West against the East. Mr.
G. W. Reynolds, one of the most influential of Chicago
bankers, headed a vigorous protest by Western money on
the ground that the Western banks did not hold the sort
of securities, especially railway bonds, covered by this bill.
Mr. La Follette, who had been in bitter opposition ever
since 1904, was the spokesman of a general Western discontent, and he, as well as Mr. Reynolds, made railway
bonds the target. Obviously the bill had no purpose but one
that was wholly base. It was designed to put money into
the pockets of the wicked railroads, whose bonds would
soar the moment the bill was passed.

As the new year came in, the secret but real purposes of
the Republican leaders were in a tangle. All were complicated by the question, Who should succeed the President? Could his own candidate, Mr. Taft, prove the lucky
man? In this connection Mr. Foraker and his championship of the negroes of Brownsville became a serious matter.
He had taken the world into his confidence. He had appealed to whom it might concern to do justice to the poor
black men cruelly discharged from the army on insufficient
evidence by an unjust President. A dinner of the Gridiron
Club was the scene of an extraordinary passage at arms—
verbal arms—between himself and Mr. Roosevelt.

Out of all this had grown a hubbub of innuendo. It had
long been apparent that Republican leaders were aiming
to make headway in the South. The President needed all

the support he could muster among the white Republicans of the Southern States. A famous indiscretion of his—the Booker Washington episode, when a noted negro was treated by Mr. Roosevelt in a way that was construed in the South as the full recognition of social equality—this episode had estranged many Southern whites. But now, in the discussion of Brownsville, there was a marked reluctance, even among Southern enemies of the President, to aid Mr. Foraker in forcing his hand. Northern enemies were quick to draw a conclusion; the expulsion of the Brownsville soldiers was mere politics, a play to the gallery to make sure the hold of the administration on the Southern Republican machines.

On the other hand, the enemies of Mr. Foraker were equally quick to detect a cloven hoof. Was not the negro vote a very serious factor in some close and uncertain Northern States? Might not any man whom circumstance had made a hero among the negroes be a formidable candidate for the Republican nomination? A criss-cross of hidden motives is to be taken for granted in politics and while it may not be put into words—candor not always being a political virtue—it is to be remembered when interpreting remarks about the ill-used negroes who had been denied their rights.

During three months, while professing to believe that some sort of emergency, antipanic legislation was immediately necessary, the Senate played politics and talked to the country on all these issues by turns. Mr. Foraker thrust into the turmoil a bill making any of the discharged soldiers eligible for reinstatement upon his mere oath that he was not an offender at Brownsville.[10] The same day Mr. Aldrich conferred with the President.[11] Mr. Foraker's bill went to the Military Affairs Committee, where it lay until the Aldrich Currency Bill passed the Senate.

The pivotal figure in the fight over the Aldrich Bill was Mr. La Follette. January had passed; February had passed; and March was about to pass. It was known that Mr. La Follette, his eye blazing at the provision about railway bonds, was preparing a philippic. But he little understood the great parliamentarian opposed to him. Aldrich has never been excelled in his use of the strategic retreat. He had satisfied himself that the larger interests of the hour necessitated such a move. He had asked Mr. Reynolds to come to Washington, which he did, and Aldrich had been convinced that the opposition by the Western banks was based on genuine alarm.

Though he had no sympathy with the railroad animosities of Mr. La Follette, Western senators had persuaded him that the railway bond feature of the bill might endanger their seats. Mr. Allison was one of those who thought the Radical wing of the party would create a crisis in the West unless this feature of the bill disappeared. There was still another consideration. Just when Aldrich became a worker for the nomination of Mr. Taft is not apparent. But whenever that happened it was now to be taken for granted. He was manœuvring for Taft's nomination.[12] Conceivably, the success of the administration programme at Chicago, the nomination of Mr. Taft, might hang upon preventing a Western bolt on the issue of the monetary bill. Suddenly, without warning, on the eve of La Follette's speech, Aldrich withdrew his railway bond provision.[13]

La Follette delivered his philippic but its sting was gone.

The ironical interweaving of issues was further illustrated by the introduction of another Brownsville bill. It provided for possible reinstatement of the negroes but made this dependent upon the pleasure of the President.[14]

Back to the Aldrich Bill. La Follette robbed of his railway bond issue was now insisting that another sinister purpose animated the unscrupulous Aldrich. He was pushing a clumsy, inadequate measure in order to head off genuine monetary reform. One day—it was March 24—Senator Beveridge walked over to Senator Aldrich, while the debate on the bill was in full cry, reminded him that "the desire was general that there should be a commission which would make a careful, honest and scientific study of the whole subject of our monetary system"; he thought that the opposition might be quieted if Aldrich would pledge himself to carry out such a study; he "put the proposition up to him— If I should rise and ask the question would he answer it favorably. With greatest possible heartiness he said that he would. Thereupon I arose and put to him the question" whether he would support a monetary commission.[15] Aldrich instantly, unconditionally approved the plan. Mr. La Follette, whose distrust of Aldrich was unconquerable, would not change his attitude. But the Senate was satisfied and a few days later the Aldrich Bill was passed.[16]

And then, six weeks more of financial inaction, while the Aldrich Bill hung fire in the House.[17] The Senate made use of this time for a pyrotechnic debate upon Brownsville. Senator Borah, newly arrived in the Senate, a very sincere and direct man though given to impatience, demanded hotly that the Republican party should not "connive at a crime so thoroughly proved as this because of anticipated political exigencies."[18] There were long speeches and far too much applause from the galleries. Then, of a sudden, the tempest in the teapot simmered down. Senator Foraker himself moved that the subject be postponed until the next session of Congress—which was done.[19]

What had happened behind the scenes? There can be no doubt that the guess of the New York *Evening Post* came very near the truth: "According to the official version, 'Mr. Foraker's change of programme is due to the generalship of Senators Aldrich, Hale, Allison and Crane, who have read the law and the prophets of the Republican party to the senator from Ohio. They pointed out that, while it was perfectly proper for him to use the Brownsville affray to prevent the nomination of Mr. Taft, his nomination being now assured, further insistence on a vote would place Mr. Foraker in the position of seeking the injury of his party, for which he could, if he persisted, expect no further consideration.' . . . Politics is at the bottom of it all, they say, as it has been the ruling factor in everything that Congress has done or failed to do at this session."[20]

It was now the middle of May. The National Convention

was scarcely more than a month distant. It was imperative to get a party agreement on the financial bill before the convention met. The House had rejected the Aldrich Bill and passed instead a sharply different measure, called the Vreeland Bill. This bill reached the Senate two days after the Brownsville compromise.

What followed was just what any shrewd politician could have foretold—rejection of the House bill by the Senate; conference between committees of the two Houses; a hurried compromise and the faces of everybody saved.[21] The measure received its final form in a private conference of Aldrich, Cannon, and Vreeland in Aldrich's rooms at the Arlington Hotel.[22] The result was the Aldrich-Vreeland Bill.

It made possible the formation of associations of cooperating banks; the banks comprising these associations might issue notes safeguarded either by certain classes of securities or by commercial paper—that is promissory notes not having more than four months to run, the chief stock in trade of the Western banks—and the whole association was to be jointly liable to make good the notes. The only bonds covered by this bill were those of States, cities, towns and counties. The bill also provided for the creation of a Monetary Commission.[23] Though Aldrich had altered his position fundamentally, Mr. La Follette was immovable. Driven by Aldrich's strategy from his position on railway bonds, driven from his position on the Monetary Commission, he clung doggedly to the idea that the bill was in the interest of money pure and simple, that its general was an enemy of the people. He determined that it should not pass. "The La Follette filibuster" is still remembered. By speaking interminably and having other senators relieve him he kept the bill from being voted on until May 30. Then occurred one of the famous moments in the history of senatorial obstruction. Senator Stone had relieved La Follette and had been succeeded by the blind Senator Gore on the understanding that he was to stop at a certain moment and Stone was to resume. But Stone, who had gone out for a brief rest, did not return on time. Gore paused as he had agreed, thinking Stone was present. Before he discovered his mistake Senator Gallinger demanded a roll call on the bill, the clerk, who had promised to co-operate if the opportunity arose, instantly called Aldrich's name, and Aldrich answered. Twenty senators were on their feet protesting. But the Vice-President, who also was waiting his chance to co-operate, ruled that the roll call had begun. La Follette could not regain the floor.[24]

The bill passed. The same day the Monetary Commission was appointed with Aldrich as chairman.

Within a month Aldrich was congratulating Mr. Taft on his nomination for the presidency and Taft was replying in his own hand, "I am anxious to see you and talk with the levelest-headed man in the country. I am very grateful to you for your assistance and good-will." [25]

CHAPTER XXI

THE MONETARY COMMISSION

On the 1st of August, 1908, the New York *Times* printed an article which announced the speedy sailing of the Monetary Commission; *The Times* added that it had "become known in Wall Street that Senator Aldrich" had no intention to create a new currency measure but would endeavor merely to perfect the Aldrich-Vreeland law. *The Times* was both right and wrong. Though Aldrich was going abroad determined to give a fair hearing to all sorts of views upon banking science, his own views as yet stood firm. He had not ceased to be the embodiment of the American tradition. He had no suspicion that he was entering upon the most astonishing experience of his life.

When he sailed in early August he was still in sharp disagreement with a young banker, who held what was then considered radical views, with whom two years later he was to unite in the repudiation of all that he had once believed. Frank A. Vanderlip had had the audacity to describe his country as the home of the "economic illiterates." Another iconoclast was Paul M. Warburg, who had come to America from the great seminary of German finance, and who had been looking at America for now six years with the clarity of vision natural to a newcomer, a man of intellect, seeing things in perspective. Both these able young men felt that the banking community of America no less than the business and the political community was economically illiterate. Mr. Warburg had the temerity of youth. When the difficulties preceding the panic of 1907 began to be discernible in the economic distance, he broke silence and published two essays contrasting American finance with European. Many letters were sent to him roundly abusing him for his "un-American views." But one letter was from Mr. Vanderlip. Though a vice-president of the National City Bank, where conservatism was intrenched, he applauded Mr. Warburg. With differing views upon many phases of their intricate subject these men were fellow soldiers in the cause of financial reform.

In the eyes of both these enthusiastic innovators—as in the eyes of a few more—"the ghost of Andrew Jackson was still all-powerful and anybody having the temerity of hinting at the desirability of organizing some central banking system in the United States was bound to be branded as a dreamer or a fool." [1] From the point of view of the banking reformer, as late as 1907, there was nothing to choose between Jackson and Aldrich. One had destroyed the old Bank of the United States and produced the "decentralization" which had resulted in depriving the American banking community of its supreme organ and in scattering the bank reserves of the country "in 20,000 individual bank vaults." The other had stood firm for continuing the decentralization. Furthermore, Aldrich, hitherto, had turned a deaf ear to the shibboleth of the reformers, "flexible currency." For the young men, the law and the prophets were in two propositions: America must have a central bank, or something like it, co-ordinating the whole financial system into a compact whole; it must acquire a financial mechanism that would give it "flexible currency," that is, its volume of money should expand and contract automatically as the demand for money rose or fell. Back of these two ideas, involved in them, lay, of course, a hundred detailed questions of banking science and political expediency. But on these two everything else hung.

A meeting that had a significance unguessed at the time took place in the autumn of 1907. It was brought about by Mr. Schiff, Warburg's senior partner in the noted firm of Kuhn, Loeb & Co. "Mr. Schiff, on that occasion had called Warburg into his private office, where Senator Aldrich had come to inquire about the law under which German Reichsschatz-Scheine were being issued. Mr. Schiff, not being familiar with the details of that matter, had asked Warburg to furnish the information, which he did. The picture Senator Aldrich made that day formed a lasting impression. His strong face with its high color, his sharp nose, his bushy white mustache and eyebrows that shadowed very piercing eyes, and above all his strong and clear forehead, the head erect upon the broad shoulders. As Aldrich walked out of the office, Warburg said to himself, 'There marches national bank currency and there goes currency reform.' As soon as he had left, Warburg ventured to ask Mr. Schiff if, now that a personal acquaintance had been established, a personal letter might not follow on the disadvantages of 'national bank currency issued against government bonds.' Mr. Schiff warned him to be cautious and not to precipitate that issue; 'if you do, he will never look at your again.' " [2]

So much for the unconverted Aldrich of 1907. The Aldrich who had emerged from the turmoil of the panic was different only in that he was now going to take time to think out the two basal questions. This commission of his should serve to convince him on these two points. Were the young fellows right in demanding a central bank and the general articulation of the whole banking system of America? Was there anything after all in their abuse of that old idea, bond-secured currency? Should it, after all, give place to the idea of elastic currency, of currency based on commercial assets? What Mr. Warburg did not then understand, what the country did not as yet understand, was the reason why Mr. Aldrich had been so slow to take up his subject. Because this was a political rather than an economic reason —the reluctance to rouse the sleeping dogs—the posture of his mind was not quite so rigid as the young reformers thought.

He had been very shrewd in making up the commission. It had three parts: those whose names were valuable but who would not want to go to Europe and so would not hamper the work; those who would like to go to Europe but would be willing enough to be excused from real work; those who meant business. The latter, for him, were the whole commission. Three men who were not technically members of the commission were his chief advisers. He had asked

Mr. Morgan to send him an expert in practical banking, and Mr. Morgan had selected H. P. Davison. He had asked President Eliot to send him an expert in banking theory. President Eliot had named A. Piatt Andrew, then an assistant professor at Harvard. Aldrich himself asked G. M. Reynolds, of Chicago, president of the American Bankers Association, to cut short a vacation in Italy and join him as third supplement to the commission.[3] These three and Aldrich were the heart of the matter.

The adventure was not without its amusing side. Mr. Andrew, who has a sense of humor has preserved the comedy. "On the journey over, the conglomerate makeup of the commission was very patent. Many of its members were no real students of monetary matters; and with this fact in mind, Aldrich had asked Andrew to bring along a number of copies of several elementary books on the subject. These were read, and somewhat discussed among the members on the way across. The first interviews at London were rather comical, as a consequence, for a few of the members would make page references to these elementary text-books at the conferences with the English bankers, and thereby make no small display of their kindergarten stage."[4]

In London the officials of the Bank of England were slow to take the commission seriously. It now became apparent that Aldrich had been studying banking history far more closely than any one had suspected. He was better posted on the Bank of England than were some of its officials. "He would sometimes in a very quiet and gentle way correct their misstatements to the amusement of Reynolds and Davison."[5]

The work of the commission was conducted on the familiar senatorial plan that had become a tradition through the countless "hearings," before Senate committees, of advocates of this and that. The four men who were doing the real work of the commission—Aldrich, Andrew, Davison, Reynolds—prepared for their interviews with unflagging care. The banking conferences which they attended were searching dissections which ranged through many problems

of financial science and were handled by men who were past
masters of their subject.

This was just the sort of thing in which Aldrich delighted.
Never in his life, before or after, was his bent for settling
things man to man, mind to mind, given such full and rich
play. Here, for once, he realized his ideal of conduct, the
total elimination of mass psychology. To deal with a great
problem of statecraft as a problem in pure mind—for him,
what could be more delightful! The experience must have
been all the more tonic because even in the midst of it he
did not permit himself to forget the peculiar pettiness of
the methods of American politics. He knew that the charge
of illicit profit was one of the favorite trumps that your
ordinary politician would always be quick to play, on the
faintest chance of circumstantial evidence. The use of
money by the commission must be watched with a jealous
eye. Though some of Mr. Aldrich's children were in Europe
he insisted that they should not stay at his hotels lest the
cry be set up by his enemies that the government was paying their expenses. He was careful to have every one know
that Mrs. Aldrich's expenses were paid out of his own
pocket.

There were other far-off echoes of politics in America.
Mr. Foraker was now the bitter enemy of Mr. Roosevelt
and included in his animosity Mr. Taft. In Ohio, wheels
within wheels, politically speaking, made the situation a
prey to the slightest indiscretion. Mr. Taft fearful that the
situation might be turned into a catastrophe wrote to Mr.
Aldrich urging him to bring his influence to bear upon Foraker who is "rather damning me with faint praise," and at
the same time flouting the Roosevelt political heritage, despite the fact that "our whole stock in trade in this campaign is the adherence to the Roosevelt policies." [6] Aldrich
replied playfully saying he was on the point of opening
"My dear Bill" but had "concluded that that this might be
too familiar." [7]

To Foraker he wrote a masterly letter—so complimentary
in its blunt recognition of what this strong man had the

power to do, and in its emphasis on the need of the party to have him more circumspect. "You and I have always been Republicans and believe in the party without reference to the particular persons who may be its candidates for office. I wish you could bring yourself to believe that you could take an important part in the campaign urging party success on account of the great principles for which the party has stood, and leaving the settlement of differences of opinion between yourself and the President to be discussed and decided, as they must be, by the verdict of history. . . . Above everything I want to see you returned to the Senate. . . . The tendency in the West to elect a class of men to the Senate who mean nothing but mischief and destruction, if their ideas are adopted, should awaken in every patriotic mind a fear of the consequences." [8]

Did he think of the contrast of himself and the Western Radicals, one night when the commission dined with Pierpont Morgan at the London house which had become his principal residence? Mr. Morgan got them deeply interested in his famous collection of pictures. He told them that he wanted to give it to the Metropolitan Museum. But under the tariff as it then stood getting the pictures into the United States would cost a million and a half in the way of duties.[9] The next year Mr. Aldrich put free art into the tariff bill of 1909. Eventually Mr. Morgan gave the pictures to the museum.

The Morgan bank in London helped arrange the conferences with officials of the Bank of England. These discussions with the great lords of international finance, the rulers of the greatest central bank of the whole world, laid effectually in Aldrich's mind the ghost of Andrew Jackson.

That grim spectre of organized unintelligence had always been odious to the disciple of Hamilton and yet, as he was beginning to see, he had, unaware, played into its hands. These calm Englishmen who were puzzled at times by the relative simplicity of the American point of view were opening his eyes to his own inconsistency. They were teaching him something else equally important. They were reveal-

ing to him the enormous value of a fully articulated banking system in international trade. Ever since 1900, Aldrich had been veering round from preoccupation with
domestic business toward having a major interest in foreign
business. He had invested heavily in rubber, especially in
an attempt to grow and manufacture rubber in Mexico. He
had studied the possibilities of the Congo region. The idea
of the Orient as a field for American investment rambled
in and out of his thoughts. England, the supreme international trader was showing him what was necessary to take
the trick.

Intent as Aldrich was upon this great business, other
thoughts were entwined with it.

He read voraciously. With Mr. Andrew he explored the
bookshops buying freely all over the field of economics.
This year he began that extensive collection which afterward became the foundation of the Aldrich Library in the
Harvard School of Business. He was very keen upon prints
of Sir Robert Peel. A new enthusiasm was permeating his
mind. Peel was becoming his model. To close his own public life by creating a great statute that should preserve his
memory was henceforth to be his fixed ambition.[10]

But London did not complete the change in his financial beliefs. To Senator Burton—then Mr. Burton, of the
House, a member of the commission—Aldrich still appeared
to be wedded to the old idea of a bond-security currency.
Nevertheless, "the asset idea began to get some hold in Aldrich's mind in London, where the testimony of the bankers"
led him to suspect "that after all there might be something
in this basic idea which Fowler had been espousing so
long." [11]

It was at Berlin that his conversion was completed. At
Berlin, he had to overcome a previous impression. Some
of the less significant members of the commission had
parted with Aldrich in London and had preceded him to
Berlin. The German bankers had formed unfavorable impressions of the caliber of the Americans. Matters were
not helped at first by the fact that Aldrich did not speak

German and had to use an interpreter. And this gave rise to another touch of comedy. The interpreter, a woman, translated not only the answers of the German bankers to the American questions but the asides among themselves not intended for the American ears. The discovery that these remarks had been understood, joined with the assurance of perfect confidence, put things on a better foot. Aldrich used his interpreter with great skill. President Butler remembers a dinner with German financiers where Mr. Aldrich was so quick, so sure, detecting so promptly the heart of each point, that the interpreter was all but forgotten. The great event which happened at Berlin must be told in the words of the other participant, Mr. Reynolds.

The most important point regarding the Berlin experience is the fact that there came to Aldrich there an understanding and a conviction which revolutionized his process of thought on note issues. The experience and practice of German bankers in meeting the needs of the commerce of their country demonstrated to Aldrich the validity of the use of commercial assets as a basis for currency. This idea, formerly so obscured by its political presentation in America, came home to Aldrich with great force from its demonstration in a non-political, practical, atmosphere. The first known of his conversion to this idea was a voluntary statement made by him to Reynolds one evening. He pulled the Chicago banker down beside him on a sofa, as was his wont, and there they talked, beneath the bend of the stairway in the old Hotel Adlon in Berlin. Aldrich there told Reynolds of his definite acceptance of the commercial asset idea; and from it he never wavered in the arduous months of monetary reform activities which followed.[12]

Two months later he was again in New York. The commission met at the Metropolitan Club, where several experts were to appear before it. Mr. Warburg had been invited to attend this meeting. Mr. Reynolds and Mr. Davison now virtually members of the commission were also present. Aldrich was so full of his purpose, so intensely alive, that the visiting experts by contrast seemed to lack lustre, to be relatively inert.

When the "hearing" was over, Aldrich asked Mr. Warburg to remain. They sat alone facing each other across a table. Mr. Warburg did not know that Mr. Aldrich had read certain writings of his in which, while confessing his own faith in a central bank, he had argued that the American people would never tolerate such an institution, that the idea would have to be modified to blend with American tradition. It was a surprise when Aldrich said to him after a moment of silence, "Mr. Warburg, I like your ideas—I have only one fault to find with them." Astounded, the younger man asked what he meant. "You are too timid about it," said Aldrich. Mr. Warburg fired up in defense of his courage. Aldrich—he of the piercing eyes, and the broad clear forehead, and the head erect upon the broad shoulders, who had taken so many risks in desperate political battles, who had driven his enemies so often before him—replied, "Yes, that is true, but you say that we cannot have a central bank, and I say we can." [13]

CHAPTER XXII

MR. LA FOLLETTE SPLITS THE PARTY

I

MR. LA FOLLETTE was an unhappy man. His career in the Senate so far had been a disappointment. The soaring Radical hopes of 1904 had come down to earth in 1906 like the stick of the rocket. The compromise of the Rate Bill seemed to him relatively a disaster. The restoration of the Roosevelt-Aldrich alliance burnt his soul. His desperation over the Aldrich-Vreeland Act was the expression of a genuine belief that the powers of evil were in the saddle. It was not so much the particular measure that was the thing, it was the fact that the Conservatives were again dominant. His keen mind sensed the real heart of the whole matter. This was the hierarchal conception of economic society, the faith in the downward percolation of good fortune from the upper classes through all the others. It was still the Conservative creed; it was also, the fixed objective of La Follette's hate.

Besides, like so many men of genius, he could not separate his convictions from his ambitions. Earnestly believing that his section was being victimized by the East, he believed with equal earnestness that he was its Moses, was entitled therefore to a high place in the Senate. And he had been cruelly used, largely through the influence of Mr. Aldrich. He had been refused admission to the important committees. There was something almost, if not quite, satirical in his relegation to committees that were palpably second rate. In the fierceness of his mortification, it was not he alone that Aldrich and his henchmen were snubbing. The affront was as much sectional as personal. The West, the region where the average of wealth was low, was being treated contemptuously by the statesman who incarnated the gorgeous East—or, as La Follette would have said, the despotic East.

A further detail of his unhappiness he doubtless never ad-

341

mitted to himself. He lacked some of the essential qualities
of the leader. Some, he had. He had the intellectual imagination which was able to pierce through surface appearances to
the real heart of controversy, that enabled him more than
once to sense issues quicker and more clearly than other men
did. But with this went a lack of intellectual realism. He exaggerated conditions, he twisted evidence, he had little sense
of the value of temperance. In a word, he was an instinctive
special pleader. It is doubtful whether he had emotional imagination, whether he could read men's hearts, penetrate
surely to their springs of action—except when they agreed
with him. Aldrich misunderstood him, and yet in a way over-
estimated him. He regarded him as insincere—which was
certainly a great mistake!—but, in view of his unquestioned
talent, thought him also one of the most dangerous men
of his time. He was firm as flint in the resolve to keep him
down.

La Follette, eaten up by his belief that the West was being
wronged, looked about eagerly to find followers in a crusade
against the power of the Easterners both in the Senate and
out. There were a dozen younger senators, all from the West,
all being kept under more or less by Aldrich, who, in the La
Follette reasoning, ought to be glad to accept his leadership.
Some of them had found places in the great Radical drive of
1906; but when Aldrich out-generalled them, they had followed Roosevelt in a good-humored acceptance of the compromise. They did not stand by La Follette effectively in his
attempt to make resistance to the Aldrich-Vreeland Bill a
test case of revolt.

La Follette carried his revolt into the National Convention. It was generally agreed that the country was not satisfied with the tariff and the Conservative leaders offered a
promise to "revise" the tariff without delay.[1] But they refused to commit themselves as to the nature of the revision.
This agreed entirely with Aldrich's wish. He held a middle
position between the two wings of the party.[2] La Follette
through one of his followers attempted to commit the party
to a radical programme which included the popular election

of senators and "downward" revision of the tariff. But the
Convention rose against him in overwhelming repudiation
of his views.

So the year 1908 wore through, this tense, unhappy man
brooding upon his wrongs. Meanwhile, another man on
whom La Follette had kept a longing eye passed through the
most fateful experience of his life. This was Mr. Dolliver.
Genial, magnetic, completely the orator, full of beautiful delusions of the sort that captivate the crowd, a magician with
his audience, he was just the man to make a movement go.
In vain, hitherto, La Follette had tried to enlist him in the
effort to build a Western bloc in the Senate opposed to Aldrich. He had laughed it aside.

In this year 1908 Mr. Dolliver made his last stand in Iowa
against the rising power of Mr. Cummins. But even then, his
heart had shifted its allegiance. Allison's sudden death within a few weeks of the defeat of Cummins was the unsuspected
stroke of fate for Dolliver. He at once put into effect that last
advice of Allison's—the advice to change sides the moment he
was gone—and instantaneously stretched forth his hand to
Cummins. He assisted in Cummins' election as senator.
Within a few weeks the Iowa delegation in the Senate was
changed from two senators reputed to be Conservatives, to
one senator avowedly Radical and another who was his
cordial friend.

Though the Republican platform had evaded committing
the party on the tariff, ardent Westerners attempted to get at
that result by another way round. They knew what the West
wanted. They proposed to make this so plain that when
Congress met, the demand would seem too formidable to be
denied. They promised Western audiences that the tariff as
a whole should be reduced but that Western products should
not suffer in the process. Lumber was a test case. It carried
a duty now of $2.00 the thousand feet. To make sure that
Canadian competition should be excluded Mr. Dolliver is
said to have roused the Western hope by promising that this
rate should be maintained.[3]

Whether Mr. Aldrich truly gauged their motives is a question. His mind was preoccupied. Finance was now his over-mastering interest. As to tariff, he wanted to form some sort of working agreement that would quiet the controversy, get the whole subject out of the way, and clear the road for constructive work reforming the national monetary system. But when he said that this was his purpose people would not believe him. He was named chairman of the Committee to Select Committees for the new Congress that President Taft called in extra session almost as soon as he was inaugurated. Aldrich's chief concern was the Finance Committee. He particularly wanted Senator Nelson of Minnesota to serve on that committee. Nelson, who was much less of a protectionist than Aldrich, interpreted the invitation as an attempt to commit him to whatever policy Aldrich was contemplating upon tariff. Aldrich went to see Nelson and spent two hours trying to persuade him that finance not tariff was the great matter. Therefore, he wanted him on the committee. Nelson was obdurate.[4]

The accidents of death and elections had opened five places in this committee, so nearly the most powerful of all. Both Mr. La Follette and Mr. Dolliver gazed longingly at the Finance Committee room. It is the custom of the chairman of the Committee on Committees at the opening of a Congress to send to each senator a formal inquiry what committees he desires. La Follette answered with a sarcastic letter reviewing his previous experience and as good as saying that there was no chance of his getting what he wanted.[5] He was quite right. He grimly accepted his fate, more convinced than ever that Aldrich was the devil.

Mr. Dolliver replied to the Committee on Committees in a different temper. It was always hard for him to distinguish between his hopes and his prospects. There is a tradition that he was taking himself seriously as a presidential candidate. Why not? He was one of the most moving speakers in the West. Now that he was in full accord with the masters of the moment in his powerful State, why not hope for the best? Surely he had a better chance than McKinley had in 1890. If he could attach his name to some great measure which

would captivate his section—in other words, do at last what
he had failed to do in 1906—a McKinley-like career might be
duplicated by a Dolliver.

His next move proved to be a rash one. He wrote to Mr.
Aldrich, "As an act of friendly interest in the promotion and
success of my colleague in the work of the Senate, I desire to
withdraw from the Committee on Interstate Commerce, in
case the committee appoints Mr. Cummins to that position.
I hope this can be done." [6] He wrote again arguing at length
his own claim to a place on the Finance Committee.[7]

Aldrich accepted his resignation from the Interstate Commerce Committee and gave his vacated place to Mr. Cummins. But nothing could persuade him to appoint Mr. Dolliver on the Finance Committee. Mr. Dolliver believed that
he had promised to do so. Mr. Aldrich insisted that this belief
was a misunderstanding. When Mr. Cummins went to him
in behalf of Dolliver, Aldrich frankly told him that he and
Dolliver could not work together in preparing a new tariff.[8]

Apparently Mr. Dolliver expected to the last moment that
he would be given the place he coveted. When the roll of the
Finance Committee was announced including five new members but without Mr. Dolliver, the disappointment was more
than he could bear. He felt, also—just as Mr. La Follette
felt—that his exclusion formed another instance of the
tyranny of East over West, that Aldrich's real purpose was
to produce a tariff inimical to the West. Mr. La Follette tells
what followed in his autobiography.

"Meeting Dolliver in the corridor one day after the appointments were announced, I said to him, 'Jonathan, are you
pretty nearly ready to have that conference with me?' He
answered, 'Yes, I am coming over to see you.'

" 'Well,' I said, 'Come now.'

"And he went with me to my committee room. We spent
several hours together." [9]

At last, the gods had given Mr. La Follette his opportunity.
The magnetism which he lacked was now his to command.
Mr. Dolliver was ready to exert all his powers in forming a
Western bloc. "After that I don't know how many times

Dolliver, when our little group would be conferring, would
turn toward me and say, 'Bob has been taking the gaff all
these years, and isn't going to take it alone any longer.' " [10]

II

Mr. Taft conferred with Mr. Aldrich and Mr. Cannon as
to the date of a special session and it was fixed at March 15.[11]
None of the three, that moment, were troubled by the clouds
on the horizon. Mr. Aldrich had not announced the committees, a Western bloc was not in any of their thoughts. Nor
was it in the thoughts of the country. As late as when the
committees were announced the New York *Times* entirely
missed the true significance of what Aldrich had done. It
enlarged upon the skill with which he had "scotched opposition with committee assignments," the only exception being
La Follette "and he is in a class entirely by himself." [12]

But there was a warning note. The spirit of insubordina-
tion—as Aldrich or Cannon, even Taft would have said—was
stirring in the House. Thirty young Republicans joined the
Democrats in an attempt to break the autocratic power of the
Speaker. They failed. But their effort was the far away beginning of great things. Again, the unsuccessful Radical
drive of 1905 and 1906 must be borne in mind. Mr. Roosevelt
to some extent had disappointed all these young men, but he
was still their hero. They were very jealous of his reputation.
They were determined to have his successor carry out his
policies.

Those policies as the young "insurgents" interpreted them
were mainly Radical. The attempt to put Mr. Cannon in a
corner was in the nature of a menace to Mr. Taft. If he did
not satisfy them that he was a true blue Rooseveltian—look
out! But none of the Insurgents contemplated at this time a
break in the party. Their temporary alliance with the Democrats was mere strategy. The conservative Republicans com-
manded 180 votes in the House. These could be relied upon
not to do anything sensational in revising the tariff. After a
brief gesture of revolt the Insurgents closed their first chapter by lapsing into the background.

Mr. Aldrich, thinking not only of the tariff but of his central bank on the other side of the horizon, had to keep his eye on the House. What use in framing any bill that the House would permanently obstruct? He did not see things eye to eye with the majority in the House, and it was safe to predict that House and Senate would draw up tariff bills distinctly different and that the real tussle would come when they were combined in conference. As for himself, he made no concealment of where he stood. Primarily, he was not concerned either with upward or downward revision. As his mind turned away from tariff to finance he contented himself with the same theory on which his first great effort was based, the idea of a general "equalization" of all industries in competition with like industries abroad—that is, giving every American industry at least an equal chance in competition with foreign rivals. In the course of the debate he phrased his basal idea in an interesting new way.

The Senator speaks of the consumer and I ask who are the consumers? Is there any class except a very limited one that consumes and does not produce? And why are they entitled to any greater consideration? The consumers of Nebraska owe their prosperity to the fact that the protective system gives them in the United States a market for all their products. I have seen the price of farm products steadily advancing, and the increased cost of living to-day is due almost entirely to the increased selling price of farm products.[13]

He was as resolute as ever to keep the balance in favor of manufactures instead of agriculture. But again, as in 1888, in 1890, in 1894, and 1897, his strongly practical mind was not to be deceived by the clamor of shorter-sighted men of business. With a touch of irritation he exclaimed,

I have no doubt that the (Finance) Committee would have done better with the aid of the Senator from Nebraska (Burkett). Undoubtedly it was a great misfortune to the Republic that the senator was not a member of the committee. The town is full of people and the hotels overflowing with persons anxious to ask us to change schedules. At least 999 out of every 1000 wants an increase and no day passes without a deputation calling on the committee with such a request.[14]

The heart of the problem had been approximated by Mr. Dodge months before. "Of course, the East wants the tariff off wools and hides and products of the soil generally; but the West is absolutely opposed to it and will make a strong fight against it." [15] Though too broadly put, this was mainly true. The task of Aldrich was to strike a resultant that should serve four purposes: express his own desire for a moderate readjustment of manufacturing interests; to do so in a way that might end in compromise with the narrowly Eastern interests that were clamoring for very high rates; to keep in harmony with the President who was strong for free raw materials and had taken up the cry for "downward" revision; and to do all this in such a fashion that there should be no serious rupture within the party, no prejudicing in advance the monetary legislation that was soon to follow.

Two bills were prepared simultaneously, the Payne Bill in the House and a Finance Committee Bill in the Senate. The Payne Bill reached the Senate April 10. Two days later, Aldrich introduced his bill as a substitute for the Payne Bill.

Three weeks had passed since the committees were announced. All this while Mr. La Follette had been silently maturing his plans. But there had not been any definite sign in the heavens of the gathering storm. Now, suddenly the storm broke. April 22, 1909 is a memorable day. Mr. Dolliver and Mr. La Follette threw themselves furiously on the Aldrich Bill. The papers next day spoke of the "profound impression" created by this attack.[16]

What had happened behind the scenes was quickly apparent. Once again that bewildering issue of the true constituencies—as distinguished from label constituencies—had created in the country and in the Senate a condition of unstable equilibrium. The dying advice of Allison to Dolliver was profoundly significant. The real boiling of the Western caldron—what had been threatening ever since 1890 and the silver revolt, what Mr. Byran had capitalized ever since 1893, what had seemed to disappear in the Spanish War—was at last a reality. Also, there was stirring everywhere a later phase of Rooseveltism. One's thoughts revert to that pre-

sumptive concordat between Roosevelt and Aldrich which
was probably part of the compromise of 1906, to that and to
the double rôle of Roosevelt thereafter, to his co-operation
with the Conservatives in Congress, while pursuing a Radical
course outside Congress in all those matters which were not
yet ripe for legislation. One remembers his Councils of Governors, his subtle relations with the press, his constant propaganda for sweeping changes in the political-social balance of
power. At bottom these were class movements. He was organizing the middle class, preparing it for a struggle with the
Conservatives. His alliance with Aldrich in that last stage
was somewhat like an armed neutrality. Both knew that
eventually it would break, and again there would be war between them. The ardent young men, whether Eastern or
Western, who were captivated by Roosevelt gave no heed to
the temporary re-establishment of the Aldrich-Roosevelt alliance. And here the Aldrich taciturnity played into their
hands. Had not Aldrich despised publicity, had he not been
so contemptuous of the power of the press—his great and
constant fault as a political strategist—they could not have
created the impression which they did. Earnestly, in a con-
scientious delusion, they portrayed him as the arch enemy at
all points of their own great leader, as the enemy of the people generally. The time was ripe to respond to such a gospel.
The literature of protest had schooled the middle class to
believe that aristocrats and Conservatives were emanations
of Satan—only one point less wicked than their opposites,
the Socialists and the labor men.

Could the discontented West with its creed that agriculture should be shown more favor than manufacture, could
it join forces with the social revolt the country over? Specifically, in 1909, could the representatives of these two tendencies combine in the Senate?

There were two other Senate groups that had also to be
reckoned with in creating an anti-Aldrich faction. The
Southerners were, of course, traditional opponents of tariff.
It was in their party that the cry "downward revision" had
originated. But did it mean the same thing for them as for its

advocates in the West? That remained to be seen. On certain points they were as quick as any one to juggle the phrase, to apply it with mental reservations. Lumber, for example, touched Southern pockets. To exclude it from the effects of "downward revision" was in many minds as righteous a duty south of Mason and Dixon's Line as west of the Missouri River.

Still more problematical was a group known as "the range senators" who spoke for the extreme Northwest. Most of them were very reluctant to enter a definite Western bloc. Generally they were content to remain in one economic constituency with the East. Their votes were needed by Aldrich. The condition of securing them was a duty on hides. The danger of losing them to La Follette was in the Cleveland doctrine of free raw materials, the doctrine which the President had espoused, which also the Eastern Rooseveltians inclined to accept as well as the Eastern manufacturers of shoes and harness.

Mr. La Follette had not succeeded—he never succeeded—in drawing together out of all these elements an opposition sufficiently strong to checkmate Aldrich in the Senate. He did something much more serious. He, with the aid of the brilliant orator who was now his first lieutenant, formed a resolute if small group that inaugurated a civil war inside the Republican party. In a way it was the extension of the minor civil war—the Wisconsin Civil War—that La Follette and Spooner had been fighting for years, that had ended in Spooner's defeat.

The Western bloc—perhaps one should narrow the term and say the La Follette bloc—which was called sometimes "the Insurgents" sometimes "the Progressives" was not numerous.[17] At the last roll call, there were but seven diehards.[18] But three of them—La Follette, Dolliver, and Beveridge—were in their peculiar ways men of genius. Another man of genius, Mr. Borah, though now definitely in the group of the range senators, was facing toward his ultimate alliance with the Progressives and was often with them in 1909. A formidable array were these four whose extraordinary talents, nine times out of ten were combined to obstruct, confuse, pervert the Aldrich programme. Around them gathered a fluctuating Republican opposition that never exceeded twenty.

It were a tiresome and fruitless labor—unendurable by any but the stoutest hearted historical specialist—to pursue in detail the furious controversy of the six weeks following April 22. Never were the speeches in Congress more brutally personal, or more frankly for home consumption. So flagrant was the merely political character of debate that Senator Tillman at last made an impatient appeal to Aldrich to prevent such speeches. But Aldrich was powerless to do anything but express his sympathy with the Senator from South Carolina. It was Tillman, by the way, who perpetrated a delightful satire upon protection, asking for a duty on tea because he had "about four constituents who are interested in this matter and I would like to see the South Carolinians get protection." [19] A letter urging it upon Aldrich was dated April 1.

No tariff has had a more interesting concealed history than the tariff of 1909. Far more important than anything that took place on the floor of the Senate or in the House were long rides through Rock Creek Park "in the cool of the evening," on which Aldrich and the House leaders discussed possibilities; other night rides, the President and Mr. Payne "roaming all over the countryside," in the President's automobile, anxiously casting up chances; talks in the portico of the White House late into the darkness when Aldrich and the President shut themselves from the press; dinners with political managers on the White House Terrace; games of golf when Mr. Taft's geniality drew out,—or instilled—the same quality in senators and representatives.

The least explicit part of this duel to the death is the strategic purpose of the La Follette bloc—the Progressive diehards. Doubtless they hoped at first to carry with them a considerable proportion of the Republican "regulars" and to combine them with the Democrats. But this hope could hardly have been their true reliance. Their whole clew is still to be revealed. It is hidden in a cloud of recriminations,

charges, denials, counter charges, screaming and fulmination.
Out of all this unseemly fury issues doubtfully the only explanation that now appears plausible. As they could not
command a majority of the Senate, they appear to have believed for a while that the President could be manœuvred
into supporting them, and that with the threat of a veto they
might force Aldrich to make the concessions they demanded.
Some of them have gone so far in their anger as to make
charges of virtual bad faith against Mr. Taft—as if that were
credible!

The truth is that in their ardor they had forgotten their
own ambiguity, advocating "downward revision" with mental reservations. They would not believe that Mr. Taft could
be as sincere as they while interpreting the phrase in a widely
different manner. It was from this difference of interpretation
—brought into glaring light in the last stage of the controversy—that a deadly, irreconcilable breach between the
President and the Progressives developed. But long before
that, their reliance upon the veto as a weapon in their own
armory had vanished into air.

III

A certain sort of writer would say that the battle "ran true
to form." People with a better sense of language can guess
what he would mean. The issues were the old familiar ones;
the problems of adjustment, such as had come up so often
before. For example, there were four conflicting demands as
to lumber. The President wanted free lumber; the House by
a narrow vote fixed the rate at $1.00 the thousand feet; the
Aldrich Bill went into conference with a rate of $1.50; the
Westerners demanded $2.00. Eventually, after a long and
bitter intrigue, in which all the power of the President was
exercised, the rate was compromised at $1.25.[20]

A typical contention was the quarrel over hides and leather.
This was another case of the strange bedfellows. The President for one motive, the Eastern shoemakers for an entirely
different motive, struggled hard to put hides on the free list.
The incident was a repetition in other terms of the classic

quarrel between raw and refined sugar. The Western cattle men wanted high protection for hides precisely as in 1890 and 1894, the Louisiana sugar growers wanted high protection for their raw product.[21] And just as the Sugar Trust aforetime wanted to get raw sugar as cheap as possible so now the Eastern shoemakers wanted to get hides as cheap as possible. In harmonizing the two interests Aldrich followed much the same course he had followed in connection with sugar. His bill carried a duty of 15 per cent on hides, but this was offset by compensating duties on manufactured leather. Aldrich had no objection to free hides—his bias toward the manufacturers rather inclined him that way—but he sorely needed the votes of "the range senators" who on their side wanted to co-operate with him. But here again the President was the eventual victor—Aldrich co-operating in a very curious way —and while hides at last went into the free list the votes of the range senators were saved upon other points.

But it was not in the schedules of duties that the truly significant part of this first debate lay. Almost as soon as the bill was introduced, both Insurgents and Democrats proposed to add to it an income tax.[22] By so doing they created for Aldrich a problem much more difficult than the problem of rates of duty. He was now, as in 1894, opposed to an income tax. But he saw the danger that would arise before him— monetary legislation being now his real goal—if he allowed himself to be put into any false position on this delicate subject.

Three distinct elements might be brought together behind such a measure—the new Western bloc, the Democrats, and the Eastern Rooseveltians who would regard an income tax as in the line with the policy Mr. Roosevelt had bequeathed them. It was the cue of all these to paint Aldrich as the exponent of heartless wealth, seeking to prevent its just taxation. Here was a revival of La Follette's course with the Aldrich-Vreeland Act. Were such a cry to go unanswered over the country a predisposition to prevent Aldrich's monetary legislation would be as certain as two and two.

One day—it was the eighth of June, in weather peculiarly

oppressive—Aldrich asked the Senate to adjourn earlier than usual. The tired Senate all but worn out by work and weather consented. But pretty nearly every one sensed at once that something was going to happen. On this eighth of June Aldrich held several private conferences. The most important was with the President. It had taken place before the Senate adjourned.

In the opinion of senators who were close to Mr. Aldrich after his return from his call on Mr. Taft, the Rhode Island leader was very nervous. Walking about restlessly and talking to Senators Dixon, Jones and other doubtful senators as if under some kind of strain.[23]

There were disquieting rumors that the Senate Progressives were about to be reinforced by a considerable number of senators that Aldrich hitherto had counted upon. He appears to have been afraid that the situation might be breaking from his hand, that at the last moment the vote might be a surprise and a Democratic-Radical-Western coalition make a bargain among themselves and seize control of the Senate. If that were possible, the income tax would be the chief counter in the bargain. From the moment he admitted this affair, Aldrich's chief concern was how to drive a wedge between Democrats and Republican Radicals on the issue of finance as now expressed in this question of taxation.

His first move in this new stage of the game, the one that resulted from this interview with Taft, was the thrusting forward of a measure which both of them had been considering a good while. The income tax had been trumpeted as a means of relieving a deficit which though inherited from Roosevelt would be increased by the reduction of the tariff. Aldrich had advocated instead a tax on the earnings of corporations to be inforced two years. The President approved.

Aldrich now made use of this proposal as his first move toward splitting the alliance of Democrats and Insurgents. In hasty interviews after his return from the White House, he submitted it, on behalf of the President to several senators. Hitherto the corporation tax had not appeared to be one of

the major pieces in the senatorial chess game. When Aldrich
thrust it forward as a measure he intended to emphasize, it
seemed, coming from him, an astonishing proposition. It put
his whole course in a new light. But it did not take the trick.
Through Mr. Cummins he submitted it to the western bloc as
a substitute for the income tax. They refused to consider it.
Ultra conservative senators were also opposed.[24]

Nevertheless a new chapter had begun. Aldrich had reached
a bold, new conclusion upon the necessities of the situation.
His power to make far reaching realignments of ideas in his
own mind was in full strength and was leading him toward
his most brilliant parliamentary *coup*. During another month,
while the wrangling over schedules grew, if possible, still more
acrimonious, Aldrich studied every senator who was in the
least an uncertain quantity. The corporation tax was paraded
before the world as a great stroke of the President's, as convincing proof that he was wedded to the Progressive policies
of Mr. Roosevelt.[25] As if to make sure its passage an "avalanche of corporation objectors" poured into Washington to
protest against it.

Aldrich and Taft had still other bolts in their quivers.
There began to be much talk in the Senate and out, whether
after all an income tax law could be so phrased as to pass the
Supreme Court. Was the purpose of all this contention about
it merely the striking of a pose? For Democrats, with their
long adherence to the idea, there might be some satisfaction
in that. But for Republicans—for Rooseveltians—what?
Would they play into the hands of their enemies to get nothing substantial in return? The President summoned the more
tractable Insurgents to the White House and argued with
them upon the futility of passing an act that the Supreme
Court was so likely to treat as it had treated the former income tax law.[26] He made little impression.

And then came the great stroke of the episode. It was
given out to the newspapers that on the third day thereafter
Mr. Aldrich would submit to the Senate two proposals. One
would provide for an amendment to the Constitution empowering Congress to levy an income tax.[27] The other would

propose the insertion of the corporation tax in the tariff bill.[27] A message from the President made these measures official.

Another masterly strategic retreat. The skillfulness of it was immediately recognized. "In the compromise on which Senator Aldrich finally decided," wrote the correspondent of the *Times,* "and in which he has the full support of the President, the Insurgents and regulars alike see an extraordinary instance of Mr. Aldrich's abilities as a parliamentary leader. He will probably introduce the constitutional amendment first, forcing the Democrats, who have such an amendment proposed in their platform, and most of the Insurgents, to vote for it.

"With that amendment adopted, the income taxers would be in the embarrassing position of either surrendering or seeming to vote against themselves by trying to levy a tax they have just declared needs a constitutional amendment. Then if they vote against the corporation tax substitute they know that they will be working for the defeat of a measure Mr. Aldrich has accepted only under strong necessity and against the only 'progressive' measure they are likely to have any hopes of carrying this session.

"The combination thrown around the struggling Insurgents is one Mr. Aldrich is believed to be capable of devising and one from which to-night the Insurgents see no outlet." [28]

There was none. When Aldrich opened his new series of manœuvres by introducing a resolution which provided for a constitutional amendment empowering Congress to lay income taxes, the Democrats as well as the Republican Radicals of the East saw that the ground had been cut from under them. Five days later when a vote was to be taken on inserting the corporation tax in the tariff bill the Democrats as well as the Eastern Radical Republicans deserted the Westerners. The vote was 59 to 11. Eight Republicans and three Democrats went down with their doomed ship.[29] Among them were Cummins, Dolliver and La Follette. Then came the vote on the constitutional amendment. The resolution was passed, 77 to 0, but fifteen senators were silent.

It was now July—a terribly hot July. Washington was an

oven. The furies of the tariff debate, echoed back through a
thousand newspapers from every corner of the land, had got
upon the nerves of almost every one. The appalling speeches
in Congress—a record, one by Mr. La Follette five hours long,
a famous one by Mr. Dolliver, attacking the cotton schedule[30] with unexcelled bitterness, and dozens of others—
charged the breathless air with hysteria. The situation was
not improved when the Aldrich Bill passed the Senate, was
rejected by the House and was sent to a conference of the two.
Almost the only serene men in that scorching city were the
President and Mr. Aldrich.

It has been no secret for more than a month past that many
of the older senators are in great need of rest if they expect to
last out the session. To this statement, however, Mr. Aldrich is
a striking exception. Every afternoon on the adjournment of
the Conference he steps over to the private office, where a barber
is waiting for him, and he reappears a few minutes later, smiling,
as fresh as ever. If there is anything in the President's activities that displeases the Senator from Rhode Island that astute
leader gives no sign, and from whatever quarter the wind blows
he blows along in front of it apparently as gay as ever.[31]

These two entirely understood each other. Mr. Aldrich had
told the President that the bill as it stood was not what he
wanted but that it was as near what he wanted as he had been
able to make it. To him the bill meant first of all: a general
"equalization" of the protective system adjusting it to the
changed conditions that had developed since 1897. The schedule about which he cared most was the cotton schedule so
dear to the Rhode Island manufacturers.[32] Upon this he
would resist any serious changes. There were administrative
features in the bill that he was ready to accept—a new prin-
cipl of tariff assessment; the principle known as the maximum and minimum,[33] the court of customs appeals[34] and
the tariff commission.[35]

Aldrich felt that his hands were partially tied. He did not
feel free to initiate departures from the trades he had agreed
to; for example, his agreement to 15 per cent on hides. But if
the President could bring pressure to bear that would give

good color for reopening these discussions, Aldrich would co-operate with him in the effort to alter the terms of his agreements without imperilling their general purposes. The President undertook to make his own fight to force raw materials into the free list. As to the men with whom Aldrich had made his trades—"Aldrich is quite with me," wrote the President, "but he is complicated with some of the obligations that association in the Senate imposes on him in passing his bill, but I told him yesterday that he could put it on me and send the men in—that I would take the burden." [36] And again, "I told him he could use me as he pleases, and that I would threaten him if he wished me to, with a view to making some of these people come over." [37]

The long squabble of the conferees of the two Houses was one of those complicated legislative bargains which are the disgrace of American politics, but which in our cumbersome system of government appear to be inescapable. The President was the central figure. His policy was first to win over the House and use it as a club over the Senate, and then to drive into a corner the "doubtfuls" of the Senate, the men who would struggle hard for their local interests but who also were in deathly fear of being read out of the party. He was able to get to the House behind him partly because its bill came nearer to meeting his views than did the Senate bill, partly because the House was angry over the substitution of a complete new bill by the Senate, partly because the talking for home consumption had had its effect. Again, Aldrich the Bogey Man had been paraded before the eyes of the nation. A fictitious Senate Bill was dangled before the easily persuaded constituents of the representatives. An amusing and yet a sinister detail is in the violence of the press because—it has generally been assumed—the Senate Bill proposed a tax upon print paper somewhat higher than that of the House. Had Aldrich eliminated that one point his path might have been smoother. The popular uproar was felt in the House. Its members, bombarded by letters and telegrams, became more and more sensitive to criticism, more and more inclined to follow the President in his battle for free raw materials.

A month passed during which the gradual drift of the conference was toward the President's programme. The keys to the situation were the range senators on one hand, the Eastern leather men on the other. Aldrich and his friend from Massachusetts, Senator Crane, followed the President's lead aiming to bring the two groups together.[38] Day after day rumor shrank the hides duty. By degrees both sides were persuaded that their safety lay in compromise. At length it appeared to be attained—free hides and corresponding reductions in the duty on manufactured leather.[39]

July was gone and things seemed well on the way to a conference report fairly satisfactory to the President. Suddenly, Mr. Cannon rashly attempted to turn the conference drift in a new direction. He was the special advocate of a high duty on gloves. He announced that if the bill did not put the glove duty at a very high rate he would contrive to adjourn the House without taking action.[40] At the same moment apparently the range senators formed a deal with the lumber men and it was given out that if the lumber duty did not stay at least as high as $1.50 the hides men would bolt.[41] Whether Mr. Aldrich secretly sympathized with this last moment reconsideration, or whether he lost his nerve, is a matter of speculation. He hurried to the President and urged him to meet the new combination by accepting $1.50 on lumber. Mr. Taft had given up hope for free lumber. He had announced $1.25 as his ultimatum. Mr. Aldrich brought him the news of the Cannon threat while he was at Fort Meyer outside Washington watching one of the experiments of the Wright brothers who were trying to prove that airplanes were possible things. The President was unruffled. He repeated his ultimatum. He added a threat of his own: if Congress adjourned without passing a tariff act he would promptly call it in extra session and compel it to start all over again. Then, as if nothing had happened he blandly changed the subject and asked Mr. Aldrich, "Do you suppose those boys will be able to get their motor in shape for a flight tonight?"[42]

Here was a threat which even so bold a political gamester

as "Uncle Joe" Cannon dared not trifle with. The country was too much on edge. He stepped into the background. Senator Borah got together most of the range senators and they held their final council of war. Presently, Senator Bourne came to Mr. Aldrich bearing their capitulation. They would vote for $1.25 on lumber.[43]

The game was up. The President had won the better part of his main points.[44] At the same time Aldrich seemed to have held the party together. When the vote came, the only Republicans in opposition were the seven Progressive die-hards.[45] What did they count for?

And yet——

The New York *Sun*, the steady supporter of Aldrich, was alarmed. It prophesied that a real civil war inside the party had begun. "The conflict, political observers believe, will continue until the leadership of one faction or the other is driven from power." [46] A few days later the *Tribune* expressed views even more ominous. The *Evening Post* had taken up the subject of Aldrich's expected monetary views and used the familiar sneer about no good thing coming from Nazareth. The *Tribune* protested. The measure he had in view should not be damned in advance merely because his name would be connected with it.[47]

These dreary prophecies were near the truth. But in the joy of the moment, getting rid of the tariff on any terms, they met the reception that Cassandras generally meet. The mood of the moment, as Aldrich felt it, was better expressed by some jingling rhymes that came to him from an unknown correspondent.

WHEN ALDRICH HAS THE GOODS

With etamine, and warp, and woof,
　Some mercerized, some dyed,
Or painted, dressed, or on the hoof,—
　(My! how those figures lied!)
In counter-jumping, sales-girl ways,
　In the Senate neck o' woods,
　　The others show the samples,
　　But Aldrich has the goods.

Untrue and unimportant each,
  Those "facts" Progressive flew;
A rapid-fire, Chautauqua screech,
  A waste and shoddy crew;
And figures never lie, oh, no!
    But goodness! see the broods
      Of liars showing samples
      When Aldrich has the goods.

So wind 'em up and let 'em run,
  Fakirs and false alarms;
(Slow death is what they would have done
  To mills and mines and farms!)
And, Boy; remember drool is cheap
  By babes in the tariff woods;
    So let 'em drool their samples,
    For Aldrich has the goods.

CHAPTER XXIII

FACING TOWARD THE FEDERAL RESERVE

I

A PHASE of Aldrich's power of concentration was his ability, when he dropped a subject, to seal it up alive, so to speak, in a vital compartment of his mind, and to preserve there all the momentum which the subject had acquired. He could return to it, later, open this sealed compartment and resume the subject just where he had dropped it. He could turn on again instantaneously, as one would turn on a faucet, all the energies which had been arrested. Having put the Monetary Commission out of his thoughts while the tariff possessed them, he now did the same by the tariff. At one turn of his mind he was back again in the full tide of the financial problem.

Shortly after Congress rose, Mr. Aldrich called the Monetary Commission together for a consultation. He was considering letters from Mr. Reynolds urging upon him a speech-making trip through the West. Tossing the matter into the hands of Mr. Davison, he was off to Europe for a holiday.

Again the European ramble was brightened by delightful "unofficial talks" with men in the highest places; "with the ministry in Paris with reference to the changes made in our tariff, especially in regard to our Maximum and Minimum duties"; similar talk in London, at luncheon with Lloyd George and Winston Churchill.[1]

While Aldrich was absent from America there was ominous warning that the country could not be persuaded easily to abandon its financial traditions. The annual convention of the American Bankers' Association demonstrated anew how deep-seated was the influence that Mr. Vanderlip and Mr. Warburg had fought so long, that now Mr. Aldrich was going to fight. The association had a committee on Federal Legislation. This committee was watching the Monetary Commission. It reported to the convention that it was doing so, and urged the association to be "alert to this situation," to be opposed to "any form of a central bank yet suggested by legislators," to insist on preserving "the individuality of our banks," and to insist that any mode of issuing "currency to prevent and dispel trouble should be such as would enable individual banks to meet such conditions largely within themselves. . . ."[2] In other words, the American Bankers Association was still the happy hunting-ground of the ghost of Andrew Jackson.

The American Bankers Association was very powerful, both in finance and in politics. It had a lobby at Washington which was one of the potent factors in that unacknowledged congregation of occupational councils which is the fourth estate in federal legislation. The influence within the association of its Western members was very great. Western influence had dictated the report which condemned the idea of a central bank. Again, as in the Aldrich-Vreeland controversy, the West and the East were eying each other askance.

But there was more of menace in those doubtful glances than in 1908. Since then, Aldrich had beaten La Follette on the tariff; since then, Taft had joined forces with the archenemy of the Insurgents; and now, the whole country was ringing with their outcry denouncing the administration, and all its friends. Aldrich was being painted as Goliath of Gath, the terrible enemy of the chosen people whose spear was as a weaver's beam. And every one of the die-hard Insurgent senators was a Westerner. No wonder Mr. Reynolds—a Westerner who was not in sympathy with the Insurgents; president of the "A. B. A.," but in opposition to the signers of the anti-Aldrich report; who understood the extent and the fury of the Western alarm—no wonder Mr. Reynolds urged Aldrich to go out into Macedonia and fight for the new gospel in the very citadel of its opposition.

Meanwhile Mr. Davison had made arrangements for the Western trip suggested by Mr. Reynolds. Two weeks after

Aldrich's return from Europe he was on his way West. For the first time in his life he had set out on a tour of propaganda.

Eight men in a private car sped over the rails as far west as Omaha and made stops at Detroit, Chicago, Milwaukee, St. Louis, Indianapolis. It was a roaming house-party, "thoroughly homelike, as if a family, with Aldrich seated at the head of the table, serving the gentlemen about him and doing it all with an attitude that might be described as fatherly." His companions were somewhat amazed by his "uniform courtesy even when routed out of bed for interviews before breakfast." [3] For this unfailing geniality he had his reward. He took the West by surprise; in part, at least, it would be fair to add, by storm.

The Washington *Star* summed up the impression he was making by an amusing cartoon. A cowboy was shaking hands with him. In the Westerner's left hand was a picture of Aldrich as Mephistopheles. The cowboy was saying, "Howdy, senator, I sho didn't recognize you." [4] Perhaps this cartoon was inspired by the remark of a "man in Des Moines who told the Senator he must be an Elk because he shed his horns so easily," which vastly amused Mr. Andrew, to whom history is further indebted for preserving the delicious remark of a hotel clerk at Des Moines, to the effect that "for real enthusiasm the Senator's meeting beat anything that had happened since the school-marms' convention."

True to the dominant impulse of his mind, Aldrich was out to present his subject to the country in general terms. He aimed to persuade his audiences on but three points: that a sweeping reform of the banking system was imperative; that it must take the double direction of greater co-operation and of flexible currency; that the scientific difficulties in the way were very great and that there must be cautious, deliberate give and take among many points of view before a satisfactory conclusion could be reached. There were many luncheons with small groups of leaders. Much of the speech-making was done at dinners. They were elaborate dinners of many courses.

Aldrich sat through these formidable feasts, exhibiting the abstemiousness for which he was noted, talking delightfully but merely sipping his wine, and when the time came throwing all the powers of his mind into the transformation of his dry technical subject into something direct and lucid. He accomplished this result through his extraordinary gift for stripping a general proposition of its accretions, for cutting a broad highway of clear thought through a wilderness of details. His speeches were never memorized. They "got over" as personal utterances—the sort of speaking that all Americans love.[5]

He was steadfast in the assertion that whatever was done it would not be a banking system in the interests of any one section, especially it would not be in the interests of Wall Street, and it would be kept out of politics. He confessed that he had formerly thought that note issue was the heart of the matter but now saw that what really counted was the organization of credit. He appealed to farmers because they were now "the great creditor class of the country."

He amused an audience by reminding them that "out of the 90,000,000 of people in the United States, I suppose at least three-quarters of the heads of families think they are entitled to submit a plan and have it considered—which I presume is true. These men of course would have honest criticisms to make of what we are doing. But we shall also be confronted by men whose sanity on general subjects would be conceded; but whom much thought upon this question has made mad." [Laughter.] The new alignment of his own thoughts, his passing over from internal to external issues, formed the last word of this preliminary statement.

"I want to see all that changed. I told you I had a plan to suggest, and I have. I have a plan the details of which I cannot work out to-night; but it is one that will make the United States the financial centre of the world, which it is entitled to be. [Great applause, and cries of "Good!"] It is entitled to be by its resources and by its wealth and accumulated capital. It will be, if we are only wise and intelligent in the discussion and disposition of this matter. Are you willing to help me and help this commission make it that? [Great applause.]

"This is the only plan I have, gentlemen. This is the end and aim of my ambition in this regard. I want to live long enough to see the credit of the United States under all circumstances, every day in the year and for every year, as sound as human agencies and human methods can make it. And I appeal to the intelligent men who have made this community so great, and who will make this neighborhood and this country so great, to help us.

"This is my appeal." [6] [Great and long-continued applause.]

Returning East he speedily took up with the three men who in addition to Mr. Andrew were now his closest advisers—Mr. Vanderlip, Mr. Warburg and Mr. Davison—the ticklish question, what sort of formal pronouncement should be made to the country.

They could all agree with him that the whole matter should be postponed until the session of Congress was out of the way. He wanted to keep the affairs of the Monetary Commission free if possible from political entanglement. An opportunity to tell the country that such was his purpose was given by an invitation to address the Commercial Club of Cincinnati. He could not go but sent Mr. Andrew in his place. Mr. Andrew assured his audience that the commission was still engrossed with its investigations, "and as for the chairman, I know that he still preserves a mind open to conviction in every direction upon the subject. I have frequently heard him say that if he were given a blank sheet of paper with *carte-blanche* power to write upon it the details of an ideal financial system for this country, he would have to resign the task because he was not yet certain what ought to be done." [7]

II

There was no year that was more truly for Aldrich a crowded hour of glorious life than this which was his sixty-ninth. It was a stormy year. All his enemies were gathering for his undoing. First of all, his old sleepless foe watched patiently from the office of *The Commoner*, convinced that while God moves in a mysterious way it is surely, eventually on the lines that a Bryan can approve—which would mean for one thing the downfall of Aldrich. Far, far away—but not too far for some people to be thinking about it—there was a vast shadow brooding over Africa, a shadow with eye-glasses and a familiar profile, that was destined to be all three Fates in one. And near at hand, chiefly in Congress, a furious political storm. The die-hards of senatorial insurgency were out to be revenged both upon Aldrich and the President. Mr. Taft had made his speech at Winona praising the new tariff and in defiance of unpopularity insisted upon talking of Aldrich as his friend and as a great man. All this added several drops to the bucket of Insurgent animosity. His quarrel with Mr. Pinchot—sworn comrade of them all—over the policies of the secretary of the interior, Mr. Ballinger, was one of the things that caused the bucket to spill over. There followed one of the most astonishing campaigns of vituperation that even the annals of American politics can boast. During both sessions of the Sixty-first Congress, and in the short vacation between, the uproar continued. In the main, the Insurgents allied themselves with the Democrats and embraced with fury whatever cause could be rendered dangerous to the President or to Aldrich.[8]

There was little in the legislation of 1910 that may be called Aldrich's own. Broadly speaking he had shot his bolt as a senator. His heart was now in the Monetary Commission. His attendance that winter except at crucial moments was irregular. Nevertheless he was a true blue administration man on whom the President could always count—as in February, when he thought there was a good opening for a Postal Savings Bank Bill on which he had set his heart, and he telegraphed Aldrich who was in Florida to come to its aid;[9] again, in March when he was afraid that a movement was afoot to abolish the Customs Court;[10] and yet again in May to save his programme for additional battleships.[11] Aldrich stood by the President on the subject of instituting a tariff board.[12] He gave rein to a sharp mood telling the Senate that the government was ruinously extravagant. "If I were a business man and were given permission to manage the affairs of the government, I would run them for $300,000,000 less than it is now costing." [13]

At a dramatic moment when the Insurgents were blocking the President at every turn, Mr. Dolliver read to the Senate a letter from his friend Pinchot sharply criticising the administration. It was a challenge to Mr. Taft to remove him if he dared. The challenge was accepted. And then an ominous thing occurred. Mr. Pinchot took ship and sailed away. But that was not all. The shadow with the glittering eye-glasses had moved over Africa and was now resting upon Europe. It was in the hope of enlisting Mr. Roosevelt in their factional quarrel that the Insurgents called down the blessings of Heaven on their informal ambassador. Mr. Pinchot had once been a protégé of the Tribune of the People.

In the midst of the storm occurred the fall of Mr. Cannon. The Insurgents played again that dangerous old game of uniting with their party enemies in order to humiliate their party rivals. In a famously picturesque congressional pow-wow, the Speaker was deprived of much of his power. New rules were adopted and the Democratic-Insurgent coalition took possession of the House.

III

All this, in the early part of the year 1910. Aldrich paid little heed to it. He had ridden out worse storms before. Life at Washington this year was delightful. The Aldriches had a pleasant house on Massachusetts Avenue. No people in the capital had more prestige. Everybody they wanted to see, wanted to see them. Their intimate circle embraced the White House coterie, the ambassadors, the American magnates. Mrs. Aldrich's diary shadows in scanty line a life of stimulating delight. "January 6, dined at Count Moltke's, party of sixteen." "January 9, first Sunday in

Lent, Nelson went to Saint Matthew's church for high mass, celebrated by Cardinal Gibbons, afterward with the Cardinal at the Rectory and spent the rest of the afternoon with Mrs. Rodgers and Josephine Patten for bridge." "January 18, left for Florida at 10 o'clock P. M." "January 20, a very pleasant day" (in Saint Augustine). January 23 (at Miami), Mr. Aldrich and two daughters are out at sea fishing. (It was the next day that Taft telegraphed him about the Postal Savings Bank Bill while Mr. Dolliver was storming at the President in the Senate.) "January 25, another perfect day, all went out together fishing." Not allowing the President's anxiety to hurry him, Aldrich shifted from Miami to Thomasville and visited the beautiful plantation of Oliver H. Payne, "with the most attractive collection of old English prints."

While Taft was complaining bitterly in private letters about the Insurgents, Aldrich was making his leisurely way back to Washington. After that, more meetings with people who were good company. "February 5, we are dining with Mabel Boardman" (who came nearer perhaps than any other woman in Washington to having a political drawing-room in the great old sense of a hundred years before and the days of Mrs. William Bingham). There is endless cheerful private life, children and grandchildren coming and going. Everywhere, clever and distinguished women, as well as men of eminence, and always bridge without end. Six weeks at Washington, then away to Warwick. On March 22, "William here to assist in staking out the cellar for the new house."

What a lot behind that simple entry! At sixty-nine, at last, Aldrich is entering on the realization of his landed dream. A great mansion is to replace the pleasant old house that has served the family hitherto. His son, William Aldrich, a rising young architect, will direct its erection.

Turning their backs on the hysterical Congress, the family celebrated another marriage. Shortly after that, a conference in an atmosphere as remote from the atmosphere of Washington as anything could be. From the beautiful

Fenway Court in Boston, the owner of that noted mansion had written Mr. Andrew that she would be delighted to have Senator Aldrich and Professor Taussig meet at her house to effect an economic "conversion." When the great men had come and gone and had discovered that they could stand together, Mrs. Gardiner wrote again to Mr. Andrew, remarking that though she had not been well, she was now "really better. Aldrich has just gone and was truly enchanting. He has cured me. His speech was perfect and as clear as possible, even to me." [14]

That was in the opening of April. The same month there were two happenings which, at the time, appeared to have no connection, but out of which history grew—far-reaching history.

In Italy, the excitable Mr. Pinchot threw himself, metaphorically, on the bosom of his former master. In the name of all that was good and noble, would not the Tribune come to their assistance, work another miracle, and give the Insurgents the control of the party. It was the loyal tribesman trusting utterly in the power of his medicine man. Mr. Roosevelt listened, pondered, but would not commit himself.

Mr. Aldrich, to whom Mr. Pinchot and all his fellows were as wraiths of windy mist—that unfortunate delusion of his!—had determined not to stand again for re-election. He wrote to the governor of Rhode Island announcing that because "of a decision long since made, I cannot under any circumstances be a candidate for re-election to the Senate." [15]

The announcement had been expected. Reports to this effect had long been going about. His day in the Senate was done. The old friends were gone. The Four were a far-off, half-forgotten memory. Of those remote days when the Elder Statesmen dominated both Houses, people hardly spoke—so shadowy they seemed to be! His friend Hale had also announced his retirement. Both knew that their rule was over and while that fact, at least in Aldrich's case, had not caused the retirement it clothed his decision in fateful majesty. We have known men and nations, and the curtain is coming down.

Perhaps the Providence *Evening Tribune* reported him correctly when it said that he felt that his job at Washington was a thankless one and he was tired of it,[16] or the New York *Times* which pictured him as "tired of being the pack-horse, that is, of being held responsible for all legislation because he was so powerful," and as intolerably lonely because of the breaking up of "the Old Guard." [17]

The last of the Elder Statesmen, it would be very natural for him to have such feelings. Then, too, his health was troubling him. And yet, he was never more hopeful, more resolute to achieve great things, whether in public as a statesman of finance—America's Sir Robert Peel—or privately in the glorious beauty of his gardens, in the stateliness of the prospective great house. The Providence *Journal* gave the true word when it quoted him as saying:

I would retire from Congress with the greatest reluctance if it were not for the thought that I can continue with the National Monetary Commission.[18]

What was practically his last act in the Senate was that extraordinary evidence of superiority to circumstance which was quoted in the second chapter as the key-note of his career. In May, 1910, twenty-four years after his first stand on the long-and-short-haul clause, his lieutenant, Mr. Smoot, came to terms with the Democrats, and agreed to put through an amendment to the Mann-Elkins Bill contrary to Aldrich's wishes.

Aldrich was taken by surprise. A brief adjournment, and hasty conferences in his committee room came too late. When he and other senators returned from his room, Smoot was in the midst of a group of Democrats who were helping him to patch together the amendment that was to abolish the work for which Aldrich had stood so long, so firmly. Aldrich stood alone awhile in the centre aisle looking at the group, and the correspondent of the New York *Times* says that he showed an instant of bitterness, but it was only an instant.

"In another moment he had counted his dead and was walking toward the group in the middle of which the Insurgent amendment was being framed under the shaking hands of Senator Smoot. When he reached the group Mr. Aldrich was smiling, and after watching Mr. Smoot's nervous efforts to hold a sheet of paper and cut it at the same time, he reached over, steadied the sheet with his hand, and pointed out some minor corrections in verbiage which the excited plotters had overlooked. From then on it was evident that whatever came from the group to which Mr. Aldrich had finally added himself would pass overwhelmingly." When the vote came Aldrich good-humoredly made no opposition.[19]

There is no more interesting picture of him than one that was drawn by a clever newspaper man just before his retirement was formally announced.

He is what might be termed a spirited, vivid, delicate speaker. . . . Delicate waves of expression come over his face as he talks. . . . There is something sensitive, polished, finished, about him—I can't describe it; it's most difficult . . . he reminds me in some indefinable way of a race horse, a finely trained race horse. . . .

When Senator Aldrich delivers himself of sentiments, he does not raise his voice, but the delicacy and subtlety of his delivery become emphasized. One is always impressed, however, with a certain suggestion of equanimity which his manner has with it always. It is probably this quality which keeps for him the poise and keenness of a young man as he speaks to you.[20]

CHAPTER XXIV

JEKYL ISLAND

In the autumn of 1910, six men went out to shoot ducks. That is to say, they told the world that this was their purpose. Mr. Warburg who was of the number, gives an amusing account of his feelings when he boarded a private car in Jersey City, bringing with him all the accoutrements of a duck shooter.[1] The joke was in the fact that he had never shot a duck in his life and had no intention of shooting any. His five companions, whatever their past might have been, were as far as he from a sporting purpose in this journey. The duck-shoot was a blind. Mr. Aldrich and representatives of three extremely significant New York banks were taking this elaborate mode of getting away by themselves without putting anybody on their track. It was Mr. Davison who had devised the plan. Their objective was a hunt club on Jekyl Island off the coast of Georgia.[2]

Why all this mystery?

The preceding summer had been a trying one for Mr. Aldrich. This year 1910 contained a good deal of ill health —no very definite malady, but frequent indisposition, carried bravely, even jauntily, in his usual way. A Canadian fishing trip revived him considerably, and the autumn included a flying visit to Aix les Bains.

A stormy political year was 1910. Mr. Roosevelt came home and plunged at once into politics though still refusing to be the acknowledged leader of the Insurgents. But they did not falter in the civil war within the party. They were confident apparently that they could force him to come into their camp as the only means of saving the Republican party from destruction. All of them, this summer, made denunciation of the Conservatives their key-note. But they were not without their sorrows. A pathetic incident of their revolt was the break-down of Mr. Dolliver. Worn out by the intensities of his ardent nature, his endurance suddenly snapped. Only a week intervened between his doctor's warning and his death. His friends, in the bitterness of their hearts, held Mr. Aldrich indirectly responsible for this tragedy—so violent had been Mr. Dolliver's disappointment over the wreck of his great designs the previous year, so passionate his belief that he was fighting a despotism.

His mantle fell upon Senator Bristow. It was he who made the next attack upon Aldrich. In the tariff of 1909 the duty on manufactured rubber had been increased from thirty to thirty-five per cent. Mr. Bristow pulled out some high stops in the organ of platform controversy and played a stormy fugue upon the theme of the diabolical Aldrich who made this wicked increase because he was a great investor in rubber. He accused Aldrich of having formed since the passage of the tariff a Rubber Trust that was now paying enormous dividends, that controlled the supply of crude rubber, and had forced up prices on every rubber article "from automobile tires to babies' rattles." [3] Mr. Bristow's charges were taken up by that astute Democratic newspaper which was so keenly interested in widening the Republican split, by *The World*. It demanded an explanation from Aldrich, dogged him with reporters, and when he refused to explain drew the most sinister conclusions.[4]

So furious was the attack, so fast and far was it extended through the press, that the Republican leaders became alarmed. Aldrich was urged to reconsider his refusal to explain. He delayed long but at length overcame his repugnance to standing on the defensive. Besides the party danger, another argument counted for much with him. The reputation that was being fastened upon him might prejudice any scheme of financial reform that he should later propose.[5]

Finally he gave way. In an open letter to the chairman of the National Republican Campaign Committee, he went into the matter at length. He had long been interested in the production of rubber from plants grown in Mexico, but all the companies in which he was interested operated outside the United States and were not affected by the American tariff. They produced crude rubber only, the price of which was fixed in Europe. They had not formed any new connections since the passage of the Payne-Aldrich Tariff and were not part of any combination resembling a trust. They had had nothing to do with fixing the price of any manufactured article. Instead of controlling the rubber output they produced but a small fraction of it.[6] Though Mr. Bristow attempted to explain away the reply, and though *The World* tried to keep up the attack by means of sneers and innuendoes, Aldrich's letter was widely accepted as unanswerable. Presently, the attack died out. But it had done its work. All the lurking opposition to him had been charged with new life. Once more, he had been painted successfully as the Bogey Man, the enemy of the people.

The summer faded stormily into the autumn, and the unbelievable happened. The Insurgents reaped their sowing. The divided Republicans lost the congressional elections. The Democrats got the House. A few months and the children of Andrew Jackson would again be in the saddle. Would they know how and where to ride?

Such was the train of events that had seemed to Mr. Davison, perhaps also to Mr. Aldrich, to justify the mystery of the fictitious duck-shoot. Newspaper notoriety must be guarded against. The party comprised Mr. Aldrich with his secretary, Mr. Shelton, and the four men destined to be hereafter his privy councillors—Mr. Andrew, Mr. Davison, Mr. Vanderlip and Mr. Warburg. None of them as yet was prepared to formulate a new banking bill. For the moment all of them wanted an undisturbed opportunity to think and argue far from the inquisition of prying newspapers. Possibly, Aldrich's health was a further consideration. A month earlier, while hurrying across a street in New York, he had to jump for it to avoid a taxi, was struck by a street-car, thrown down, and very badly bruised.

The journey began on a night train and early the next morning Aldrich opened upon the purpose of their adven-

ture. It was instantly apparent that their views were far
from uniform. At first it seemed as if they were all at cross
purposes, all emphasizing their differences. Presently Mr.
Vanderlip suggested that they begin at once setting down
on paper the points they held in common. This sensible
suggestion was accepted. Bit by bit, often after hot discussion, they reached a general, but still tentative, agreement upon the main difficulties of their problem.[7]

The curious episode came very near—in fact, it shaved
by a hair—defeating its purpose and attaining the worst
sort of publicity, amusing publicity. The game had gone so
far that they were playing at being incognito, and spoke of
each other by first names. Even Aldrich before the end of the
play had become "Mr. Nelson," In the station at Brunswick,
Ga., where they ostentatiously talked of sport, the station
master gave them a start. "Gentlemen," said he, "this is all
very pretty, but I must tell you we know who you are and
the reporters are waiting outside." But Mr. Davison was
not flustered. "Come out, old man," said he, "I will tell
you a story." They went out together. When Mr. Davison
returned, he was smiling. "That's all right," said he, "they
won't give us away." The rest is silence. The reporters disappeared and the secret of the strange journey was not
divulged. No one asked him how he managed it and he did
not volunteer the information.[8]

The incident was characteristic. In managing people,
Mr. Davison had the magic touch. It was fortunate that
he had. These men were all so much in earnest, and all
were such strongly defined characters, that their discussion
of a vital issue could scarcely escape at times becoming
heated. But always, just in the nick of time, Mr. Davison
would give a little twist to the argument that shifted it off the
danger field, or he would cut in with precisely the right humorous story, and the storm cloud blew over. One instance
in particular. They had all agreed from the start that the
new central institution however formed should be empowered to issue an elastic currency. There arose the highly technical question, whether other banks should be permitted to

hold such currency in their vaults and count it as part of
their "reserve" money. Mr. Warburg thought that this
privilege should be granted; Mr. Aldrich that it should not.
So hot was the debate between them that Mr. Davison
was afraid to let it go on. He sprang up from his comfortable seat in a large easy chair, took Warburg by the arm
and drew him out of the room. He urged him to let the
matter drop for the present. Mr. Warburg, who playfully
described himself as a "fanatic" for what he considered
sound finance, was hard to persuade, but at length consented. When Mr. Aldrich issued his "Plan" shortly afterward, he stuck to his guns upon this point. Eventually he
dropped it. This was brought about,—though just how is
not known,—as a result of the long debate upon the new
scheme that occupied the year 1911.[9]

A very tense controversy filled the days and nights at
Jekyl Island. The financial privy council went at it first
thing in the morning and kept at it until midnight. Mr.
Vanderlip thought of the episode afterward as the most
stimulating intellectual experience he had ever had. They
were all impressed by the range and acuteness of Aldrich's
mind, also by the relentlessness with which he pursued an
argument to its bitter end. They felt also the great force of
him as a politician. But in this respect, one detail struck
them as singular. All the others were far more conscious
than was he, of the wide-spread personal animosity that had
been kindled against him throughout the land. He seemed
almost oblivious of it.[10] He was wedded to a belief in the
irresistible power of the Conservative leaders inside the Republican party. The business constituency that stood behind them seemed to him the only constituency worth considering. It was the backbone of the party. The Insurgents
were negligible; the recent elections, but a passing vagary
of the electorate. As to the Democrats, they were on the
other side of the horizon.

Nearly ten days of this arduous mental tournament. And
then, they felt they were near enough in accord to draw
breath and look about them. One day was devoted to ex-

ploring the waterways of the vicinity, or to actual duck
shooting. The next day, reconsideration began. Mr. Vanderlip was pressed into service as a committee on statement, and under his skilful hand a comprehensive memorandum of their agreements rapidly took form.[11] The
moment it was finished, back to New York; and after that,
the break-up of the party. They had spent Thanksgiving
Day in their seclusion by the lonely sea.

Aldrich entered this discussion at Jekyl Island an ardent
convert to the idea of a central bank.[12] His desire was to
transplant the system of one of the great European banks,
say the Bank of England, bodily to America. Upon this
basic issue a great deal of the discussion turned. The others
felt that whatever might be the theoretical justification of
such a view, American conditions would compel some sort
of a compromise. Mr. Warburg, thorough-going as he was
in his European tradition, led the insistence upon modifying European ideas in transplanting them to America.
Upon this point as on every other, Aldrich took the position
that what he was after at the moment was a tentative
working plan that would be free from financial vagary, and
would serve as the basis of general discussion the country
over. What was finally agreed upon took the form of a
great federation of banks with pooled reserves, that was to
serve as the custodian of the government's funds and that
should be known as the National Reserve Association. Its
board of directors was to be a sort of financial parliament
regulating all those banking activities that were too complicated to be dealt with by the simple old-style type of
wholly independent bank. The Association as a whole was
to serve as a bank of rediscount—that is, it was to be empowered to discount a second time the commercial paper
which members of the Association had already discounted.
It was to transact business only with banks and these banks
must be members of the Association. It was to be able to
render the currency flexible because, in rediscounting, it
could issue new money that might stay in circulation so long
as the "paper" for which it was issued was not redeemed but
that would be taken up and cancelled when the paper on

which it was based was reclaimed. But they were not thinking of their problem solely in terms of currency. Stated in
another way, their aim was to make credit flexible.

A host of technical questions—such as whether there
should be any limit to the amounts that might be redis-
counted, or that difficult question whether the new money
of the Reserve Association should be counted by its member banks in the part of their funds known as reserve,
though brought up, were left unsettled. They were regarded as the beginning not the end of a discussion. The
project in this first tentative form, was slightly retouched
a few weeks later and was issued to the world in a pamphlet
which outlined what at once became known as "The Aldrich Plan."

Of the controversies, aroused by those features of this
plan that were issues of financial science, more hereafter.
Two features not fundamentally scientific were destined to
overshadow all others. Aldrich insisted upon requiring the
association to maintain a uniform rate of rediscount
throughout the United States. This the bankers regretted.
But his argument which was fundamentally political, appears to have silenced them. He regarded this provision as
the only way to anticipate and refute the charge that great
financial centres would, without this provision, inevitably
influence the new bank so as to establish rates in different
regions favorable to their own operations, unfavorable in
some cases to the locality.[13]

There was another matter which proved to be the rock
on which the scheme eventually split. How was the Reserve Bank to be controlled? The experience of the two
United States Banks, in our early history, pointed a warning. The experience of a life time spoke in Aldrich's unconditional reply. It was to be kept out of politics. It
must not be controlled by Congress. The government was
to be represented in the board of directors, it was to have
full knowledge of all the Bank's affairs but a majority of
the directors were to be chosen, directly or indirectly, by the
members of the association.

CHAPTER XXV

THE CONQUEST OF MACEDONIA

I

MR. ALDRICH was now several weeks into his seventieth year. On the whole it was his most remarkable year. But it began inauspiciously. Six weeks after Jekyl Island, the correspondence of his young associates suddenly bristles with alarm. Senator Aldrich had been peremptorily ordered South by his physicians. He had obeyed "very reluctantly." A nervous break seemed imminent. Mr. MacVeagh wrote that he would have come to see him before he left Washington, but "you were having all the visitors you could stand." [1] About the middle of January he was back at Jekyl Island.

A good deal was accomplished in the six or seven weeks between the last day of the Jekyl Island duck-shoot and Aldrich's return. Promptly after his arrival in the North he spoke before the American Academy of Political and Social Science at Philadelphia. He spoke guardedly intimating that what the country needed was a unified system of banking, but one that would not destroy the State banks, that would not compete with any existing banks, that would nevertheless provide a mode of concentrating reserves and preventing panics, and would give the country a flexible currency. [2] Mr. Andrew also addressed the academy. The two played into each other's hands. Andrew was equally guarded but dropped several well-chosen hints.

The time had not come to use frankly the term "central bank." But Andrew described the great central banks of Europe "with vast resources of lending power," which "through the practice of rediscount furnish to the banks an agency for making available in times of need those sterling assets in the form of first class commercial paper which in the United States at such times can find no market and can only be translated into cash when they mature." One result of Jekyl Island appeared in the promise that there was no intention to create "a vast institution like the Bank of England, which is not in any way subject to governmental examination, regulation or control." [3]

All of the Jekyl Islanders were mulling over in their minds that outline of a banking system which Mr. Vanderlip, at the island, had put upon paper. At the same time they were beginning to cast out their nets with a view to capturing other big fish of finance. Particularly, they wanted to draw into the toils Mr. Forgan, of Chicago, the "dean," as he was named of American banking. The President gave a dinner at the White House "to discuss some phases of monetary reform" at which Mr. Forgan was the principal guest.[4] Two days previous Mr. Aldrich had come down with tonsilitis; another day and "he had a spell of feeling very nervous but nothing serious resulted." [5] Serious warnings for so self-contained a man!

And still the close hard work on the last revision of what was soon to be known as "The Aldrich Plan" continued. But at last illness had the Senator firmly gripped. The last meeting of the inner council was minus its leader. He was too ill to attend. Andrew, Warburg, Davison and Vanderlip met in Andrew's apartment at Washington for the final interchange of notes on details hitherto unsettled. The Chicago friends, Reynolds and Forgan, were consulted by long-distance telephone. The conclusions of this conference were sent to Aldrich who in his sick room passed the final judgments.[6] The "Plan" was to appear immediately as a pamphlet. It was to be accompanied by a letter which Aldrich asked his councillors to frame. They had a hard day's work on it, "with Vanderlip whipping it into final shape," and Aldrich accepted it "with a very few changes near the end, changes in which he showed his master hand." [7]

The pamphlet which now appeared, its letter of introduction dated January 16, 1911, bore the superscription—"Suggested Plan for Monetary Legislation, Submitted to the National Monetary Commission, by Hon. Nelson W. Aldrich, chairman." It outlined a general system of cooperative banking based on the Jekyl Island conclusions and using the term, the National Reserve Association.

But Aldrich was far too astute to assume the ex cathedra tone, to offer the Plan with a gesture of authority. He wrote a letter of his own to Mr. Vreeland and had it printed as a preface to the general letter prepared by his four lieutenants. He apologized for his enforced withdrawal from Washington, directed the calling of a meeting of the commission for purposes of discussion, and asked Mr. Vreeland to "present to the commission the suggestions which I send you forthwith," as a "tentative plan" for "discussion and criticism," not only in the commission but among "the commercial organizations of the country."

That last remark was the heart of the matter. The commercial organizations of the country were beginning to take active interest in banking reform. The writings of the younger reformers had gradually sown the field. The conversion of Mr. Aldrich had made the situation dramatic. For this powerful politician to recant the creed of a lifetime, to do so with an outspoken frankness that lesser politicians dared not use—what could be more impressive?

At the moment when his health wavered, the National Board of Trade was about to hold a general conference at Washington. Represented there would be the Chamber of Commerce of New York, the Merchants' Association and the Produce Exchange. These three, through the patient diplomacy of Mr. Warburg, sent a joint committee. Mr. Warburg was a member. He had primed the committee with a resolution indorsing the general agreement reached at Jekyl Island. The resolution was carefully confined to a statement of general principles. One of the delightful experiences of Mr. Aldrich in these trying days, was the news that the general principles of the Aldrich Plan had been approved by the Board of Trade Conference.[8]

Another delight of the early days of his retreat to Jekyl Island was a letter from Mr. Forgan, telling him quite cordially that he was in sympathy with the new movement.[9] But there were doubts in Mr. Forgan's mind. From the start the Plan encountered two sorts of objections, scientific and political. Mr. Forgan's, of course, were scientific. It was partly to meet his objections that Mr. Aldrich from his Southern retreat directed his secretary to call a meeting of bankers at Atlantic City.[10]

The conference was held and opened its session with a gracious telegram to Jekyl Island. They appreciated the honor of his invitation "to consider your outline" but before doing so "we desire to express our keen disappointment and regret at your inability to be present. Although absent in person, we recognize your spirit and influence as with us, which will aid us greatly in our deliberations." But they were pleased "at the opportunity to congratulate" him on his Plan as containing "the proper and correct principles of reform." [11] Of course this was a small and picked body— again, the unfailing Aldrich belief that the small body of leaders are the men who count—but they represented great power. The chief incident of the conference was the full conversion of Mr. Forgan. He propounded a long list of technical questions. He debated them at length chiefly with Mr. Vanderlip. So unmistakable was the sense of the meeting that at last Mr. Forgan and Mr. Vanderlip reached a cordial agreement.[12]

The conference indorsed the Plan with a few suggested changes described in its own announcement as "unimportant." [13]

II

Meanwhile a sick man at Jekyl Island was forcing himself back to health through rest, through the ocean solitude, through the power of the will. Mrs. Aldrich was with him, also Miss Lucy Aldrich and his son, Richard. Mrs. Aldrich's diary affords brief glimpses of lonely, delightful life, at the remote club, where but few others were present, with the glittering winter sea that is the splendor of those latitudes near at hand. Shadowy afternoon waters filmed over with a brightness felt rather than seen; turquoise sky wholly different from the fierce blue of the North; and everywhere, inland, a riot of vegetation; giant oaks that ought to have Greek denizens; the whole sealed up in dreams—the "low country" of the Georgia-Carolina coast. Walks, drives, ocean trout fishing, bridge at night. "The Senator walked for a mile along the beach alone." He is "improving gradually playing bridge as usual in the evening." He is teaching the ladies auction bridge. There is a delightful day when son William arrives "to bring complete plans of the new house at Warwick. Decided upon location of telephones and electric lighting."

And there was good talk upon great affairs. Professor and Mrs. H. Fairfield Osborn were there and Mr. Aldrich talked with them at length upon the services to his country of Mr. Morgan. A flash of the inner man came out in his chance remark that there must be a better banking system in America because, as he said to Professor Osborn, "we may not always have a Pierpont Morgan with us to meet the country's crisis." He watched Congress from afar, almost grieving—he was too much the stoic to let himself really grieve—because he could not take part in the stirring events of the moment.

He wrote the President that nothing else in his long public life had been so great a disappointment, but added with characteristic fatalism "there seemed to be no alternative." He admitted, "I must stay here until I am stronger. Every attempt to do my work or to think seriously on any subject brings back my sleeplessness." [14]

Taft earnestly assured him that his improving health was verifying "the diagnosis and prognosis of your physicians that there was nothing the matter with you organically and that all you need is to rest your nerves and to rid yourself of the notion that you are breaking down." [15]

Again the President wrote, "I long for your presence. I feel about as Scott said of Rhoderick Dhu,—A blast upon your bugle horn were worth a thousand men." [16] In a letter that is like a sigh the discouraged President, whom the Insurgents in Congress were tormenting ruthlessly, said of "the new tariff board bill" which appeared to have cleared the breakers in the House, "I wish you were here to put it through the Senate." [17]

Upon one subject the President could not refrain from seeking his assistance. This was the scheme for reciprocity with Canada, a scheme which the Insurgents were bitterly opposing. In a way, the fight was the old one of 1909. La Follette and the Westerners saw in lower duties against Canada the injury of certain Western interests, especially lumber and food products; now as then, they were not for reduction of duties except so far as this might benefit themselves. And again there were the strange bed fellows of politics. A group of Eastern manufacturers were equally fearful. But it was with the fight of the Insurgents against the President chiefly in mind that Aldrich wrote to Taft:

"With reference to reciprocity as you know, I believe we should make the most liberal trade arrangements with our neighbors and with the Central and South American States and China. We are impelled to do this by our selfish interests and by our neighborly obligations. We must have for the future of our industries and our trade closer commercial relations, better transportation and banking facilities with all these countries. They must be in the future our most profitable customers if we are to have any, and we are the natural customers of what they have to sell. All this seems perfectly plain to me and I believe that for yourself and the party and the country you cannot insist too strongly upon the policy. As to the Canadian agreement I have not seen the text and I cannot speak by the book. I am inclined to think it is more liberal in its concessions than I should have had the courage to make. However, I do not and cannot

know all the conditions and circumstances and therefore am
not disposed to criticise. Of one thing I am quite clear,—the
Finance Committee should report the bill to the Senate
promptly and it should be acted on at this session. Every
consideration from a party and protection standpoint makes
this necessary. I am quite willing you should say this for
me to any one on the Committee who is in doubt." He closed
with a very gracious line, appreciating the President's confidence, "which I hope never to forfeit. I wish I could serve
you more efficiently, but if my strength returns—as I am
sure it will—I am sure I can help in the future." [18]

That letter made a stir among the Conservatives to whom
the President in confidence delivered Aldrich's message.
Some of them were as short sighted with regard to their own
brand of protection as La Follette was with regard to his.
Senator Smoot, for example, has never been able to understand what induced Aldrich to send that letter.[19] And yet,
Aldrich had been steadily swinging over—at least since 1900
—away from preoccupation with domestic trade and toward
a vivid interest in foreign trade.

Early in March the Aldriches were on their way to Washington. Aldrich was himself again. His friends were delighted to find him hale and hearty. At once the crowded
round of his habitual life was resumed. Business luncheons,
social dinners, conferences at the White House, many sessions of the Monetary Commission, sittings to Zorn for his
portrait, social duties, bridge parties, delightful conversations with charming women—one especially, an intimate of
the Aldrich family, of whom Mrs. Aldrich entered in her
diary that this lady "brought N. W. home from Mrs. D's
last night and as usual tore her friends to tatters"—and
every little while flying trips to New York or Providence.
Small wonder Mrs. Aldrich exclaimed, "As a family we seem
to be constantly on the road, rushing from one place to another, a fatiguing and profitless kind of existence."

To her indomitable husband it was only a normally busy
life. The sleeplessness at Jekyl Island could hardly be remembered.

III

In one of his letters to Jekyl Island, President Taft had said that "the coming two years furnishes the much needed time to educate the bankers of the country to the wisdom of your proposed Plan. Meantime if you formulate your scheme into a definite bill backed by the Commission, I can recommend it and present it with the arguments in its behalf to a Democratic Congress and in this way perhaps prepare the way for its being adopted as a plank of the next Republican platform. So that if we are successful in the next election we can put it on its passage in a Republican Congress as the performance of a platform pledge and promise." [20] This was not quite Aldrich's view. He had hopes of keeping the whole movement out of politics. Nevertheless, he was quite confident that before the matter should be ripe to be voted upon, the Republicans would again be omnipotent.

Like so many masterful men whose tenure of power has been too long, too masterful, he had become obsessed by an illusion. He believed that the alliance of Democrats and Insurgents was of no consequence, that a serious division of the Republicans was unthinkable; therefore, that his problem was not between parties but within a party. If he could win over the dominant element among the Republicans, he would win everything. The Republican Conservatives were still the real people in America. Now as in 1902, the solid, propertied classes were the men who would save the day. In his view the wise thing to do, this while, was to convert the business classes—and, of course, incidentally, the bankers—to a belief in the rightness of the Plan.

His thinking was about what one of his partisans put into words when he said to the convention of the National Association of Clothiers, that as often as the financial system of the country broke down, "the business man seeking credit is refused and pays for this condition. You who are business men bear the burden." [21]

This was also Mr. Warburg's view. At Jekyl Island he

had been eager to begin at once upon a campaign of education. He was to discover that the task was far more difficult than he thought. Even Mr. Aldrich whose knowledge of politics had caused him to scoff at Warburg's faith in a quick victory, even he was much too sanguine. Both over-estimated the power of the class to which they were intrusting their cause. In this respect the one deep pessimism in Mr. Aldrich's thought, his distrust of mass thinking and of political contrivances, was to find itself justified in ways he did not foresee.

Other powerful forces were also at work. By the time Aldrich was in full sail going strong once more in the social-political whirlpool, an organization for financial propaganda had been formed. It traced back to the conference of the Board of Trade in January. Mr. Warburg introduced a resolution authorizing the establishment of a Citizens' League "for the purposes of promoting banking reform upon the principles outlined in the resolution just passed and embodied in the Aldrich Plan." [22] The committee was appointed with Mr. Warburg as chairman.

After many labors the committee brought about the formation of a National Citizens' League. Its headquarters were in Chicago. The choice of location was due partly to a desire to conciliate the West, even more to avoid association in the popular mind with Wall Street. One had no need to be a prophet to see that keeping the issue out of politics was going to be difficult. Every effort would be made to give it a sectional and class aspect. There was danger that the alignments of 1908 and 1909 would be craftily revived and the whole matter dissolve away amidst the blinding smoke of a purely political battle.

The league was non-partisan. It was careful to abstain from emphasizing Senator Aldrich, while advocating the adoption of some system of central banking analogous to that proposed in the Plan.

Professor Laughlin of the University of Chicago was given charge of the league's propaganda. Mr. H. Parker Willis, later to have a distinguished part in forming the Federal

Reserve Act, was retained to write a popular book on "Monetary Reform." First and last, hundreds of thousands of dollars were spent by the league in popularizing financial science.[23]

IV

It was against the background of the league and its widespread activities that Mr. Aldrich conducted his own campaign, like the first violin against the background of the orchestra, in 1911. He continued to be a very busy man the whole year through. While considering innumerable criticisms of the Plan, weighing carefully the political value of each objection, considering deeply who must be placated, but at the same time making it perfectly plain that there was an irreducible minimum—chiefly the idea that the new bank must not be under political control—which under no circumstances he would concede; he found time also for his customary rounds of diversion—salmon fishing on the Moisie River in June; building the mansion throughout the summer; a trip to Europe in August. The latter was really a working trip. He went abroad with masses of memoranda upon the various suggestions poured in upon him since his return from Jekyl Island. He came back with a revision of the Plan embodying such of those suggestions as he was willing to accept.

The most significant event of the year, from the Aldrich point of view, was a conference of the Monetary Commission and the Currency Committee of the American Bankers Association. Again, Mr. Forgan was a conspicuous figure. He was pleased by what happened. He made a report in which he assured the "A. B. A." that the conference was most satisfactory and that all the suggestions of the Bankers' Committee had been accepted by the commission. In his suggestions, the inescapable distinction between scientific considerations and political considerations again opened like a chasm. When the bankers urged that "rediscount functions" be enlarged, or that notes of the National Reserve Association should be counted as part of the legal reserves of national banks or that any of a dozen similar points be reconsidered, they were thinking obviously as financial scientists. They were thinking as politicians serving a class interest when they protested against the mode which Aldrich had devised for effecting a working connection between the government and the new bank. They issued an ultimatum. Convinced that the support of the bankers was essential to the conversion of the business classes, Aldrich accepted their terms. He made a great—perhaps a ruinous —concession.

IV

Aldrich had now reached the final outcome of his thinking in political science. The new conservatism had arrived, in his mind, at a conclusion quite different from the position of the Radicals upon the one hand or of the mere Plutocrats upon the other. Between the theory of pure democracy—nose-counting democracy—and the theory of pure aristocracy (Hamilton's theory, which once upon a time, had been Aldrich's theory) he had discovered middle ground. A conception of occupational groups as the basis of the State had been dimly recognized by a few Americans and had been talked about rather uncomprehendingly. Old-style conservatives of all parties had refused to consider it. Aldrich in his gradual, tacit way had allowed it to permeate his thought. He still retained all the sharp social limitations that were always his. In essence he was as much the aristocrat as any of the great English conservatives that had arisen in his time, as, say, Benjamin, Earl of Beaconsfield. But like Beaconsfield he based his conception of aristocracy on a profound knowledge of life. He was worlds away from the crude American plutocrat who thought that God had a golden shadow, that somehow the possession of money gave one the immunity of the celestials. Aldrich knew, as all great statesmen know, and as no mere politician seems to know, that in politics the last thing to tolerate is hocus-pocus. Consistency, frankness, courage, joined with utility, were the foundations on which always he would ground any theory he might propose. He demonstrated all this in the candor with which he now laid his cards on the table.

He believed that the solution of the modern democratic problem was to be found in three purposes: to accept the old machinery of the popular State and use it as the expression of the collective will of the nation; at the same time, to vest immediate power in great occupational groups that were also great accumulations of capital; to give the former not the initiative in the affairs of the latter but intimate knowledge of those affairs, and for practical purposes a selective veto upon their proposed courses of action. He had thought out for himself as a means of harmonizing the complexities of the day a double application of La Rochefoucauld's maxim, "Who administers, governs." [24]

This theory underlay that burning question which was destined to be the final crux of the whole debate—how was the new bank to be governed? Aldrich had displayed once more his innate possession of a larger horizon than the mere plutocrat could comprehend. The original Plan, after providing for a national Board of Directors provided also that "The Executive officers of the Reserve Association shall consist of a governor, two deputy governors . . . (they) shall be selected by the President of the United States from a list submitted by the Board of Directors. The Governor shall be subject to removal by the President of the United States for cause." It was this provision that the committee of the "A. B. A." headed by Mr. Forgan had refused to ratify. It was in accepting their ultimatum that Aldrich made his most extreme concession to the grasping political demands of the bankers. The Revised Plan, embodying their ultimatum, read thus: "The Governor shall be selected by the President of the United States from a list submitted by the Board of Directors and shall be subject to removal by a two-thirds vote of the Board of Directors for cause. . . . The deputies shall be elected by the Board of Directors and may be removed for cause at any time and their places filled by the Board."

By this transfer of the power of removal from the President of the Board, Aldrich won over the bankers completely. Did he show himself lacking in strategy? Had he the right to believe—as evidently he did—that mere knowledge of the Banks' inner workings, the mere power of publicity, gave the President so much revising power, that the question of removal of the Governor, though apparently important was really trivial? The bankers did not attempt to force a reconstitution of the Executive Committee of the Board and in that committee Aldrich had given the comptroller of the currency a place ex officio. Nevertheless this concession of the power of removal, because of the way politicians might ring the changes upon it, was a dangerous move even as the price of securing the support of the "A. B. A."

Aldrich expounded his Revised Plan in several public addresses. In the middle of November he was at Kansas City attending the Trans-Mississippi Congress. His reception was all he could desire. To a sympathetic audience he explained in popular terms the procedure contemplated in the Revised Plan. His purpose at Kansas City was to commend the Plan to the agricultural interests. He dwelt upon a subject prominent in his own thoughts, the international aspect of monetary reform. The American farmer needed the whole world as his market and in order to possess it he must be equipped with a modern, scientific system of banking. In part Aldrich was speaking as a scientist simplifying a difficult scientific proposition; but he was also speaking as a politician. He had satisfied himself of the points upon which the Western farmers needed to be fortified against the political arguments, which as he knew only too well were soon going to be brought into play. It is worth noting that he had become cautious about the term "central bank." He sensed across the horizon a coming battle upon that term.

After recounting the aims of the National Reserve Association, he adds "We propose to do that not by an organization like a central bank, but by an organization that affords a concentration and mobilization of cash reserves, and at the same time secures a decentralization of control." He alluded to that part of the Plan which distributed the actual business of the association among fifteen regional branches, and to that other part of the Plan which made it impossible for any one region to control the Board of Directors of the whole system.

The necessity to persuade the West that control of the system would not be vested in the East had inspired another provision upon which he laid heavy stress. Subsequently there was furious debate—including the most sinister imputations—over the provision in the original Plan, which was retained in the Revised Plan, that the rates of discount fixed by the Reserve Association "shall be uniform throughout the United States." Whether this provision was sound, or unsound as financial science, became the theme of a controversy that delighted the trained athletes of the scientific arena. What Aldrich thought about it as pure science is unknown. He had adopted it for political reasons.[25] He put those reasons into words in his speeches at Kansas City.

"This Plan takes away from New York and from the other cities that have enormous accumulations of capital the undisputed power to say to Kansas City, and to the banks of Kansas City, and to the banks of Kansas and the neighboring communities, what rates they shall pay for rediscounts of their paper, or whether the accommodations shall be granted that are so essential for their existence or development." Again: "but so far as the National Reserve Association is concerned, and its control over this matter, every local bank in this community will be entitled to the same rate of discount as the largest bank in this community, will be entitled to the same rate of discount as the largest bank in Chicago or New York. And this is as it should be. The farmer, the producer in every part of the country, is entitled, through his local bank, to equal facilities and equivalent rates in so far as the great national organization is concerned, to those afforded the most favored

class in any community. The tendency of this enforced
uniformity will be to insure greater steadiness and reasonableness of rates everywhere. It will surely be felt in the
communities you represent through a gradual equalization
of rates for the same classes of paper in different parts of
the country." [26]

He was taking his life in his hand, frankly, without concern, as he had done so often before.

On his way to Kansas City he had paused in Chicago and
there had addressed the Western Economic Society dealing
with his Plan more in a scientific than in a political vein.
But even there politics had crept in. As was natural to
him, he was bluntly candid, arguing that the shareholders
who were to own the new bank should control it despite
those people who "thought that the owners of property are
the people who ought not to manage it." [Laughter.]

He supplemented these remarks with a few sentences
which as he uttered them must have brought back to his
mind those stimulating days in London when he turned the
corner in his own development—those brilliant days that
must have reinforced all his innate impulse to insist that
the bulwark of a nation is a class of trained and intelligent
administrators, just what England so conspicuously has.
"But, after all, we shall depend upon the wisdom of the
management, in whose hands we place the power to raise
the rate of discount and to refuse discounts, the power over
examinations into the conditions of banks, and if, in the
face of all that, you admit the possibility of failure in this
regard you have less confidence than I have in the bankers
and business men of the United States." [27]

There spoke the final inner Aldrich. Just what that inner Aldrich was really facing; just how his conception of
the American nation differed from the conception held by
his indomitable enemy, that other man of genius, Bryan;
how the two were to fight the matter out—no one fully
comprehended in November, 1911.

There were few people who did not think it was Aldrich's
star that still, in the main, ruled the ascendant. Before the

end of the month the American Bankers Association in convention at New Orleans approved the Aldrich Plan. There was but one dissenting vote. A delegate from Texas announced that he entered his objection from conviction and with regret.[28]

V

Fixed as he was in his illusion that the Democratic-Insurgent coalition was of no consequence, Aldrich had refused to give heed to the powerful forces gathering for his defeat. And yet, the storm of vituperation had not quieted. The feeling against him was so wide-spread and so violent, it was kept active so craftily, that many people in the National Citizens' League clamored for a divorce between him and the reform movement. The New York *Times* laughed at "the fear the leaders of the new movement have for the name of Mr. Aldrich."[29]

The Democrats were lying low and biding their time. In 1911 it was the Insurgent revengefulness that kept up the hue and cry against Aldrich. They were also trying to break down the Administration. This gave the Democrats an opportunity to hold the balance of power. They supported Canadian reciprocity while the Insurgents furiously attacked it, and prevented a vote on it, in the last session of the expiring Congress. Taft, determined to force it through whatever the result, called a special session which dragged on in miserable displays of mere chicanery—each party trying to "dish" the other—throughout the summer. A temporary alliance of Conservatives and Democrats passed the Canadian Reciprocity Bill. With each day the Democrate grew happier over the widening breach among the Republicans. True to congressional traditions of the balance of power they transferred their votes to the Insurgent side when the latter under Western pressure favored tariff reductions prejudicial to the Eastern interests.

Senator La Follette made characteristically fierce attacks upon Aldrich. Another Insurgent, Senator Cummins, resolved to put an end to the Monetary Commission. After much debate, frequently ill-natured, a bill destroying the commission was passed. Salaries were to cease at once; the commission was instructed to report to Congress January 8, 1912; it was to go out of existence March 31.[30]

This made it necessary, as the year approached its close, to draw up a formal bill and send it to Congress as the fruit of the commission's labor. Upon the scientific questions involved, the commission—or at least a large majority—was pretty well in harmony. Aldrich's position was that none of these things were being finally settled; that the bill was to form a platform for discussion and gradual adjustment—his attitude toward almost all bills—and that criticism was now invited. Politically his attitude was sharply different. Two provisions at least had nothing to do with financial science; two other provisions nominally scientific —doubtless really scientific in the minds of the commission —could, and certainly would, be transformed eventually into pure politics. On these four, the fate of the bill would depend. They were:

The character of the national board of directors;

The uniform rate of discount for the whole country;

The relation between the Bank and the government;

The opportunities that might be found in the system for control of it through purchase of bank stock.

Upon the first of these problems there had ceased long since to be any discussion among the advocates of the Aldrich Plan. The new Bank was to form a single institution, a "national" institution in the same sense in which the Republican party had been using the word "national" since 1860. In a way, a narrow way, Aldrich's last word as a politician was the same as his first. He came into public life in the full glow of the early Republican faith in a single, consolidated nation. All his life he had held to that faith and had consistently believed he was expressing it. His crucial strategic mistake through which the Insurgents had built their power was a refusal to modify that traditional idea, to think in terms of sections. To this extent he was repeating in 1911 the position which had inspired his fateful

victory in 1909. He was inviting and defying the same furious Insurgent opposition.

As to the uniform rate—waiving its scientific rightness
or wrongness—it was an obvious attempt to give the na-
tionalism of the general idea a local justification.

With regard to the formal control of the new Bank, Aldrich's principle of governmental knowledge without direct
governmental control was to be applied in the Revised Plan
not only through the appointment of the Governor by the
President but also through the presence in the national
Board of Directors of three great officers of the government
—the secretary of the treasury, the secretary of commerce and labor and the comptroller of the currency.
The comptroller was to be a member of the Executive
Committee of the national Board of Directors. The secretary of the treasury was to be chairman of a special board
of supervision.

By this device Aldrich hoped to reconcile the country to
his refusal to put the bank under political control. Was it
not quite sufficient, he reasoned, to give the government—
that is, the party in power—such intimate knowledge of
all the affairs of the Bank that it could give instantaneous
publicity to any of the Bank's decrees, could at any moment
lay all its affairs before Congress? How much more intimate such a relation between Bank and government than
that which obtained between the Bank of England and the
great nation whose financial affairs it conducted. Extraneous as the thought might be in the mind of Mr. Bryan,
it must have meant much in the mind of Mr. Aldrich. It
is not accidental that his speeches this year contained frequent references to England's Bank Act of 1844, frequent
evidence that England's experience was steadily at the back
of his head.

All these considerations had been pretty clearly determined before the commission took up the task of putting
a bill into legal form. The fourth consideration was another
matter. It evoked a singular discussion. Aldrich had described the National Reserve Association by saying that

"the organization suggested is a co-operative union of all
the banks of the country . . . a federation of banks with
functions clearly definite."

The individual banks were to be combined in local associations, the local associations were to be federated in district associations—fifteen in all—and these jointly were
to elect the national Board of Directors by which the entire
system was to be administered. Obviously, if some great
combination of capital—a "money trust," as the phrase
was—undertook to buy its way to control of the Association it could do so only through purchasing the control of
a vast number of local banks.

In Aldrich's view the original plan rendered this practically impossible. He calculated that such purchases
would necessitate the investment of five or six billions of
dollars. In 1911 such sums were unthinkable. He had
another argument. There was a provision in the Plan
which enabled him to say that the question had been asked
—"What would New York or any part of the country do
with this organization if they should secure the control of
it? They cannot make any money out of its operations
because all the dividends over five per cent go to the government." In the Revised Plan he had added a third safeguard against the imaginary "money trust." The Revised
Plan made it impossible for more than four of the forty-
five directors to be chosen from any one district.[31] Thus
he had offset—as he thought—the concession forced upon
him by the "A. B. A.," the transfer from the President to
the Board of the right to remove the Governor.

Events took a new turn in December. All the friends of
the reform movement, Aldrich included, were persuaded
that the West was really afraid that Wall Street would
gobble up the new Bank. The three safeguards of the Revised Plan were not enough. The arguments of Aldrich at
Kansas City must have further reinforcement. The secretary of the treasury took a hand by incorporating in his
annual report a warning that the new law must "deny with
great precision to any bank included within its provisions,

whether national or state, the right to own stock in any other independent bank. . . . The prohibitions should be so explicit that its spirit as well as its letter could be enforced. We must prevent perpetually the concentration of the banking power in the hands of the few."

Upon this point there were discussions—not apparently in the tone of serenity usual with Aldrich—during the last days of the year when the commission was struggling to get the bill into shape before January 8. The President, the secretary, the solicitor-general, all took part. It was one of those maddening problems of legal phraseology which the layman cannot understand. The solicitor, after a three-hour interview with Aldrich, "had thrown his hands up and confessed that the situation could not be covered by law."

For once, Aldrich came near losing his temper. He wrote Secretary MacVeagh, saying that the Monetary Commission had "exhausted itself trying to draft such a clause" and as the secretary thought the matter could be disposed of so easily, would he be good enough to draft the needed clause. MacVeagh, who seems also to have grown hot under the collar, replied that he would not attempt to frame such a clause, but that the whole movement would collapse unless the public had more complete assurance that Wall Street was indisputably barred, from ever in any way gaining control. The commission, though fearful that they might "insert a section in their bill which could be shot full of holes" by the lawyers, fearful also that such a clause might actually weaken the bill, determined to take the risk. As MacVeagh had advised they would try to make plain their intent, and trust "it would serve a useful purpose whether it was good law or not." [32]

Out of all this last-minute legalistic hubbub came the final provision designed to quiet the cry of Wall Street control. The bill which the commission at last submitted to Congress though following pretty closely the Revised Plan, added the provision that in any case where forty per cent of stock in each of two or more banks in the same local association should be "owned directly or indirectly by the same person, persons, copartnership, voluntary associations, trustee or corporation" these banks should be regarded as a unit and have together but one vote.[33]

The commission closed its labors by a display of courtesy. Several members signed the report submitting the bill for the sake of making the action unanimous though reserving the right to oppose the passage of the bill if they wished to do so. Satisfaction with the result was not confined entirely to Mr. Aldrich's own group. Senator Teller when he signed the report said that he regarded this as the most important act of his life.

CHAPTER XXVI

POLITICAL FOOTBALL

I

AND now through that irony of fate which is everywhere in politics, Aldrich's fortunes were delivered into the hands of his old adversary. The man whom he had always refused to take seriously, whom he had begun thwarting sixteen years before, had come at last to a position of great influence. Mr. Bryan was not quite the master of the Democratic party but in that party he held firmly the balance of power. Though it was tacitly—even openly—admitted that he could not be the Democratic nominee, it was also admitted that he could dictate the choice of a nominee. It was this fact that disturbed the dreams of a newcomer in politics whose rise had been as sudden, as amazing, as sixteen years before had been Mr. Bryan's own. Woodrow Wilson—translated so recently, so unexpectedly, from the presidency of Princeton to the governorship of New Jersey —was the favorite for the nomination of the Democratic conservatives—if, that is, any Democrats, at that moment, would have accepted the horrid term. Setting terms aside there were two wings to the party and Professor Wilson and Mr. Bryan were symbols of the two. It would not be fair to say they divided the party as Aldrich and La Follette had divided theirs in 1908, but there is a vague half analogy between the double leadership of the two years.

These remarkable men stood over against each other on the threshold of a political revolution in such sharp contrast that it was natural for their followers to compare them to Light and Darkness—interchanging the labels according to the point of view. Mr. Wilson had formed his mind in the mental chastity of the university classroom and the high frivolity of seminars in historical speculation; the views of Mr. Bryan emanated from the romantic myopia of machine politics refined by the ardent seriousness of Chautauqua reading circles. Both were Calvinists, but Mr. Wilson breathed easiest in the spiritual dryness of Princeton, New Jersey; Mr. Bryan in the spiritual humidity of Lincoln, Nebraska. They were instinctively antagonistic. The utterance of Mr. Wilson which perhaps has the best chance of immortality is his devout wish that somebody might knock Mr. Bryan, because of his financial heresies, into a cocked hat; Mr. Bryan was deeply distressed because Mr. Wilson's candidacy had been floated upon the Democratic tide by the editor of *The North American Review* who was believed to be a financial friend of the Morgans. For Mr. Wilson the voice of God in politics was the voice of the college professor magnified into a roll of thunder; for Mr. Bryan it was the composite wail of all those whose incomes were not large enough to enable them to cease from troubling. The one man was a clear, cool, undaunted mind, slightly lacking in realism, slightly subject to intellectual mirage; the other a passionately conventional dreamer, the perfect utterance of a class and a tradition. Both were absolutely sincere. Neither was capable of doing justice emotionally to the other. Though both desired to play fair, it was destiny—temperamental destiny—that, if they were forced to co-operate, one would have to devour the other. The question was—which?

We may assume that Governor Wilson saw his danger as early as January, 1912. He made a speech that month which surely was intended to placate Mr. Bryan, to persuade him that Wilsonian doctrine was as fiercely anticapitalistic as he could wish. On the same morning, January 9, 1912, the newspapers printed the Report of the Monetary Commission and Governor Wilson's speech which had been delivered the night before when leading Democrats dined together in honor of Andrew Jackson. Mr. Wilson's remarks had been carefully prepared; they evaded any commitment of the speaker to the perilous idea of political control over the nation's banking: Nevertheless, he said, the country was "scrutinizing so narrowly the new proposals with regard

to banking and currency which are being put forward by the
Monetary Commission. The country will not brook any
plan which concentrates control in the hands of the banks,
because it knows that the bankers themselves are not iso-
lated and that the banks are tied in by a thousand enter-
prises, by community holdings and by interests in many
intricate ways. The outside public must in some thorough
and effective way be put in a position to keep its credits
and its financial opportunities free and undictated. The
bankers of the country may have the highest and purest
intentions; many of them I know are scrutinizing the new
proposals in the right spirit, with an intent to serve the
country. But no one class can comprehend the country; no
one set of interests can safely be suffered to dominate it.
We must safeguard these matters at every hazard, for always, even above the purpose of efficiency, must come the
principle of freedom." [1]

Of course this was a hit at the Aldrich Bill, but a very
guarded hit. People who were close to Governor Wilson
got the impression—at least in some instances—that he
"was in sympathy with the Aldrich plan. The matter of
control and the Board of Governors (Directors) was the
one question still undecided in his mind." [2]

In this impression they were not far wrong. Doubtless,
he then thought, as he subsequently said, that "the Aldrich
Bill was probably about sixty or seventy per cent correct." [3]
Governor Wilson was enough of a statesman to perceive that
the scientific aspect of the bill and its political aspect were
two sharply different problems, each of course conditioning
the other, but each to have its own mode of solution. He
must have seen what so many of his followers saw, that their
party cue was to utilize the reform momentum generated
the previous year, satisfying the scientists that they would
not block reform, and yet keep their own masses from taking
fright lest the spirit of Andrew Jackson should not again be
allowed to rise from the dead. Could the latter effect be
brought about without their committing themselves to political control of the banking industry? It was highly

doubtful. The real financiers among the Democrats—such
men as Mr. Carter Glass, chairman of the House Committee on Banking and Currency, or Professor H. P. Willis,
who was later to be his right hand man in financial legislation—these men were silent, watchful, uncertain how the
popular cat was going to jump.

It started jumping in the Democratic National Convention. The Democrats did the same sort of thing that the
Republicans did in the platform of 1904, coming out strong
on generalities and craftily evading particulars. But they
made one thing plain. There was no doubt where they stood
as to Aldrich. "We oppose the so-called Aldrich Bill or the
establishment of a central bank, and we believe the people
of the country will be largely freed from panics and conse-
quent unemployment and business depressions by such a
systematic revision of our banking laws as will render temporary relief in localities where such relief is needed, with
protection from control or domination by what is known as
the 'money trust'." [4]

How curiously similar, in different terms, to the systematic evasions of 1904! Not a word on the issue that was at
the back of all their minds—as much so as was the social
issue in Republican minds in 1904—the question whether
the new banking system which had now become inevitable,
should or should not be subjected to political control?

II

In the early days of 1912 Aldrich had the rare experience
of being made the subject of a sympathetic magazine article.
Munsey's January number drew his portrait. He was a
stoic; abuse rattled off him as if it were dry sand; his maxim was "Deny nothing; explain nothing"; he had unshakable courage; he was modest, using only eight lines for his
biography in the Congressional Directory; he had a contempt for self-advertising; he had a passion for accuracy;
he was tirelessly industrious; his sense of organization enabled him to build up a project as if he were building a

skyscraper, to stand under every stress and strain of attack.[5]

Aldrich could not take the Insurgents seriously. He could not believe that they would ever control the situation. As to foreseeing a split in the party—impossible! And without a split—what did the Democrats count for?

Even when the thunderclap came, when Mr. Roosevelt yielded to the desperate appeal of the Seven Governors who begged him to stand for the Republican nomination, even when he announced that his hat was in the ring, Mr. Aldrich was not disturbed. Apparently, his illusion that the Conservatives controlled the party and that the party was unbreakable was as a rock. He threw care to the winds and sought recreation in his favorite fields. In April he was in London; later, Paris; then Aix-les-Baines, long a familiar place to him; after that Paris again. London this year seemed peculiarly attractive. The weather was very fine. He was buying with ardor for the library of the great house —not only in economics, but generally, taking a critical interest in editions and bindings. Delightful as London was, he felt that Paris was still "the most wonderful and attractive city in the world." There, also, book-buying had his chief attention. The few letters that record this spring, reflect his preoccupation with books and contain here and there a characteristic comment—as when he touches on a French book that might be questioned in New England because of its frankness, but which was "much less dangerous from what you would call a moral standpoint than the veiled and demoralizing suggestions of Bernard Shaw." He was always repelled by anything that seemed to him to have the quality of innuendo. Frankness, in art as in life, was for him the heart of things.

At Paris, Zorn painted a second portrait of him. The first, done at Washington, had disappointed the family. The great painter had not done justice either to himself or the subject. This other picture done in the full flush of one of Aldrich's happiest springtimes was nearer a success. At least, it was worthy of the astute hand that painted it. But

Zorn had his troubles. The clew to them is a remark of
Cecilia Beaux's. Meeting Zorn one day, she asked him
what he was doing. He told her he was painting Senator
Aldrich. "I don't envy you," replied the gifted woman,
"his expression changes every minute."

The powerful face that looks out from Zorn's second canvass is, of course, an interpretation. It is unforgetable.
The emphasis, to be sure, is heavily on the power of the
man; scarcely at all on the winsomeness; not in the least on
the mobility which Miss Beaux had observed, nor on the
hint of caprice which Platt had in mind when he allowed
himself one touch of fretfulness in the words, "He is always
doing inexcusable things." The painter had become infatu-
ated with the man's power and there it is, stark, even terrible! The seventy years are forgotten—not concealed, merely put aside as immaterial. The face is neither young nor
old, though its note, in every line, is triumphant experience. The eyes are those of a general in action. The spirit
that the Scandinavian had perceived was the inner viking,
the elemental power, that dwelt aloof far behind the veil of
his modernity, the captain who came to life in the moments
of crisis, who so often had driven the field before him.

Few people, if any—except the lonely painter—felt themselves this spring in the presence of the viking that lay concealed in Aldrich. It was the gay, modern companion of
whom the others were aware. He was in a gleeful mood.
His letters are concerned with the pleasant little things of
every day. In the midst of much motoring about Aix-les-
Bains, he finds the landscape "really heavenly, and this
word is not too strong."

III

The opening days of June, 1912, are the very peak of
Aldrich's career. Events were to show that it was an illu-
sive peak, a pinnacle of misapprehension, but that was not
apparent at the time. The confidence that the Insurgents
would not get control of the Republican party was shared
by most of his countrymen. The eventual audacity of the

Insurgents was so far beyond the horizon of practical politics that few people even so much as dreamed of it. Confident that his party would carry the election the following autumn, confident that the next Congress would give him a free hand to perfect his Plan, Aldrich came back to America in as happy a mood as he ever knew.

It was reinforced by the fulfillment of his long personal dream. In these opening days of June the mansion was at last prepared for occupancy. Mr. and Mrs. Aldrich took possession of it on the thirteenth of the month.

Over forty years had passed since he fixed upon this site as the end of the rainbow of his personal fortunes. What thrilling successes had come to him, one after another, that long while. And the great reverses! But it was not his nature to remember reverses. The realization of the private ambition coming at the very moment when it seemed that his public ambition was also on the eve of fulfillment, gave peculiar brilliancy to the whole landscape of his desire.

Aldrich House occupies the site of the old Hoppin House, on the crest of that beautiful ridge which lies north and south, its principal prospect toward the west and the Bay. The style of the mansion is the simplest phase of that architectural temper which France derived from the Renaissance. The interior is somewhat more ornate, more definitely renaissantine. There is a spacious entrance hall, Italian in mood; a great marble stair; noble proportions and lofty ceilings, in drawing-room, dining-room, library; lesser rooms in plenty; a lovely outlook from every window.

The furnishings expressed the owner. Though the flavor was of the Renaissance it was not florid. A pervading taste united all the details in a rich moderation. The chief paintings were some admirable Flemish portraits and a severe semi-primitive of the Renaissance that no one without a real eye for pictures would have selected, and that any one who had such an eye would treasure. Among minor things, porcelain and the rest, there was the same pervasive unity of a definite taste.

To none of his furnishings had he given more careful

thought than to the rugs. All were of his own choice, and all were characterized by the delicacy of their color schemes. There are dealers in Paris who still wax eloquent talking of Monsieur Aldrich and his discrimination as a buyer of rugs. The conventional rating of such things counted with him not at all. His own keen eye, his own responses, controlled his purchasing.

The most delightful feature of this house at Indian Oaks is the great terrace along the west front facing the sea. Beneath it the sloping lawns fall away, a considerable descent, studded with noble trees to the water's edge. The mansion is placed sufficiently high to command the breadth of the bay and the long stretches of lowland that extend from the farther shore to the horizon. The prospect from the terrace is filled with the sense of immense space as well as with the sense of immediate loveliness.

Though the new house had not arisen, eight years before, when Mr. Platt wrote his sad last letter about Warwick, the prospect from the old house which he knew was much the same . . . "all its beauties I can just see as I write— the bay and its sails and the yachts, the shrubs and the flowers and the garden and the house and the porch— it is a beautiful picture."

And now Platt was dead. And Allison was dead. The Four were a memory. But the great house was here, and the moment of final triumph was almost here. As the survivor of the unique brotherhood stood upon the terrace of Indian Oaks, ghosts were there beside him, ghosts of a great friendship worthy to become immortal, of hopes and problems which the Four had not solved, which were now to fade and be forgotten, absorbed into the achievement of their bold companion.

Wonderful hours, in this brief span of unclouded hopefulness, for the master and mistress of Indian Oaks. The shining afternoons—New England in June, so crystalline, and yet so shadowy, so imaginative!—with the long beams striking over the roof of the mansion and lengthening westward and farther westward along the deep blueness of the bay. And at night—surely they must have walked together on the terrace, under the early moon, their gardens all about them, tranced and silent, golden as in a dream; the bay and the far shore mysterious, illimitable.

IV

Meanwhile the unbelievable had been preparing to come to pass. The Progressives—as the Insurgents had now definitely named themselves—were growing daily in the faith that they were the Sons of Thunder, that nothing could resist them. They went to the National Republican Convention determined to rule or—make history. There was a savage fight over contested seats. Two hundred and ten were claimed both by Progressives and "regulars." In some cases the Progressive claims were mere gestures. But in a dangerously large number the fight was real. Both sides nailed their colors. Every contested seat was denied to the Progressives. But the narrowness of the "regular" majority in the convention was sufficient to shake the stoutest heart; on the crucial vote over seats it was but 13 out of 1071. Immediately after the "regulars" had triumphed, a Kansas delegate presented a statement from Mr. Roosevelt. He accused the National Committee of "scandalous disregard of every principle of elementary honesty" in passing upon credentials of delegates; denounced the convention as having "now declined to purge the rôle of the fraudulent delegates placed thereon by the defunct National Committee"; declared that the convention represented nothing but successful fraud; and issued some portentous commands. "This action makes the convention in no proper sense any longer a Republican convention representing the real Republican party. Therefore I hope the men elected as Roosevelt delegates will now decline to vote on any matter before the convention. I do not release any delegate from his honorable obligation to vote for me if he votes at all, but under the actual conditions, I hope that he will not vote at all." [7]

What moment at all comparable in the history of the Republican party since the bolt of the silver senators in 1894!

Facing this grim menace—and remembering the margin of only thirteen votes that had saved them—the Conservatives took up the apalling task of committing themselves to a policy. Was it possible to win the Progressives back?

With the exception of a few paragraphs, the platform was written by Aldrich's stanch friend, President Butler. An experienced political strategist, he did not deceive himself upon the gravity of the situation. There was only the slimmest chance that even the most dextrous use of the cards could take the trick, but the most should be made of that chance. He had phrased the financial plank with a view to securing an indorsement of "the principles of the Aldrich plan without mentioning his name and arousing unnecessary antagonism." [8] The plank skilfully recognized the political points that were being used as the basis of attack upon the Aldrich Bill—the hubbub over the term (rather than the reality) "central bank," the real concern over the safeguarding of member banks in the Association, the fear of Wall Street control on the one hand, the fear of political control on the other. After promising "better currency facilities for the movement of crops in the West and South" and new banking arrangements for the "better conduct of our foreign trade" the main lines of the coming political battle upon finance were indicated thus: "In attaining these ends the independence of individual banks, whether organized under national or State charters, must be carefully protected, and our banking and currency system must be safeguarded from any possibility of domination by sectional, financial or political interests." [9]

But the Progressives were obdurate. Before the convention adjourned a group of seceders organized themselves as a rival convention and offered the nomination to Mr. Roosevelt. He accepted. Six weeks later he had appeared before a formal convention of what was henceforth to be known as the Progressive party. Addressing that convention he made his now famous "confession of faith," closing with the words, "We stand at Armageddon, and we battle for the Lord." [10]

There were now three parties in the field. No one could deny that the situation, for the Republicans, was grave. For all the leaders it was an anxious summer. What Aldrich felt, he kept as usual to himself. As to the management of the campaign, he was entirely out of it. Therefore, come what might, he would not let it torment him. The fisherman in him became his refuge. Few men were more devoted to that cryptic art. His family remember how tenderly he fingered his fishing tackle, what personality there was for him in a well-made fly. He had contracted recently for fishing rights on the Moisie River in Canada. He was there this summer, the dangers of the hour resolutely put behind him. His catch is recorded—123 salmon in thirteen days. Not bad for a man of seventy-one.

The furious summer wore through. While the Rooseveltians were chanting "Onward Christian Soldier" and the "Battle Hymn of the Republic" the President wrote privately: "When we lost Aldrich and Hale and the old leaders in the Senate and the House, we then only came to understand what leadership meant. Now we have no leaders and, with the exception of a dozen in each house, the rest are mediocre."

Aldrich took no part in the general campaign. From "the new château," as Mr. Andrew had playfully described Indian Oaks, he watched silently the ebb of the Republican tide. His health was bad again. In the early autumn he was "quite ill last night with a severe attack of indigestion" and was confined to his bed for a time.

At last the shocking truth could not be denied any longer. The power that Aldrich had defied three years before, had completed its work pulling down the temple of Republican power. The Progressive secession was going to result in the election of Governor Wilson. The whole matter of financial reform would be taken out of Aldrich's hands. His belief, once unshakable, that he could carry on the work the following winter was as the vain imaginings of a dream.

The circle of destiny was complete. It had begun in that other presidential contest twenty-eight years before when

Aldrich, Roosevelt, and Dolliver all emerged together. Now Dolliver was dead. Aldrich had wrecked his hope in 1906 and 1909. But his spirit had had its revenge. He had helped to fashion the instrument with which Roosevelt had cleft the party asunder. Now Roosevelt was wrecking Aldrich's hope. No one as yet had any premonition of the third retribution, of how the triangular fatality was to be made complete in 1914; nor of how, after that, Aldrich and Roosevelt were eventually to be reconciled through the kind offices of misfortune.

The results of the election of 1912 need not be recited.

Did Aldrich, gazing at the incredible completeness of the Democratic victory—House, Senate, the President—did he recall the bitter remark of that cavalier nobleman to the triumphant Parliamentarians at the close of the English Civil War—"If you don't fall out among yourselves you may go and play."

Others had labored and they had entered into their labors.

CHAPTER XXVII

THE HARVEST

I

It proved to be a bitter harvest for Mr. Aldrich. The two years allowed by Mr. Taft for the education of the public had come and gone. But how different the result from everything that he and Aldrich had expected. A college professor had become President! And behind him, the Warwick of the hour, with an expression that was not quite a smile, a look as mysterious as that which the orientals put upon the face of Buddha—Mr. Bryan. What next?

Mr. Bryan's purposes during the six months following the election are among those hidden things that will inform some day one of the most interesting of American biographies. This much we may guess: he was resolved, at the proper moment, strategically, to turn the flank of the reform movement, take the whole thing by one great *coup* out of the hands of the scientists and place it irrevocably in the hands of the politicians.

The story of these six months—of which the world to-day has but a small part—begins soon after the election. At the opening of the year 1913, when Aldrich was in Egypt, Mr. Glass, chairman of the House Committee on Banking and Currency, and the noted economist on whom chiefly he relied, Mr. Willis—now Professor Willis of Columbia—were hard at work in the honorable temper of genuine scientists.[1] Both of them disagreed with Mr. Aldrich and with his most significant advisers, with Mr. Forgan, Mr. Warburg, and Mr. Vanderlip, on many questions of pure science. In making over the Monetary Commission Bill—or effacing it, as perhaps they would say—they contemplated many devices not to be found in that bill. But what one would like most to know, following their course in shaping a new measure of their own, is—how far was Mr. Bryan kept in view? Of

413

course their bill had to conform to the general Democratic
tradition. Just as Aldrich, the dyed-in-the-wool Republican, had had to nationalize his measure as much as possible for his own peace of mind, so, conversely, Mr. Glass, the
dyed-in-the-wool Democrat, had to denationalize his scheme
as far as political modernism would allow. Not a ghost of
a chance would it have, in a Democratic Congress, with Mr.
Bryan looming awfully in the background, unless its centralizing tendencies were reduced to a minimum. This was
done by breaking up the power of the national Board of Directors and by making each of the banking districts the seat
not of a mere branch of the central bank but of a semi-inde-
pendent bank, central to that district.

A controversy arose, delightful to all lovers of the subtleties of debate, as to just what was the difference between
a "central bank" and "a system of central banking." Politically, here was a real distinction. It lies at the bottom
of what professed to be a purely scientific discussion. Mr.
Glass—whatever were his scientific convictions when he entered this discussion—made his sacrifice to the ghost of Andrew Jackson by devising a plan which did not propose one
central bank for the whole country, but instead, contemplated the creation of a dozen or so—eventually fifteen—
through replacing the "branches" of the Aldrich Bill by a
system of "regions." The country was to become a union of
fifteen States, financially speaking, and each financial State
was to have a central bank, but the relations of these banks
in certain respects were not to be sharply determined in the
statute; they were to be left to be determined in the future
through the operation of circumstance and the pressure of
opinion working upon and through a Federal Reserve Board
pretty closely analogous to the Board of Directors of the
National Reserve Association, but chosen in a widely different way.

There was a further political—or constitutional—distinction between a "central bank" and "a system of central
banking." Mr. Glass and Mr. Willis disagreed with Mr.
Aldrich on the question of a uniform rate of discount. They

proposed to give to each of their fifteen financial States the right to fix its own discount rates through its own reserve bank. But they did something else that the historian finds extremely interesting. They left open a door to the free operation of centralizing tendencies, should such arise through stress of circumstance. Their plan required each "regional" bank to have its discount rates "approved" by the Federal Reserve Board. A similar course was the distinctive feature in the action of a constitutional convention, one hundred and twenty-six years before, dodging the question of the relation of the States in the Union, leaving it all to be determined any way heaven willed through the incalculable forces of the time that was yet to be. And yet people say that history does not repeat itself!

It is quite probable that this solution of the problem if it could have been divorced from politics would have seemed to the nationally-minded statesman pretty nearly as satisfactory as his own. At any rate, he did not challenge it, except on the assumption that it would be used to authorize a number of local and contradictory rates. He reasoned that in so doing political and sectional favoritism were bound to appear.[2]

The original draft of the Glass-Willis bill gave the banks a large share in control of the new "system of central banking." The national Board of Directors was to consist of thirty-two members, twenty-six representing the banks, six representing the government. In the Executive Committee the relation of the two elements was reversed. This committee was to include the six government directors together with three of the bank representatives.

Such was the plan of control of the system when the new bill was confidentially printed and submitted to Mr. Bryan. Now Mr. Bryan stepped forward and for the last, culminating time asserted his will as holder of the balance of power in the Democratic party. He would tolerate nothing but thorough-going government control of the whole system. The Federal Reserve Board must be redefined. It was to contain none but government appointees.[3]

At the time Mr. Glass and Mr. Willis were both aghast. Mr. Willis remained to the last opposed to this admission of complete political control. Mr. Glass, eventually became reconciled, apparently as mere political necessity. But it mattered nothing what these financial scientists thought or did not think. The moment the bill was submitted to Mr. Bryan, politics that had been lurking all the while in a dark corner of the room stepped into the light, and with an air of undeniable authority assumed command. *Do this or your bill dies,* was in substance, for this while, *vox dei.*

President Wilson and Mr. Bryan faced each other during a moment of doubt. The President had been newly translated from the closet of the political philosopher to the quarter-deck of the ship of State. The experience that had made him a deep and acute thinker had not yet undergone a transformation. His nervous system was not yet hardened to endure the fierce strains of the practical statesman. The prospect of a serious duel with the Warwick of the Democracy at the very outset of his tenure of office was one that he could not endure with firmness. The moment of doubt was very brief. President Wilson accepted Mr. Bryan's ultimatum. He issued a subsidiary ultimatum to the authors of the bill. It was a case of the house that Jack built. This is the concession that Mr. Bryan forced upon President Wilson who put it into the ultimatum that he issued to Mr. Glass and Mr. Willis who framed the bill.

II

During the long winter and spring, when Aldrich was adjusting himself to the caprice of Fortune, he had sought the road once more. He glimpsed Algiers; he took his family far up the Nile; again he wandered the less frequented ways in Italy. On the surface there was nothing in the tone of this journey to distinguish it from so many that had preceded. Ostensibly it was on account of Mrs. Aldrich's failing health, the possible good she might get from a winter in Egypt. But was this all? Was there no restlessness in her husband's spirit? Would it have been easy for him to stay quietly at home this winter, absorbed in developing the estate? Even so unusual a temperament as his has its limitations.

An event of the Egyptian journey was a dinner with Kitchener. The American guests were Aldrich, his youngest daughter, and Pierpont Morgan. The greatest sphinx of Egypt talked fluently with Aldrich on the subject of desert reclamation. The event is humanized by the recollections of the Senator's daughter. She sat between Lord Kitchener and Mr. Morgan. They talked across her on large objective themes as if oblivious of everything but their own thoughts. But Kitchener had a way with him that defied all the ordinary rules of impression. His young guest, who thought him a great man before she went to the dinner, came away more convinced than ever that he was superbly incomparable.

The Aldriches were at Rome when Mr. Morgan came down with his last illness. He and Aldrich had become close friends. The powerful mind of the financial giant had filled to some extent the gap made in Aldrich's life by the passing of his old comrades of politics. When the time came for the Aldriches to go to Monte Carlo, the two men took leave of each other reluctantly. Mr. Morgan was eager to go along. But his doctors were uncompromising. They asked Mr. Aldrich to telegraph back from Monte Carlo giving a disagreeable account of the weather.

That commission disturbed Aldrich. Trifling as it was, and urgent as it seemed to be, the deception grated upon him. He was much relieved when nature took thought of his scruples and welcomed him at Monte Carlo in a downpour of rain.

Back in America he beheld from a distance the rapid progress which had been made in the monetary problem toward a victory for Mr. Byran. Moisie River and the game salmon were again the Aldrich refuge. This year Mr. Davison was one of his companions. Less than three years before they were together on the momentous duck-shoot at Jekyl Island. How the world had changed since then!

What a victory had been won, and how successfully the fruit of it had been taken over by their enemies. But they were both in a way stoics—humorous stoics. They did not talk of their disappointment or if at all only between themselves. The members of their families, who had accompanied them to Canada, were not aware of the slightest shadow upon the general conversation.

There were young people in the party—one of Aldrich's daughters, the same who dined with Kitchener, and friends of hers—and her father played cards with them every night. For this while the austerities of bridge were forgotten. They were replaced by more amusing games, the sort one may take lightly, with twenty people playing at once. Aldrich generally kept score. He played as merrily as the youngest in the crowd.[5]

III

During the later summer and early autumn, in his retirement at Indian Oaks, Aldrich observed with growing unhappiness the crystallization of the power of Mr. Bryan. His ultimatum had compelled the authors of the Federal Reserve Bill to put the new banking system under direct government control. Though Mr. Bryan had insisted on other changes that were not so frankly political—especially one with regard to note issue—it was his political victory that became at once in Aldrich's mind the conclusion of the whole matter. He was a man of much more powerful imagination than Mr. Bryan. He saw what Mr. Bryan could not see—or at least what Mr. Bryan could not believe in—the grim possibilities of the power which Mr. Bryan was creating.

The Democratic king-maker was the victim of an illusion. He had waited so long for power that when at last it came to him he could not believe that "the People"—in accurate English, the Democratic party—had not come into its own forever, that the millennium had not arrived, that the kingdom of God and his Saints (as conceived in the office of *The Commoner*) was not henceforth the everyday thing of this painful earth.[6] If only history, and the facts of human nature, could have meant more to him! If only he could have sympathized with hard-headed John Winthrop who refused to ask the Long Parliament to legislate in favor of Massachusetts because there might be a change of parties in the future and meantime "a precedent would have been established" for parliamentary interference in the affairs of the colony.

Mr. Aldrich, in some respects, was own brother intellectually, of that hard-headed, aristocratic Puritan of the Seventeenth Century. Both of them had that power of trained imagination without which any statesman so easily goes on the rocks. In Aldrich's vision there might well have been included a prophetic forecast of the sort of control of the Federal Reserve System that was eventually put into effect when Mr. Bryan's enemies returned to power. President Harding has been accused of "debauching" the system through his brutal use of the President's power of appointment. The real responsibility is upon Mr. Bryan and Mr. Wilson.

These visions of what might happen under the "Bryanized Banking Bill" threw Aldrich for once completely off his guard. He thought he had himself under control, but he was deceiving himself. When he responded to an invitation to address the Academy of Political Science, October 15, 1913, he over-estimated the power of his will. The prepared address was deliberately in his usual urbane tone.[7] He made his public acknowledgment to the scientific purposes of the framers of the bill, saying that they had "in a majority of cases accepted remedies and adopted ideas based on experience of other countries and on sound economic principles. . . ." He took issue with them as pure science upon the subject of note issue.[8] Firmly but courteously he condemned the surrender to the radicals in the matter of control.[9] Had he confined himself to what he meant to say he would have been the Aldrich of old. But it was straining human nature too far. In spite of himself his bitterness broke forth. Turning aside from his manuscript he made some impromptu remarks that were described by his enemy, *The World,* as a "long and bitter" attack. His friends agree that he spoke with bitterness. He dwelt upon the idea that in giving the government control over the reserve system, the Democrats were violating their own Jacksonian tradition and breaking their tacit promises to the country, "in order that Mr. Bryan may proclaim to the world a triumph of transcendant importance for his monetary and governmental theories." [10]

CHAPTER XXVIII

AFTERWARD

Othello's occupation gone!

The succession of political ironies since Aldrich sailed with the Monetary Commission had ended in his exclusion from public life. A return to the Senate was inconceivable. The Commission had been abolished and its place given over to his enemies. Had the new President been of a different sort, there would have been room for Aldrich on the first Board of Directors of the Federal Reserve Bank. But that was not President Wilson's way. Aldrich was safely off the stage. Let a sacrifice to Fortune be duly made—a heartfelt sacrifice!

Mr. Aldrich turned his face resolutely to private life. His family are unanimous that no cloud darkened the household because of their father's great disappointment.

As it turned out but two years were left to him. It is always dangerous to an active man to be arrested in full career, to be forced into idleness against his will. What were his seventy-two years to this intensely vigorous spirit if he had something more to do? But all the avenues of his inclination were shut, and most of his old comrades were gone. The great house, the gardens, his yacht, and the old love of travel, these were all, outside his family feeling, that he had now to rely upon. A pleasant, beautiful life it was, at Indian Ooks,—the life of the distinguished private gentleman, who was once a power in the land. But what a difference from the life of the Master of the Senate in the days of the Elder Statesman!

To his family, at least, he maintained the aspect with which they were familiar. Perhaps he maintained it to himself. But there is a little evidence which makes one doubt. Mr. Warburg who met him at Paris in the spring of 1914 is unconditional that he dropped his defenses and spoke

with bitterness of his political enemies. Then, too, his health
was giving way. His doctors saw a menace in the condition
of his heart. Nevertheless, he was insistent as ever upon
travel. The winter of 1913–1914 was taken up with a ramble
in Spain. His son, Winthrop Aldrich, who accompanied him,
had been freighted by the doctors with a supply of heart
stimulants.

A brilliantly diverting moment in Aldrich's experiences
was this Spanish summer which is photographed in a letter of his son's. "My recollection of my visit to Spain with
my father in 1914 are quite vivid and I do not remember
that he appeared to be in any way suffering from the strain
through which he had been. We had altogether a most delightful journey. Mr. Willard, who was then ambassador
to Spain, was most kind to us, and my father had a number of interviews with the Prime Minister and with leading Spanish bankers. My father was very much interested
at the time in Spanish art, particularly the works of Goya,
and under the guidance of the younger Beruete and of
Sarolla, who was a personal friend of my father's, we spent
many days in the Prado and in seeing the private collections
of a number of old Spanish families. We went first to
Madrid where we spent about ten days, and then to Toledo,
Seville, Granada, and returned to Madrid by way of Cor-
dova, and again spent about two weeks in Madrid, taking
motor trips into the country roundabout. My own impression is that my father enjoyed this trip very much and was
in the best of health and spirits all the time." [1]

Whether there was a real improvement in health, or a
great act of will, Mr. Aldrich, in the following summer,
seemed to be entirely himself again. Once more there was
a summer of the familiar sort—salmon fishing in Canada,
beautiful days at Indian Oaks, cruising on his yacht in the
home waters. His family life appeared to be completely
sufficient for his happiness. He got the greatest pleasure
from the company of young people. His youngest daughter
and her friends were encouraged to have no compunctions
about invading his library. Amidst a vast array of books

on economics he would sit at his desk listening with bright eyes and a droll mouth to the sparkling chatter of saucy girls.

The World War broke. Miss Lucy Aldrich brought the news to him on the yacht. He sat for a space without a word looking hard at nothing. Then he said, "It will be a three years' war at least."

Miss Aldrich asked him why he felt so sure. He replied, "Because I have been in Germany and I know her financial condition." He added that the United States could not escape being dragged in.

The autumn came—the ringing autumn with the world crumbling toward the East. He remembered another autumn fifty-three years before, since which America had not faced a genuine war problem. What would happen now?

The autumn passed. Huge armies dug in along the western front and the long slow agony got well under way. At Indian Oaks there was one more family event of first magnitude, the wedding of the youngest daughter in December, 1914. Mr. Aldrich appeared his old blithe self, the man they had all known so long. The guests did not perceive any failing of energies. He was still so immensely vivid, with an artist's interest in every detail of the occasion.

That winter there was another southern wander, Mrs. Aldrich and Miss Aldrich with him—Jekyl Island, Florida, Nassau. No one detected in him any decrease of zest. At one place he told his daughter he had to get away because everybody there was too old for him.

He was in the North again in March. On the first of April the stables at Indian Oaks were burned. They were spacious buildings in which were stored temporarily a number of objects of art recently received from Italy. Mr. Aldrich was at home and exerted himself rashly. What his servants remembered afterward was his anxiety lest any of them take undue risks attempting to rescue the contents of the stables. He went to New York, where he had taken a house for the winter, and at once entered upon plans for rebuilding.

Meanwhile something had happened which is quite obscure, of which nothing is known except through one remark to Miss Lucy Aldrich, now his constant companion. He said to her that he had been asked to go to Europe on a financial mission and had promised to go.

Whether there is any connection between this and the final incident of his career, is still to seek. Aldrich was not the only statesman to whom Mr. Wilson's government, in the fury of the World War, denied a function. Mr. Roosevelt also, in this terrible crisis, was condemned to a tragic idleness.

There was a time when Americans did not shrink from quoting—sweet are the uses of adversity! In the spring of 1915, the friends of a vigorous war policy were stirring everywhere in America, hoping to draw together all those who were the natural enemies either of Mr. Wilson or of his policy of inaction. It has never been told just what was hoped of a conference that was arranged between Roosevelt and Aldrich. Both were sounded and both were agreeable. Mr. and Mrs. Cornelius Vanderbilt were among the most ardent enemies of official neutrality. A luncheon at their house in New York was made the occasion for a meeting of Aldrich and Roosevelt. After luncheon they spent an hour together alone in Mr. Vanderbilt's library. Mrs. Vanderbilt remembers that when they came into her drawing-room, after their talk, Roosevelt had his arm either on Aldrich's shoulder or in some similar attitude of comradeship. She also remembers Aldrich saying to her, "We are going to work together again." [2]

But this time there were no uses of adversity after all. Mr. Aldrich's thread was spun. The night following his interview with Roosevelt he was at the theatre with Miss Aldrich and she noticed that he looked very tired.

The next forenoon she went with him to examine a collection of books that was to be sold at auction. He left several bids. There was nothing alarming in his appearance. A remark of hers upon the pathos in this cold ending of a collector's loving zeal brought out a flash of the Aldrich that used to be, the unconquerable optimist who would never think of life in terms of loss. "At least he had the fun of collecting it," was the reply that may be counted his last word upon the vanity of human wishes.

The Aldriches this winter occupied a house on Fifth Avenue at the corner of Seventy-second Street. Here that same afternoon, Mr. Aldrich suffered a very acute attack of what appeared to be indigestion. By nightfall, he seemed much better.

"At least he had the fun of collecting it." The words insist on lingering in memory. Holding one's ideas lightly is the last word of his career as well as the first. His indomitable spirit was never quite out of sight of the sense of humor. The mood which had always ruled him was the mood in which he came to his journey's end.

When his physician called, early next morning, there seemed to be no immediate cause of alarm. Directly he had left, Mr. Aldrich said that he was going to get up. The nurse barely persuaded him not to do so. A few moments he lay still. His eyes closed. Then, without any struggle, in an instant, life passed, April 16, 1915.

NOTES

A. MSS. (Senator Nelson W. Aldrich.) Consists of two parts: (*a*) miscellaneous collection of political and personal letters scattered through 1876–1914, valuable chiefly in fields of currency and banking, tariff, and local Rhode Island politics of 1880–1888; (*b*) notes of interviews, inquiries, sources, and biographical data assembled for this biography; custody of Mr. Winthrop Aldrich, New York City.

Allison MSS. (Senator William B. Allison.) Approximately 200,000 letters, 1864–1908, chiefly to Allison, most valuable for indications of changes in the political viewpoints and usages of the Middle West over this long period; custody of Edgar R. Harlan, Curator, Historical, Memorial and Art Department of Iowa, Des Moines.

A. P. The Associated Press.

Bishop. "Theodore Roosevelt and His Times." By Joseph Bucklin Bishop. Scribners, 1920.

C. MSS. (Senator William E. Chandler.) Voluminous collection of personal and political letters to and from Chandler, 1876–1919, scattering items beginning 1858, important for brief diary notations, bimetallic movement of 1897, outbreak of war with Spain, railroad rate controversy of 1906, and local New Hampshire politics; custody of Senator George H. Moses, Washington, D. C.

Cleveland MSS. (President Grover Cleveland.) Described in great detail in Robert McElroy, "Grover Cleveland," II, 387–392; custody of J. Franklin Jameson, Chief of the Division of Manuscripts, Library of Congress, Washington, D. C.

Coolidge. "An Old-Fashioned Senator (Orville H. Platt)." By Louis A. Coolidge. Putnam, 1911.

Correspondence. "The Correspondence of Theodore Roosevelt and Henry Cabot Lodge." Scribners, 1925.

Cummings MSS. (H. S. Cummings.) Small collection of letters on local New Hampshire politics with occasional references to national affairs; custody of Otis G. Hammond, Director, New Hampshire Historical Society, Concord.

D. MSS. (General Grenville M. Dodge.) Twenty-three record books, 1853–1915 and 409 volumes of letters, 1851–1915, valuable on railroad expansion west of the Mississippi and on political developments in the Middle West; custody same as Allison.

Dawson. "Life and Character of Edward Oliver Wolcott." By T. F. Dawson. Private, 1911.

F. MSS. (Senator Joseph B. Foraker.) Approximately 50,000 letters chiefly to Foraker on Ohio matters and in national affairs confined to railroad rates, joint statehood, and Brownsville, with some data on campaigns of 1884–1888, and 1908, contains copies of correspondence with Hanna, Roosevelt, Sherman and Taft which was privately printed; custody of Miss L. Belle Hamlin, Librarian, Historical and Philosophical Society of Ohio, Cincinnati.

G. MSS. (Senator Jacob H. Gallinger.) Small collection miscellaneous items embracing a few letters referring to national issues; custody same as Cummings.

Glass. "An Adventure in Constructive Finance." By Carter Glass. 1927.

H. MSS. (President Benjamin Harrison.) More than 250 boxes of letters chiefly to President Benjamin Harrison with some memoranda by him, most important for relations with cabinet and senators; custody of Mrs. Benjamin Harrison, New York City.

Halford MSS. (Colonel Elijah W. Halford.) Four books, 1889–1893, commenting briefly upon the daily events as far as viewed through eyes of a friend and private secretary to President Harrison; sidelights on Harrison's problems; custody of Colonel Halford, Leonia, New Jersey.

Hay MSS. (Secretary of State John Hay.) The so-called "Hay Diaries" which Henry Adams edited and officially styled as "Diaries and Letters," value somewhat marred by use of initials, chiefly interesting for references to senatorial behavior on foreign relations; custody of "Office," Library of Congress, Washington, D. C.

Herald. The New York *Herald.*

Holls MSS. (Frederick W. Holls.) One large carton of memoranda and letters to and from Holls chiefly devoted to New York affairs in the nineties, most important for sidelights on international relations and on the political work of Americans of German birth; custody of Roger Howson, Librarian, Columbia University.

J. of C. The *Journal of Commerce,* New York.

L. MSS. (James O. Lyford.) Small collection letters to and from Lyford chiefly devoted to New Hampshire politics, with some references to national affairs; custody same as Cummings.

Ledger. The Philadelphia *Ledger.*

La Follette. "La Follette's Autobiography." By Robert M. La Follette. Author's print, 1913.

M. MSS. (Senator Justin M. Morrill.) Relatively small collection letters chiefly to Morrill, most interesting of recent period being those on tariff movements of the eighties; custody same as Cleveland.

McK. MSS. (President McKinley.) About thirty-six chests containing private files and letterpress books of McKinley prior to and during his administration as President, letterpress books of his secretaries, Mr. J. Addison Porter and Mr. Geo. B. Cortelyou, and miscellaneous data and papers; custody of Geo. B. Cortelyou, New York City.

Michener MSS. (General L. T. Michener.) Scattering collection of memoranda and letters chiefly devoted to Indiana politics with some reference to Harrison administration; custody of Mrs. Michener, Washington, D. C.

M. and P. "Messages and Papers of the Presidents." Compiled by James D. Richardson. Washington, 1897 and 1909.

Morton MSS. (Vice-President Levi P. Morton.) Small miscellaneous collection chiefly New York politics, most valuable for sidelights on cloture contest in Senate, 1890–1891; custody of Victor H. Paltsits, Chief of the Manuscripts Division, New York Public Library, New York.

P. MSS. (Senator Orville H. Platt.) Twelve volumes political letters to and from Platt, most valuable concerning insular affairs in 1901, and Cuba, campaign of 1904, tariff revision, railroad rate legislation, Panama and joint statehood, 1903–1905, besides sidelights upon conservative reaction to Roosevelt administration; custody of George S. Godard, Librarian, Connecticut State Library, Hartford.

R. Congressional Record.

R. MSS. (President Theodore Roosevelt.) Immense collection letters to and from Roosevelt on all manner of subjects, 1900–1909, valuable for study of almost any situation in that administration; custody of Mrs. Theodore Roosevelt, Sr., Oyster Bay, Long Island.

R. E. B. (Roosevelt Engagement Book.) Incomplete list of formal appointments.

S. MSS. (Senator John C. Spooner.) Sixteen large boxes letters to and from Spooner, 1885–1907, relating to local Wisconsin matters as well as national affairs; most valuable for Spooner's connection with Roosevelt administration's insular policies, 1901–1904; custody of Charles P. Spooner, New York City.

Sherman MSS. (Senator John Sherman.) Immense collection letters to and from Sherman on political and personal subjects; most interesting in recent period for Republican party affiliations; custody same as Cleveland.

Stanwood. "History of the Presidency." By Edward Stanwood. Houghton, 1916.

Sun. The New York *Sun.*

T. MSS. (President William H. Taft.) Immense collection letters to and from Taft covering more than twenty-five years; most valuable for study of any situation in administration; custody of heirs of Chief Justice William H. Taft, Washington, D. C.

Taussig. "Tariff History of the United States." By F. W. Taussig. Putnams, 1923.

Times. The New York *Times.*

Tribune. The New York *Tribune.*

Willis. "The Federal Reserve System." By Henry Parker Willis. Ronald, 1923.

W. MSS. (Paul M. Warburg.) Letters and pamphlets important for study of banking reform in United States; custody of Paul M. Warburg, New York City.

World. The New York *World.*

Note: The term "custody" as here used refers to the person who controls a manuscript collection, from whom permission to use must be obtained.

CHAPTER I

IN THE WAKE OF THE CIVIL WAR

1. Mr. Aldrich has left extremely few letters that are truly intimate. The two packages mentioned in the text, separated by an interval of seven years, are almost unique. The passage quoted is from the earlier package written to his future wife during their engagement.

2. Ibid.

3. Recollection of Mrs. Wightman.

4. His credentials from the Providence authorities to arrest "one Hopkins" and his commission from the governor of Louisiana are in A. MSS.

5. Aldrich to Joshua Addeman, April 22, 1865, loaned by Mr. Addeman.

6. Providence *Journal*, Jan. 2, 1866.

7. Records, City Hall, Providence.

8. Providence *Journal*, May 6, 1869.

9. Providence *Journal*, May 13, 1872.

10. Ibid., March 24, 1876.

11. Providence *Tribune*, April 14, 1910; also recollections of Joshua Addeman.

For the personal details and traditions mentioned in this chapter, I am indebted not only to his immediate family but to several other relatives and friends, from whom Dr. Nichols, in a long exploration of his early environment, collected much material now in the Aldrich MSS. Especially helpful were Mr. Frank Greene and Mrs. Lucy Greene, cousins of Mrs. Aldrich, another cousin Mr. Gideon Burgess, Mr. Addeman, Mr. J. N. Tucker, Judge Charles Matteson, and Mrs. Wightman.

CHAPTER II

SHADOWS BEFORE

1. Providence *Tribune*, April 10, 1910.

2. Ibid., also Rhode Island *Manual*.

3. Ibid.

4. Congressional Directory, 1879.

5. *R.*, May 28, 1879.

6. These intimate details are clearly recollected by his family and by various old friends.

7. Told in his speech at Kansas City, Nov. 14, 1911.

8. Providence *Journal*, Sept. 14, 1881; Springfield *Republican*, Oct. 4, 1881; Newport *Mercury*, Oct. 8, 1881; recollections of Judge Matteson.

It is difficult to say just how much of a local power Mr. Aldrich was at this time. General Brayton was temporarily in eclipse. The letter cited in Chapter III shows that he felt himself under obligations to Aldrich.

9. See Chapter XXV.

10. *Tribune*, Oct. 17, 1881.

11. *R.*, Jan. 23, 1882, pp. 555–6.

CHAPTER III

A STRUGGLE FOR A CONSTITUENCY

1. Coolidge, 153–7. *R.*, March 9, 1882.

2. Aldrich to Chandler, June 28, 1883, A. MSS.

3. Same to same, July 4, 1882, A. MSS.

4. This was done by the familiar subterfuge of an "amendment" to a House bill.

5. Aldrich's opinion of the final result of the tariff debate is indicated by an autograph memorandum on a printed copy of the Conference Report, "63 of the items included herein were taken from the dutiable and put on the free list by act of March 3, 1883. Of the 712 items enumerated

only 75 items represent increases." A. MSS. His statement with regard to the conference is in *R.*, Jan. 2 and 9, 1889, pp. 452, 455, 624–6. See also, *R.*, Oct. 18, 1888, pp. 9549–50.

6. *R.*, Jan. 27, 1883, p. 1657.

7. Ibid., Jan. 26, 1883, p. 1624.

8. Ibid., Feb. 3, 1883, p. 2029.

9. Ibid., Jan. 27, 1883, pp. 1662–5. He had recently taken part in an investigation of trade conditions which concerned itself largely with labor costs. Studies of this sort were always part of his natural bent. Their climax was the report on prices in 1892. See Chapter V, note 20.

10. Ibid., Jan. 15 and 16, 1883, pp. 1193–4, 1229–30.

11. Ibid.

12. Ibid., Feb. 5, 1883, p. 2078.

13. Ibid., Feb. 7, 1883, pp. 2217–18. The gunpowder duty was proposed by Bayard and was held to be in the interests of the Duponts. Aldrich, here, is revealing his position, protecting manufacturers, but he is also beginning an insistence upon frankness in admitting motives that was alien to the time. See the discussion of double affiliation in politics in Chapter VII.

14. Ibid., Feb. 7, 1883, p. 2217.

15. Foraker to Sherman, June 9, 1884, F. MSS. Unpublished letters in the Foraker manuscripts add interesting details to the account given in Foraker's "Notes of a Busy Life" but do not alter the main lines of the narrative. Apparently Aldrich went to the Convention as an Arthur man. S. P. Colt to Aldrich, June 9, 1884, A. MSS.

16. Brayton to Aldrich, Feb. 7, 1880, A. MSS.

17. Told to the author by the scholar's brother, Professor Dana Carleton Munro.

18. Six signers to Charles F. Folger, May 27, 1882, C. MSS. Aldrich said of the Tariff Commission "there was a representative of the wool growers on the commission; there was a representative of the iron interest on the commission; there was a representative of the sugar interest on the commission; and those interests were very carefully looked out for and preserved. . . ." *R.*, Feb. 6, 1883, p. 2149.

19. *R.*, Feb. 12, 1883, p. 2507.

20. *R.*, Jan. 30 and 31, pp. 1795, 1883, also Feb. 12 and 13. Hitherto the duty on sugar had been little more than a revenue duty, but such as it was, it favored the refiners. Nine-tenths of the sugar used in America was imported. Taussig, 275–6. Aldrich proposed a reduction of duty on raw sugar (*R.*, Jan. 30, 1883, pp. 1786, 1795 ff.). As he would have worded the law, "All sugars not above No. 13 Dutch standard in color, all tank bottoms, sirups of cane juice, or of beet juice, melada, concentrated melada, concrete and concentrated molasses, testing by the polariscope not above 75 degrees, shall pay a duty of one and twenty-five hundredths cent per pound, and for every additional degree or fraction of a degree shown by the polariscopic test they shall pay four hundredths of a cent per pound additional." There was a battle over this provision, the Louisiana men standing for a higher duty including .05 per cent additional instead of .04. Curiously enough Mr. Havemeyer favored the higher rate, though it was to his interests to make the duty on raw sugar as low as possible. The trust was not yet established and the refiners were at odds among

themselves. Eventually, the Aldrich main rate was raised to 1.40 per cent but the additional rate was allowed to stand. Meanwhile Aldrich had proposed to reduce the duties on high-grade sugars as follows: above No. 13 and below No. 17, Dutch Standard, 2.45 cents per pound; above No. 16 and below No. 21, 2.75 cents per pound; above No. 20, 3.10 cents per pound. These rates were changed respectively to 2.75, 3.00, and 3.50. See *R.*, especially Jan. 30, 1883, pp. 1795, 1798, 1830; Jan. 31, 1843, 1844; Feb. 12, 2507, 2508; Feb. 13, 2510, 2555. The debate on the subject developed much bitterness and started the long-standing accusation that the sugar refiners were tampering with the Senate. Bayard protested that "as to all this talk of unfairness or not speaking out openly, it is not worthy of this place or this occasion." Aldrich to M. D. Spalding, Jan. 6, 1883, A. MSS.: "I think it safe to say that the sugar refiners of the country will be united in at least one thing, and that is in opposition to this (Aldrich) plan. Havemeyer's agents are here to-day and are very active in trying to secure a reversal by the committee of their action. The tendency seems to be in both Houses toward the use of the polariscope; and I am inclined to think that it would be wiser for me and for those who agree with me about the necessity for a substantial reduction in the duties on sugar to try to arrange some plan which all could support for the use of the polariscope. . . . Havemeyer, I think, is satisfied with the committee's report on everything except the limit, which of course he thinks should be 13 instead of 16. He says the duty on high grades is much too low, in which I presume you will agree with him." Aldrich to G. S. Hunt & Company, Jan. 6, 1883, A. MSS: "I tried to secure a greater reduction than that voted by the committee but failed. I am inclined to think that the rate fixed by the Boston refiners is lower than we shall be able to obtain. I think the reduction should be at least one-fourth cent per pound more than that reported by the Finance Committee."

21. C. E. Warren to Morrill, Sept. 12, 1885, Morrill MSS.: "I found some of Senator Sherman's friends (in Ohio) in the effort to defend him in the matter of the reduction of the wool tariff (in 1883) engaged in traducing, as I think and asserted, both yourself and Senator Aldrich of Rhode Island. They asserted among other things that the reduction of the tariff, so far as your committee was concerned, was done against Mr. Sherman's wishes and by a conspiracy of Eastern Woollen manufacturers." Wool has always been the subject of much bickering between the growers and the manufacturers. Aldrich insisted that he stood for only a fair protection of manufacturers in proportion to the protection of the growers. *R.*, Feb. 6, 1883, pp. 2149–50. See also, Belmont, "J. S. Morrill," pp. 301–2.

22. Providence *Journal*, Dec. 4, 1885.

23. *R.*, May 6, 10, 12, 1886.

24. A. MSS.: Aldrich to Littlefield, Jan. 6, 1883, "I have no idea about what Jonathan (Chace) intends to do in regard to the Pawtucket postmastership. I think it is the unanimous feeling of the other members of the delegation that they will not under any circumstances undertake to decide the matter for him. . . . I do not think that I ought to interfere, and I am sure that I shall not." Aldrich to H. A. Pierce, Jan. 16, 1883: "It has always been understood that by courtesy the appointment of all postmasters belongs to the member representing the district, and any in-

vasion of this right would not be wise or fair to the parties interested."
Aldrich to J. E. Lester, Jan. 28, 1883, ". . . in the matter of the Olney-
ville post-office. I shall, however, have to insist upon preserving the
strict neutrality which I have hitherto preserved in this matter; and I
feel sure that the slightest detraction from it now would be destructive of
my peace of mind." Wayne MacVeagh to Aldrich, March 5, 1906, refers to
a conversation in which he and Aldrich had fully agreed that Senators
should regard patronage as a purely executive matter, "not interfering
with patronage until the name reached the Senate."

25. The election was followed by a sharp, almost furious newspaper
debate over what had been done behind the scenes. The conflicting interests of *The Star* and *The Journal* of Providence were part of the mainspring of this affair. There were charges of a deal between Aldrich and
Brayton. Aldrich denied the implications of the newspaper charges. But
this does not affect the general question of the relations between the two
men. Altogether, the controversy leaves the matter at the end about
where it was in the beginning. The best argument for an understanding
of some sort is Brayton's later service to Aldrich. The real questions remain: was Aldrich powerful enough in 1886 to compel Brayton to support him? did Aldrich have to make terms with Brayton? did Brayton
have enough gratitude to give his support freely?

26. W. E. Curtis to Aldrich, June 8, 1886, A. MSS.

CHAPTER IV

ON THE VERGE OF GREATNESS

1. *R.*, July 31, 1886, p. 7816. The bill had been reported by the committee at a meeting of a bare quorum. Aldrich moved to recommit.

2. *R.*, Dec. 15, 1886, p. 171.

3. *R.* The passages are from a speech printed in the Appendix, also as
a pamphlet, "Remarks of Mr. Aldrich of Rhode Island, in the Senate of
the United States, Friday, Jan. 14, 1887, Washington, 1887." The part
of the Act of 1887 that seemed most in point at the time was its anti-
pooling provisions. Aldrich and the New Englanders generally had little
thought except for the possible regional favoritism implicit, as they believed, in the measure. It is very interesting to note how closely Aldrich's
position on this original Interstate Commerce Act foreshadows his position twenty years later on the Hepburn Act which amended it. See
especially pages 1, 2 and 28 of the speech in pamphlet form. Aldrich referred to the original debate early in the later controversy in reply to statements by Senator Clay. "Mr. President, the bill (of 1887) in terms said
that all rates should be reasonable and just. That, of course, is not and
cannot be a subject of contention on the part of anybody; but that the
Congress went beyond that and gave, or intended to give, the Interstate
Commerce Commission any power to fix rates is not within the range of
possibilities. Those who were members of the Senate at that time, as I
was, and my friend from Iowa (Mr. Allison) and other senators around
me were, had a clear understanding on this subject." *R.*, Jan. 22, 1906,
1361. It is a twice-told tale that the commission assumed rate-making
power and that the Federal Courts deprived it of this power by adopting
the interpretation of the law indicated by Aldrich in these remarks. Ad-

mirable review of the whole subject in Ripley, "Railroads: Rates and Regulation," Chapters XIII and XIV.

4. Speech, pamphlet form, 16.

5. *R.*, Feb. 4, 1887, pp. 1353–60.

6. Memorandum by President Butler, A. MSS.: "Aldrich considered Harrison as the finest intellect in the presidency since John Quincy Adams because of his keen mind and superior capacity as a lawyer. The same was true of the close friends of the Aldrich group, among the members of which were none who were annoyed by the chilly temperament of the Chief Executive. Rather than being estranged by the characteristics of the man, they were attracted by his strong sense of detachment and impartiality."

7. Authorized memorandum of Colonel David Corser, given to J. P. Nichols, Sept. 8, 1926, A. MSS. Colonel Corser says that these votes gave Harrison the nomination "partly through the generous behavior of Alger." *Tribune*, June 19, 1888: "There have been many rumors that Alger's friends were making a number of converts among the negro delegates from the South. Only the first ballot will show how much basis there is for these rumors. General Alger is personally conceded to be an estimable man, but the methods of his managers have destroyed whatever chance he may have had for the nomination."

8. My authority for this interesting detail is President Butler, who permits the following summary of his recollections: "The 1888 convention was the most deliberative of any in President Butler's experience. Its leaders really did take council together; they had to, because there was such a stalemate among the factions for Alger, Allison, Blaine, Depew, Sherman and others. Finally, realizing that they weren't getting anywhere, the group of which Aldrich was one gathered together to attempt a mutual understanding. Harrison offered a way out, if they could feel that they understood him and he them. So the emissaries went to Indianapolis, and they came back satisfied with Harrison as a compromise candidate."

Whether Aldrich went to the convention an avowed Harrison man is open to question. There was a feeble attempt to nominate Allison and Aldrich was named in the newspapers as one of his supporters. The Rhode Island delegation at first voted for Allison. But the movement was too feeble to have deceived Aldrich, and it is plausible to regard the Rhode Island vote as merely complimentary, while plans for a break toward Harrison were being quietly matured.

9. McClure, "Old Time Notes of Pennsylvania," II, 573.

10. Morrill to Aldrich, Oct. 6, 1888, A. MSS. The Aldrich Substitute is Senate Report 2332, published as a pamphlet, Government Printing Office, 1888; the same sheets with a different cover form the pamphlet mentioned in the text.

11. Without waiting for the Mills Bill, the Finance Committee had conducted hearings and also corresponded with manufacturers on the tariff. Herbert Radclyffe, Secretary of the Home Market Club of Boston, to Allison, July 12, Allison MSS.: "I have been able to send you a complete copy of the suggestions of the (executive) committee (of the Club.)" James M. Swank, Manager American Iron and Steel Association, to Allison, Aug. 16, Allison MSS.: ". . . I have at last been able to sit down to

a thorough study of the Mills Bill, which I promised Senator Aldrich I would do for your committee. I will mail the senator some comments to-morrow." Chas. C. Harrison, Franklin Sugar Refinery, to Allison, Oct. 19, Allison MSS.: "At our conference upon the 'sugar question' three weeks ago, further consultation was expected."

As the Senate cannot theoretically originate a money bill this one by a bare-faced fiction was treated as an "amendment" to the Mills Bill. Its programme was kept before the Senate until after the election. This, of course, gave rise to the charge that it was done in order to make deals with manufacturers who might be induced to contribute to campaign funds. Senator Cockrell used familiar political language when he said that "the frying pan was kept not far from the Senate Finance Committee, so that when the manufacturers and others came voluntarily before the committee, they had an opportunity of visiting that frying pan and seeing what was wanted."

Aldrich's report gives 45 pages to analysis of the Mills Bill and adds a summary of the substitute bill proposed by the Finance Committee. The most significant features, other than higher rates, are the reduction of the duty on sugar and the substitution of specific or compound rates for ad valorem rates "wherever practicable, or where the necessary data could be obtained." The chief reason assigned for discarding ad valorem duties was the prevention of fraudulent valuation in the customs, a matter in which Aldrich took much interest.

The rivalry of the two bills reveals between the lines an amusing competition for Southern votes. The Democrats with their low tariff programme aimed to please the Southern masses by a great decrease in the rigor of the internal revenue laws. The Republicans built upon the hope that Southern industry was creating Southern protectionists while at the same time they denounced the professed changes in the internal revenue.

12. Letter head of the Committee.

CHAPTER V

MIRAGE

1. W. B. Weeden to Aldrich, June 23, 1883, A. MSS.

2. E. W. Halford, "How Harrison Chose His Cabinet," *Leslie's Weekly*, April 19, 1909.

3. Blaine to Harrison, Feb. 13, 1889, H. MSS. Blaine subsequently changed his advice. In August, Harrison asked for views and Blaine urged him not to call an extra session. Hamilton, "Biography of James G. Blaine," 692. The politicians generally, early in the year, had opposed an extra session. It is fair to assume that Blaine in August saw that the opportunity had gone by. What point in calling an extra session in September with months of tariff dispute in prospect? The mistake of Harrison was in not anticipating the wisdom shown by McKinley in 1897, and failing to call an early session. E. W. Halford to J. P. Nichols, April 20, 1929, A. MSS.: ". . . Naturally the first two months of the administration my entries were unusually full of all manner of things occurring, and about which the President and I talked a good deal.

"I find no allusion whatever to the question of a special session of Congress up to May when the Senate finally adjourned. . . .

"Nor for some days after is there any mention of a 'special session of Congress.' . . ."

4. Harrison to Blaine, Feb. 11, 1889, H. MSS.

5. Especially, speech of Aldrich in the Senate, Sept. 30, 1890. Though this speech was his summing up, these views had been expressed in various forms at all stages of the debate. The statements of theory in this chapter are all from the speech of September 30.

6. Ibid.

7. Ibid.

8. The abler Democrats of course made their attack seriously upon the fundamental idea of the bill—the frank recognition of the manufacturing interests as the mainspring of prosperity. Aldrich did not evade the charge that he aimed to raise the prices to the consumer. "Otherwise there would be no force and effect in a protective tariff." *R.*, May 2, 1890, p. 4123.

9. Quoted from a petition, A. MSS. Among the signers are Henderson, Cannon, Butterworth and Dolliver.

10. Sugar is taken as the typical item in this controversy partly because Blaine made it a point of attack, partly because it was so soon to play such an important part in Aldrich's fortunes. Eventually the growers were given a bounty and the duty on refined sugar became half a cent. See note 16, and also note 27, Chapter VII.

In the popular attack upon the bill other schedules counted for as much or more. The tin-plate schedule was singled out because of the effect it might have upon the small objects of household use.

The woollen and cotton schedules, as has been pointed out by all writers on the subject, form important landmarks in the upward trend of protection.

11. *R.*, Feb. 25, 1892, p. 1433. Edward Stanwood in his life of Blaine pooh-poohs the story.

12. Dawson, "Life of Wolcott," II, 578; *R.*, June 17, 6166. A concise review of the episode with references to the *Record* is Wellborn's "The Influence of the Silver Republican Senators," 1889–1891, *Mississippi Valley Historical Review*, March, 1928.

13. The complicated strategy of these interlocking measures may be traced with tolerable clarity through the *Record*. Crucial moments are indicated by the following abbreviated calendar: Dec. 4, 1889, Sherman introduced Anti-Trust Act (S. 1); Jan. 20, 1890, House Silver Purchase Bill (H. R. 5381) introduced; Jan. 28, Senate Silver Purchase Bill (S. 2350) sent to Finance Committee; March 3, speech by Reagan for unlimited coinage; April 8, Anti-Trust Bill passed the Senate; April 12, Tariff Bill (H. R. 9415) introduced in House from Ways and Means by McKinley; May 21, House passed Tariff Bill; June 7, House passed its Silver Bill; June 7, Republican caucus advocated purchase of 4½ million ounces of silver monthly, with redemption in bullion; June 11, Finance Committee reported to Senate the House Silver Bill amended and announced that the bill would be offered in place of the Senate Silver Bill "at the proper time"; June 13, Senate laid aside S. 2350 and substituted the amended H. R. 5381; June 14, "Force Bill" (H. R. 10958) introduced in House by Lodge; June 16, Senate and House at loggerheads on Anti-trust bill; June 17, Wolcott threatened Rhode Island, Plumb Free Coinage amendment adopted, and

Silver Purchase Bill passed Senate; June 18, Senate accepted conference report on Anti-trust Bill; June 19, Harrison's reciprocity message; June 25, House refused to concur in amendments to Silver Bill; July 2, Force Bill passed House; July 7, conference report on Silver Bill compromised by requiring monthly purchase of 4½ million ounces to be paid for by treasury notes redeemable in gold or silver; July 10, report accepted by Senate; July 18, conference report accepted by House; August 12, Quay introduced resolution postponing Force Bill until next session, and limiting debate on tariff to end of August; Aug. 28, Aldrich introduced reciprocity amendment to Tariff Bill; Sept. 10, Tariff Bill passed Senate; Sept. 23, Quay stated that his resolution, not yet voted upon, had served its purpose, and it was postponed indefinitely.

The obvious problems that are suggested by the chronology are, for the most part, still unsolved. For example, the Force Bill. The text follows the usual interpretation. It is conceivable that the Force Bill was a far-sighted move designed to bring on the situation which was dealt with by Quay's astute resolution of August 12. Against the latter interpretation is the fact that the Republicans the previous year had committed themselves to bring in such a measure; in favor of the interpretation is the strategic value in the introduction of the bill at the precise moment when it appeared.

14. M. and P., 5509.

15. There has been much controversy over the origin and course of this reciprocity dispute. It seems clear that what Professor Taussig calls old-style reciprocity—keeping the duty on but offering to remove it—was the Blaine-Harrison programme as late as the message of June 19. "The basis of the original amendment was the retention of the sugar duty till reciprocal treaties could be negotiated. When that basis was changed and the repeal became a fixed fact it is difficult to see what other plan than the Aldrich amendment could be devised." Hale, in the Senate, Jan. 28, 1892, *R.*, p. 612. The amendment putting a duty on sugar was submitted by Hale June 19. It was eventually set aside to clear the way for voting on Aldrich's reciprocity amendment. See note 13.

16. P. C. Cheney to L. T. Michener, March 23, 1893, Michener MSS. The whole matter of the quarrel over sugar is still relatively obscure. As Blaine was convinced that free sugar would lose the support of the crowd, and as other shrewd politicians were convinced that a duty on sugar would alienate the crowd, there is need for much more close study of the subject than has yet been given it.

17. June 17, Plumb's amendment carried this day 42 to 25; 17 not voting, Aldrich, of course, in the negative. This was the day of Wolcott's threat. See chronology in note 13. The complexity of the situation is well illustrated in Newlands to Harrison, June 5, 1890, H. MSS.: "The Republican bimetallists know that they can pass a free coinage bill through both Houses by the aid of Democratic votes. They think it doubtful whether a majority of the Republican votes would be for free coinage. Though they insist that the actual sentiment of a majority is in favor of it. Whilst their constituents are uncompromising with reference to free coinage, and will support them in opposing the majority, however large, of the Republicans opposed to it, they prefer to favor a measure which will secure the party's support in Congress, if it can be done without viola-

tion of the bimetallic principle. They contend that redemption in bullion in whatever form it may be, and however guarded, is an abandonment of the bimetallic principle and is a surrender to the monometallic gold standard; that practically it demonetizes silver and makes it a mere commodity held as security for additional circulation. They object to a currency which can at any time be retired and cancelled. They insist that all silver bullion going into the Treasury should come out only as money, either in actual coin or certificates calling for coin. They will be willing to yield their views as to free coinage and substitute a limited purchase of bullion, provided there is no redemption in bullion. They also insist that the notes issued in lieu of and representing silver shall be legal tender.

"They declare, however, that they will not vote for this compromise measure, or for any compromise measure until its passage is assured; that otherwise they will stand with their constituents for free coinage and go before the country on the issue."

18. There was strong opposition among the Republicans. Edmunds to Aldrich, July 11, 1890, A. MSS. Apparently the opposition was overcome. A caucus decided for cloture, July 14, the day the Silver Purchase Act was passed. Memorandum in Halford MSS. For possible evidences of a feeble move in direction of cloture see R., Aug. 13.

19. Edmunds to Morrill, Sept. 9, 1890, Morrill MSS.: "I do not think that my proposition for a recess will avail anything. I have heard that the Democrats say that it would violate their trade with Quay, etc., about which I know nothing and hope I never shall." A memorandum in the Halford MSS., dated Aug. 15, 1890, says that Aldrich "opposes the election bill on the ground of the business interests being against it." Nevertheless in January, 1891, after the "land-slide," he took part in the effort to push the Force Bill through the Senate. Senator Stewart had introduced a bill for free silver which passed the Senate and was eventually killed in the House. Aldrich submitted a resolution for changing the rules so as to make cloture practicable: ordered printed Dec. 29, 1890, Mis. Doc., No. 33. The resolution was rejected, the Force Bill defeated, the Silver Bill passed, all in a sharp parliamentary scuffle closing late in January. See R., New York newspapers, Dawson's "Wolcott," Coolidge, Wellborn.

20. Aldrich gave a great deal of attention to the report on "Retail Prices and Wages" which was published as a pamphlet entitled "Report by Mr. Aldrich from the Committee on Finance, July 19, 1892." 52nd C., I S., Sen. Rept. 986. It had been authorized by a Senate resolution of March 3, 1891. The report consisted of an extensive collection and analysis of statistics by Carrol D. Wright, then Commissioner of the Department of Labor, and an introduction by Aldrich summarizing its significance. Mr. Wright was assisted by Prof. R. P. Faulkner. The report at once became the subject of sharp controversy, the Republicans aiming to show that it disproved the Democratic charges against the McKinley tariff, the Democrats maintaining the reverse. See Aldrich, R., July 26, 1892; Carlisle, R., July 29; Nation, Aug. 4, 11, 18; Quarterly Journal of Economics, Oct., 1892; Taussig, in Yale Review, Nov., 1893. Aldrich's speech was used as a campaign document and widely distributed. An article by Aldrich, "The McKinley Act and the Cost of Living," Forum, Oct., 1892, was an argument to show that protection raised wages

and lowered expenses. The report, together with the still more extensive one on wholesale prices produced by Wright the following year, Professor Paxson calls "almost epochal as the beginning of the statistical control of legislative policy."

CHAPTER VI

THE RESURRECTION OF ALEXANDER HAMILTON

1. The issues of *The World* for March, 1892, are very largely concerned with the Rhode Island campaign. Aldrich was painted as an enemy of the people, and the creature of the Sugar Trust. This newspaper campaign is a classic of the "new" journalism. A good illustration is the issue of March 25 with an editorial on the "disfranchising" of Rhode Island towns and a long article on "Aldrich and Boodle."

2. *World*, March 18, 1892.

3. Aldrich to Harrison, March 20, 1892, H. MSS.

4. McKinley to Aldrich, March 22, 1892, A. MSS.

5. *World*, March 21, 1892.

6. Ibid., March, 26.

7. G. F. Parker, "Writings and Speeches of Grover Cleveland," 321–328.

8. *World*, April 4, 1892.

9. Specimens in Brown University Library.

10. The explanation in the text is also the view of W. Tyler Page, who has contributed a memorandum on the subject, A. MSS. Though Mr. Page does not touch the real problem, the explanation of the shift in the city vote, his views fit into the circumstantial evidence which makes it fundamentally a labor revolt. A newly organized Central Labor Union figured actively on the Democratic side. Providence *Evening Telegram*, Oct. 2, 1902, ff.

11. Harrison to Aldrich, June 14, 1892, H. MSS.

12. The contract between Aldrich and his associates, preserved in A. MSS., is dated Feb. 2, 1893. They secured controlling interests in the two street railways of Providence, and in one at Pawtucket. Their stock was transferred to the United Traction and Electric Company organized under the laws of New Jersey with Aldrich as president. He continued as president until 1902. In an argument before a committee of the Legislature, April 27, 1896, Aldrich said that "the United Traction and Electric Company was organized for the express purpose named in its charter, of acquiring and holding and operating street railway, electric lighting and other plants, not only in the cities of Providence and Pawtucket and vicinity, but in a dozen different States, and in the District of Columbia." These statements were called forth by a typical quarrel over transfers, a common theme of dispute at the time between street railways and municipalities. It was carried to the legislature. Aldrich's argument before the legislative committee opposed transfers unless compensation was made to the companies. The legislature granted free transfers but exempted the companies from paving operations for five years.

13. Gresham to Chandler, May 21, 1891, C. MSS.

14. Aldrich's son, Mr. E. B. Aldrich, states that in order to effect the traction deal bonds were sold in 1892, bringing in about nine million dollars. Of this, some two and a half millions were paid out almost immediately to

cover purchases of stock. The remainder formed a cash balance in hand when the panic came. It enabled Aldrich and his associates to meet the crisis through creating the emergency labor market. So much work was provided that the achievement is still remembered in such sayings as "no one was out of a job in Rhode Island in 1893." This appears to be an exaggeration. See Reports of the Railway Commission of Rhode Island for the years 1893 and 1894; also Bradstreets, *Journal of Trade, Finance and Public Economy*, Dec. 23, 1893. Professor Kirk in his able study, "A Modern City—Providence, R. I., and Its Expenditures," is concerned chiefly with the activities of the city government.

15. Quoted from Roosevelt's first annual message. For reasons why it may be assumed that Aldrich inspired these passages, see Chapter XIII.

CHAPTER VII

THREE FRIENDS AND A DIFFICULT SITUATION

1. A. D. Gaston to Allison, July 9–20, 1895, Allison MSS.
2. Congressional Directory, 53rd Congress. The other two members were Brice of Ohio, and Harris of Tennessee. It is interesting to note the change in the committee the next Congress when the Republicans returned to power and Aldrich dropped the chairmanship which went to Jones of Arkansas.
3. McElroy, "Grover Cleveland," II, 26.
4. Ibid., II, 36.
5. Stanwood, "Presidency," I, 499.
6. *R.*, Oct. 30, 1893, p. 2958.
7. McElroy, "Grover Cleveland," II, 108.
8. Whitelaw Reid to Chandler, Jan. 23, 1894, C. MSS.: "My judgment has been that it is not wise for Republicans to attempt improving the Wilson Bill. It is a thoroughly bad bill, on which the Democrats themselves cannot agree, and over which they should be allowed to fight at leisure and assume the whole responsibility. As a result I hope you may be able to beat it in the Senate. At any rate you will be able to beat the party that passes it next Fall at the polls." James H. Wilson to Chandler, March 11, 1894, C. MSS.: "As Allison said, you must discuss every item and paragraph of the Tariff Bill! The Income Tax is an odious one which will bring you the support of every man who has a little money, while free wool, notwithstanding their desire for lower wages, will bring you the support of most of the farmers." Morrill to Edmunds, May 1, 1894, M. MSS.: "I hope our friends in the Senate will not 'filibuster' against the Tariff Bill. Discuss fully and point out its evils one by one, and then let the Democratic party pass it if they will."
9. E. Morris to Morrill, Dec. 11, 1893, M. MSS.
10. *R.*, roll calls of June 27, 1894.
11. *R.*, roll calls of June 15, 16, July 3, 1894.
12. S. N. D. North, Secretary, Association of Wool Manufacturers, to Aldrich, Oct. 7, 1895, expressing the confidence of the Association in his leadership.
13. H. C. Warmoth to Allison, Aug. 7, 1894, Allison MSS.
14. Clarkson to Allison, Feb. 6, 1896, Allison MSS.
15. Manderson to Morton, April 4, 1894, Morton MSS.

16. H. L. Terrell to D. S. Lamont, March 6, 1894, Cleveland MSS.

17. *World*, March 1, 1894.

18. *Tribune*, March 7, 1894.

19. *R.*, March 9, 1894, pp. 2762–3.

20. *World*, March 8, 1894; *R.*, March 7, p. 266; March 12, pp. 2833–5.

21. For example, see his use of the Seignorage bill of late February, and of the Russian Thistle Bill, the next month.

22. Chandler diary, May 2, 4, 8, C. MSS.

23. Philadelphia *Public Ledger*, May 17, 1894.

24. *Press*, May 14; repeated in *Tribune*, May 15.

25. *Sun*, repeated in *Tribune*, May 17; *Tribune*, May 18.

26. *R.*, May 16, p. 4796; May 17, pp. 4848–51.

27. Concord *Evening Monitor*, May 17, 1894.

28. *R.*, May 31, p. 5530.

29. *Tribune*, June 5, 1894.

30. *Tribune*, June 10.

31. The bill as it came from the House made a clean sweep of sugar duties, placing both raw and refined sugar on the free list and abolishing the bounty. How the schedule was remade was told by Senator Blanchard. A conference of Democratic Senators agreed upon the duty of 40 per cent ad valorem on all sugar, $\frac{1}{8}$ of a cent per pound additional on refined, and $\frac{1}{10}$ of a cent per pound additional on sugars from countries that gave export bounties. The Louisiana men wanted more but acquiesced. *R.*, July 20, 1894, p. 7746. The final text of the bill contained this schedule with the exception of the bounty which was abolished. See Taussig, pp. 305–315. The position of Aldrich and his group is brought out in the debates of June 2, 4 and 5. On the latter day, Aldrich was momentarily absent when the crucial vote was taken. Later he explained his absence, and stated how he should have voted if he had been present and how he meant to vote in the future. *R.*, June 8, p. 5963.

32. *R.*, June 3, p. 5755. A certain sort of student will brush this remark aside and say that it was mere strategy, that Aldrich was still aiming to defeat the bill by making it unpalatable to the Louisianians. I do not think so—being convinced that Aldrich was both the statesman and the politician, and that it is superficial to interpret him as only the parliamentary juggler—but that is immaterial. Those who will have it that there was no purpose in the opposition but to defeat the bill, must base their argument on the assumption that Aldrich, ordinarily so astute in reading the purposes of the Senate, did not on this occasion see things as they were. If that be so, he may have been trying to force a situation in which the Louisianians would abandon Gorman. Hill, more definitely the politician, may have had only this motive in getting rid of the sugar bounty—which was part of the Louisiana demand (note 31). The bounty was got rid of but the Gorman-Louisiana alliance was not broken.

33. June 5, C. MSS. Any way you take it, this incident—whether you believe as I do that Aldrich understood the inner situation and was merely defining his attitude, or hold with those who believe he had no more insight than Hill and was merely playing a game to defeat the bill—remains one of the choice bits in the American political comedy. It cannot be divorced from its basic significance—the party that was officially anti-protectionist out-Heroding the arch protectionist.

34. Senate Reports, 53 C., 2 S., serial 3188, Aldrich testimony, p. 432; Quay testimony, pp. 497–8. Quay denied having had knowledge what the sugar schedule was to be.

35. *World*, June 12, 1894; *R.*, June 11, p. 6101.

36. *R.*, July 5, p. 7136.

CHAPTER VIII

REALIGNMENT

1. E. E. Perkins to J. M. Forbes (by copy transmitted to Allison), July 14, 1893, Allison MSS.

2. Cablegram, May 1, 1894, Allison MSS., signed by Sherman, Allison, Voorhees, Hoar, Aldrich, Frye, Davis, Cullom, Lodge, Brice, Platt, Gorman, Murphy, Hill. Also in Foraker, "Notes," I, 471. A promise to attempt an international agreement had been incorporated in the repeal act. It is to be observed that the Democrats who signed this cablegram were the same who were conspicuously Eastern in their sympathies in the tariff debate of 1894.

3. Martin, "Life of Choate," II, 9–13.

4. Feb. 26, 1896. Senator Carter gave warning that the Silver men would not support the Republican nominee for President unless he stood for free silver. *R.*, Feb. 26, p. 2157.

5. H. R. 2904, *R.*, Dec. 27, 1895; p. 345, also Jan. 7, 1896, p. 484. This bill had been passed by the Republican House following Cleveland's message, Dec. 20, describing the government's need of money. The refusal of the silver bloc to allow any such bill to pass the Senate led Cleveland to tell Morgan that it was useless for him to try to effect legislation.

6. *R.*, Feb. 1, pp. 1215–16. The bill was killed in the House. *R.*, Feb. 14, p. 1735.

7. H. R. 2749. *R.*, Feb. 4, p. 1267.

8. *R.*, Feb. 25, p. 2101.

9. *R.*, Feb. 25, pp. 2103–5.

10. His choice for President appears to have been Reed. Brayton to Aldrich, June 12, 1896, A. MSS.: ". . . is voting all right now and will for Reed. . . . Rhode Island will stick to Reed until the last and have so wired him."

11. Memorandum authorized by President Butler, A. MSS.: "Aldrich went to St. Louis to participate in framing the currency plank. There he worked together with a small group to persuade Hanna that McKinley should come out for a gold plank. McKinley did not know his own mind and Hanna feared the vote west of the Missouri. It took considerable argument to reassure Hanna, but Aldrich, Henry C. Payne and W. R. Merriam persuaded him after many hours and long-distance connection with Canton." A dreary controversy has arisen as to who wrote the "gold plank." Probably no one in particular, though many men evidently contributed to bringing it about, and each thought he was the crucial factor. The Republicans must be taken at their word when they claimed that they had not as yet committed themselves to mono-metallism. Even Pierpont Morgan took this position; he was in favor of saying: "We are entirely opposed to the coinage of silver as full legal tender money, and to any change in the existing gold standard, except by international agree-

ment to which England, France and Germany must be parties." Reed to McKinley, June 13, 1896, McK. MSS. The McKinley MSS. contain an undated draft of a plank which states that the party "would welcome international bimetallism but in the absence of the co-operation of other nations it will oppose the free and unlimited and independent coinage of silver at the ratio of 16 to 1."

At least equally worth claiming is the authorship of the clause beginning "we pledge." ... H. Kohlsaat to Chandler, Dec. 26, 1899, C. MSS.: "I have always understood it was put in through Senator Teller, by the sub-committee on Resolutions; it did not have the desired effect as you know.

"Personally, I objected to it when it was shown me Tuesday, June 16, but was overruled." Hansborough to Gallinger, Aug. 4, 1896, G. MSS.: "I endeavored to impress upon him (Foraker) the importance of pledging the party to use its efforts honestly in behalf of bimetallism. ... I called his attention to the fact that we were not likely to control the next Senate and that we should do something to give the people of the Western States some ground of hope. Foraker agreed with me. ... You will remember that the first draft of the platform ... did not contain anything pledging the party to bimetallism. I again saw Senator Foraker ... he said to me ... you will have no cause for complaint when we are through." Chandler was convinced that Lodge inserted the words "which we pledge ourselves to promote," and Lodge was of the same opinion. Chandler to Lodge, May 27, 1901, and Lodge to Chandler, June 21, 1901, C. MSS.

CHAPTER IX

THE DAY OF THE ELDER STATESMEN

1. There was talk in their day of a "Big Five" composed of the Four named and Hale. But the facts do not bear out that impression. As will be plain from later chapters, the Four acted consistently as a unit, and Hale is only incidentally a member of their cabal. The confusion on this point has arisen through enumerating all Aldrich's lieutenants and thinking of them as in close co-operation with him at all times; also, in confusing social with legislative companionship. Socially, these five were very close throughout. Legislatively, Hale became a mainstay of Aldrich's only after the Four began to fall asunder; in the later days Smoot was his right-hand man. See Chapters XIII and XVII.

2. Barry, "Forty Years in Washington," 106.

3. Senator Beveridge repeated this remark to the author.

CHAPTER X

CONCILIATION

1. M. and P., 6265.

2. Shortly after the election, the Republican leaders held a caucus at Washington. "We ... appointed a committee of five to look after the passage of some legislation regarding an international conference." Gear to Allison, Dec. 8, 1896, Allison MSS. Wolcott carried the views of this committee to McKinley, who wrote to the other members: "I have received your letter of Dec. 17 presented by Senator Wolcott and thank you

for it. My interview with Senator Wolcott has been very satisfactory. He will tell you of it. I am sure the bill you propose looking to an international conference is both wise and timely. . . ." McKinley to Geo. F. Hoar, Wm. E. Chandler, John H. Gear and Thomas H. Carter, Dec. 28, 1896. Concord *Evening Monitor*, March 4, 1901. Wolcott sailed for England soon after, and on Jan. 10, 1897, C. MSS., wrote Chandler from London, "To-morrow evening I am to meet Mr. Balfour, Lord Lansdowne (formerly Governor-General of Quebec), Mr. Asquith, Lord Rothschild, Mr. Greeley, the Speaker of the House of Commons, and one or two others. On Tuesday I am to have a confidential meeting with the leaders of the Bimetallic League from France, Germany and here, the Continental members coming here for the purpose." Before this letter reached America, the Republican senatorial caucus approved a resolution looking toward an international silver conference: Chandler diary, Jan. 15, 1897, C. MSS. The next month Wolcott was in Paris conferring with the French bimetallists, all of whom were intensely interested in the American situation, even reading the *Congressional Record*. Edward Tuck to Cummings, Feb. 24, 1897, Cummings MSS.

3. Wolcott to Chandler, Feb. 1, 1897, C. MSS.

4. Tuck to Chandler, March 4, 1897, C. MSS.

5. Chandler's diary, April to July, C. MSS. The whole of this episode is still obscure but there seems to be no doubt that the bimetallist senators were all conferring privately while the House was preparing the Dingley Bill, and were devising a programme that should propitiate the French.

6. Wolcott to Chandler, Nov. 13, 1896, C. MSS.

7. *Tribune*, April 17, 1897.

8. Though the details of this strange episode hitherto concealed remain to be discovered, a letter from Chandler to Allison, July 4, 1897, C. MSS., implies a definite programme with regard to the bill, agreed upon by Aldrich, Wolcott, Chandler, and at least six other senators previous to Wolcott's second departure for France which occurred May 8. A memorandum enclosed in this letter contains the passage quoted. The memorandum formed a protest from Senators Carter, Clark, Warren, Wilson, Shoup, Hansborough and Chandler. It continued: "The French Government perceived the conclusions of the sub-committee [of the Finance Committee] as shown in the amendments they made to the tariff bill as it came from the House, and the ministry accepted them as fair and just.

"But the retreat of the sub-committee from various amendments, as the bill has been considered in the Senate (see note 20), has created alarm and distrust, and is liable to unfavorably affect the pending negotiations, especially in this way—by raising the suspicion, unjust although it be, that there has been intentional deception from the beginning.

"Therefore, as the cause of Bimetallism is of paramount importance, the foregoing request is made—that the sub-committee will adhere completely, in the Senate and in conference, to the understanding with Senator Wolcott, there being no doubt that such action can be sustained by a majority vote in both Houses, as it is certain that it will be approved by the President."

The evidence that Wolcott, in his over-confidence, gave very definite promises to the French consul-general (note 14) seems quite plain. Wolcott to Chandler, May 7, 1897, C. MSS., introduces Bruwaert to Chandler. Wolcott to Chandler, May 30, 1897, C. MSS.: "We have been apparently infinitely helped by the tariff action of our Senate Committee, and by Bruwaert's cable to the government that I was instrumental in bringing about fair treatment of French products. . . . I shall speak of this plan or agreement as 'epistle.' If you get it signed, or if any question arises, it may be necessary for you alone or with Allison, or Aldrich, or whomsoever you think best, to see to it that our action is approved and not questioned or repudiated." Chandler to Wolcott, July 19, 1897, C. MSS., contains the reference to this agreement that had embarrassed Aldrich because it could not be stated "openly to any one" (note 19).

9. Aldrich to Frick, March 29, 1897, Harvey, "Frick," 294. Thos. S. Harrison to Dalzell, June 25, 1897, transmitted to Allison through Harrison and Geo. C. Tichenor, Allison MSS.: "In the interviews that I had with Senator Aldrich he gave no reason why he had recommended lower rates than he did in the act of 1890, which he then warmly supported, other than that he thought the lower rates could now be endured, due to the changed conditions. . . ." Lodge to Aldrich, June 9, 1897, A. MSS.: "As you are against increases generally, this (hides schedule) is a good case to stop one." Hanna to Holls, March 26, 1897, Holls MSS.: "At half-past two, I went with Senator Platt to the White House. In the ante room waiting were Senators Aldrich and Wetmore of Rhode Island. We all had to wait half an hour while the President was engaged with some members of the [cabinet. During the interval we talked much about the tariff. Senator Aldrich assured me that it would be very much changed in the Senate. . . ." G. C. Tichenor to Allison, June 14, 1897, Allison MSS.: "This (wool rate) my dear senator, is entirely too high. . . . You will recollect that this paragraph was discussed considerably by the sub-committee consisting of yourself and Senators Aldrich, Platt and Wolcott, and I distinctly recall that some of you thought that the 'differential' should not be more than ten per cent, and the majority of you, not more than fifteen per cent. How it came to be *twenty* I don't know." Rhodes, who was close to the leaders of that day, asserts that it was Dingley's intention to cut nearly all duties considerably below the level of 1890, thus affirming, unaware, Chandler to Bruwaert, June 20. Rhodes, IX, 37. Mr. Olcott in his life of McKinley makes a similar statement, I, 351, and Mr. Cortelyou sees no reason to question it, though neither does he affirm it.

10. *R.*, May 25, p. 1227. Aldrich had reported the bill May 24. See note 20.

11. S. N. D. North to W. Whitman, June 10, 1897, H. R. Committee on Ways and Means, Tariff hearings, V, p. 5494. North had been brought to Washington by Aldrich as expert secretary to the Finance Committee. The "meetings" to which he refers were really party caucuses held at the Arlington.

12. Dawson, "Wolcott," I, Chapters V–VI.

13. Wolcott to Allison, June 4, 1897, Allison MSS.

14. Wolcott to Chandler, May 7, 1897, C. MSS. See note 8.

15. Chandler to Bruwaert, June 20, 1897, C. MSS.

16. Chandler diary, July 4, 1897, C. MSS. The same day Bruwaert wrote Chandler a note enclosing a memorandum, apparently a list of

articles upon which France must be satisfied. The list includes silks, woollens, gloves, olive oil, perfumery, and free allowance upon travellers' clothes.

17. Horace Porter to McKinley, July 13, 1897, McK. MSS.

18. Wolcott to McKinley, cable, date missing, McK. MSS.

19. Chandler to Wolcott, July 16, 1897, C. MSS.

20. Hay to McKinley, July 16, 1897, McK. MSS. He also reports that London is all agog over the Behring Sea negotiations, which were then in their first most dangerous stage.

The letter of Wolcott upon the hurried visit of Thiebault to London (note 22) describes the French ambassador as having grown "lukewarm" on the subject of the negotiations. At the beginning of the episode there was high talk in France about what "the two great republics" could accomplish in a monetary way, if only they stood loyally side by side, irrespective of the rest of the world. It remains for some close student of the French end of this obscure but so important episode to determine just what the French Government was really driving at, and just why they took the course which they eventually took.

The chronology of the episode is important: March 29, Aldrich's letter to Frick; March 31, House bill passed; April, much log-rolling and secret conferences of bimetallist senators; April 16, Hanoteaux interview; May opens with some sort of programme agreed upon in private among the bimetallist senators; May 4, Aldrich tentatively reports bill from Finance Committee but the bill is speedily taken back by the committee because it is instantly apparent that there will be strong opposition; May 8, Wolcott sails; May 24, the reconsidered bill submitted by Finance Committee; May 25, Aldrich speaks on the bill; June witnesses fierce opposition by reckless coalition inside party; June 1, Aldrich's last appearance in the Senate until July 20; June 8, Republican caucus rejects Aldrich's sugar schedule; Aldrich present at this caucus; June 12, caucus takes the bill out of the hands of the Finance Committee; furious meetings described by North (see note 11); July 12, Thiebault's conference with Wolcott in London; July 20, Aldrich returns to the Senate; July 22, bill passed. Aldrich accepted defeat with his usual stoicism; made the best of a bad job and voted for the bill.

21. Chandler to Wolcott, July 20, 1897, C. MSS.

22. Wolcott to Chandler, July 14, C. MSS.

23. Chandler to Wolcott, July 19, C. MSS.

24. Same to same, July 22, C. MSS.

25. Bruwaert to Allison, July 22, 1897, C. MSS.: "The French ministry has given to the delegates of the United States its most cordial support on the silver question in pledging our country to the bimetallic policy of the President and they will be at a loss to understand how the promises made to them by Mr. Wolcott could not be realized."

26. Hay to McKinley, Oct. 11, 1897, McK. MSS.

27. Statement of Aldrich's secretary, Mr. A. B. Shelton, A. MSS. His enemies criticised Aldrich very sharply for his frank use of the Wool Manufacturers Association in conference on this schedule. It was quite in line with his established practice. The schedule was in part at least a concession to the Westerners who forced up the rates on coarse wool and were agreeable to still higher rates on manufactured wool. A long and

candid statement of how the schedule was formed is in North to Payne, Dec. 3, 1908, 60 C—2 S., H. Doc. 143, Vol. 5, pp. 5496–98.

28. Chandler diary, Sept. 10, 1897, C. MSS.

29. Wolcott to Chandler, Oct. 1, 1897, C. MSS.

30. *R.*, Jan. 20–28, 1898; article on Aldrich, Concord *Evening Monitor*, Jan. 23, 1898; Platt to Aldrich, Jan. 16, 1898, A. MSS.

CHAPTER XI

ENTER IMPERIALISM

1. Both parties played rather disgraceful rôles—by any other standard than that of American politics—with regard to the Cuban agitation. The Republican line politicians used it to embarrass Cleveland in 1896, the Democrats to embarrass McKinley in 1897. In Feb., 1897, the Four led the opposition to a resolution recognizing Cuban belligerency. The subject was interwoven with the tariff but elicited no attention from Aldrich. See *R.*, 1897, April 1, 5, 6, 7, 8, 13, 20; May 3, 10, 11, 18, 19, 20.

2. Chandler to Aldrich, Dec. 20, 1912, C. MSS.

3. Chandler to C. R. Miller, Sept. 24, 1896, C. MSS.

4. The country was sharply divided, as mountains of evidence make plain, but it seems fair to say that the more intellectual part of the nation was generally opposed to war. Many letters in the McKinley MSS. reaffirm this view. Typical of them all is President Eliot, and 85 others, to President McKinley April 4, 1898: "We, members of the Faculty of Arts and Sciences of Harvard University, heartily commend and support you in your efforts to maintain peace." *The World*, trying to draw the clergy of the country into its propaganda, received this from Bishop Walden of the Methodist Church, Feb. 4, 1898: "Our nation may well be satisfied with the President's declared policy as to Cuba. Our government should not determine its action by Spain's course alone, but by thorough consideration of all known facts and the probable results of its own action. The people will strongly sustain all conditions which result from Spain's inability to enforce order and the Cubans' inability to achieve independence. If war with Spain would cause more suffering within our country than exists in Cuba, such war with its inevitable demoralization would not promote liberty, civilization and Christianity." Business took much the same view. John F. Dryden, president, Prudential Insurance Company, to McKinley, April 11, 1898, praising his course and hoping for peace.

5. *The World* and *The Journal* were the leaders in working up a war furor. Every possible argument was used including the old cry that England was at work and if we did not intervene she would somehow make Cuba a commercial vassal.

6. Concord *Evening Monitor*, March 24, 1898. A companion of Senator Thurston, Colonel David Corser, has authorized the following statement, A. MSS.: "General Blanco and other officials of the Spanish Government in Cuba refused to permit the press representatives of Mr. Hearst to investigate affairs on the island. Hearst made a personal trip to Washington and asked a number of the senators and representatives if they would go to Cuba at his expense and by so doing make it possible for the actual facts to reach the public through the press. Among those who

consented to go and ascertain the facts were Thurston and Gallinger. The party started from New York by boat, but met a severe storm at Cape Hatteras. Many of them, in fact most of them, thereupon decided to return to Washington. But in Richmond, Senator Gallinger was met by one of Mr. Hearst's representatives and urged to go on with the work in spite of the dangers and difficulties pertaining thereto. Finally Gallinger consented with the understanding that Colonel David Corser would come down from Washington and accompany him. This he agreed to do.

"Arrived in Cuba, Blanco and the other Spanish officials did not dare to refuse senators of the U. S. the right to look about the island. So the trip was made and it was one of horrors at that, made all the more horrible by the death of Mrs. Thurston.

"Arrived back in Washington, Gallinger and Thurston told the Senate, with immense effect, what they had seen; and while perhaps Thurston's speech was the more effective, beginning as it did with a 'message from the dead' Gallinger could not but be glad that Mrs. Gallinger had declined to continue with him farther than Richmond." Similar information is to be found in the newspapers of the time.

7. Platt to H. Wales Lines, March 25, Coolidge, 271.

8. Holls' diary, April 2, 1898, H. MSS.

9. Platt to J. H. Flagg, April 7, 1898, Coolidge, 278. Not only may Platt be taken as the spokesman of the Four during the storm in Congress over intervention, his letters, as Mr. Coolidge points out, are almost a diary of the event. The phraseology of this letter is singularly close to that of the original House resolution, and to the paragraph in the war message suggesting action by Congress.

10. Chandler to Dana, April 17, 1898, C. MSS. R., April 16.

11. Platt to Flagg, April 6, 1898, Coolidge, 277.

12. R., April 13 and April 16. The final provision, generally called "the Teller resolution," was added during debate, being agreed to without a division.

13. R., April 15. See Appendix, 287.

14. Ibid., April 16, p. 3991.

15. Ibid., p. 3948.

16. Ibid., pp. 3991-2.

17. Ibid., p. 3993. Conferences with the House after hot debate ended in the acceptance of the resolutions as they passed the Senate, except that the Turpie amendment was struck out. R., pp. 3993, 4041-3, 4017-19.

18. Chandler diary, April 25, C. MSS.

19. Hanna to McKinley, Nov. 10, 1898, McK. MSS. Some students will have it that the Republican leaders went into the war for the purpose of avoiding defeat in these elections. Possibly, of course. But the evidence cited is tenuous.

20. R., for June, 1898, especially 15, 17, 30, and also July 6. During two weeks before voting the Senate discussed the subject from every point of view. Though the final vote was not taken until July 6, the vote that aligned the factions for and against was taken on June 20 (p. 6157).

CHAPTER XII

THE FERMENT OF 1901

1. Speech by Aldrich in the Senate introducing the bill Jan. 4, 1900. The bill was a "substitute" for one sent up by the House, *R.*, pp. 652–5.

2. Significant of the time is this from Henderson to Aldrich, May 5, 1899, A. MSS.: "I am in the field for the speakership and want Rhode Island. I know that your two members have nothing against me and are my friends in the general sense. Can you not make them so for me in this great contest?"

3. Published as a pamphlet by the Academy—special series, No. 9, Annual Meeting of 1900. *Annals*, XV, 155–168.

4. *World*, Dec. 4, 1900.

5. This relatively small matter has been exaggerated out of all proportion to its importance by one of those parochial quarrels over authorship to which American politicians are peculiarly prone. The most recent discussion of it is naturally the best. A. L. P. Dennis, "Adventures in American Diplomacy," 259–266.

6. Professor Dennis, who reprints Roosevelt's letter to John Hay, calls it "the best brief criticism of the treaty as it stood," p. 160.

7. This is the accepted version of an obscure event. I state it without challenge because I have no authority for saying anything else. The unpublished materials that have been searched for this volume throw little light on the subject. But if guesses were of any value, I should be willing to argue that Aldrich was in sympathy with the opposition, despite the fact that the newspapers of Dec., 1900, represent him as standing for the treaty. The bare facts are: treaty negotiated early in 1900 and provisions made public; "On Sunday, Feb. 11, I had Governor Roosevelt, Asst. Sec. Hills, Nicholas Murray Butler and Albert Shaw at the house to discuss public affairs, with the result that the governor issued his manifesto against the Hay-Pauncefote treaty, which I hope has killed the latter, and also his declination of the vice-presidency," Holls to A. D. White, March 5, 1900, Holls MSS.; the treaty under discussion during most of 1900; accusations against the railroads and to the effect that Senator Hanna will hold up the treaty unless a bill of his own for subsidies to merchant marine is passed; men like Holls and President Butler opposing the treaty as a renunciation of the Monroe Doctrine; early in Dec., Holls "went to the Finance Committee room and had a long talk with Senator Aldrich. . . . He told me that he had promised the President to help along ratification and he must keep his promise. 'Senator, you never would have negotiated such a treaty if you were secretary of state,' he said. 'No, indeed, I would not. I don't approve of it at all, but I don't think it is as important as you seem to think. I have promised to vote for it anyway, and I am going to carry out my promise.' I told him he could not carry the treaty through. He smiled and said he thought he could. I told him I knew of four Republican senators who would oppose it. He doubted it." Holls diary memorandum, Dec. 9–12, 1900, H. MSS.; Dec. 13, Senate adopts the Davis Amendment to the treaty, Aldrich voting with the majority; Dec. 20, Senate adopts Foraker Amendment without roll call; Senate ratifies amended treaty. Professor

Dennis summarizes the original treaty, pp. 159–160, and gives a summary of the difference between it and the second treaty, pp. 164–165.

8. Again, we meet an obscure episode which has generally been either passed over or accepted at newspaper valuation. Aldrich's attitude and his motive are discussed in Chapter XIII, in connection with the final disposition of the French treaty. There was pretty resolute opposition to the treaties outside Congress. Such organizations as the Home Market Club and the American Manufacturers Association were against them.

9. What has sometimes been called "the Iowa idea," was expressed by the State Republican Convention, Aug. 7, 1901, when it adopted a resolution drawn by George Roberts, the purpose of which was "to declare the general policy of the Republican party upon that subject (reciprocity) and to give the influence of the State for a cautious but forward movement for more liberal trade relations between the United States and other countries." George Roberts, "The Origin and History of the Iowa Idea," in the *Iowa Journal of History and Politics*, II, 69–82. Holls to A. D. White, written the day of McKinley's second inauguration, H. MSS.: "The Middle West, which is the seat of power in this country, and which New York and the East understand less than ever, will stand no nonsense whatever on the subject of the Nicaraguan Canal. It was this part of the country which swept us into the Spanish War against the unanimous protest of the East, and it will sweep us into other difficulties if shortsighted and incompetent men like Hay continue to fool with our relations, especially with Great Britain."

10. Mr. Cortelyou, in an interview with Doctor Nichols, May 3, 1928, authorized the following statement which is apparently contradictory of the views of McKinley's biographer, Mr. Olcott: "McKinley considered himself as building for the *future* adoption of the idea—not in his own time. He did not consider the demand for it sufficiently wide-spread to secure its adoption. He hardly expected that his speech would work the ratification of the pending Kasson treaties, nor in any sense was his speech intended as a throwing of the gauntlet down to the recalcitrant members of the Senate, Aldrich included, who were defeating those treaties. Therefore, it is entirely erroneous to suppose that there was any open clash between McKinley and Aldrich because of the reciprocity treaties. Their relations were not affected by them. As McKinley had little expectation of their ratification, he never asked Aldrich to work to that end. The people with whom Aldrich clashed on those treaties were not the inner members of the administration group."

CHAPTER XIII

THE GENTLEMEN'S AGREEMENT WITH MR. ROOSEVELT

1. Mr. Shelton himself is authority for this characteristic detail. Memorandum, A. MSS.

2. *Sun*, Sept. 6, 1901.

3. Reed to Aldrich, Sept. 25, 1901, A. MSS.

4. Aldrich to Allison, Sept. 3, 1901, Allison MSS.

5. Statement of Mrs. J. D. Rockefeller, Jr.

6. Roosevelt to Allison, Sept. 27, 1901, Allison MSS.

7. James Wilson to Allison, Sept. 21, 1901, Allison MSS.

8. Roosevelt to Spooner, Sept. 30, 1901, S. MSS.

9. Hay to Roosevelt, Sept. 30, 1901, R., MSS.

10. Wharton to Allison, Oct. 30, 1901, Allison MSS.

11. Charles M. Pepper to Allison, Oct. 2, 1901, Allison MSS.

12. Wharton to Allison, Oct. 30, 1901, Allison MSS., Roosevelt "said he had consulted several protectionist senators about it, yourself among them, all of whom had approved." Lodge had also approved. Lodge to Roosevelt, Oct. 17, 1901, Lodge, I, 507.

13. Cortelyou to Aldrich, Oct. 18, 1901, A. MSS.

14. Platt to Aldrich, Oct. 26, 1901, A. MSS.

15. *Sun*, Oct. 29, 1901; *World*, same date.

16. *The World* seized the opportunity to renew its opposition to Aldrich by contrasting him unfavorably with Roosevelt.

17. Allison to Roosevelt, Nov. 2, 1901, R., MSS.

18. Roosevelt to Allison, Nov. 7, 1901, R., MSS.

19. Aldrich to Roosevelt, Nov. 16, 1901, R. MSS. He does not say this in so many words, but alludes to a previous understanding with the President contradictory of Allison's advice. As the only definite contention of Allison's was that the Senate must not ignore the treaties it seems safe to assume that what Aldrich had advised was just the reverse and that he had already told Roosevelt where he stood. Otherwise his allusion is meaningless. The assumption fits into the newspaper reports of the conference of Oct. 28 and is borne out by Roosevelt's letter to Aldrich, Nov. 18, by his message, and by the later history of the treaties. The chairman of the Senate's Committee on Foreign Affairs, Senator Cullom, was a friend of reciprocity and "proceeded to urge the consideration of the treaties at every meeting of the committee for many months." Opposition to reporting the treaties was stubbornly maintained on technical legal grounds due to the peculiarities of the Dingley Act. Cullom discussed the whole matter in an extended address in Jan., 1902. "Aside from the reciprocity treaty with France, none of the treaties were considered by the Senate itself. I pressed them as best I could, but Senator Aldrich, Senator Hanna, and other advocates of high protection, were so bitterly opposed to them—no one in the Senate aside from myself seeming to have much interest in them—that they were dropped and allowed to expire by their own terms." "Fifty Years of Public Service," 374. There was a coalition of interests opposed to reciprocity. The wool growers were afraid of Argentine competition; tobacco growers felt the same about Porto Rico; sugar growers, both the beet and cane interests, could not look on Cuba as a problem in philanthropy; New England manufacturers saw a danger in France. See also Chapter XII, note 8.

20. Roosevelt to Aldrich, Nov. 18, 1901, R. MSS.

21. J. B. Osborne, "Expansion Through Reciprocity," *Atlantic Monthly*, Dec., 1901, 88:722.

22. Richardson, *M. and P.*, 6645-8.

23. *Tribune*, Dec. 4, 1901.

24. Crane to Aldrich, Dec. 4, 1901, A. MSS.

25. *R.*, Feb. 17, April 7, 1902, pp. 1827, 3810.

26. *R.*, March 17, p. 2909. The Four split for other reasons over the Oleomargarine Bill which Aldrich voted against while Allison, Platt and Spooner voted for. *R.*, April 3, pp. 3607-14.

27. *R.*, June 16, p. 6843.

28. *Tribune*, Dec. 7, 1901. Treaty reported unanimously.

Tribune, Dec. 12. Senator McLaurin held an anomalous position because of his views on the tariff. An encounter between himself and Senator Tillman on the floor of the Senate grew out of accusations as to how votes were secured for the treaty. When the Senate placed the two in contempt, Aldrich utilized the opportunity to protest against their voting on the Philippine Bill. Later, after censure, he voted for restoring them to their privileges. *R.*, Feb. 22 and 28, pp. 2087–90, 2203–7.

The progress of the treaty debate is well indicated in *The Tribune*, Dec. 5–17. The *Record* is invaluable. This is one of the instances—none too frequent—when the face of The *Record* may be taken as truly exhibiting the event. The new treaty gave the United States control of the canal in time of war and permitted its fortification.

29. *R.*, pp. 2131–4.

30. *R.*, Feb. 13, 24, pp. 1682–1701, 2131–4.

31. Coolidge, 369–383.

32. On June 2, the President had a conference with the Four and other administration supporters. On June 3, Aldrich lunched with him. On June 9, the President gave a dinner party which has historical significance. The guests were the Four together with Senator Foraker and General Wood, R. E. B. They discussed the situation in Congress and reached a momentous conclusion. The President would frankly take a hand by sending to the Senate a message on the subject.

Roosevelt to Spooner, June 10, 1902, Roosevelt MSS.: "If I hear from you this evening that I ought to send in the special message tomorrow morning, it will be sent in. . . . If I do not hear from you I shall take it for granted you do not desire it sent in until Friday morning. Accordingly I shall get back Thursday evening and send in the message as we agreed upon it last night, on Friday morning. Will you please show this note or tell the facts to Messrs. Aldrich, Allison, Platt of Connecticut, Foraker and Hanna. . . . If I do not hear from any of you gentlemen I shall take it for granted that the programme is unaltered. . . ."

It was asserted in the newspapers that a conference was held at the White House on the night of June 12 and that Aldrich was not present. The reality of this conference is still to be established, also the validity of an inference that Aldrich opposed sending in the message at this time. These rumors may be found in *The Times*, June 11–21.

33. See note 37.

34. The *Record* for March and April shows the rapid approach of the controversy to an acute stage. Teller presented to the Senate the memorial of the beet-sugar interests of Colorado opposing Cuban reciprocity, March 7. The Cuban Reciprocity Bill was introduced in the House, March 19. On March 27, there was a sharp altercation in the Senate over the conduct of the Philippine war. In the House, debate dragged on intermittently until April 18 when the bill was passed. The next day the Senate referred it to Platt's Cuban Committee from which it never returned.

A resolution of Teller's for investigation of the sugar interests in Cuba was referred to the same committee on the same day. The committee reported a substitute April 25 designed apparently to evade an implied obligation to obtain reciprocal concessions from Cuba (see *R.*, pp. 4423 and 4667). This substitute resolution was referred to the Contingent Expense Committee, reported the next day, and greeted by Teller with, "It is not what I wanted, and what I think we are entitled to have, but it is all the committee were willing we should have, and of course we have to accept what the majority of the committee said was proper." *R.*, p. 4708. Throughout this episode the American Protective Tariff League backed up the sugar growers in their efforts to prevent Cuban reciprocity. See also, Coolidge, 374, 381; Latane, "America as a World Power," 187–9. *R.*, p. 4708.

35. *Tribune*, June 12; see also *R.*, June 11, 12, 16, 17, July 1, also H. Doc. 679. This was given by F. B. Thurber. The investigation was conducted by a sub-committee of the Committee on Relations with Cuba.

36. *R.*, June 13, p. 6720.

37. Republican conferences called by Allison as chairman of Republican Steering Committee, June 17. Allison MSS. See also newspapers, June 21. Nicholas Murray Butler to Holls, July 17, 1902, Holls MSS.: "I was at the White House for three days in the middle of June and was present at most of the conferences with the Senators and political leaders at the time that the senatorial caucus finally declined to act on the Cuban Reciprocity Bill. The situation is very complicated. . . . The fight was a fight on the President as much as on reciprocity, and it was conducted largely by men who professed to be for the administration policy. I never saw greater duplicity and shameless treason to a man and to a cause than was shown by some of the men who, in the public eye, have their records straight in the matter."

38. *R.*, June 19, p. 7074.

39. *R.*: passed Sen., June 3, p. 6231; passed House, June 26, p. 7487.

40. The attitude of Platt may be taken, I think, as probably the attitude of them all. Stanch believer in capitalism as he was, he thought the case thoroughly good policy, good both for the country and the party. Coolidge, 430. In his famous defense of Roosevelt at New Haven in the autumn of 1904, he made it part of his argument. Furthermore, "Spooner held the opinion of Platt that the prosecution of the case was the only thing to do since the law stood as it did on the statute books. It is believed that Aldrich and Allison also shared this view. At any rate the Northern Securities Case does not mark any particular line cleavage as between the wishes of Roosevelt on the one hand and the Big Four on the other." Statement of C. F. Brooker to J. P. Nichols, Aug. 3, 1926, A. MSS.; similar statement by H. Wales Lines.

41. Roosevelt to Platt, July 12, 1902, R. MSS.

42. Same to same, July 21, R. MSS.

43. Hay to Roosevelt, July 24, R. MSS.

43. R. E. B., June 19.

44. Hanna to Roosevelt, July 24, 1902, R. MSS.

45. Henderson to Allison, Sept. 16, 1902, Allison MSS. Also, fear that reciprocity meant tariff revision.

46. Miss Kathleen Lawler, Platt's very competent secretary, prepared the following statement for this volume: "It is not known that Aldrich advised the President in the matter (of the coal strike); but it is known definitely that his close associate Platt assumed a great deal of responsibility. Platt had been greatly exercised over the dangers of the situation

fearing, as he said in his November speech of 1904, at New Haven, that violence and possibly revolution might result . . . he was too modest to mention that his council clarified the President's sight to a great extent. Throughout those anxious days of Sept. and the first part of Oct., 1902, Roosevelt was in constant communication with Platt, Platt making special trips to both Oyster Bay and Washington, with a barrage of letters and telegrams passing in between."

47. N. E. Kendale to Allison, Aug. 9, 1902, Allison MSS.

47. Wetmore to Aldrich, Aug. 7 and Aug. 20, 1902, A. MSS.

48. Notes in A. MSS.; Providence *Journal*, Aug. 24. The date of the visit was Aug. 23.

49. Cortelyou to Hanna, Aug. 25, 1902, R. MSS. Practically the same note was written the same day to Allison.

50. Roosevelt to Aldrich, Sept. 6, 1902, A. MSS.

51. Aldrich to Allison, Aug. 26, 1902, A. MSS., asking Allison to come; Allison to Roosevelt, Aug. 28 (copy), A. MSS., hoping he may be let off; Hanna to Roosevelt, Aug. 29, R. MSS., accepting; Roosevelt to Hanna, Sept. 1, R. MSS., fixing the date; Roosevelt to Aldrich, Sept. 1, A. MSS., asking whether he shall let Allison off; Allison to Aldrich, Sept. 9, A. MSS., saying he is coming; Roosevelt to Lodge, Sept. 10, R. MSS., giving him the date of the conference. Also R. E. B.: "Sept. 16, 1902, 11 A. M. Senators Hanna, Lodge, Spooner, Allison and Aldrich." Why Platt was not present does not appear.

52. Roosevelt to Aldrich, Aug. 26, 1902, A. MSS.

53. The telegram from Henderson contained the fierce remarks already quoted about "the trust evil" and the free trade Republicans. Henderson to Allison, Sept. 16, 1902, A. MSS. How quick was the response of the group at Oyster Bay may be judged by another telegram of Henderson's sent the next day saying "a telegram from the President and a long one from the National Committee strongly indorsed by Senators Aldrich, Spooner and Lodge together with your telegram disturb me not a little, but it is too late to reconsider, and I believe that I could satisfy any of them if I could sit down with them alone that I am justified in my course. I could spend all my time straightening out Republicans on . . . (internal factional quarrels) trusts and tariff and I have neither the time nor the strength for such work. Can fight Democrats and Populists but not the other class." Henderson to Allison, Sept. 17, 1902, A. MSS. Mr. Henderson's stubborn retreat into obscurity is something of a mystery. An interesting interpretation of his course is given in Dodge to Henderson, Oct. 16, 1902, D. MSS.: "There is one thing certain, people, especially here in the East, give you credit for having laid down a great future in support of a principle as they make a vast difference here between your position and the Iowa platform. I admit I cannot see much difference between your position and that of Allison, or that of any of the others who have explained it, but whether there is a difference or not, people in the East generally assume that there is, and praise you for the position that you take though they would have preferred to have you stick and fight it out."

Already, without admitting it, East and West have begun interpreting each other according to preconceptions. The battle of 1909 is only seven years distant.

54. This summary of the conclusion reached at the Oyster Bay conference is based on the report of the speech of Roosevelt at Logansport, Indiana, Sept. 23, 1902, carried in all the papers of Sept. 24. See especially New York *Times*. The underlying assumption of the text rests on the following: Allison to Roosevelt, Sept. 24, 1902, R. MSS.: "I have read your Logansport speech which is an admirable statement of Republican doctrine. This will do much to clear the atmosphere and will generally be accepted as sound and wise"; Spooner to Roosevelt, Sept. 26, 1902, S. MSS.: "Your speech at Cincinnati, and especially your speech at Logansport, have done immeasurable good and will bear rich fruitage"; Roosevelt to Allison, Sept. 27, R. MSS.: "I am particularly pleased that you liked the Logansport speech. I thought I had substantially the idea that we agreed upon at the time you were at Oyster Bay."

That priceless little note of Roosevelt's settles the matter, and yet, strangely enough, a version of the event, nearly correct has been in print, overlooked, ever since the morning after. A despatch from Oyster Bay, Sept. 16, apparently Associated Press, appears in *The Daily Times*, Dubuque, Iowa, Sept. 17, 1902: "Senators Hanna, Spooner, Allison, Aldrich and Lodge, and Postmaster-General Payne (?) spent several hours with President Roosevelt to-day and discussed with him the entire political situation having special reference to the condition of the Western States which the President is to visit on his approaching trip . . . it was decided to make no attempt to revise the tariff at the coming session of Congress . . . that the President is to maintain his position as to trusts, and further that he is to insist on his demand for reciprocity with Cuba. . . . 'The conference was entirely harmonious,' said one of those who participated, but who declined that his name be published, '. . . the coal strike was not talked about.' "

55. *Sun*, Oct. 28, 1901.

CHAPTER XIV

INDIAN SUMMER

1. Authorized memorandum of interview with Miss Kathleen Lawler, prepared for this volume, A. MSS.
2. Memorandum in Aldrich's handwriting, A. MSS.
3. Platt to A. Brainard, Feb. 10, 1904, P. MSS.
4. Memorandum of Miss Lawler.
5. Authorized memorandum of interview with G. G. Hill, A. MSS.
6. Ibid.
7. Memorandum of Miss Lawler. These invaluable notes were destroyed soon after Platt's death by another secretary to whom Mrs. Platt intrusted the task of weeding out from his papers whatever was of "no historic value."
8. Ibid.
9. Memorandum of Mr. Hill.
10. *R.*, Jan. 30, 1903, p. 1458.
11. Grosvenor to Aldrich, Oct. 25, 1902, A. MSS.
12. E. W. Brush to Aldrich, Oct. 16, 1902, A. MSS.
13. Aldrich to Roosevelt, Oct. 22, 1902, R. MSS.
14. Hay to Henry White, Nov. 28, 1902, "Hay Letters," III, 262–3.

15. Lodge to Roosevelt, Feb. 17, 1903, "Letters," II, 2.

16. Roosevelt to Taft, March 13, 1903, T. MSS. A portion of this letter, with phraseology slightly altered, appears in Bishop, I, 237–8.

17. Hay to Roosevelt, Dec., 1902, R. MSS.

18. Root to Dodge, Jan. 22, 1903, D. MSS.

19. *R.*, Feb. 28, 1903, pp. 2784–5.

20. *R.*, March 2, 1903, p. 2909. For text of the bill, *R.*, Feb. 24, 1903, pp. 2550–51.

21. Memorandum of L. White Busby, A. MSS.

22. *R.*, March 3, 1903, pp. 3058–9. Tillman read to the Senate Cannon's remarks and made an extended reply defending his course and condemning the action of the House. *R.*, March 5, 1903, 3 ff.

23. R. P. Falkner to Allison, March 28, 1903, Allison MSS. Also H. H. Hanna to Aldrich, March 23, 1903, A. MSS.

24. Shelton to Allison, April 23 and 24, 1903, Allison MSS.; Aldrich to Allison, April 28, 1902, ibid.; Platt to Aldrich, May 4, A. MSS. Platt was unable to attend because of ill health.

25. Fowler to Aldrich, May 2, 1903, A. MSS.

26. Platt to Reed, May 23, 1903, Platt MSS.

27. See note 16. This is the early part of the same letter. It is printed in Bishop, "Roosevelt," I, 237–8, with phraseology slightly altered and with the later part concerning the Philippine tariff omitted. Just what Roosevelt had in mind when he spoke of Aldrich as accepting antitrust legislation is not clear. The most plausible assumption is that he and Aldrich crossed swords over Littlefield's Antitrust Bill and reached an agreement that it should die (see *R.*, Feb. 27, 1903, pp. 2745–6); also that there should be a compromise with regard to the function of the Bureau of Corporations. The House wanted a bureau authorized to "gather, compile, publish, and supply useful information concerning such corporations doing business within the limits of the United States as shall engage in interstate or foreign commerce." To Aldrich at the opening of 1903 this could seem only a firebrand. Though evidence is lacking it is safe to conclude that he opposed it (see *R.*, Jan. 19, 1903, pp. 944–6). If that is so, the language of the Roosevelt letter to Taft may be taken to imply that the President and the Conservative senators came to terms and that the result is embodied in the substitute provision exempting railroads from the operations of the bureau and limiting the power of publication by means of the words, "the information so obtained, or as much thereof as the President may direct, shall be made public." For the final debate in the House, see *R.*, Feb. 10, 1903, pp. 2003 ff. Littlefield voted against the amended bill.

28. Lafe Young to Aldrich, March 20, 1903, A. MSS.

29. Roosevelt to Allison, May 19, 1903, R. MSS.

30. Roosevelt to Aldrich, March 16, 1903, A. MSS. Similar letters to the other leaders in the R. MSS. Also "Correspondence," II, 4.

31. Roosevelt to Dodge, April 22, 1903, D. MSS.

32. Charles E. Perkins to Allison, June 2, 1903, Allison MSS.

33. Taft to Roosevelt, April 27, 1903, Taft MSS.

34. Roosevelt to Hanna, May 29, 1903, R. MSS. Croly, "Hanna," 427, same date, and Bishop, I, 246–7, give a very different letter in which Roosevelt defends his course.

35. Platt to Beveridge, May 30, 1903, P. MSS.

36. June 11, 1903, A. MSS.

37. Professor H. P. Willis in a very interesting talk with the author remarked that Aldrich was not "dense" on the subject of finance and added that "he was never dense about anything," but that he appreciated the enormous difficulties to be encountered in financial reorganization and therefore was slow to act. Professor Willis made use of the famous remark, "After me, the deluge."

38. Roosevelt to Aldrich, July 22, 1903, R. MSS.

39. Roosevelt to Cannon, Aug. 13, 1903, R. MSS.; Platt to Hanna, Aug. 15, 1903, P. MSS. The Cuban treaty had been ratified by Cuba and had been accepted—one can hardly say "ratified"—in a brief special session of the Senate called in March. Since the rejection of reciprocity the previous June a new House had been elected. The temper it would display could be forecast with tolerable certainty. Hence there was no resisting the skilful strategy which threw the responsibility for the next step on the popular body. Roosevelt to Millard, Sept. 19, 1903, R. MSS.: "Surely you have forgotten what I explained again and again, and stated publicly in the press last year, that the special session was called in pursuance of a statement on my part that I would do so, without which statement it would probably have been impossible to secure the ratification of the Reciprocity Treaty by Cuba. I am committed to it."

See also "Correspondence," II, 65–66 and 68. Also Platt to Hanna, Aug. 15, 1903, P. MSS., urging an early session, agreeing with the President "that supplemental legislation to make the Cuban treaty effective should be passed before Dec. 1, which is the time when the sugar crop begins to move in Cuba."

40. Aldrich to Roosevelt, Aug. 11, 1903, R. MSS.; R. E. B., Aug. 12, R. MSS.

41. Roosevelt to Cannon, Aug. 13, 1903, R. MSS. Platt to Aldrich, Aug. 15, 1903, P. MSS.: "I told (Hill) that we really did nothing but talk the matter over among ourselves and with the President and . . . we felt as he felt that it is very essential that we should have a good understanding with the House."

42. Platt to Aldrich, Aug. 17, 1903, P. MSS.

43. Allison to Aldrich, Aug. 22 (1903), A. MSS.: "I saw Cannon in Chicago and had a pleasant talk with him. He thinks it will be impossible or improbable that any plan could be put through at an extra session and gives good reasons for the belief. . . . He personally thinks there is at this time no emergency in sight that would require hasty action. He talks well, and I think on the lines we marked out something can be done. I do not think he wants to hastily make up his Banking and Currency Committee, though he did not say so."

44. Roosevelt to Cannon, Aug. 24, 1903, R. MSS.

CHAPTER XV

HOW THE REPUBLICANS UNDID THEMSELVES

1. See the Special Message of Jan. 4, 1904. *M. and P.*, 6827 ff., especially 6830. The intricate subject of the subterranean diplomacy of the summer of 1903 has no place obviously in the present volume. That Al-

drich knew about it, I have no doubt. I would risk a great deal that it was a topic of conversation that night when the Four were at Oyster Bay, Aug. 12. The President subsequently told the country that in Aug. he began to consider what to say to Congress in event of the failure of negotiations. But Doctor Nichols was unable to find anything bearing on the subject in the Aldrich MSS., the Platt MSS., and the Allison MSS. That all the Four were in the main sympathetic with the President's policy is apparent, first, from their support of the Spooner Bill which laid the foundation of that policy, and, secondly, from their support of the treaty with Panama following the Isthmian Revolution.

Holls to Roosevelt, Jan. 20, 1903, Holls MSS.: Advising "an immediate, well-considered and deliberate diplomatic campaign for the annexation of the State of Panama" he continues, "I believe that this can be brought about by the right kind of diplomacy in Bogota and in the State of Panama, and I think this government would be perfectly justified in showing friendliness to the efforts which are constantly being made in the State of Panama to achieve independence from the rest of Colombia." The President's argument in defense of his eventual action is in the Annual Message of Dec. 7, 1903, and the Special Message of Jan. 4, 1904. See *M. and P.*, 6806–15 and 6827–52.

The complicated melodrama of the shareholders of the French Canal Company, and their spectacular representative, Mr. Buneau-Varilla, is shadowed in R. E. B. where the date of his interview with the President is given as Oct. 7, 1903. Mr. Buneau-Varilla, in his "Panama," gives the date as Oct. 9.

2. W. F. Osborne to Platt, Nov. 7, 1903, Platt MSS.

3. R. E. B., Nov. 8, 1903.

4. R. E. B., Nov. 10, 1903.

5. Washington *Times*, Nov. 10.

6. *Tribune*, Nov. 17, 1903.

7. Aldrich had conferences with Roosevelt on Nov. 20 and 24, and Dec. 9. R. E. B.

8. Senator Cullom, chairman of the Committee on Foreign Relations, was taken ill and asked Platt in the words quoted to take his place. Cullom to Platt, Dec. 28, 1903, P. MSS. Roosevelt's satisfaction with Platt's speech is reflected in Loomis to Platt, Feb. 4, 1904, P. MSS.

9. *Post*, May 20, 1903.

10. *Nation*, Nov. 12, 1903.

11. *R.*, Dec. 14, 1904, p. 263. The words though used a year later express Aldrich's attitude in 1903. Few issues of the period were more intricate than the pure food controversy. It reappeared in the session of 1905–6. The Four steadily opposed it until the provisions which Spooner and Aldrich so sharply criticised were eliminated. They then permitted it to pass. See note 2, Chapter XVIII.

12. Memorandum of G. G. Hill, A. MSS. The President was not alone in the belief that the Hanna boom was reviving. Halstead to Foraker, Dec. 6, 1903, F. MSS.; Platt to S. J. Fox, Dec. 18, 1903, P. MSS.: "I have no faith that Mr. Hanna could be elected or Mr. Hay, or any other man except Roosevelt." Senator Warren made this interesting statement to Doctor Nichols: "Aldrich was very close to Hanna and presumably might have favored the latter's candidacy if he had not realized his impaired

health. As it was, Aldrich is believed to have understood that Wall Street hoped Hanna would remain an ostensible candidate until some other could be set forth in successful opposition to Roosevelt. . . . Hanna explained to Aldrich and one or two others of the dominant senatorial group that he was remaining half-way in the field to satisfy the request of Wall Street lest the party funds suffer irreparable damage in 1904." A. MSS. If Senator Warren meant to imply that Aldrich was carrying water on both shoulders, he flies in the face of all the evidence. The Four had made up their minds. Platt's correspondence at this time is bristling with irritation at "the Wall Street crowd" because they cannot see that they must support Roosevelt whether they like it or not.

13. Memorandum given to J. P. Nichols by Kathleen Lawler, May 18, 1926, A. MSS.

14. R. E. B., Senators Aldrich, Lodge, and Beveridge present, Jan. 26, 1904; Aldrich present, the attorney-general and Governor Crane also Jan. 27. Platt to Brooker, Feb. 10, 1904, P. MSS.: "All the prominent men who were promoting it (the Hanna boom) have given up unless it be Harriman."

15. Memorandum of speech, A. MSS.

16. Roosevelt to Allison, May 5, 1904, Allison MSS.: "Thank you for the tariff plank." Lodge to Allison, May 11, Allison MSS.: "I think I have the reciprocity plank just as you worded it that day and I have compared it with the Iowa platform which you sent to the President. I think your wording at our little meeting is better than repeating the Iowa plank." Same to same, May 18, Allison MSS.: "I have tried to get the platform as we agreed upon it that morning in Aldrich's room." *World*, May 3; *Herald*, and *Tribune*, May 5; R. E. B., May 1 and May 3; Memorandum enclosed in Lodge to Platt, May 11, P. MSS. The phraseology adopted by the convention contained also the famous sentence: "The measure of protection should always at least equal the difference in cost of production at home and abroad."

17. *R.*, Jan. 30, 1903, p. 984.

18. *Tribune*, May 5, 1904. The interpretation of the text seems to me to be warranted by the subsequent course both of Aldrich and Platt. In Aldrich's speech to the New England Jewellers (note 15) he frankly accepted the idea that virtual monopoly was inevitable under modern industrial conditions. He took this position while facing the most powerful opposition he ever confronted. He still believed that the interests of Labor and Capital could be harmonized but he was not willing to surrender his general theory of the hierarchical industrial society. Platt was equally resolute. See note 31 in connection with his opposition to a national eight-hour law; also, Platt to C. E. Newton, Feb. 5, 1904, P. MSS.: "I am credited by the labor people with having prevented the passage of this eight-hour bill in the last two sessions . . . I do not hesitate to say that I am opposed to it." Both Aldrich and Platt were opposed to compromise with LaFollette, when the fight between him and Spooner became acute.

19. Memorandum of speech, A. MSS.

20. Aldrich to David Barry, Feb. 21, 1904, A. MSS. Another newspaper, the Pawtucket *Times*, was also brought under Aldrich's control. Memorandum by E. B. Aldrich, A. MSS.: Colt to Aldrich, July 11, 1904, A. MSS.

21. Platt to Spooner, May 23, 1904, P. MSS.

22. Spooner to Platt, June 2, 1904, S. MSS.

23. Lenroot to Chandler, June 10, 1904, C. MSS. For unavailing conferences in which Aldrich was involved see Chandler MSS.: diary, June 2, 1904; Chandler to Aldrich, June 2 and June 4; and Chandler to Hauser, June 5; for the La Follette position, Hauser to Chandler, June 8.

24. Lodge to Chandler, June 13, 1904, C. MSS.

25. Chandler to Lodge, June 10, 1904, C. MSS.

26. Lodge to Chandler, June 13, 1904, C. MSS. Memorandum by G. G. Hill, A. MSS.: "Roosevelt was very much impressed by the strength of the La Follette faction and fearful that it should prove so strong as to divide the delegation on the question of the presidential nomination. He found it hard to decide which group it would be best for him for his own welfare to indorse. He could not make up his own mind until Hill by his request wired him that Spooner had pledged himself to withdraw the stalwart electors in Wisconsin if by any chance the Half-Breeds succeeded in getting their (La Follette) electors on the ballot. On the strength of this pledge Roosevelt decided to withdraw all opposition to the Spooner delegation and Payne immediately put the order into execution."

27. Roosevelt to Allison, Aug. 2, 1904, Allison MSS.

28. Roosevelt to Spooner, Aug. 26, 1904, R. MSS.

29. Roosevelt to Platt, June 29, 1904, P. MSS.

30. Roosevelt to Aldrich, Aug. 1, 1904, R. MSS. They had a conference, Aug. 23, R. E. B.

31. Brooker to Platt, Oct. 4, 1904, P. MSS. Secretary Metcalf wrote Platt, Nov. 1, 1904, P. MSS.: "No manufacturer need fear that the Department has sided, or is siding, with either those who advocate or those who oppose the measure."

32. Roosevelt to Cortelyou, Oct. 6, 1904 (copy), C. MSS.

33. Memorandum, A. MSS.; sentence not quoted in Providence papers. He praised the university for being "intensely practical in all its relations to the body politic."

34. Aldrich to Hale, Aug. 28, 1904, A. MSS.

35. Text of speech, A. MSS.

36. Platt to H. R. Reed, Sept. 2, 1904, P. MSS.

37. Aldrich opened with a subscription of $1,000 as shown by his private accounts, A. MSS. In a once famous article, "The Treason of the Senate," Graham Phillips said that "the Aldrich machine" spent about $200,000 in this campaign. He gave no authority for the statement. Major James W. Abbott made the following statement to Doctor Nichols and it is now in the Aldrich MSS.: "This efficient aid (of Catholic school children addressing campaign envelopes) was one reason why Mr. Brayton did not find it necessary to use the generous contribution of $300,000 made available by the National Manufacturers' Association and the American Protective Tariff League for the re-election of Senator Aldrich, to whom they owed so much prosperity, and for whose campaign they were glad to contribute whatever was needed. Another reason why General Brayton was able to return the fund was because Aldrich himself contributed unknown amounts to the State campaign that year."

38. Memorandum of Major J. W. Abbott, A. MSS.; special edition of *The Catholic News Agency,* Oct. 17, 1904, copy in A. MSS.

39. Memorandum of Ex-Senator Marian Butler, A. MSS.: "As for the relationship of Aldrich to these contributions, little is known but the general impression is that when Murray Crane would go personally and solicit contributions, Aldrich remained in the background. His influence was exerted by the fact that it would become known that he was sympathetic to such contributions."

CHAPTER XVI

COUP D'ETAT

1. E. J. Hill to Platt, Nov. 11, 1904, P. MSS.
2. C. A. Schierin to Roosevelt, Nov. 21, 1904, P. MSS.
3. Platt to E. J. Hill, Nov. 12, 1904, P. MSS.
4. *Review of Reviews*, 32:526.
5. Platt to Aldrich, Nov. 12, 1904, P. MSS.
6. R. E. B., Nov. 16, 1904.
7. Aldrich to Platt, Nov. 23, 1904, P. MSS.
8. Aldrich to Platt, Nov. 18, 1904, P. MSS.
9. Aldrich to Platt, Nov. 19, 1904, P. MSS.
10. Platt to Aldrich, Nov. 21, 1904, P. MSS.
11. See note 7.
12. R. E. B., Nov. 21, 1904.
13. Roosevelt to Platt, Nov. 22, 1904, P. MSS.
14. See note 2.
15. What happened in the phrasing of the message of 1904 is still obscure. The evidence is contradictory. Platt to Aldrich, Nov. 21, 1904, P. MSS.: "I saw the President when I was in Washington, and while he is going to simply say in his message that he will call the attention of Congress to the tariff question later, his mind, I judge, is pretty fully made up to the policy of having a joint commission, to be composed of members of the Committee on Ways and Means, and the Finance Committee, appointed to consider the subject, with a view to reporting to an extra session to be called in September." Roosevelt to Platt, Nov. 22, 1904, P. MSS.: "I agree with you entirely that there should be only a few and moderate changes, and I should suppose that by means of a joint committee which could determine upon a course of policy this winter while we are all here, we could keep those changes down." Authorized interview given by Senator Cummins to J. P. Nichols, March 19, 1925, A. MSS.: "The governor of Iowa, A. B. Cummins . . . went to see Roosevelt a few days before the meeting of Congress. They inquired of him as to what the message might do for tariff reform. In reply he drew from a desk drawer the completed draft of his message, and read the tariff sentence asking if it met their wishes. It was to the effect that a programme for tariff reduction would be set forth in a special message. The reply to this was that it was eminently satisfactory. But two days later when the message was given to Congress it did not contain the sentence on tariff reform. . . . Cummins went to the President and reproached him for the omission. Whereupon he frankly explained that Aldrich and Cannon had told him very forcibly that they would not allow the President's interstate commerce programme to go before Congress unless he would abandon tariff revision. Roosevelt was closely wedded to the idea of re-

form in railroad rebates and therefore chose to take out the tariff clause. This had to be done by wire all over the country, as the message had gone out for future release. Roosevelt felt that he had done the preferable thing from the standpoint of practical political conditions." The most interesting part of this statement, the implied bargain with Aldrich, is the most puzzling. If Senator Cummins remembered Roosevelt accurately—nearly twenty-one years had elapsed—there may be here a further support of the suggestion in the text that Aldrich and Cannon had a confidential agreement about the Esch-Townshend Bill. In part, Senator Cummins is sustained by Platt to F. T. Maxwell, Dec. 7, 1904, P. MSS.: "You will observe that the President has not mentioned the tariff in his message. It is possible that some representations which I made to him may have had influence in this respect. As the message was sent out to the press it contained an allusion to the tariff, saying that he would call the attention of Congress to the matter by special message hereafter, but it seems that he sent word to the newspapers to 'kill' that part of the message. So that it does not appear in it. I trust the matter will be allowed to rest." Memorandum of L. White Busby, given to J. P. Nichols, March 17, 1925, A. MSS.: "When making up his messages to the two Houses of Congress, it was Roosevelt's regular custom to send them, in finished draft, to the Speaker for final vise. In the case of the 1904 message, the President inserted one paragraph advocating tariff reduction. When the message was returned from the Speaker's room it was amended in but one particular, and that one consisted of striking out the reference to the tariff." Mr. Richard Hooker, who is a first authority upon the time, made the following statement, A. MSS.: "There were no rumors current at the time that he (Roosevelt) had turned to transportation—stressing since he had agreed to stress that since he was not to be allowed to stress the tariff . . . there was not the slightest indication of the existence of such an arrangement, and it would have been almost impossible for its existence not to have become known to that small group of correspondents who were the confidants alike of Roosevelt and the Aldrich group."

16. Richardson, *M. and P.*, 6902.

17. Chandler to La Follette, Dec. 24, 1904, C. MSS.

18. Chandler to Roosevelt, Jan. 6, 1905, C. MSS.

19. Houser to Chandler, Jan. 23, 1905, C. MSS.

20. R. E. B., Jan. 7, 1905.

21. *Tribune*, Jan. 6, 7 and 11, 1905. See also *Times*, Jan. 7.

22. R. E. B., Jan. 11, 1905.

23. R. E. B., Jan. 23 and 28, 1905.

24. Platt to Van Ingen, Dec. 13, 1904, P. MSS.

25. *R.*, latter half of February, for trial of Judge Charles Swayne. Also Coolidge, 573 ff.

26. Platt to Reed, Feb. 13, 1905, P. MSS.

27. Gray to Platt, March 10, 1905, P. MSS. In response to a telegram from Platt, Gray cited action of Evarts, as secretary of state, Feb. 28, 1881; of Blaine, July 23, 1881; Chinese arrangement of Sept. 7, 1901. He enclosed a memorandum by J. B. Moore to the same effect.

28. Both Roosevelt's San Domingo protocols were read in substance to Congress by Bacon who incorporated them in resolutions. *R.*, Jan. 23 and Feb. 13, 1905.

29. *Review of Reviews*, 31:400.

CHAPTER XVII

THE MAN ALDRICH

1. For most of these details I am indebted to Miss Lucy T. Aldrich and Mrs. Stewart N. Campbell (Miss Elsie Aldrich), who were with their father at this time. The audience with the King was reported in the papers.

2. White to Aldrich, Sept. 29, 1905, A. MSS. He adds: "I consider you the real author of my interview. . . . I was much touched at the interest you showed in my welfare and success when you were here at Rome. . . ."

3. *McClure's Magazine*, Feb., 1905.

4. Bryan to Chandler, March 31, 1905, C. MSS.

5. La Follette to Chandler, March 8, 1905, C. MSS.

6. Sternberg to Roosevelt, April 5, 1905, R. MSS., says that the Emperor "would be most grateful" if Roosevelt would intimate to England that he would like to see harmony in Morocco. See also Bishop, I, 469, and Lodge, II, 170, 172.

7. April 23, P. MSS.

8. Repeated by Senator Beveridge to the author.

9. Mr. Slade to the author, Nov. 5, 1929.

CHAPTER XVIII

CLEARING THE DECKS

1. *The Independent*, April 27, 1905, lists six opinions on the Esch-Townshend Bill: against, Elkins, Kean, Foraker; for, Cullom, Dolliver, Clapp.

2. Tillman to Chandler, June 4, 1905, C. MSS.

3. Elkins to Aldrich, July 15, 1905, A. MSS.

4. E. P. Bacon to Chandler, April 28, 1905, C. MSS.

5. Esch to Chandler, May 2, 1905, C. MSS., citing his article in *National Magazine* for April.

6. Dodge to Allison, May 12, 1905, D. MSS.

7. Chandler to Townshend, Oct. 5, 1905, C. MSS.

8. Chandler to Esch, Oct. 14, 1905, C. MSS.

9. *Nation*, Jan. 5, 1915.

10. May 10, 1905.

11. It should be familiar to every reader that President Roosevelt was praised at the time and has had much praise since for a reason that can be made plausible only by realizing the boldness of his "advance" from the message to the Iroquois speech. The contention is that Radical sentiment had grown so powerful as to threaten the country with State ownership of railroads and that he headed this off by his concessions to the Radicals. See "President Roosevelt's Railway Policy," by W. Z. Ripley, *Atlantic Monthly*, Sept. and Oct., 1905.

12. Lodge to Chandler, Oct. 18, 1903, C. MSS.

13. R. E. B., Aug. 30; Roosevelt to Aldrich, Aug. 31, R. MSS.

14. This seems plain from a letter of Secretary Shaw to the President: "I also join with Senator Aldrich in his belief that negotiations should be confined to the articles named in Section 3 of the act of 1897." Shaw to

Roosevelt, Sept. 16, 1905, A. MSS. Also, Allison to Roosevelt, Sept. 24, 1905, R. MSS. Aldrich to Roosevelt, Sept. 25, 1925, R. MSS.

15. Beveridge to Allison, Sept. 16, 1905, A. MSS.

16. Roosevelt to Allison, Nov. 9, 1905, R. MSS.

17. Tillman to Chandler, Oct. 19, 1905, C. MSS.

CHAPTER XIX

THE SENATE WINS

1. "Correspondence," II, 337 and 346. On Jan. 26, Roosevelt wrote Aldrich at length, beginning with: "I thoroughly enjoyed my talk with you the other evening and regard it as important"; and closing with: "Taft says I was wrong on one point which I was inclined to acquiesce in about the Philippine sugar schedule, but I told him as well as Moody that nothing definite had been agreed to; that it was simply a purpose to see if we could not get a policy which would mean a substantial advance and with which there could be something like a general agreement." A. MSS.

2. Serious confusion has arisen through failing to distinguish, one from another, the various Pure Food bills that have been considered by Congress at various times. The one that was under discussion in the spring of 1904 (S. 198) provided "that the introduction into any State or Territory . . . of any article of food, or drugs, which is adulterated or misbranded . . . is hereby prohibited; and any person who shall ship or deliver for shipment . . . or who having received shall deliver in original unbroken packages . . . or offer to deliver to any other person any such article . . . shall be guilty of a misdemeanor . . . fined not exceeding two hundred dollars . . . or be imprisoned not exceeding one year or both." Senate Rep. 1209, 58 C., 2 S. This bill, like its predecessors, was blocked by Aldrich and his friends.

On Dec. 6, 1905, Senator McCumber and Senator Heyburn both introduced Pure Food bills, which were sent to the Committee on Manufactures. A bill emerged from the committee carrying the same number as the Heyburn Bill, S. 88. It was printed, slightly amended, in the *Record*, Jan. 10, 1906, pp. 897–8. Though similar in many respects to the bill of the previous spring, it contained this vital difference: to come within its scope a dealer must "knowingly" commit the offenses described. It further provided "that no dealer shall be convicted under the provisions of this act when he can establish a guaranty signed by the wholesaler, jobber, manufacturer, or other party residing in the United States from whom he purchased said articles, to the effect that the same are not adulterated or misbranded within the meaning of this act, designating such article." There was a vigorous discussion turning on the word "knowingly," Jan. 10, and again Jan. 18, when Gallinger was very sharp on "these young fellows of the Department of Agriculture," Doctor Wiley and others, who were for extreme measures. Other notable debates, Feb. 19, 20, 21. The bill passed amended, Feb. 21. *R.*, pp. 2770–3.

As indicated in the text Aldrich did not vote on the passage, nor on some of the most important amendments. The strategy of the passage is still obscure. Senator Beveridge said to me, telling the story that Mr. Sullivan has made current ("Our Times," II, 533), that he did not know why the bill was thrust forward when it was. All he knew was that Aldrich came to him in Feb., 1906, and told him that if the friends of the bill would bring it up at once, it would go through. The obvious guess is that Aldrich was clearing decks in every possible way and compacting alignments for the final battle over the Rate Bill.

The Pure Food Bill did not pass the House until June 23 (*R.*, pp. 9075–6). Its last stage is the most curious of all, and so far as I know quite unexplained. The full text of the bill as it passed the House is given in *The Journal of Commerce and Commercial Bulletin*, June 25. As rephrased by the House the offense still consisted in having "knowingly committed" the forbidden acts. The further protection of the guaranty clause was unimpaired. After the ensuing conference the members from each chamber assured their associates that the other chamber gave way on all important points. The conference report was accepted by the Senate, June 29. The final text cuts out the word "knowingly" and restores the blanket provision of the bill of 1905, to the effect that any one performing the acts described, "shall be guilty of a misdemeanor" punishable by fine and imprisonment. However, the clause protecting the retailer who can produce the guaranty described in the Senate bill remains. *J. of C.*, June 30, 1906.

I have nothing to suggest by way of explanation except—very cautiously —that the final change may have been part of that general pacification discussed in note 5, Chapter XIX. After all, for practical purposes, the bill had been robbed of its original sting by the guaranty clause. Furthermore, the elections of 1904 were an ancient tale and compromise was now imperative.

While the bill was in progress, H. B. Needham, in *World's Work*, Feb., 1906, made a famous attack on the Senate as the citadel of special interests.

3. *R.*, Jan. 25, 30.

4. *R.*, Jan. 31.

5. *R.*, Jan. 8, 31; Feb. 13, 14.

6. This explanation of the course of Mr. Allison is based on the trend of events as here delineated, on his own remarks in the *Record*, on the intimate relations between himself and Mr. Dolliver, and on the La Follette "Autobiography." "The organization (back of Mr. Cummins) is complete and candidates are being brought out, and if he succeeds, Dolliver is doomed. . . . Senator Dolliver had better be getting busy. . . . In case he (Cummins) fails with Dolliver, he is now scheming to oust Allison." Shaw (quoting C. W. Johnson) to Allison, March 16, 1906: Allison MSS. How definitely Dolliver's position was menaced at this time is hard to say. Doctor Nichols in 1924 made a "field survey"—as they say nowadays—among survivors of the Dolliver-Cummins embroglio and found very contradictory recollections.

7. See the Roosevelt news in the papers of Feb. 9, 15, 16, 17, 19, 24; March 2, 3; and the speech of Senator Stone, *R.*, April 5.

8. H. R. 12987. The various printings ordered by the Senate show all the fluctuations of its text.

9. One of the ironies of American politics is the fact that the bill was railroaded through the House by the fiat of that arch-Conservative, Mr. Cannon and his machine. Like so many of "Uncle Joe's" devices this piece of strategy can be explained only by inference. Had he not been

perfectly sure that the Senate would not shrink from battle over the bill, the Speaker could not have slept easily after the bill had left the House —despite the unpopularity which seemed to be in store for any one who opposed it.

10. *R.*, March 28, 1906, p. 4382. It might be said in defense of Mr. Dolliver's intention that he was afraid to risk any sort of specific amendment for fear it would go much further than he wished. If that was the case, he has paid the penalty always paid by the man who fails to see the danger in a false reason.

11. Boston *Evening Transcript*, Feb. 24, 1906.

12. *R.*, April 2.

13. *Times*, March 2, 1906. *The Tribune* of the same date was not so explicit: "The President is determined to carry the battle on until the victory is won, no matter where it leads. The end must be attained if not by means of a bill of the sort now under consideration, then in some other manner that will hold water in the courts."

14. *J. of C.*, Feb. 10, 1906. The President may have referred to this clash when he wrote, "Aldrich did what I have rarely seen him do: he completely lost both his head and his temper." Bishop, II, 2. If the comment does not refer to this clash it sets one guessing about the conference between the President and Aldrich, Feb. 15, of which no details have escaped the reticence of both the principals—at least, so far as the world knows to-day.

15. *Tribune*, Feb. 14; R. R. G., Feb. 16.

16. *Tribune*, Feb. 15. The significance of this move is not fully seen until it is recalled that Senator Lodge on Feb. 12 had made a statement which seemed to commit the President to broad review. *Tribune*, Feb. 13. The day on which the newspapers gave out that the inference drawn from the Lodge remarks was unwarranted, was the day on which Dolliver took position against any clarification of the bill's intent. The risk he was taking is evident from the utterance of the President the next day, Feb. 15, which plainly intimated a willingness to consider amendments if they suited his eventual purpose. *Tribune*, Feb. 16. An Associated Press despatch, Feb. 19, appears to be inspired, saying: "The President has emphasized that the main point is appeal to the courts. The Hepburn Bill itself, he believes, allows such appeal as does every other proposed bill in both Houses. The proposals from Senators Aldrich, Foraker, and others, who hold similar views looking to a complete retrial of the case by the courts, both as to the law and the facts, the President does not believe in. He believes as outlined in his speech before the Iroquois Club, in Chicago last May, that the appeal to the courts should be only to test whether the order of the commission was in whole or in part confiscatory, and also to test the legality of the order."

17. *Tribune*, Feb. 15. The two Democrats who were the key to the position were Foster and McLaurin.

18. *J. of C.*, Feb. 16. In all likelihood, what Aldrich proposed this day was virtually the bill which Knox read in the Senate at his request on Feb. 22.

19. *Ledger*, Feb. 16.

20. *Tribune*, Feb. 16; A. P., same day.

21. Stone, *R.*, April 5; A. P., Feb. 15.

22. A. P., Feb. 16.

23. Stone, *R.*, April 5. The bill which Cullom would have accepted as an alternative had been prepared by Dolliver but was not given any real hearing. The Committee thrust it aside.

24. *J. of C.*, Feb. 16.

25. *Tribune*, Feb. 15, 16.

26. *Tribune*, Feb. 17.

27. On Feb. 19, two conferences were held in both of which Dolliver and Clapp took part. Between whiles, Mellon was running around Washington confabing with senators. On Feb. 20, Knox seems to have communicated to Moody the substance, at least, of a new proposal—apparently the bill he read to the Senate on the 22d which must have had some sort of difference from whatever it was that Aldrich laid before the President on the 15th—which Moody considered overnight and refused to accept. Until then Knox seems to have hoped to win Roosevelt over to broad review. Why, is not apparent.

28. Feb. 21. It was reported that the President had also said that he would keep out of the fight and let the two factions settle it between themselves. *Tribune*, Feb. 22. The next day, Dolliver contradicted this report and gave out that in a later interview the President had again expressed his determination to have the unamended bill. *Tribune*, Feb. 23; *Ledger*, same date.

29. *R.*, Feb. 22. The spirit of this bill ruled the Aldrich-Knox strategy to the very end.

30. *Tribune*, Feb. 23; *Ledger*, Feb. 23. See note 16. At no moment is the evidence less explicit. Whether he believed he had got some definite pledge from the President subsequent to the interview with Knox, or whether he was going on a confident guess as to what the President really desired, remains to be determined.

31. An inference, but inescapable in the light of his general ambition and the facts that follow. See also *Ledger*, Feb. 24, and La Follette, 405, 433.

32. *Ledger*, and *Tribune*, Feb. 24; Stone, *R.*, April 5.

33. *Ledger*, Feb. 24.

34. *J. of C.*, Feb. 24; *Nation*, March 22.

35. Sen. Rep., 1242 (Ser. 4904). When the bill was reported five members of the committee—Aldrich, Crane, Foraker, Kean, and Elkins, chairman—signed a statement disapproving its return without amendments and stating some at least of their own views. Ibid., part 2 (Ser. 5060).

Aldrich, Foraker, and Elkins all made explanations when Tillman submitted the bill. Aldrich: "A majority of the Republican members of the committee did not join in the favorable report . . . for the reason . . . that clear and adequate provision should have been made for subjecting the orders of the commission affecting rates to judicial review . . . with these amendments" four of the five Conservatives including himself "were ready to give their support to the House bill." *R.*, Feb. 26, p. 2969.

Senator Newlands who voted in committee with Tillman and Dolliver told the Senate that he regarded the bill as "fragmentary legislation" because it did not provide for national incorporation of railroads and a fixed limit for dividends. Sen. Rep., 1242, p. 12.

Senator La Follette who regarded the bill in somewhat the same light attempted to amend it so as to provide for the evaluation of railway property. Though this question became very conspicuous later it seems to have had no weight at the time and is here ignored.

The various amendments dealing with other matters besides the two basic issues were proposed at various times and were subjects of sharp dispute after the bill went into the conference stage. They revealed the curious fact that the Senate on all these questions of mere extent of jurisdiction was more liberal than the House. One cannot refrain from dropping here the historical objectivity and saying bluntly that the liberalism of the House was mainly gesture—a bid for votes. It was all calculated to pay the very lowest price for the popular support it was trying to buy.

36. Mr. Bailey himself has sometimes been called "a railroad senator." It is probable that he was as near that as a senator from Texas could be. Nevertheless, he is plainly in this debate circumscribed by what might be termed the semi-traditional Democratic position, contrasting with Tillman on the one hand and on the other with such cut-and-dried old-fashioned Democrats as, for example, Senator Pettus. Bailey's course in this controversy has given rise to much speculation. See also note 50.

37. Professor Story, criticising this chapter, put a vital point with admirable lucidity. "Did not the Conservatives perceive that there was a new drift toward the 'statesmanship of control' over public policy which was being transferred rapidly to the courts, and which, then and since, they have been desirous to facilitate in order to escape legislative and administrative control?" I have hesitated about raising this point, because, so far as it concerns Aldrich, his habitual reticence embarrasses the biographer. By way of mere dicta, I may say that in my judgment he was steadily moving away from faith in assemblies and toward faith in more permanent and less popular machinery of control.

38. *R.*, March 19, p. 3959.

39. Lodge, II, 217. See also notes 36 and 50.

40. *R.*, April 2, pp. 4562–3. Whether Aldrich was sound or not in his ideas of constitutionality, it is plain that the heart of the matter, so far as theory was concerned, appeared to him to be this blending of powers, making an administrative body the judge of its own actions. The mere historian, in a matter of constitutional law, speaks under correction and finds it easy to get on the wrong track. But is not there an analogy here to that consolidation of powers intended to be counter-balancing of which the students of the Roman Empire have made so much? Be that as it may, the President, it should be remembered, had frankly confessed his repudiation of the older view of checks and balances, frankly told the country to think less about their liberties and more about administrative efficiency. Which, perhaps, was justifiable advice. Every one sensed the necessity for new institutions. The significance of this controversy, from the historian's point of view, is in the contest between the temper of political reconstruction and the temper of political evolution.

41. *R.*, April 3.

42. *R.*, April 30, pp. 6115–16.

43. *R.*, March 28, p. 4384. The speech of Spooner, March 22, had prepared the way for Knox.

44. I go upon the assumption that Mr. Dolliver was in truth playing

the part of Menas, because there is no contemporaneous evidence now accessible to the world which would justify the conclusion that he acted under instructions from the President. What secrets may be locked up in the Dolliver papers I do not know. Twenty years after the event, Senator Clapp, in an interview with Doctor Nichols, was positive that Roosevelt had given Dolliver encouragement to act as he did. He was equally positive in a letter to Doctor Nichols, Nov. 3, 1927, A. MSS.

45. *Tribune*, April 2, 3.

46. R. E. B., March 31. Newspapers of April 1. *R.*, April 3, 4, 5; May 12, 14.

The purpose of the President in calling this long conference is still largely conjectural. It is reached by analyzing what he did as seen in the perspective of the moment. Nothing could be more rash than the interpretation of it as a "surrender" by *The Nation*, April 10. Such reasoning confuses him unwarrantably with Dolliver.

47. The original bill (Section 4 amending Section 15 of the law of 1887) provided that orders of the commission should go into effect within thirty days and be observed by the roads "unless the same shall be . . . suspended or set aside by a court of competent jurisdiction." These were the words about which debate had raged. Was there a court of competent jurisdiction? The Long Amendment struck these words out. Practically the same phraseology occurred in Section 5 (amending old Section 16) where again, the Long Amendment struck it out substituting a provision that orders of the commission should take effect "within such reasonable time as shall be prescribed by the commission and shall continue . . . unless suspended or set aside in a suit brought against the commission in the circuit court of the United States sitting as a court of equity . . . and jurisdiction is hereby conferred on the circuit courts of the United States to hear and determine in any such suit whether the order complained of was beyond the authority of the commission or in violation of the rights of the carrier secured by the Constitution. . . ." Ordered printed, by the Senate, April 2. See also the extensive defense of the amendment by Long the next day.

48. Roosevelt to Lodge, May 19, 1906; "Correspondence," II, 215; Tillman's speech, *R.*, May 12; Chandler to Tillman, *R.*, May 14. A considerable part of the subsequent Roosevelt-Tillman-Chandler dispute hung on the conflicting recollections of the President and Mr. Chandler as to what each said that night.

49. Tillman's speech, *R.*, May 12; Chandler to Tillman, May 12; *R.*, May 14.

50. *R.*, p. 6777. The reasons for Senator Bailey's change of front are obscure. His account of his relations with Tillman, of a conference they had with Moody (April 15) and of his own later position are in *The Record* in remarks confirming other remarks made by Tillman. He described his purpose as "to protect the orders of the commission from judicial interference until the court is ready to render a final judgment." His original amendment provided that any dissatisfied party might enter the circuit court, "alleging that such rate . . . will not afford a just compensation . . . or that the regulation is unjust and unreasonable" and if the court "shall find that such rate . . . will not afford a just compensation . . . or that the regulation . . . is unjust and unreasonable, it shall enjoin the enforcement

of the same; provided . . . no rate . . . prescribed by the commission shall be set aside or suspended by any preliminary or interlocutory decree or order of the court"; printed by order of the Senate, March 21. Nevertheless, Tillman stated, and Bailey did not correct him, that in their conference with Moody, April 15, "There was absolute accord from the first on the proposition that the court review should be limited to the inquiry whether the commission had exceeded its authority or violated the carrier's constitutional rights." *R.*, May 12, p. 6775. There seems no doubt that "constitutional rights" meant to Tillman only the right of protection against confiscation, which was exactly the meaning given to the term by the President in the Iroquois speech.

51. Ibid.

52. Roosevelt to Lodge, April 6; Lodge, II, 214; remarks by Lodge, *R.*, April 3, p. 4649. Though Roosevelt and Lodge had parted company on the Rate Bill, there was no breach in their cordial relations. Roosevelt to Lodge, April 28, "Correspondence," II, 215.

53. Reported in the papers of April 15. On the basis of the known evidence there seems to be no reason to hunt a subtler motive behind this speech than the one indicated in the text. But this assumes that Roosevelt, on April 14, was still confident of victory, and did not know the situation as well as Aldrich did. If at that date he knew that the Democrats were breaking from his hand, it would be still more plausible to assume that the speech was a skilful anticipation of subsequent events, preparing his followers to look upon what ensued as a strategic retreat—which undoubtedly was how later he conceived it himself.

54. Repeated to the author by Mr. Barry.

55. *R.*, March 27.

56. *R.*, April 6.

57. *R.*, April 11, p. 5043.

58. *R.*, April 19.

59. Ibid.

60. *R.*, April 25, pp. 5805–6.

61. The early history of these amendments has not been recovered. Mr. Fulton, instrumental in phrasing them, was evidently in his own mind the main author. *R.*, May 11. Mr. Hooker regards him as important. The amendments evidently grew by stages, even after their publication in the papers of May 9. They were submitted to the Senate the previous day. In the form in which they were first given out, the words, "in its judgment" were to be cancelled. On this point Mr. Dolliver had made a last desperate stand. Mr. Allison took his part. It was agreed to allow these words to remain. *Tribune*, May 8. But before the amended bill came to a vote this action was reversed and "in its judgment" was again struck out.

62. *Tribune*, May 2, 1906.

63. The argument for the reality of the compromise here assumed is inferential. It begins with the "feel" of the time. Almost every one recognized that the course of both sides was hard to explain. The narrow review senators trumpeted to the world that they had not surrendered, and the broad review senators did not contradict them. Professor F. H. Dixon indicated both the contemporaneous impression and also the contemporaneous bewilderment when he said: "The Conservatives practically won

their contention, and the so-called compromise which was effected. . . ." Ripley, "Railway Problems," revised, 545. "The curious feature of this compromise is that no one can be absolutely sure of its meaning." H. S. Smalley, *Annals of the American Academy of Political and Social Science,* March, 1907, p. 297. The interpretation of *The Tribune* that it was verbiage pure and simple may be dismissed as frivolous. The constituencies of the fifteen precarious senators were not made up altogether of fools. If "verbiage" had been the only material compromise, ten able lawyers in a close constituency might have wrecked the whole thing.

Frankly admitting that the clew is still to be found, I submit that the debate in the Senate on May 11 betrays the secret which all the Republicans, for election purposes, had agreed to keep. Most difficult to explain on any other ground is the silence of Aldrich, Knox, Spooner, and Foraker, while Allison, Long, Cullom, and Fulton asserted their belief that the amendments stood for narrow review, for just what the Long Amendment had previously stated. While the issue had been upon the text of the bill as affected by the Long Amendment the Conservative lawyers had been unable to keep silence. The indiscretion of Allison precipitated a discussion upon the venue clause of the bill in the course of which Senator Bacon completely turned the position of the narrow reviewers and pilloried them in a palpable lack of candor. Allison, talking obviously for the benefit of Iowa, assured his invisible constituents of his faithfulness to the presidential programme; the others followed suit. Bacon entangled them in an exact comparison of the old and the new texts and upon the exact legal meaning of the phraseology in each case. A radical difference was thus brought out between the alteration of the text now proposed and the one that had been proposed by Long. Bacon's aim, apparently, was to show that the Long text, which he, like Tillman, desired, was honest, narrow review, while the new text was not. If I am not reading into him more than is there, he was trying at first to make the narrow reviewers admit that they had some other purpose in supporting this amendment than the one they were stating. He pointed out that the new amendments lacked the specific limitations that would tie up the courts to narrow review, and scoffed at the argument that the silences of the amendment deprived the courts of certain powers left unmentioned. Mr. Fulton, it seems to me, let the cat out of the bag, though the others had come near to doing so. An incautious statement of Fulton's was snapped up by Bacon as an admission that the amended bill would give the courts unlimited power of review. To extricate himself, Fulton replied that he had not meant that; he had meant to say that if the statute gave the courts unlimited powers, still there was no danger that they would make use of them. Almost in so many words he said that he felt perfectly safe in leaving to the courts full discretion as to what power they would accept. Here, then, is the real compromise assumed in the text: an agreement to phrase the statute so as not to prescribe anything to the courts in the way of limiting their action, but to leave the whole question of constitutionality, of who is to determine the standard of "just and reasonable," to the courts' own unhampered discretion.

Again, the silence of the Conservative lawyers seems to be most significant. Bacon's skilful exposure of the narrow reviewers, when he forced them to vote down a specific statement of the very interpretation they professed to hold, played directly into the Conservative game; Aldrich and all the others thus went on record at the last moment as voting against narrow review.

The question then arises, was there nothing more in the programme of the narrow reviewers than merely to put themselves in a defensible position at the next election? Let us recall the President's intimation on March 1, his general position upon the need of a new attitude toward our institutions as indicated in note 40, the promise of a general programme of reform in the speech of April 14, the literature of protest, the specific clashes in the Senate such as that between Aldrich and Fulton, April 2; do we not, out of all of this, get the hint that the narrow reviewers were looking upon the passage of the bill as the beginning not the close of a controversy, that they intended to carry the issue to the people and eventually either by coercion of the Supreme Court or through a constitutional amendment secure the interpretation they desired? The mere historian cannot refrain from thinking upon Seward and his threat "we will change the personnel of the court and so reform its opinions."

It is important to remember that the turn of chance the next year put all these questions in a new light and gave to the later history of the issue a direction not foreseen in 1906. Furthermore, one must be very careful not to read back into the frames of mind of 1906 anything that requires for its explanation the reactions that may have arisen since the decisions of the Supreme Court in 1909 and later.

64. Remarks by Senator Beveridge to the author.

65. This sentence is a close summary of the view he later expressed in a letter to Lodge, April 11, 1910, "Correspondence," II, 370.

66. Memorandum authorized by Richard Hooker, A. MSS.

67. *Tribune*, May 5.

68. Tillman's speech, *R.*, May 12, and the Chandler letter which he read on May 14; Roosevelt to Lodge, May 19, 1906, "Correspondence," II, 215–219.

69. *R.*, May 11, pp. 6685–90.

70. Ibid.

71. The amendments which extended the field—in distinction from the character—of the commission's activity were probably in Aldrich's eyes the real contribution made by the bill toward solving the problems of the hour. These included besides the commodities clause a wide extension of the definition of common carrier, bringing under the term express companies, sleeping-car companies, and, above all, pipe lines. With regard to all these, Aldrich took a cool middle course, upon which he and Platt appear to have reached their final position the previous year; these reforms were inescapable, therefore they must be accepted and put into execution with the minimum of friction.

One of the amendments focussed the difference between the attitudes of the Senate and the House. The Senate added a provision abolishing free passes except for the use of railroad employees or for purposes of charity. The House struggled hard in conference to preserve the old system of passes as a free dole to all the friends of the railroads, including members of Congress.

Aldrich proposed a few minor changes. The only one that may have had significance concerned the transport of gas. Aldrich opposed placing it under the control of the commission, and the Senate acquiesced practically without debate.

72. *R.*, May 18, pp. 7087-8.

CHAPTER XX

RESTORING REPUBLICAN HARMONY

1. Repeated to the author by Senator Beveridge. It was in the same connection that Aldrich let fall the remark, "If Platt had been here this wouldn't have happened."

2. La Follette, 434, quoting Dolliver.

3. Report of the Joint Commission of the Massachusetts Legislature, Boston, 1911; also Senate Document, 563, 63C-2S, pp. 854 ff.

4. Dinwiddie to Warburg, Jan. 11, 1911, W. MSS.

5. It is not possible, from present knowledge, to speak with certainty upon the inner history of the last stages of that mass of legislation which was brought to a standstill by the rates controversy and resumed after the compromise on the Hepburn Bill. The face of *The Record* was never more inscrutable. No one will have trouble with himself in concluding that almost any confidential agreement among the factions is a respectable hypothesis.

The Meat Inspection Bill passed the Senate without debate, May 25. The night before, Aldrich had dined with the President. The bill was close to the President's heart. It provided that labels on canned meats should be dated, and put the cost of inspection on the packers. The House mitigated its severity by striking out both provisions and putting the cost of inspection on the government. While the bill was pending in the House, the Packing House Report was published by order of the President, and Lodge stated in the Senate that this would not have happened if the House had not softened the bill. In conference the House stood firm, and eventually the Senate yielded, accepting the conference report, June 29.

The measure upon which Aldrich was most outspoken was the Free Alcohol Bill, which was designed to promote the use of alcohol in arts and manufactures free of tax. The bill passed the House, April 16, and was referred, in the Senate, next day. It shared the fate of the other measures which by common consent were sidetracked until the fight over the Rate Bill was finished. Following his victory, Aldrich was so prompt in calling up the Alcohol Bill that again one suspects an agreement which is lost. On May 23, he reported the bill, out of order, saying, "The bill is an important one." He advocated amendments putting off the date of going into effect to Jan. 1, 1907. The bill passed the next day; the House accepted the amendment, May 28; Roosevelt signed, June 7. While the bill was pending the anti-Aldrich papers construed the delay in the manner to be expected. They ignored, as most historians have done, the Rate Bill strategy. *The Nation*, May 3, 1906, described Aldrich as determined to defeat free alcohol because it was not in the interests of the Standard Oil Company. Senator Teller, of the minority in the Finance Committee, poohpoohed the idea that the Standard Oil Company cared anything about it, one way or the other. *R.*, May 24, 1906, p. 9342. Aldrich's amendment was for the purpose of allowing the manufacturers of wood alcohol to dispose of their stocks before the new law took effect.

The significance of the delay in all this legislation, and the virtual certainty that a new working agreement had been formed with the President, is further indicated by the calendar of the Employer's Liability Bill. It passed the House, April 2, and was committed by the Senate, April 3. It lay in committee along with the other suspended measures, and was not reported until May 18; considered by unanimous consent, on request of La Follette, and amended, May 31; passed, June 1, without roll call; passed the House, June 6; signed, June 11.

Aldrich played into Roosevelt's hand in connection with the purchase of supplies at Panama. The President had announced that he would buy in the cheapest market. There had been a great outcry that purchases should be made only in the United States. On May 23—five days after the Rate Bill had passed both Houses—Aldrich introduced a resolution (S. R. 60) instructing the President to purchase only products of the United States, unless their cost should be "extortionate or unreasonable." The Democrats pounced upon the resolution and party lines were once more sharply drawn. Senator Stone sneeringly described the resolution as a mere device to save the President's face. Aldrich coolly announced that it was for the purpose of "enlarging the President's discretion." R. 7228, 7527, 7718.

6. Foraker's version of this event is in a long letter to his son. "Notes of a Busy Life," II, 249–254. The Gridiron incident is ignored in Bishop's "Roosevelt." Also, R., Jan. 15, 1907, p. 1130. Foraker to Stone, Feb. 13, 1907. A letter to Chandler from the chairman of a Colored Campaign Vigilant Committee, May 29, 1908, C. MSS.: "Since the time of the assembling of the Republican National Convention is rapidly approaching, you will confer a favor if you will see the anti-Taft allies, and secure some financial aid for members of the Colored Campaign Vigilant Committee who are to attend a meeting of the committee . . . in Chicago . . . for the purpose of protesting against the nomination of Secretary William H. Taft, or Theodore Roosevelt. . . ."

7. *Tribune*, Feb. 13, 14, 21, and 26, 1907.

8. Mr. Bishop has an important chapter on this subject, the fourth of his second volume. Also Miss Tarbell, "E. H. Gary," Chapter VIII.

9. S. 3028. *R.*, Jan. 7, 1908, p. 504. Nothing was more characteristic of Aldrich than his unwillingness to introduce legislation that could not pass. Furthermore, he appears to have begun thinking in new terms. Warburg to Aldrich, Dec. 31, 1907, W. MSS.: "Since I had the pleasure of seeing you, I have carefully considered the interesting scheme which you outlined for creating an additional currency using as a basis Clearing-House Certificates."

10. S. 5729, *R.*, March 11, 1908, pp. 3122–48.

11. R. E. B.

12. The relation of Aldrich to the nomination of Taft is the subject of much chatter. There is a story that "the Aldrich group"—a convenient vagueness!—were animated first of all by the desire to prevent a third term for Roosevelt, that they tried to find one of their own number strong enough for the race, and that they accepted Taft as a safe compromise to head off Roosevelt. I know nothing about it—that is to say, none of the evidence that has come under my eye is of the sort that I am willing to label "knowledge." Doctor Nichols thinks that circumstantial evidence

is all in favor of the theory indicated. It may be. My only guess, so far, in this connection, is that if there was any opposition by Aldrich to the choice of Taft, it did not outlive the conference with Roosevelt on March 17. (See note 13.) A very plausible guess—plausible, that is, to any one assuming the anti-Taft theory—would be that Roosevelt and Aldrich formed a working agreement on that occasion—Roosevelt to support the Aldrich Bill, and Aldrich to support Taft. But every student of politics knows that the plausible so often refuses to happen.

13. There is much confusion as to what influences were brought to bear upon Aldrich to induce him to change his attitude upon railway bonds. *Tribune*, March 17: "President Roosevelt has reached a thorough understanding with the leaders of his party in Congress, and they are willing to do everything possible to promote his programme, with the single exception of postal savings banks. . . ." *Times*, March 19: "Aldrich eliminated the railroad bond feature of his currency bill in order to prevent La Follette from gaining the credit throughout the West for beating that obnoxious measure." The same issue of *The Times* asserts that Aldrich had conferred with the President, March 17, and that Roosevelt after some delay had "let it be known that in his opinion Aldrich would have to abandon the railway bond feature. Aldrich's only hope of putting his bill through lay in the sturdy support of the President, and when that was not forthcoming, surrender was inevitable." The day before *The Times* had said that Aldrich's motive was not as first supposed to embarrass La Follette but to help Allison and Long, and that he dropped railway bonds at their personal appeal. *Tribune*, March 18: "It is explained that several Republican senators would have been seriously embarrassed in their States by the retention of the railway bonds provision, while its elimination by the House was almost certain. It was deemed wiser, therefore, to strike the provision from the bill. . . ." American *Review of Reviews*, April, 1908, 37:400: "Senator Allison and other sagacious leaders of the Middle West were of opinion that their States would disapprove of the railroad bond feature." *The Independent*, April 2, 1908, 64:770: the withdrawal of the bond feature "was due to the opposition of Republican senators from the West." See also *R.*, March 17, pp. 3421, 3435–53.

Mr. Reynolds, in an authorized interview given Doctor Nichols, A. MSS., attributed Aldrich's change of front to his own earnestness backed up by Medill McCormick and the Chicago press. A conference was arranged at Washington between Reynolds and Aldrich. "Reynolds made clear to Aldrich that the Western opposition to his emergency bill was based upon fundamental differences between banking East and West and could not be shaken—in fact would and could defeat the bill as it stood." Aldrich promised to change the bill, introducing commercial paper as a basis of currency—a plan he had originally believed in but had abandoned because "the New York banking group had argued so strongly for bonds as to dissuade him, under the impression that he held a mistaken opinion"—and Reynolds promised that the Chicago press would cease opposition.

Out of all this the only details that are biographically significant are the facts that Aldrich when he came to Washington at the close of 1907 was meditating the use of commercial paper as a basis of emergency cur-

rency, that he was persuaded by New York to switch to bonds, that
Western influence, partly friendly, partly hostile, induced him to switch
back to his original idea.

14. S. 6206. *R.*, March 19, p. 3557; April 1, p. 4213.

15. Beveridge to J. P. Nichols, Jan. 27, 1927, A. MSS.
One of those foolish displays of vanity to which politicians seem peculiarly susceptible involves the question, who first suggested the formation
of a Monetary Commission. Apparently, it was not Aldrich. See also *R.*,
March 24 and 25, pp. 3803–6, 3852.

16. *R.*, March 27, p. 4025.

17. Mr. Fowler was chairman of the Banking and Currency Committee.
He had a bill of his own that was more advanced financial science than
the Aldrich Bill but which had no chance to pass the House. He seems to
have been reluctant to burn his bridges by reporting his own bill, and at
the same time even more reluctant to report the Aldrich Bill. Mr. Fowler's
bill provided for a banking currency based on commercial paper, and is
regarded by Professor Willis as the turning point in the development of
sound financial ideas in Congress. "The Federal Reserve System," 46–49.
The recognition of commercial paper and of co-operative banking in the
Vreeland Bill was due in part at least to the Fowler Bill, though the
Western banking influence represented by Mr. Reynolds was very insistent upon the former.

18. *R.*, April 20, p. 4970.

19. *R.*, May 13, pp. 6185–7. This episode is discussed at length in
"Notes of a Busy Life," II, Chapters XLI–XLIII. At the next session a
bill was passed that represented a compromise engineered by Aldrich. A
court of inquiry appointed by the secretary of war was to decide whether
the discharged soldiers were "eligible for re-enlistment." *R.*, Jan. 29, 1909;
Feb. 1, 23, pp. 1578, 1664, 2932, 2947.

20. *Evening Post*, May 14, 1908.

21. See note 13. A similar confusion clouds recollection with regard to
the unrecorded details of conference negotiations.

22. Memorandum of talk with Mr. Vreeland, May 3, 1926, made by
J. P. Nichols, A. MSS.: "After several days of continued disagreement,
Mr. Vreeland received from Senator Cannon a request that he come to
the Arlington Hotel the next morning at ten o'clock for a conference in
the room of Senator Aldrich. Arrived there, Mr. Vreeland found that no
one else was present but these three. An hour and a half, approximately,
was devoted to convincing Mr. Aldrich that his bill could not pass the
House, and that the party would be at an extreme disadvantage in the
coming campaign if no bill whatever were passed. Thus it came about
that Senator Aldrich gave his consent to a compromise measure which
was not satisfactory, wholly, to any of the groups concerned. In this respect, of course, it was like all legislation. The three gentlemen thereupon
agreed to the measure as it was reported from the conference. Senator
Aldrich for his part agreed to insertion of some of the Vreeland provisions,
permitting commercial paper to be used as a basis for emergency currency, this on behalf of those Western and Southern banks which did not
regularly keep in stock the municipal and railroad bonds permitted by
the Aldrich Bill. On the other hand, Mr. Vreeland agreed to the insertion in the bill of those rigorous restrictions as to the amount of such

commercial paper, and its use, which Senator Aldrich felt necessary to safeguard the currency. These restrictions were so rigorous that Mr. Vreeland felt they came near to vitiating those provisions of the bill referring to commercial paper; but without these restrictions Senator Aldrich would not give his consent to the use of commercial paper in any way. By such arduous means the compromise measure took its form."

23. Condensed in Beckhart, "Discount Policy of the Federal Reserve System," 583–5.

24. The basis of this account is a memorandum authorized by Colonel Corser, Sept. 14, 1926, A. MSS. A memorandum of G. G. Hill, June 9, 1926, A. MSS., repudiates the popular story that Gore was induced to sit down by the trick of pulling his coat tail.

25. Taft to Aldrich, June 27, 1908, A. MSS.

CHAPTER XXI

THE MONETARY COMMISSION

1. The Warburg files contain a vast mass of material relative to banking reform in the United States. The statements in this chapter relative to Mr. Warburg are drawn mainly from an unpublished memorandum setting forth his relations with Aldrich, cited here and later as Warburg Memorandum, W. MSS.

2. Ibid.

3. Memorandum by A. Piatt Andrew, A. MSS.

4. Ibid.

5. Memorandum by G. M. Reynolds, Nov. 11, 1927, A. MSS. Mr. Reynolds was president of the Continental National Bank and of the American Bankers Association. The "A. B. A." had not been friendly to the Aldrich-Vreeland Act.

6. Taft to Aldrich, July 12, 1908, T. MSS.

7. Aldrich to Taft, Aug. 21, 1908, T. MSS.

8. Aldrich to Foraker, Aug. 21, 1908, A. MSS.

9. Memorandum of interview with Mr. Vreeland by J. P. Nichols, May 3, 1926, A. MSS.

10. Memorandum by A. Piatt Andrew, A. MSS.

11. Memorandum by Senator Burton, March 10, 1926, A. MSS.

12. Memorandum by G. M. Reynolds, A. MSS.

13. Warburg Memorandum, W. MSS.

On Nov. 18, 1908, Aldrich dined with the Merchants' Association of New York and made an address. He told them it would be at least two years before the commission would have a bill to report. "As for himself, Senator Aldrich said he had given up many of his former views on banking and had entered upon the study of the question with a mind free to accept new conclusions." *Times*, Nov. 19, 1908.

CHAPTER XXII

MR. LA FOLLETTE SPLITS THE PARTY

The suggestive comment on La Follette, by Professor Paxson, mentioned in the preface is as follows: "I think there are some points at which you would have given a slightly different proportion to the story had you sweated over Western politics and economics as I have had to do. I am far from being a La Follette-ite or a Rooseveltian, but I think you do not quite do justice to the Western demands that La Follette brought to a focus. My own interpretation of La Follette, apart from his political gestures, is that he was a defender of capitalistic society against itself. He was never a Socialist or a destroyer. He believed, I think, that unless checked by a hand sympathetic to capital as such, capital was almost certain to suicide in U. S., and to bring on an effective opposition of Socialism. If I am right, he was trying to protect Democratic government from the upset that unrestricted capitalistic conservatism might inspire. But this is a long story which I may only suggest without elaboration." I think every reader will agree with me that Professor Paxson ought to give us an analytic biography of this extraordinary and most interesting man. He is so well fitted to do so.

1. Stanwood, II, 172–3. The official Republican position was still "the imposition of such duties as will equal the difference between the cost of production at home and abroad, together with a reasonable profit to American industries."

2. It has been very generally forgotten that there were at least five different attitudes toward tariff revision in 1908: out-and-out demand for "downward" revision in the true Democratic sense; demand for raises in duties by the manufacturing interests of the East, and by special groups in the West; demand for readjustment of the tariff in the interests of the West as opposed to the East; demand for removal of duties on raw materials, in pretty much the spirit of Cleveland in 1887; demand for readjustment of duties to redistribute both burdens and profits in accord with conditions that had developed since 1897. La Follette represented the third of these, but sought as will appear to compromise it with the first. President Taft stood consistently for the fourth; Aldrich for the fifth. He was repeating his position in 1890 when he said that the McKinley Bill included many items "not contained in any prior tariff act, items covering articles and industries which had no existence, even at the time of the adoption of the act of 1883." At the same time he was not in favor of the reckless protection which ignored his own theory that protection was a harmonious "equalization" of industrial interests. "Friends of Mr. Aldrich are of the opinion that on many of the rates (of 1909) he would gladly have seen real reductions, and it is a well-known fact that he used all his influence with individual senators to keep them from protecting their local products with rates too obviously constituting increases." *Times*, April 16, 1910. "It is believed that Aldrich and other Republican leaders in the Senate could not have forgotten the election results of the tariff of 1890 and 1897; but the constituent industries insisted that the rates must be raised even at the cost of a congressional election." Memorandum authorized by Senator Warren, A. MSS. "It is believed by some few members of the Senate Finance Committee at the time that Aldrich, at the outset of the making of the new tariff, had no intention but that it should really be a reducing tariff. . . . At a hearing of the glass industry, Senator Aldrich was apparently somewhat surprised at their attitude, and inquired whether they really expected to be able to obtain increases in the pending bill. . . . The New England constituents, who had always been so successful in obtaining increases proved too strong for Aldrich's

intentions to decrease in 1909 . . . in so far as the weakening of party loyalty made necessary exceptional voting arrangements with senators outside the party, just so far was it necessary to give their constituent industries exceptional recognition." Ibid., Senator Burton. "To an observer on the ground at the time of the big tariff struggle the Aldrich tariff doctrine may be described as a belief in tariff for everybody." Ibid., Governor Preuss. Exactly opposite views have been more frequently expressed. Senator Smoot, memorandum, A. MSS., thinks Aldrich had no objection to any of the increases, but adds that "the biggest increases of all secured by any one senator were those Dolliver himself obtained." O. K. Davis, "Released for Publication," 167 ff., restates the insurgent view that the Payne-Aldrich Bill was full of secret increases not perceptible to the world.

3. Authorized memorandum of Senator Clapp, A. MSS.

4. Authorized memorandum of Governor Preuss, A. MSS. Because of Aldrich's opposition to the La Follette bloc it must not be inferred that he was indifferent to reconciling the West. Quite the contrary, as shown by his overtures to Nelson. He included McComber, Smoot, Flint and Cullum in the Finance Committee.

5. La Follette to Aldrich, March 17, 1909, A. MSS.

6. Dolliver to Aldrich, undated, A. MSS.

7. Same to same, March 16, 1909, A. MSS.

8. Authorized memorandum of Senator Cummins, A. MSS. The question has been raised, Was Dolliver entitled to the appointment, and did Aldrich exceed his rights in refusing it? Senator Clapp, for example, while regarding the question of broken promises as "unimportant," thought that "in view of what Dolliver had previously demonstrated, therefore, he merited the position under the unwritten law of the Senate." Authorized memorandum, A. MSS.

9. La Follette, 432–3.

10. Ibid., 435.

11. *Times*, Feb. 17, 1909.

12. March 23.

13. *Times*, May 9, 1909; *R.*, May 8, p. 1846.

14. Ibid.

15. Dodge to A. B. Farquhar, Dec. 3, 1908, D. MSS.

16. *Times*, April 23.

17. There is much confusion over these terms. Both are found in the newspapers of 1909.

18. Beveridge, Bristow, Clapp, Cummins, Dolliver, La Follette, Nelson.

19. Tillman to Aldrich, April 1, 1909, A. MSS.

Tillman argued for tea tariff before the Senate and some people have failed to see the tongue in his cheek.

20. *R.*, April 30; May 22, 24. See "Comparison of the Tariff of 1897 and 1909 in parallel columns." Washington Government Printing Office, 1910. Plain, sawed lumber, 1897, $2.00, the M feet; 1909, $1.25, the M feet. As a whole, the lumber schedule (D) was sharply cut in 1909.

21. Taft to C. H. Krippendorf, April 12, 1909, T. MSS.: "I am very much in favor of free hides and I hope they can be kept in the free list. I agree with you, however, that it is going to be hard to do so in the Senate, where the Western States that think they are directly affected, have so much larger proportional representation than in the House."

22. *R.*, April 15, pp. 1351, 1360; *Times*, April 16, 17.

23. *Times*, June 9.

24. Ibid., June 10.

25. *Times*, June 20. Chandler to Roosevelt, July 10, 1909, C. MSS.

26. *Times*, June 15.

27. Ibid.

28. June 16.

29. *The Record* gives all stages of this brilliant and intricate parliamentary engagement. The New York *Times* is very useful, though once in a while slightly inaccurate. Bailey for the Democrats and Cummins for the Insurgents both introduced amendments providing for the insertion of an income tax in the tariff bill. June 11 appears to be the date on which they came to a complete understanding. Aldrich, doubtless, saw what was coming, which would explain in part his anxiety of June 8. His new policy was recorded in the papers June 15. Taft's message recommending an amendment to the Constitution and also the corporation tax was sent in, June 16. On June 25, Aldrich introduced an amendment to the bill inserting the corporation tax and on June 28 introduced the Joint Resolution (S. J. 60) to amend the Constitution. On July 2, a vote was taken for substituting Aldrich's corporation tax amendment to the tariff bill for the Bailey-Cummins income tax amendment. The Democrats went through the motions of standing by their allies; the vote for substitution was 45 to 31. Immediately a vote was taken for incorporating the substitute in the bill. Here the coalition broke—59 for incorporating the substitute, 11 against. The constitutional resolution was adopted July 8.

30. June 5.

31. *Times*, July 19.

32. On the night of June 4, Aldrich had defended the schedule. Perhaps no part of the tariff has been fought over so bitterly as the rates on cotton. Aldrich had called in as expert adviser Thad. S. Sharretts, with whose aid the schedule had been framed. Aldrich held that the changes were designed not with a view to effecting increases but because of the introduction of new grades of cloth from foreign mills. *R.*, June 4; *Times*, June 5. At no other time was debate quite so furious. "Why this bamboozling of the country?" exclaimed Senator Tillman. "Either the Senator from Rhode Island bamboozled us last night, or the Senator from Iowa is bamboozling us this morning. I am getting tired of all this." *R.*, June 5, p. 2855. Aldrich proposed to make this schedule approximately what he had intended it to be in the Dingley Act. *R.*, June 4, p. 2835. Court decisions interpreting that act had had the effect of lowering cotton duties below the intention of the framers. Taft to E. T. Baldwin, July 29, 1909, T. MSS.: "I have talked with Mr. Payne about it, whose attitude in favor of downward revision has been shown, I think, to be very genuine, and he believes that the present cotton schedule is substantially fair—perhaps a little high in one or two instances but that generally it is what it ought to be."

Aldrich produced in the Senate a letter signed by four officials of the New York Custom House, Marion De Vries, Thad. S. Sharretts, W. H. Parkhill, Otto Fix: "We all agree that the average ratio imposed by paragraphs 313, 314, 316, and 317 of the bill as reported from the Senate Committee on Finance are not greater than those imposed by the Act of

1897 as originally construed upon the merchandise now included in those paragraphs of the Senate bill." *R.*, June 4, p. 2842.

The following year Miss Tarbell published a celebrated attack upon this schedule. *American Magazine*, Dec., 1910. Professor Taussig, on the other hand, in the seventh edition of his "History of the Tariff," seems to consider it one of the minor features of the bill. With the lapse of time and the subsidence of partisan rancor it will not seem inappropriate to characterize the schedule as having been reached upon the line of least resistance, and having far less significance than was once imputed to it. At least, there is no reason for seeing in this schedule anything but the natural evolution of Aldrich's settled policy with regard to the protection of manufactures. In his own words: "Take the metal schedule. Take the silk schedule. Take every schedule of this bill. The intention is to have the rates progressive from the crude products, the raw materials, to the finished product; progressive as to the amount of difference in the cost of production here and in competing countries, which means that if you put one duty on iron ore you must put a higher duty on pig iron, a higher duty still on steel rails, a higher duty still on watch-springs, progressive all through the scale." *R.*, June 4, p. 2838.

The main feature of the cotton schedule was its complete abandonment of ad valorem duties. The Dingley Act laid specific duties on the cheaper grades of cotton cloth, but ad valorem duties on the finer grades. The Aldrich Bill retained the Dingley specifics but without exception changed the other rates. The controversial battle was upon whether this change had some secret purpose. Aldrich steadily insisted on the explanations indicated above and on the additional ones that these finer cloths were luxuries and that where there were close differences in cloth, frauds in classification were more easy under ad valorem than under specific duties. The appraisers held the same view.

The attack on the schedule in the Senate rested on the calculation of "equivalent" ad valorem duties. The aim was to show that the new specifics inflicted on the nation a far greater burden than the old rates did and that this was why the old ones were changed. The mode of establishing these hypothetical "equivalents" was in taking the whole bulk of the importation under a given classification, dividing it arithmetically, without regard to the fluctuation of prices or the character of supply, into the whole bulk of duty paid. The resulting quotient was the equivalent ad valorem paid under a specific rate. This reasoning proved in a government table that certain cotton cloths paid, without change of rate, an "equivalent" duty of 22.50 per cent in 1898 and 355 per cent in 1904. *R.*, June 4, p. 2837. Aldrich called up all his resources as a debater in his effort to discredit the "equivalent" argument. "Take iron ore. Iron ore may be worth in Cuba at the mines 50 cents per ton, and 25 cents a ton would be 50 per cent. If it came from Canada, where iron ore might be worth $2.50 a ton, it would be 10 per cent ad valorem. The table might show 50 per cent one year and 10 per cent the next. It would show nothing except that there had been a change in the value, or possibly and probably a change in the place from which the goods had been imported." *R.*, June 4, p. 2837.

33. Section 2, of the tariff act of 1909, stated that the duties levied were "minimum" duties. It empowered the President to increase them to

"maximum" duties against any country that discriminated in any way against the United States. The "maximum" tariff was to be calculated by adding twenty-five per cent of the cost of the imported goods to the amount of tariff levied in the "minimum" rate.

34. Section 29, of the tariff act, created a special Court of Customs Appeals to be the final court for all questions arising under the act.

35. Throughout the controversy there had been much talk about a permanent tariff commission that should somehow remove the whole subject from politics and put it on a scientific basis. The issue was so entangled with the purely political battle that it is difficult to determine what were the real motives with regard to it. The idea appears in Aldrich's thinking at several times. In this case, nothing came of it. A mere shadow, so to speak, is to be found in the last sentence of Section 2. "To secure information to assist the President in the discharge of the duties imposed upon him by this section, and the officers of the government in the administration of the customs laws, the President is hereby authorized to employ such persons as may be required."

36. Taft to C. P. Taft, July 13, 1909, T. MSS.

37. Taft to C. P. Taft, July 12, 1909, T. MSS.

38. *Times*, July 20 and 24; *Sun*, July 20.

39. Taft to Mrs. Taft, July 22, 1909, T. MSS.: "I am anxious to secure free hides, free oil, free iron ore and free coal. I would like to secure a dollar on lumber and say, three dollars on print paper. . . . I sent for Borah of Idaho, and had a talk with him and we made peace. . . . Borah agreed to come in with me on free hides if we could get some concessions on the duties on shoes and leather and harness. . . . Yesterday morning I had Crane at breakfast and he told me the Senate would be all right for the bill with free hides. . . ." See "Correspondence" (cited in note 20). Hides, 1897, 15 per cent; free, 1909.

40. Taft to Mrs. Taft, July 27, 1909, T. MSS.: "I am just now about to meet a delegation of congressmen to confer as to the lumber schedule. If we could settle that I believe we could get a conference report that would be satisfactory; but there are clouds in that matter that seem almost insurmountable. . . .

"I haven't time now to tell you the various phases of the tariff fight. The Speaker is engaged in trying to foist a high tariff on gloves into the bill in the interest of a friend named Littauer, and he has been threatening Aldrich and I believe will threaten me with defeating the bill unless this goes in. It is the greatest exhibition of tyranny that I have known of his attempting. Aldrich and I continue to be good friends, although we differ somewhat, but he is a very different man from the Speaker." See also *Times*, July 21, which makes the President at issue with Cannon as early as July 19.

41. *Tribune*, July 28.

42. *Tribune*, July 29; *Sun*, July 29. This was on July 28. The next day the President sent a long letter, in duplicate, to Aldrich and Payne, T. MSS. He repeated his terms. He would veto the bill unless they were met.

43. *Tribune*, July 30, 1909.

44. He had failed in the cases of coal and iron, which he had hoped to put on the free list. He was forced to accept forty-five cents per ton on coal and fifteen cents per ton on iron ore and $2.50 per ton on iron pigs.

This was a reduction from previous tariff which laid, sixty-seven cents on coal, forty cents on iron ore and $4.00 on iron pigs.

45. Beveridge, Bristow, Clapp, Cummins, Dolliver, La Follette, Nelson. *R.*, Aug. 5, 1909, p. 4949. At the last moment the bill was imperilled by discovering a "joker"—a provision believed to be surreptitious, which had escaped attention in the heat of debate—that was held to vitiate the hides-leather compromise. On Aug. 2, the range senators were crying out that they had been duped, that only on a few leather articles would duties be lowered. Aldrich reconvened the conference in order to rephrase the passage in dispute so as to satisfy the range senators. *Sun*, Aug. 3.

46. Aug. 2.

47. Aug. 6.

CHAPTER XXIII

FACING TOWARD THE FEDERAL RESERVE

1. Aldrich to Knox, Oct. 24, 1909, A. MSS.

2. *Proceedings*, Annual Convention, A. B. A., Sept. 13–17, 1909, Chicago, p. 246.

3. Authorized memorandum of interview with Mr. Budlong, a member of the party, A. MSS.

4. *Star*, Nov. 9, 1909.

5. Statement by Mr. Andrew. Aldrich had in a marked degree the prime talent of the advocate—the ability both to make fully clear the main point, and yet, without obscuring it, to create conviction that he had mastered the whole subject in detail.

6. Clipping in A. MSS.

7. "Banking Systems and Currency Reform." Address by Hon. A. Piatt Andrew, Jan. 22, 1910, p. 12.

8. Taft to C. P. Taft, March 5, 1910, T. MSS.: "The situation in Congress is uncertain, but with the assistance of my wicked partners, Cannon and Aldrich, I am hopeful that I can pull off the legislation that I have most at heart. Cummins, La Follette, Dolliver, Clapp and Bristow are five senators who are determined to be as bitter as they can against the administration, and to defeat anything that the administration seeks."

9. Taft to Aldrich, Jan. 24, 1910, T. MSS.

10. Same to same, March 24, T. MSS.

11. Same to same, May 21, T. MSS.

12. Taft to J. A. Sleicher, May 10, 1910, T. MSS.

13. *World*, Dec. 7, 1926.

14. Mrs. Gardner to Mr. Andrew, March 27, 1910, and April 2, A. MSS.

15. Aldrich to Governor Pothier, April 17, 1910, A. MSS.

16. April 18, 1910.

17. April 15, 1910.

18. April 18, 1910.

19. May 14, 1910.

20. Garnett Warren in New York *Herald*, March 6, 1910.

CHAPTER XXIV

JEKYL ISLAND

1. This curious episode of Jekyl Island has been generally regarded as a myth. A rumor with regard to it got into print six years later (see note 8) but was not taken seriously. Four of the participants are still living; all of them have read this chapter and are satisfied with its accuracy. Mr. Warburg has set down his recollections in an extensive memorandum which is here cited as Warburg Memorandum, W. MSS. The citation Vanderlip Memorandum refers to a long notation which I made on the basis of talks with Mr. Vanderlip who has read it and accepts it as representing him correctly. Mr. Andrew's recollections coincide entirely with those of Mr. Warburg and Mr. Vanderlip. Mr. Shelton, unfortunately, has not preserved the very full notes which he made at the time, but his memory is clear and circumstantial with no contradictions of the other recollections. There seems to be no positive evidence who originated the plan but the circumstantial evidence is good. It was Mr. Davison who proposed the outing both to Mr. Warburg and Mr. Vanderlip. It is also significant that none of the party were members of the Jekyl Island Club and that Mr. Morgan was. The incident occurred in Nov., 1910. Aldrich made an address before the Academy of Political Science at New York, Nov. 11, and another before the Academy of Social and Political Sciences, Philadelphia, Dec. 8. The Jekyl Island trip intervened.

2. I am indebted to Mrs. H. Fairfield Osborn, who took great interest in trying to determine the possible connection of Mr. Morgan with this episode. Mr. P. S. Brewster, a member of the club, searched the records at Mrs. Osborn's request and interrogated the officials of the club. The secret visit of the financiers is a club tradition and also the report that Mr. Morgan made it possible. They had the place entirely to themselves.

3. Bristow made his charges in an address at Winfield, Kans., July 9, and elaborated them in speeches at Paoli and Kansas City.

4. *World*, July 16, printed an account of an unsuccessful attempt to obtain an interview with Aldrich on the subject of the Bristow charges. "No part of the stinging speech of Senator Bristow would force Senator Aldrich to comment." Other significant articles were printed July 30, Aug. 5 and Aug. 11. The article of Aug. 5 records a second attempt to force Aldrich out of his silence.

5. George E. Roberts to Aldrich, Aug. 11, 1910, and similar letters, A. MSS. C. D. Norton, private secretary to President Taft, wrote Aldrich Aug. 10, 1910, A. MSS., referring to "the visit which Senator Crane and I paid you on Sunday . . . I hope nothing will occur to change your decision to make the statement on the rubber matter. . . ."

6. Aldrich's letter was dated Aug. 10, 1910. A transcript of the original manuscript is in the A. MSS. The letter is a careful essay of several thousand words. It was published that day. *The World*, Aug. 11, attempted to discredit it without challenging its facts.

7. Vanderlip Memorandum. Mr. Vanderlip to the author, March 13, 1929: "Will say that none of us knew certainly what Mr. Aldrich wanted in the way of a new banking bill. As a matter of fact, Mr. Aldrich knew almost as little of what he wanted as we did. He had a vast deal of ac-

cumulated information. He had a firm grip on a good many principles, but at this moment he had not crystallized his opinions."

8. Warburg Memorandum. It may be that one of these reporters was the source of an article by B. C. Forbes, printed originally in *Leslie's Weekly*, and reprinted (1917) in his book entitled "Men Who Are Making America," pp. 38–39. It told in vague outline the Jekyl Island story, but made no impression and was generally regarded as a mere yarn.

9. Warburg Memorandum. Mr. Warburg was arguing on the basis of his essay "A United Reserve Bank of the United States" (printed in *Proceedings of the Academy of Political Science*, Vol. I, 302–342). Students will profit by comparing this essay with the original Aldrich Plan, both with the second Aldrich plan, and all with the Monetary Commission Bill and the eventual Federal Reserve Act. The comparison will be facilitated by Willis, "The Federal Reserve System."

10. Warburg Memorandum.

11. Ibid.

12. Ibid. Mr. Warburg is unconditional that all of the party were surprised by Aldrich's conviction that he could force upon the nation some form of central banking. The reference to the Bank of England is my own inference from the general story of the trip of the Monetary Commission plus the fact that he refers to it now and then in his speeches. I have no information of his discussing it at Jekyl Island.

13. Warburg to Aldrich, A. MSS. To make sure upon this point I wrote to Mr. Warburg, who replied: "The matter of a uniform discount rate was discussed and settled at Jekyl Island. While Senator Aldrich was much impressed by the methods of European central banks, which have a uniform discount rate, and while this made him predisposed toward a uniform rate, I am convinced that he would have surrendered to the arguments favoring the granting of power to discriminate between the districts of the National Reserve Association, had it not been for the impelling political requirements of the case. Any proposal had to be prepared to meet the determined charge that the scheme was conceived for the purpose of benefiting 'Wall Street and the interests.' . . . The Senator, as far as I remember, did not believe it possible to pass a law that would not provide for a uniform discount rate." It is to be borne in mind that Aldrich's reasoning, at this time was all based on the assumption of a unified irresistible Republican party. What vitiated his forecast was the unexpected break-up of the party in 1912.

CHAPTER XXV

THE CONQUEST OF MACEDONIA

1. MacVeagh to Aldrich, Jan. 19, 1911, A. MSS.

2. Addresses by Senator Nelson W. Aldrich on the work of the National Monetary Commission, before the Academy of Political Science, New York City, Nov. 11, 1910, and the American Academy of Political and Social Science, Philadelphia, Dec. 8, 1910.

3. Pamphlet by Mr. Andrew: "The Purpose and Origin of Banking Legislation."

4. The President's secretary to Aldrich, Jan. 4, 1911, A. MSS. "Saturday, January 7. Dinner at White House with bankers Forgan, Riply,

Rowe, and Professor Laughlin. Aldrich absent on account of illness."
Engagement Book of A. Piatt Andrew.

5. Mrs. Aldrich's diary, 1911, A. MSS.

6. "Sunday, January 15. Vanderlip, Davison, Warburg, spent the day in my rooms getting the Aldrich plan in shape. Aldrich ill." Engagement Book of A. Piatt Andrew. Memorandum, authorized by Mr. Andrew, A. MSS.

7. Ibid.; Warburg Memorandum, W. MSS. Mr. Vanderlip to the author, March 13, 1929.

8. Annual Report, New York Chamber of Commerce, 1910–1911, p. 150.

9. Forgan to Aldrich, Jan. 26, 1911, A. MSS.

10. Mr. Shelton to various bankers, A. MSS.

11. Telegram, Feb. 10, 1911, A. MSS., signed by twenty-six names.

12. Vanderlip Memorandum, A. MSS.

13. *Commercial and Financial Chronicle*, Feb. 18, 1911, 92:430.

14. Aldrich to Taft, Feb. 17, 1911, T. MSS.

15. Taft to Aldrich, Jan. 29, 1911, T. MSS.

16. Same to same, same date, T. MSS.

17. Ibid.

18. Aldrich to Taft, Feb. 17, 1911, T. MSS.

19. Interview, J. P. Nichols with Senator Smoot, May 19, 1926, notation in A. MSS.; *Times*, Feb. 21, 1911.

20. Taft to Aldrich, Jan. 29, 1911, T. MSS.

21. Irving T. Bush, in "Banking Reform," June 5, 1913.

22. Warburg Memorandum, W. MSS.

23. Ibid.

24. Of course this interpretation of his purpose is mainly inferential. The defense of it is in the circumstantial evidence (1) of his gradual departure from his own views of 1893, (2) the general tenor of his developing attitude toward the money problem, and (3) his specific relation to the question of government control over finance. This theory of what he aimed to do seems to me to be the chief reason why this biography is worth while. To my mind the significance of his attempt to solve the money problem in a way unsatisfactory to both extremes, a way that offended Mr. Bryan for one reason and pure Plutocrats for another reason, is just the thing that will give him a permanent place among American political thinkers. I may betray a temperamental bias when I add that in my judgment practically all the partisan discussion of the time, whether in Congress or in the literature of protest, is too much in the nature of propaganda to deserve serious consideration.

25. Warburg to Aldrich, Dec. 11, 1911, W. MSS.

26. The address was published as a pamphlet by the Monetary Commission.

27. Address published as a pamphlet by the Monetary Commission.

28. Report Annual Convention, A. B. A., Nov. 20–24, 1911, pp. 385–6.

29. *Times*, July 6, 1911.

30. *R.*, 1911: S. 854, April 13, July 6 and 28, Aug. 10, 11, 12, 14, 19 and 21.

31. Sections 14–18 of Revised Plan.

32. Dinwiddie to Warburg, Jan. 3, 1912, W. MSS.

33. S. 4431, 62C-2S, Monetary Commission Bill, Section 7.

CHAPTER XXVI

POLITICAL FOOTBALL

1. *World,* Jan. 9, 1912.
2. Dinwiddie to Warburg, Jan. 26, 1912, W. MSS.
3. Willis, "The Federal Reserve System," 140.
4. Stanwood, II, 265. A curious dispute arose as to whether the platform originally contained "or" or "for" a central bank.
5. At the same time, Mr. La Follette renewed his severe criticism. A very bitter sneer attributed to him, but which prolonged search has not succeeded in tracing to its source, spoke contemptuously of Aldrich as worth fifty millions. Dinwiddie to Warburg, Jan. 11, 1912, W. MSS. The appraisal of his estate came to about seven millions.
6. Naturally, these details of the year of 1912 have been obtained from the family. I am chiefly indebted to the very accurate memory of Miss Lucy Aldrich.
7. Stanwood, II, 245.
8. President Butler to J. P. Nichols, Feb. 6, 1925, A. MSS.
9. Stanwood, II, 250.
10. Stanwood, II, 288; Bishop, II, 334–336.
11. Taft to Mrs. B. A. Wallingford, Aug. 25, 1912, T. MSS.

CHAPTER XXVII

THE HARVEST

1. The story of their labors as scientists, and a good deal of their difficulty as politicians, is in Willis, "The Federal Reserve System," and in Glass, "An Adventure in Constructive Finance." Mr. Willis' book gives all the stages of the Federal Reserve Bill. An elaborate study of Federal Reserve legislation is in preparation by Mr. Warburg.
2. See address cited in note 7, 69–70.
3. The relations with Mr. Bryan in this connection are discussed by Mr. Willis, Chapter XIII.
4. See address cited in note 7, especially page 86: "The creation of this board, with its improvident grants of executive and legislative authority, is repugnant to every fundamental principle of popular government. No instrumentality could be further removed from popular control. The functions of the board are exercised in secret and there is no provision for publicity of any kind, except an annual report to Congress. There can be no review of its opinions and no appeal from its decisions. It is doubtful whether its members could be impeached for flagrant abuse of power. They are appointed by the President and are apparently responsible to him alone for the manner in which they discharge their duties. This attempt to give to a political oligarchy the power to control the banks and currency of the country, to be exercised at its discretion, with no means of preventing or punishing abuses, is promoted by the same men who are proclaiming their purpose to destroy monopolies and to repeal all grants of special privilege. No monopoly or grant of special privilege could be so great, so far-reaching in its consequences, as that proposed by the bill under consideration."
5. Mrs. Stuart N. Campbell (Miss Elsie Aldrich) and Mrs. Connal-

Rowan, who was her companion in this episode, recall the event with sharp detail.

6. Professor Willis is my authority for this account of the mood of Mr. Bryan. Talking it over with me he was unconditional as to Mr. Bryan's delusion.

7. *Proceedings of the Academy of Political Science,* IV, 31–91. The address was delivered Oct. 15, 1913, at Columbia University. It criticised the Federal Reserve Bill in the form in which it had been passed by the House, Sept. 18, 1913. Hearings were already in progress leading eventually to modification by the Senate. Aldrich himself was one of those who appeared before the Finance Committee at a hearing—a dramatic reversal of his experience. The final bill seemed to him a distinct improvement on the House bill. The following January he republished his Academy address as a pamphlet with this introduction:

"Since the following address was read before the Academy of Political Science, the 'Federal Reserve Act' has become a law. The Senate and the Democratic caucus practically remodelled the measure, eliminating many of the objectional features of the House bill, and modifying provisions which had been subjected to severe criticism. The act as finally adopted will, I believe, be accepted by the national banks with a view of seeking in good faith to make its operation a practical success and with the hope that defects may be cured by subsequent legislation.

"Whether the measure will meet the expectations of its friends will depend largely upon the manner in which it is administered. Its success will depend, first of all, upon the character and wisdom of the Federal Reserve Board, which is granted extraordinary powers of control over vast interests and intrusted with the decision of the intricate questions which are involved in the various provisions of the act. Very much will also depend upon the conservative character of the management of the several Federal Reserve banks.

"The act adopts many of the principles of the bill reported by the National Monetary Commission, as will be seen by a comparison of the texts of the two measures. Its authors concede that effective legislation for banking reform must embody provisions for the concentration and mobilization of bank reserves through an organization of banks, and that member banks must be able through such an organization to maintain and replenish their reserves by a rediscount of commercial paper. Whether the organizations provided by the act will secure these results in a satisfactory manner can be ascertained only by experience.

"If the loaning and note-issuing power of the reserve banks is used to the fullest extent in ordinary times as anticipated by some of the authors of the act, these institutions will be found powerless in case of emergency for purposes of support or protection. The adoption of this policy would naturally lead to an expansion of credit and inflation of the currency, producing an appearance of prosperity and a boom in speculative prices, but the ultimate result would be disastrous."

8. Ibid., 37–58. He regarded the notes that were to be issued under the provision of the House bill as virtually fiat money.

9. Ibid., 81–91, interlocking with 50–61. He dissects the Democratic tradition and criticises Mr. Bryan without heat but with unsparing disapproval.

10. *World*, Oct. 16, 1913. The report is slightly confusing. It does not distinguish between the prepared address and the impromptu remarks. The sentence quoted is from the address as subsequently published, p. 91. I am greatly obliged to Professor Willis for his permission to print the following statement, which coming from him is so highly significant:

"Those most closely connected with the enactment of the Federal Reserve Act do not believe that the strong attacks made upon it by Aldrich were actuated by opposition to the bill as a whole. They believe that, had he been in the Senate at the time, he would probably have given it his final affirmative vote, after the debating was over.

"They believe that Aldrich was motivated, in his attacks on the Federal Reserve Bill, chiefly by opposition to its political features (as found in the provisions for appointment of the board members) which his legislative experience had led him to fear as a very injudicious provision. His judgment in this respect has since been vindicated by the effect of political influence upon the Reserve System. The fact is that the first draft of the bill did not have these political features, which had to be inserted because of the political exigencies facing the administration. Without the addition of those political features, the enactment of the measure would have been vastly more difficult.

"Aldrich also was motivated in an unconscious way, by the natural feeling of regret on the part of a strong Republican, that his own party should not be the one to have the credit for the actual passage of the banking reform measure. It would have been impossible for any one in his position not to have had this feeling."

CHAPTER XXVIII

AFTERWARD

1. Mr. Winthrop Aldrich to the author.
2. Mrs. Vanderbilt remembers the incident with careful exactness of detail. Mrs. Roosevelt remembers Roosevelt saying to her that he had had a very satisfactory interview with Aldrich.

INDEX